Band 96 der ORPHEUS-Schriftenreihe zu Grundfragen der Musik
herausgegeben von Martin Vogel

Michael Hewitt

The Tonal Phoenix

A Study of Tonal Progression
through the Prime Numbers
Three, Five and Seven

ORpheus-Verlag GmbH
Verlag für systematische Musikwissenschaft GmbH
Bonn 2000

© ᴏʀpheus-Verlag GmbH
Bonn 2000
All rights reserved
Printed in Germany
ISBN 3-922626-96-3

INTRODUCTION

The musical interval defined by the fourth and seventh members of the harmonic series has always posed immense problems for theorists. Manifesting in the lower regions of the harmonic series, it undoubtedly presents a strong and characteristic intervallic relation. Yet the fact remains that the ratio 7/4 signifies an interval which would seem, at first sight, to be incommensurate with the traditional tonal system of Western music. Alluding to this in the theoretical tract of his *Craft of Musical Composition*, Paul Hindemith observed that *the seventh overtone* [he obviously means harmonic] *in the series based upon C (-Bb) does not make the triad into a dominant seventh chord such as we know in practice. It is flatter than the Bb that we are used to hearing as the seventh of C.*[1] Thus giving the impression that the seventh harmonic gives a defective or 'out-of-tune' minor seventh, there is something distinctly unsettling about this, a feeling that the defect lies not with the seventh harmonic, but with the system from which it is being viewed. Hindemith expresses this feeling admirably *Is it not remarkable that musical mankind, after thousands of years of musical practice, should not have arrived at mastery of the characteristics of the seventh overtone?*[2]

Such imposing problems aside, the seventh harmonic has always taunted theorists and composers with the promise of fresh possibilities for the musical language. Occurring just after the sixth harmonic, its prominent placing in the harmonic series tends to invite the implication that it may be the inevitable and natural successor to the '3/2' and '5/4' relations which have played such an important part in the development of Western harmony and harmonic theory. Yet for various reasons it is an interval which has never lived up to it's immense promise.

This study endeavors to explain the various reasons for this, and also how, with a little thought and investigation, a new approach may be taken to the issue of the seventh harmonic in such a way as to unfold the vast wealth of possibilities which it does actually embrace. Indeed, when this has been done, it will soon become apparent that the interval 7/4 provides the theoretical key to an altogether new system of tonality, a chromatic tonal system whose logic and

---

[1] Paul Hindemith, A Craft of Musical Composition, Vol. 1 (Theory), Schott & Co., Ltd., London 1945, 24.

[2] Ibid., 39.

rationale is just as clear cut as the major and minor tonal system which preceded it in the scale of musical progression. Leading to the formulation of an altogether new musical scale, it will become apparent that the 7/4 relation is, as many have already suspected, a vital catalyst in the process of tonal growth and evolution.

ACKNOWLEDGEMENTS

Thanks are due to Professor John Harper, for his role in encouraging and supporting this study in the first place.

Thanks also to Laura Davey for her patient work translating into English the relevant quotations used from Tartini's *Trattado di Musica*.

Last but not least, thanks go to my Undergraduate composition teacher Brian Dennis, for his encouragement of that keen interest in the fascinating world of septimal intervals, which led to this study in the first place.

CONTENTS

4

LIST OF ABBREVIATIONS

AcM	Acta Musicologica
CQ	Classical Quarterly
EM	Early Music
GSJ	The Galpin Society Journal
JAMS	Journal of the American Musicological Society
JASA	Journal of the Acoustical Society of America
JMT	Journal of Music Theory
MA	Music Analysis
MD	Musica Disciplina
MF	The Music Forum
MM	Modern Music
MQ	The Music Quarterly
MR	The Music Review
MTS	Music Theory Spectrum
PNM	Perspectives of New Music
PRMA	Proceedings of the Royal Musical Association
SM	Studies in Music

THE UNITY OF TONE

The concept of unity has come to be fundamental to our understanding of tonal music. Indeed, it is often taken for granted that some of the greatest of musical works will present themselves to us as an organic whole. Therefore analytical strategies evolved in order to help the listener understand those works have generally aimed at the exposition of those features by which the unity of the whole can be more clearly understood. Whether conceived through processes of formal analysis (i.e. Koch, Riepel, or Momigny), or tonal analysis (i.e. Riemann, Schoenberg or Schenker), the most important principle to observe is that a state of musical unity is dependent upon a perceived relationship between the component parts of that unity.

Naturally this works on different levels. Heard relationships between separate movements of a symphony may give to that symphony a sense of coherence and purpose. Within the individual movements, there are relationships between various themes or sections of the chosen form, and within these a further set of relationships arising from the motivic make-up and constitution of the individual themes themselves. All of these, operating on their own respective levels, may contribute to that final sense of unity obtained of the whole.

Viewed from another, although interdependent perspective, there are various levels of tonal relationship present within a musical work to be taken into account. These, as explicated in the process of Schenkerian analysis, show that the tonal unity and coherence of the foreground texture of a piece of music may be viewed as being dependent upon other deeper levels of tonal relationship, which proceeding from the middleground to the background, culminate in the Ursatz, that pattern of fundamental unity into which the entire musical work ultimately resolves.[1]

The search for musical unity therefore, although beginning with a consideration of the whole, finds itself increasingly involved with the parts,

---

[1] As explained and set forth in Allen Forte's and Steven Gilbert's Introduction to Schenkerian Analysis, New York, Norton 1982.

which themselves are but the wholes of yet further parts. So it goes on, each level of construction serving as the enclosure for yet another. Inevitably, there is a point where this process of subdivision comes to a natural stop – that indivisible nuclear unit of European art music called the musical tone.

Yet even here there are exceptions, notably in the music written in the latter half of this century, a period known and characterized by its highly experimental outlook. *Polymorphia* (1961), written for 48 stringed instruments by the Polish composer Krystof Penderecki (b. 1933), makes considerable use of string glissandi and other such effects based on frequency mutation which are represented only graphically on the staff. Modeled upon the frequency modulation capabilities of electronic instruments, such effects fall outside of the limitations of the concept of musical tone, as it is ordinarily understood.

A musical tone is generally characterized by its invariable frequency. Effects based on frequency modulation therefore, tend to undermine traditional conceptions of musical tone. But even in this case the piece as a whole depends upon stable elements which serve as reference points from which frequency mutations occur. So even here, the building block of music that is the musical tone cannot be entirely dismissed.

Each musical tone within a work can be regarded to be a unity in its own right. Looking at a musical score, each note therein is represented as a separate event; each distinguished by its own particular note symbol. Even the symbols themselves, circular in profile, bespeak of the fundamental unity of musical tone. That state of unity is poetically described in the text entitled 'Unbegrenzt' from Carleinz Stockhausen's *Aus den Sieben Tagen* (1968) in which is written:

> 'A sound
> lives, like YOU, like ME, like HE, like SHE, like IT.
> Moves, stretches out and contracts.
> Transforms itself, gives birth, begets, dies, is re-born.
> Seeks – seeks not – finds – loses –
> Binds itself – loves – waits – hastens – comes and goes...'[1]

Casting up the philosophical view of a musical tone as a microcosm of the whole world, Stockhausen calls attention to the fact that the unity of tone promulgates itself through a process of replication. One musical tone calls for another, and in so doing, a relationship is created. In this respect each musical composition, no matter how big or small, can be seen to subsist entirely upon

---

[1] K. H. Stockhausen, Aus den Sieben Tagen, Universal Edition, Vienna 1968. The recording of FROM THE SEVEN DAYS the booklet of which contains this text may be ordered from the Stockhausen-Verlag, Kettenberg 15, 51515 Kurten, Germany.

the unity of that fundamental building block that is the musical tone. Now in so far as the selection of those tones for the purposes of musical expression depends upon the dictates and artistic desires of the composer, means that the application of rigorous scientific principles to the understanding of the tonal combinations arrived at by the composer, is itself a seeming irrelevance. Music is an art-form, and its style, substance, and genre changes from age to age. Consequently, it is foolish to look for scientific certainties in music, because as soon as a certainty does become established, it gets swept away by the tide of incessant change and flux.

Yet looking at the recorded history of music there is one feature that has a certainty value: the universality of musical tone. In all ages, epochs and civilizations, music is based upon the tone and its properties. The musical tone thus constitutes a common factor that serves to bridge both the historical and stylistic gulf between widely divergent repertories. A study of the precise nature of musical tone is therefore paramount towards the proper understanding of music. Analogous to other, perhaps more natural fundamental building blocks, such as the atom, molecule or cell, the precise composition and structure of musical tones can provide vital leads towards understanding why certain combinations or aggregates of tone have proved successful.

The structure of crystalline formations is an outgrowth of the peculiar arrangement of the molecules from which they are composed. Resulting in a series of forms displaying properties of mathematical symmetry and regularity, the crystalline forms of certain minerals offer an instinctive appeal to the human aesthetic sensibility. Similarly, many of the basic materials of music, whether they be chords, melodic figures or musical scales, can be understood to be outgrowths of the unique properties and internal arrangement of the vibrations of musical tones. These, like the crystals that represent themselves to the eye as objects of great beauty, become similar objects of fascination and beauty to the hearing sense.

Yet the concern here is not primarily with aesthetics. It is to come to an understanding of how such tonal structures are obtained. To be able to do so, it is essential to make an initial examination of the nature of musical tone - the basic unit from which such structures are built up. This may involve going over material which has already been covered in writings on acoustics. However, as this information proves relevant to the understanding of the nature of musical tone, it will be discussed here.

Here the most important point to dwell upon is the clear gulf between the impression received in the mind of a musical tone, and what actually constitutes a tone in more objective scientific terms. To the ear the tone presents itself as a unified entity distinguished from others of its kind by virtue of its exact pitch, volume, duration and tonal quality. Each musical tone thus occupies a space within a musical work which is entirely its own. It is a unitary event within a musical work that carries its own special symbol within the score.

Naturally, such an impression belies the fact that the tone is an extremely complex aggregate of vibrations which the ear somehow manages to resolve into the characteristic sensation of a note with a particular frequency. The ears capacity for such resolution, constituting the mediating principle which links the subjective notion of musical tone as a singular entity, to the objective proscription of tone as a complex aggregate of separate vibrations, is also therefore, a very important consideration in any study of the nature of tone.

These two apparently opposite conceptions of tone find an adequate resolution in the concept of the simple tone - a pure vibration characterized by its own particular speed, rate or frequency. Here the simple tone is a rather unique tonal phenomenon, for it is both a musical tone and a partial tone in its own right. It thus serves to embody the conceptual paradox of being both a part and the whole at the same time. Indeed, because a simple tone comprises only one partial means that it also has another name - fundamental tone - that frequency the perceived presence of which gives rise to the sense of pitch. In this sense pitch is the first and most basic property of tone, being possessed by both simple and complex tones alike.

Most of the tones used in music, consisting of a combination of pure tones, are appropriately designated as being complex tones. Concerning these, the physicist Robert H. Silsbee observes that: *quite generally, any complex musical tone may be represented as the sum of a number of pure tones ... If one strikes a metallic lampshade or pan lid and listens carefully, one can hear at least a couple of the distinct frequencies that make up the full complex tone. These different components, which together make up the sound produced by the flute, violin or cymbal, are called partials, and their individual frequencies are called partial frequencies.*[1]

Each of these partials, the result of a certain mode of vibration of the sounding body, can be isolated and looked at independently of the others. The first partial, otherwise known as the fundamental tone, results from the first mode of vibration, which runs along the entire length of the sounding body. The second mode of vibration which runs along the respective halves of the sounding body produces a simple tone whose frequency is double that of the first i.e. it lies an octave higher than the fundamental frequency. Subsequent modes of vibration based on correspondingly higher fractional lengths of the

---

[1] Robert H. Silsbee, Acoustics, Harvard Dictionary of Music, ed. Don M. Randel, Harvard University Press, London 1986, 7.

sounding body (thirds, quarters, fifths, etc.) and producing simple tones of correspondingly higher frequencies, can be viewed thus:

The Mathematically Regular Modes of Vibration of an Open Pipe

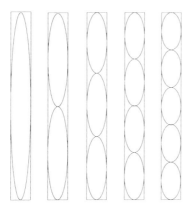

Not all partials are equally audible. As the series rises the partials become gradually fainter to the point of indistinction i.e. the ear can no longer separate individual partials from the complex mass of vibration. Aristotle observed that *a musical note constantly contained its musical octave*,[1] whilst Mersenne, in his Harmonie Universelle observed that *every string produces five or more different sounds at the same instant, the strongest of which is called the natural sound of the string, and alone is accustomed to be taken notice of, for the* others are so faint that they are only perceptible to delicate ears.[2]

Some musicians hearing is more sensitive than others in this respect. Olivier Messiaen believed that it was possible to perceive the pitch of the first fifteen separate harmonics.[3] Be that as it may, after a certain point it is impossible to recognize individual partials any longer. Nonetheless their collective effect contributes to our sense of the tone color or timbre of the instrument upon which the note is played. Arnold Schoenberg (1874 - 1951) alludes to this in his Theory of Harmony: In *the overtone series, which is one of the most remarkable properties of the tone, there appear after some stronger sounding overtones a number of weaker-sounding ones. Without a doubt the former are*

---

[1] Guy Oldham, Harmonics, The New Grove Dictionary of Music and Musicians, Ed, by Stanlie Sadie, etc., London 1995, Vol. 8,167.

[2] Ibid.

[3] Olivier Messiaen, Technique de mon Langage Musical (Volumes 1 and 2), Alphonse Leduc, Paris 1966.

more familiar to the ear, while the latter, hardly perceptible, are rather strange...But it is quite certain that they all do contribute more or less, that of the acoustical emanations of the tone nothing is lost.... Even if the analyzing ear does not become conscious of them, they are still heard as tone colour. [1]

One of the most intriguing features of the partials that comprise a musical tone is the mathematical relationship that exists between their frequencies. Here, Dr Silsbee observes that: *for many musical sounds, specifically those that are continuously produced by a single source such as the bowed violin, trumpet, oboe, or voice, a special relationship exists among the partial frequencies: they are all equal to an integer times a single frequency, called the fundamental.* [2]

This 'special relationship' can be portrayed through the example of a vibrating string. The second string on the violin is ordinarily tuned to produce note A, which according to modern Western diapason has a frequency of 440v./s. The number itself, descriptive of the frequency of the fundamental, or first partial, means that subsequent partials will then have frequencies of two, three, four, five, etc., times the frequency of that fundamental.

Conveniently, the ordinal number given to a particular partial corresponds to the number by which the frequency of the fundamental is to be multiplied. Thus the fifth harmonic partial has a frequency five times the fundamental - in this case 2200 v./s.:-

Frequencies of the First Seven Partials of the Violin A String

Partial	Frequency	String Length
First partial	1N - 440H	1M
Second partial	2N - 880H	1/2M
Third partial	3N - 1320H	1/3M
Fourth partial	4N - 1760H	1/4M
Fifth partial	5N - 2200H	1/5M
Sixth partial	6N - 2640H	1/6M
Seventh partial	7N - 3080H	1/7M

In relation to the now rather outmoded term 'overtones', it is useful to remember that the first partial is equivalent to the fundamental (of the overtone series), whilst the second partial is equivalent to the first overtone.

---

[1] Arnold Schoenberg, Theory of Harmony, Trans. by R. E. Carter, Faber & Faber, London 1978, 19.
[2] Robert H. Silsbee, Op. Cit.

Unfortunately, even the most stringent of theorists sometimes confuse these two methods of classification. Therefore, when for example Schenker asserted that the *overtones 7,11, 13, 14, etc., remain totally extraneous to our ear*[1] he means either that it is harmonics 7,11, 13, 14, etc., or overtones 6, 10, 12, 13, etc. which *remain totally extraneous to our ear*.

Because of the mathematical relationship between partials produced by instruments such as the bowed violin, trumpet, oboe or voice the partial configurations produced by such instruments are generally termed harmonic - as opposed to the inharmonic partial configurations of instruments such as the bell, gong, cymbal or even the tuning fork which do not present such a regular mathematical pattern.

The presence of a regular mathematical pattern as distinguishes harmonic from inharmonic partials would seem to be important to our sense of pitch. Hence in those cultures of the world - such as Bali, Thailand or Java - where instruments with inharmonic partials tend to predominate, it often proves difficult to pinpoint the exact pitches of the notes produced.[2] Consequently, it is difficult to expect that within those cultures there will, or should be, an evolution of pitch values which runs parallel to our own. The pitch values relevant to our own musical culture have tended to evolve from the fact that the strings and air pipes used in the standard instruments of the orchestra, produce partials which are harmonic, with the result that the auditory system can detect a common fundamental frequency i.e. a musical tone with a clear and definite pitch.

On paper the harmonic series looks a very simple phenomenon owing to the fact that the exact frequencies of successive harmonics are related as the integers 1, 2, 3, 4, 5, 6, 7, 8, 9, etc. ad infinitum. To calculate the frequency of any of the harmonics of a given pitch the fundamental frequency is thus multiplied by the number of the harmonic whose frequency is sought. Given a fundamental frequency of 220v./s. (note A), the frequency of the seventh harmonic is thus $7 \times 220 = 1540$ v./s..

The relationship between individual members of the harmonic series can be represented by the mathematical ratio between the frequencies concerned. The relationship between the fifth and fourth harmonics is thus represented by the ratio of 5/4. Moreover, it will be seen that this relationship is duplicated many times in the harmonic series - between the tenth and eighth harmonics; the twelfth and fifteenth harmonics; the eightieth and the hundredth harmonics, etc.

---

[1] Heinrich Schenker, Harmony, Trans. by Elizabeth Mann Borgese, The Mit Press, London reprint 1973, 25.

[2] Bernard Arps (Ed.), Notes on the Acoustics and Tuning of Gamelan Instruments, Performance in Java and Bali, School of Oriental and African Studies, London 1993, 197 - 200.

Completely new relationships originate only when the denominator of the ratio is odd, since if it is even, it is already divisible by two. Prime numbered harmonics therefore, are exceedingly important, as they originate new relationships in the series.

The significance of this is lost until the members of the harmonic series are represented by precise string and/or pipe lengths, or pitches on the staff. Then the study starts to have more of a bearing on actual musical issues and problems. Indeed, many curious features concerning the harmonic series may be noticed.

For the second harmonic a length of half that of the open pipe/string is required to produce the corresponding frequency; whilst for the third harmonic a length of one third is required. The differences between those respective string lengths is thus subject to a process of perpetual diminishment:

Differences Between String/Pipe Lengths in the Harmonic Series

Partial	String/Pipe Length		Difference	
First	1000	1 (Whole)		
Second	500	1/2	500	1/2
Third	333.3	1/3	166.66	1/6
Fourth	250	1/4	83.3	1/12
Fifth	200	1/5	50	1/20
Sixth	166.6	1/6	33.3	1/30
Seventh	142.9	1/7	23.7	1/42

The difference in length is obtained by dividing the first term by the second i.e. 1/4 of 1/3 = 1/12; 1/5 of 1/4 = 1/20, etc. The process of perpetual diminishment of the mean length of string/pipe required to produce successive harmonics, reflected in the sizes of the intervals between the pitches corresponding to the harmonic series, means that such differences can be viewed more clearly by representing the harmonic series in staff notation.

Partials in brackets, namely the seventh and eleventh, are considered to be 'out of tune' with the equally tempered pitches represented by our staff notation. As Martin Vogel points out *every prime number introduces tonal relations that can no longer be represented and described with the letters and signs of our conventional tone system.*[1] For this reason, the nearest convenient equivalent is usually given.

---

[1] Martin Vogel, On the Relations of Tone, trans. by V. J. Kisselbach, ed. by Carl A. Poldy, Verlag für systematische Musikwissenschaft GmbH, Bonn 1993, 21.

First Twelve Harmonics of Cello C String on Staff Notation

Partial:	1st.	2nd.	3rd.	4th.	5th.	6th.	7th.	8th.	9th.	10th.	11th.	12th.
String L.:	1n	1/2n	1/3n	1/4n	1/5n	1/6n	1/7n	1/8n	1/9n	1/10n	1/11n	1/12n
Frequency:	1m	2m	3m	4m	5m	6m	7m	8m	9m	10m	11m	12m

Correlative with the gradual diminishment of the differential of pipe/string lengths necessary to produce these pitches, the intervals between adjacent harmonics gradually get smaller. Is there any relationship between these sizes? This question can be answered by looking more closely at the intervals concerned. After the interval of the octave occurring between the first and second partials, the third partial divides the octave into two smaller intervals: whose ratios are 3/2 and 4/3 respectively. In the placing of the next few harmonic partials it can be seen that as the interval of the octave has become subdivided by the third partial, so the intervals whose ratios are 3/2 and 4/3 become similarly subdivided, this pattern perpetuating itself thereafter, each interval between adjacent harmonics becoming subdivided in the next octave of its appearance.

Because the intervals in the harmonic series get progressively smaller the lower interval of each pair is always the larger. To calculate the ratio of the differential interval between each pair of intervals:

1) Multiply the denominator of the ratio of the larger interval by the numerator of the ratio of the smaller interval.

2) Multiply the numerator of the first ratio by the denominator of the second ratio.

The former gives the denominator of the ratio of the interval that represents their difference, whilst the latter gives the numerator of the interval that represents their difference. Thus the interval which represents the difference between intervals 3/2 and 4/3 is 3 x 3 = 9 (denominator) and 2 x 4 = 8 (numerator), thus giving a resultant ratio of 9/8. In this way, 9/8 is the differential interval of 3/2 and 4/3.

Processes of Intervallic Subdivision in the Harmonic Series

1 : 2							
2 : 3				3 : 4			
4 : 5		5 : 6		6 : 7		7 : 8	
8:9	9:10	10:11	11:12	12:13	13:14	14:15	15:16
16:17 17:18 18:19 19:20 20:21 21:22 22:23 23:24 24:25 25:26 26:27 27:28 28:29 29:30 30:31 31:32							

From the diagram above it can be seen that the harmonic series represents an exponential growth pattern. Whilst in the first octave there is only one interval, in the second octave there are two. Similarly, between the sixth and fourth partials lies the fifth partial, and between the sixth and eighth partials the seventh partial. Therefore, in the third octave there are four intervals. So the pattern continues, the number of partials within each successive octave increasing according to the ratio of 1:2. This means that the increase in the numbers of partials in each octave of the harmonic series conforms to the geometrical progression of numbers 1: 2: 4: 8: 16: 32: 64: etc..

A natural scale or series of scales based on the harmonic series would thus have 8, 16, 32, 64 division's etc. Because of the gradual diminishment in the sizes of the intervals however, such scales, although quite natural, tend to be impractical. This tends to borne out by the observation that musical history seems to favour scales where the pitches rise or fall by proportionate steps, examples of which are the diatonic scale, composed of whole and half tones, and the chromatic scale, composed of semitones. But there again, there are always exceptions. Kathleen Schlesinger's *The Greek Aulos*[1] is notable in this respect, in that it argues for the use of pure harmonic scales within the music of ancient Greece. Basing her theories not on the lyre of traditional Greek musical theory, but on the discovery of wind instruments with equal boring, she showed that these would yield scales conforming to the upper regions of the harmonic series, i.e.:

Harmonic Scale Implied by Equally Bored Pipe

$$9/8 \quad 5/4 \quad 11/8 \quad 3/2 \quad 13/8 \quad 7/4 \quad 15/8$$

The result is a scale that could only be represented very imperfectly in modern staff notation.

When considering such relationships it is important to observe that the harmonic series is generated upwards from the lowest pitch. So far as musical harmony is concerned, this is crucial, for it means that the bass line of a composition possesses a critical importance as the foundation for the upper parts. That the first six harmonics define a perfect major triad in root position is significant in this respect, for in practice, the upper notes of such a chord will serve to merely reinforce the primary partials of that fundamental. The result is a sonority of great strength and stature, although so far as the minor chord is concerned, there is clearly a conflict between the flat third and the fifth harmonic. It is interesting however, that when the major triad is mirrored, so that the root becomes the axis of symmetry, a minor chord is obtained as the negative reflection of the major chord:

Minor Triad as Mirror of the Major Chord

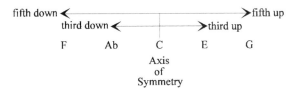

This observation raises an intriguing question. As the major chord finds a natural ratification in the harmonic series, does mean that the minor chord finds ratification in a sub-harmonic series – an exact mirror image of the harmonic

---

[1] Kathleen Schlesinger, The Greek Aulos, Methuen and Co. Ltd. London 1939.

series? On paper, it is remarkably easy to demonstrate the possibility of such a series:

Harmonic and Sub-harmonic Series

	Harmonic Series		Sub-harmonic Series	
Harmonic	Frequency	String Length	Frequency	String Length
First	1m	1n	1m	1n
Second	2m	1/2n	1/2m	2n
Third	3m	1/3n	1/3m	3n
Fourth	4m	1/4n	1/4m	4n
Etc.				

This is an interesting concept, which, like the related idea of anti-matter in physics, has fuelled much debate.[1] In the main however, it is difficult to accept this theory, for it means that the root of the minor chord would thus be the upper note - the fifth - a notion which would throw harmonic theory into a state of utter confusion. And in more practical terms, this idea is also problematic because whilst a string can vibrate at a half, a third, or a quarter of its length, it cannot vibrate at a half, a third, or a quarter of its fundamental rate of vibration. For the second sub-harmonic, this would mean that the string would have to be vibrating at double its own length - a physical impossibility. Descartes (1596 - 1650) subtly pointed this out three hundred years ago: *Sound is to sound as string to string; but each string contains in itself all others which are less than it, and not those which are greater: consequently, every sound contains in itself those sounds which are higher but not those which are lower.*[2]

By the very incontestability of Descartes observation, an equal and opposite reflection of the harmonic series can only be regarded as a hypothetical phenomenon. Vibrations lower than the fundamental tone have been discovered - difference tones for example - the original discovery of which may be attributed to the Italian violinist, composer and theorist Guiseppe Tartini (1692 - 1770),[3] have frequencies which are calculated as the difference between the frequencies of two notes. These however cannot be cited in support of the

---

[1] William Mickelson, Hugo Riemann's Theory of Harmony: A Study, University of Nebraska Press, Lincoln 1977.

[2] This is the statement which Rameau presents at the beginning of the third chapter of his Treatise on Harmony. Philip Gosset however, points out that it is part of a citation from Descartes' Compendium of Music, 60. (Rameau, Treatise on Harmony, 5, ft. 8).

[3] Tartini referred to difference tones as 'terzi suoni' in his Trattato de Musica (Padua 1754).

theory of the sub-harmonic series, as they have no objective existence, being a phenomenon of the inner ear.[1] The highly attractive, although physically implausible theory of the 'undertone series' therefore, can for the moment, be excluded from any further consideration.

The Hypothetical 'Undertone' Series

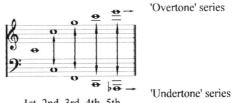

'Overtone' series

1st. 2nd. 3rd. 4th. 5th.

'Undertone' series

The most important feature to focus upon at this stage, is the fact that within the harmonic series exists an intriguing mathematical order, one which becomes all the more remarkable for a phenomenon which, as the epithet sometimes applied to the harmonic series - the 'Chord of Nature'[2] serves to imply, is a completely natural phenomenon. In order to gain a reasonable perspective of what this means, the mathematical order of the harmonic series is not an abstract pattern, but a natural design implicit to each and every musical tone. The musical tone and harmonic series are thus inseparable for they are the same phenomenon being viewed from different perspectives. The tone is the ear's fusion of the multiplicity of partials into a concrete whole, whilst the harmonic series is the plural description of that whole.

This leads on to a number of important points. Because of the naturally ordained order underlying the internal structure of musical tone, the harmonic series should not be ignored if the ramifications resulting from the combination of musical tones are to be understood. The strongest reason for this is that a musical tone is the ear's fusion of many separate partial vibrations into a singular entity. A musical interval, in which two tones are combined, thus presents a relationship between two audibly distinct and separate patterns of partial vibrations. Consequently, the qualities and results attributable to that combination of tones which is called an interval, must derive not solely from a tonal level, but from a subtonal level as well i.e. at the level of the individual partials and their relationships. This point will be more fully discussed in the next chapter.

---

[1] Hermann von Helmholtz, On the Sensations of Tone, Dover Publications Inc., New York 1954, 153-158.
[2] L. S. Lloyd & H. Boyle, Intervals, Scales and Temperaments, London 1963, 289.

Another point is that considering that the mathematically regulated order of partials that comprise a musical tone is entirely natural, means that it is nature that has provided the basic building block from which musical compositions are built. In effect this means that nature itself has an important place in any theory which would satisfactorily explain the relationships from which those compositions are built up. The harmonic series is a product of nature, and in so far that it exerts, or has exerted, an influence on our predisposition towards certain types of musical logic, means that music has thus inherited certain features of natural design which it would be unwise to ignore. Crucially, the natural order of the harmonic series impinges itself upon the brain through the human faculties of hearing, which themselves are a product of natural design. At both levels therefore, nature is participating in the musical process.

This notion need not be objectionable however. The mathematical order underlying the constitution of physical matter as exposed in Mendelehv's 'Table of Elements' is fully recognised by science, and to ignore this natural order would clearly be foolish, simply because it is the determinant of many of the basic laws and principles underlying the behaviour of physical matter itself. Similarly, through the influence of the harmonic series, the 'Chord of Nature', as recognised in eighteenth and nineteenth century musical aesthetics and philosophy, has an important place in musical experience and thinking which cannot possibly be ignored.

THE QUINTESSENTIAL PROPERTY OF VALENCY

From the last chapter it becomes apparent that a well-founded consideration of tonal music can only really begin from one point: the consideration of the essential nature of a single musical tone. The logic of this lies in the argument that as the tone is the unit from which musical structures may be built up, it makes sense to consider the nature of that unit as a first principle. Music after all, can only develop in ways that initially derive from the structural properties of its fundamental building block. In this respect, the basic model of the musical tone as provided for us by physics is extremely useful. As the demonstrable sum of the three respective properties of frequency (wavelength), amplitude (wavedepth) and quality (waveform), it is in these that the musical pitch, intensity and timbre of music are based. Add to these the span of time allotted to the tone within the musical concourse - the duration, then a basic workable model of the musical tone and its four respective properties is obtained.

As the basic unit of the language of music it doesn't really matter *which* tone is considered. In essence, all musical tones may be regarded to be the same: i.e. as replications of one another. Like a cell, which through processes of replication gives rise to an entire organism, so a complete musical composition can be understood in a similar sense. Each musical tone that occurs within it is a replication of the others. Herein lies the key to an initial definition of music which is simply this: music is the replication of tone.

Yet within this definition there seems to be a fundamental flaw. To assert that music is the replication of tone implies that music consists of nothing more than a process of monotonal repetition. Yet this is an extremely simplistic interpretation of this statement. The replication of musical tone proceeds along certain fundamental tracks that are implicit to each and every musical tone. These tracks are the four properties of tone designated by the terms pitch, intensity, timbre and duration.

Every musical tone possesses these properties and all essential differences between one tone and another are directly attributable to variations amongst them. Replication where these values remain invariable can only be defined as being static. In contrast to this there is replication characterised by movement along one or more of these fundamental tracks: alterations in the pitch, intensity, timbre, and duration, which would therefore be defined as a process of dynamic replication.

Looking at this concept in terms of dynamic levels, static replication implies a succession of tones where the dynamic level is relatively constant, whilst dynamic replication implies a movement along that track, and therefore an alteration in the dynamic level. Here there are only two possible directions of movement: towards increase or decrease.

This fundamental condition is basically true of the other properties of tone as well. In pitch, it is only possible to rise or fall; in duration to augment or contract. Timbre is perhaps more problematic because there is no objective scale of tone quality. But even here, those distinctions between bright and dark, clear and nasal, etc., show that the same basic principle is in operation, but on a more diffuse and complex level.

The language of music is generally characterised by the presence of a balance or mean between static and dynamic levels of tonal replication. This is because too much of the former is to invite a state of unending monotony, whilst too much of the latter gives the impression of a rambling chaos. To strike a successful balance between the two states is to give the impression of an intelligible order, a plan or pattern that the listener may follow. Ultimately, such a balance would culminate in an impression of that state of unity referred to in the last chapter. But of course, it all begins in the first place, with the tone and its properties.

As the basic units of a musical composition, musical tones may be viewed to occupy their own distinctive world. That world, it will be surmised, has four basic elements: pitch, intensity, timbre and duration. Each of these elements can be viewed to have three aspects: increase, decrease, and stasis. The three aspects are themselves the expression of the two states: fixed and changing. These, in themselves, are simply the two sides of the principle of replication. In this way, beginning with a single tone and the possibilities of its replication, the fundamental unity of the tonal world can be clearly defined:

The Fourfold Unity of the Tonal World

        1 Replication
        2 Static/dynamic
        3 Increase/decrease/stasis
        4 Pitch/intensity/duration

Of the four levels of replication the most important for this study is the element of pitch, for the concern here is not so much with the building up of a complete scheme of musical parameters, but understanding just why musical tones tend to build up into those pitch aggregates which characterise tonal music in general. Towards this end it becomes expedient to observe that the value of pitch occupies its own particular place in the tonal world. That place may be accorded an initial definition through the consideration of vibration numbers as devised and introduced by Marin Mersenne in his *Harmonie Universelle* of 1636-7.[1] If the sensation of pitch is attributed to the ears detection of the common fundamental of any number of harmonic partials present in a complex tone, then that pitch can be represented by a definite number, in this case, the ordinal number which represents the number of vibrations per unit second of that fundamental frequency. Each musical tone can thus be assigned a specific vibration number that remains true for all subsequent appearances of that tone.

Consequently, the dimension of pitch can be expressed mathematically in the sense that a series of rising vibration numbers would correspond to a rise in pitch, and visa versa. It was undoubtedly this initial idea which gave rise to the concept of the frequency or pitch continuum, an idea propagated both by Carl Stumpf (1848 - 1936) in his *Tonpsychologie* of 1883,[2] and later by Carl Seashore (1866 - 1949) in his *Psychology of Music* (1938).[3] Here the element of pitch is conceptualised as a straight line composed theoretically of an infinite number of points, each pitch or fundamental frequency thus representing a point somewhere along that line: -

The Pitch Continuum

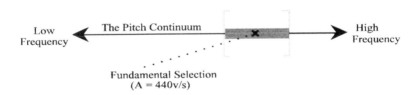

As a mode of conception of tonal space, the idea of the pitch continuum raises a number of interesting contingencies. If a musical pitch is considered as a point along a straight line, an interval may be considered to represent a finite section. An octave is thus analogous to a line of say length n, whilst an equally tempered semitone would be equivalent to 1/12n. At all points along that line, a

---

[1] Marin Mersenne, Book 1, Harmonie Universelle, Paris 1636 - 1637.

[2] Karl Stumpf, Tonpsychologie, Leipzig 1883, 122.

[3] Carl Emil Seashore, The Psychology of Music, New York: McGraw Hill 1938; Reprint New York/Dover 1967, 53.

measurement of 1/12n will yield an equally tempered semitone. The advantages of this mode of conception of musical pitch are considerable, for they foreshorten difficulties in the perception of intervallic breadth prompted by the unwieldy and often complex measurements occurring in the form of string lengths and ratios.

In terms of the former, a regular division of the pitch continuum can only be crudely expressed through a geometrical progression of numbers descriptive of the increase or decrease of string lengths required to create that division.

Octave Division of Pitch Continuum Expressed in String Lengths

16'   8'   4'   2'   1'   6"   3"   1.5"   Etc.

The same essential distance along the pitch continuum thus yields a different value each time. The concept of the pitch continuum is therefore extremely important, for it provides a direct spatial analog of the logarithmic nature of frequency relationships. Evidently, the analog itself was the nearest ancient Greek theorists such as Aristoxenus (c 375 - 360 b.c.,d. ?) who abstracted up to thirty equal divisions of a perfect fourth, ever came to the precise logarithmic method of measuring intervals which is used today.[1]

The concept of the pitch continuum serves as a great leveler of cultural bias extended towards particular tonal systems and scale structures. Although, within the confines of a particular culture, a given scale or pitch structure may carry a great weight of historical authority and inevitability, it can more realistically be viewed as a series of pitch points that have been selected from that continuum according to various criteria. Accordingly, there are an infinite variety of possibilities actually available.[2] This notion prompts a fairer view of scale structures other than the equally tempered twelve-note scale. These would include the pentatonic scale of traditional Chinese music; the twenty-two note Northern Hindustani *Sa and Ma Grāma*; the Pythagorean seven-toned scale prevalent in ancient Greek music, or the basic foundation scale of seventeen notes derived from the spiral of fifths used in the music of Arabia.

Such alternative tonal systems depend upon a body of cultural usage that gives them an aura of inevitability within their own cultures. Yet from a cross-cultural standpoint not one of these systems can be proved to be superior or more necessary than the other. Simply, there are no absolutes in terms of the

---

[1] Aristoxenus: Elementa Harmonica, Book I, 3-7: Greek Musical Writings, Vol. II: Harmonic and Acoustic Theory, Ed. by Andrew Barker, Cambridge University Press, Cambridge 1989, 126-30.
[2] Ramon Fuller, A Study of Microtonal Equal Temperaments, JMT, 35, Spring 1991, p. 230.

systems which different cultures choose for the purposes of musical expression. The equally tempered twelve tone scale is one of these, and at any time, according to the expediency of the age and time, may become superseded by another, quite different system.

Schoenberg in his Theory of Harmony alludes to this point: *Moreover, it is not to our scale alone that we owe the evolution of our music. And above all, this scale is not the last word, the ultimate goal in music, but rather a provisional stopping place. The overtone series, which led the ear to it, still contains many problems that will have to be faced. And if, for the time being we still manage to escape those problems, it is due to little else than a compromise between the natural intervals and our inability to use them - that compromise which we call the tempered system, which amounts to an indefinitely extended truce. This reduction of the natural relations to manageable ones cannot permanently impede the evolution of music; and the ear will have to attack the problems, because it is so disposed. Then our scale will be transformed into a higher order, as the church modes were transformed into major and minor modes. Whether there will then be quarter-tones, eighth-, third-, or (as Busoni thinks) sixt-tones, or whether we will move directly to a 53-tone scale that Dr Robert Neumann has calculated, we cannot foretell. Perhaps this new division of the octave will even be untempered and will not have much left over in common with our scale. However that may be, attempts to compose in quarter or third tones, as are being undertaken here and there, seem senseless, as long as there are too few instruments available that can play them. Probably, whenever the ear and imagination have matured enough for such music, the scale and the instruments will all at once be available. It is certain that this movement is now afoot, certain that it will lead to something.*[1]

Bearing such considerations in mind, it becomes necessary to make further inquiries about those pitch structures, that for various reasons have managed to emerge from the formless and primeval state that is the pitch continuum. When for example, a composer selects a pitch for the purposes of a composition, they are making a selection from the infinite array of fundamentals which constitutes the pitch continuum. Containing within itself all possible pitches it is an important part of the world in which musical tone has its substance and being: each tone, viewed as unity, occupies a place in that realm, and has its own space and position. Subsequent pitches selected for the same purpose automatically fall subject to the principle of replication. Static replication gravitates about the same point, whilst dynamic replication moves either up or down along that pitch scale.

---

[1] Arnold Schoenberg, Op. Cit., 25.

Outside of the domain of electronic music, such movements do not generally utilise the entire resources of the pitch continuum. Changes in pitch usually occur in relation to a pre-established scale of values that offer a series of discrete steps between one pitch and another. The equally tempered twelve-tone scale of European music is an infallible example of this. Generally viewed as *the* scale of Western music, its mass adoption by all concerned has been a source of many problems, for it represents a constraint against the free utilisation of the total resources of the pitch continuum.

Should therefore, a composer decide to use a different scale of values, say for example a nineteen or thirty-one note equal division of the octave, the problems involved can be considerable. Yet the natural musical instrument possessed by all of us is the voice, and unlike many other instruments it is capable within its range, of sliding up and down the pitch continuum as and when required. So why is a scale of pitch values required? That this issue is not unique to the music of the West becomes apparent from the fact that such scales, even though they may be differently organised to the twelve tone tempered scale, occur throughout the world wherever music is practiced.

The fact that such scales occur everywhere, points to the existence of a constraint or natural principle which works against the infinitude of possibility provided for by the pitch continuum, and instead serves to regulate changes of pitch so that they do conform to a scale of values. This in its turn indicates that musical tone itself may possess more than four basic properties: a fifth aspect may be implicated which provides the automatic basis for such pitch regulation.

Like the formation of matter in the universe from an infinite and formless stream of charged particles, processes of tonal coalescence and accretion from the raw matter of the pitch continuum have occurred throughout the history of music. Resulting in pitch structures like the major, minor or chromatic scales, such tonal formations often tend to harbor some kind of intelligible order; the semblance of a pattern of some kind. This indicates that processes of tonal replication do not occur in an atmosphere of infinite freedom that the basic grounds of the pitch continuum would serve to suggest. Indeed, it seems that wherever music has been developed, its emergence has been guided by a hidden principle, which although felt and sensed, seems to be hidden, obscure, or extremely difficult to formulate.

Since the very earliest times, number has been invoked as an important element of such structures, and even today, number often proves crucial as a factor in the organisation and arrangement of musical pitches. As to why number is so important, is a difficult question to answer. Certainly to attempt to study even the rudiments of music without recourse to number theory is well nigh impossible. In terms of pitch, the clearest and most potent manifestation of numbers is in the ratios of the basic intervals used in music. The octave has a ratio of 2/1, the perfect fifth a ratio of 3/2, and the perfect fourth a ratio of 4/3.

Another area in which numbers manifest is in the composition of tone itself, in which successive members of the harmonic series have frequencies which represent whole number multiples of the frequency of the fundamental. Therefore the ratios of the intervals given above are also found in the relationship between the first four members of the harmonic series. This observation has been made by a long line of musical theorists, not the least of which was the Dutch physicist Adriaan Fokker, who observed that *If both notes belong to the same overtone series - to the overtones of the same fundamental - we have an harmonic interval...intervals such as 2/3, 3/7, 9/11 are harmonic intervals.*[1]

From this clear correlation between the intervals used in music, and those implied in the harmonic series, much capital has been made, for it would seem that the internal structure of musical tone, as defined by the harmonic series, has a bearing on those intervals which have been selected and used for the purposes of musical expression, i.e. the three perfect intervals whose ratios are defined above:

The Three Perfect Intervals as Implied by the First Four Harmonic Partials

	Octave		Perfect 5th		Perfect 4th	
Note:	C		C		G		C
Ratio:	1		2		3		4

Although this may be true at a superficial level, there are other factors at work which considerably modify the picture to be obtained as to the reasons why certain primary musical intervals have emerged from and occupied such an important place in the musical cosmos. The most important factor is a property of musical tone that does not seem to have been properly defined. This is the property of *valency*: the innate capacity of musical tones to bond with each other to form metatonal structures. Intervals, scales and chords are prime examples of such structures.

The existence of such a property is not difficult to understand. Each musical tone can be viewed to be a sum of simple tones whose frequencies conform to the terms of an arithmetic progression i.e. 1, 2, 3, 4, 5, 6, 7, etc *ad infinitum*. When two or more tones are combined together, the pattern of partials present within each tone are brought into close juxtaposition with one another. When

---

[1] Adriaan Fokker, Neue Musik mit 31 Tönen, Düsseldorf 1966, 47.

the notes concerned share one or more of these partials, the ear is able to recognise a common bond between them. The existence of such bonds, pre-empted by the pattern of partials present within each tone, provides the basis for that quintessential property of tone here described as the valency:

The Five Properties of Musical Tone

        1. Pitch
        2. Intensity
        3. Timbre
        4. Duration
        5. Valency

In this sense, the power of valency is hierarchical, in that it begins with the unison, two tones of identical pitches whose partials are completely alike, and thenceforth extends to every other interval, whose place in the hierarchy is determined by how many partials are common to the notes concerned.

The idea of shared partials is not new. In the eighteenth century, Esteve and Saveur were investigating the role of shared partials in the determination of the consonant qualities of musical intervals.[1] The Swiss mathematician Leonard Euler went even further, using the idea of shared partials to generate a numerical scale by which the degree of consonance of a musical interval could be obtained.[2] A very simple demonstration can be seen with the perfect fifth whose ratio is 3/2. The third partial of the lowermost note C is at the same time the second partial of the uppermost note G. This shared note, Euler called the *exponent*, and in this case it has a value of 6:

Definition of the Exponent of the Interval of a Perfect Fifth

C		C	G
2		4	6
	G		G
	3		6

A very simple rule for the discovery of the exponent is to multiply the numerator by the denominator of the ratio concerned. Therefore, the exponent of the interval whose ratio is 4/3 is 12, whilst the exponent of the interval whose

---

[1] Mathew Shirlaw, Theory of Harmony, Novello & Company Ltd., London 1917, 283-284.
[2] Leonard Euler, Conjecture sur la rasion de quelques dissonances généralement reçues dans la musique (1764), Opera Omnia, Serie III, Band 1, Leipzig and Berlin 1926.

ratio is 5/4 is 20. For Euler, the exponent provided a precise numerical value, which he felt, was able to define the degree of tension present within an interval.

In many ways, this system is problematic, although it should be pointed out that it is not the place here to comment upon the value of Euler's theories, for these are aimed towards an understanding of the qualities and attributes of musical intervals. The concept of valency as used here applies to individual musical tones. This is because it represents the capacity of musical tones to bond with one another by virtue of the mathematically regular definition of their component partials. Euler's exponent is the first point at which a bond takes place.

The property of valency is something which is of fundamental importance to music. When a musical tone is replicated, it already carries within it the basic tracks or channels which may serve to offer it an audible connection with another tone. This might explain why, throughout musical history, and in all cultures, musical tones have tended to build up into systematic aggregations, that is, tonal structures which serve to define those basic paths or channels. This is because of the property of *valency*, possessed by each and every musical tone. Like the quintessence of the four elements of the alchemists, this force is essentially invisible in the sense that it is the glue that binds the multiplicity of tone together into a coherent and intelligible whole.

A prime example of the manifestation of the property of valency is the interval of the octave. It is common knowledge that when notes whose fundamental frequencies conform to the ratio of 2/1 are played together, a remarkable aural phenomenon occurs. The pitches blend so well that the ear takes the respective tones to be the same in some way.

Theorists have often commented upon this fact. The eighteenth century theorist Kirnberger (1721 - 1783) observed that: *notes that have been considered alike because of their great correspondence or complete agreement are those whose string or pipe lengths are related to one another as the numbers 1, 1/2, 1/4, 1/8, etc. That is, when a stretched string produces a note designated as C, half of this string under the same tension will produce a higher note that the ear accepts as just the same. For this reason they have been designated by the same letter.*[1]

Here Kirnberger makes an important point about this interval - the same note letter portrays the two notes. This is reliably evident in the Western Diatonic Scale of seven notes:

[1] Johann Philipp Kirnberger, The Art of Strict Musical Composition, Trans. by D. Beach & Jürgen Thym; Yale University Press, New Haven and London 1982.

The Diatonic Scale

Note:	C	D	E	F	G	A	B	C
Degree:	1	2	3	4	5	6	7	8
Frequency:	264H	297H	330H	352H	396H	440H	495H	528H

$$1 \qquad : \qquad 2$$

When viewed as a harmonic sonority the absolute consonant qualities of the interval of the octave are well recognised. As Kirnberger indicates, it is these qualities that have led to the notion of octave equivalence in the first place. Yet why do two notes an octave apart sound so alike? One of the most convincing explanations came from the nineteenth century German physicist Hermann Helmholtz (1821 - 1894) who observed that: If *we allow a low voice to be accompanied by a higher in the octave above it, the only part music which the Greeks employed, we add nothing new, we merely reinforce the evenly numbered partials. In this sense then the compound tones of an octave above are really repetitions of the tones of the lower octaves, or at least a part of their constituents.*[1]

For Helmholtz therefore, our perception of the aural qualities of that sonority is determined by an aural comparison of the partial structure of the two notes. If correct, such a process occurs automatically, because of the difficulty in perceiving more than a few separate partials at the very most. That this happens to both trained and untrained ears indicates that the process of comparison is something that happens within the inner ear.

Bonding Pattern of Two Musical Notes an Octave Apart

As Helmholtz observes, the partials of the upper note are repetitions of the even numbered partials of the lower note. As a result of these shared partials the ear recognises a powerful valent bond between the two notes. Therefore, although the two notes are indeed separate pitches, they are perceived as a unit

---

[1] Hermann Helmholtz, On The Sensation of Tone, Dover Publications Inc., New York, 1954, 254.

owing to the natural force of valency as revealed and manifested through the presence of those shared partials.

In this way, the ears preference for intervals with simple ratios derives from its recognition of the great strength of those valent bonds as they occur between the stronger harmonics lower down in the series. Here, the interval of the octave comes to represent the strongest valent bond possible between two notes. So strong is this bond that the ear perceives the two notes as belonging to the same pitch class.

In this respect the octave becomes an important principle underlying the division of the frequency continuum, establishing, as it does, a periodically generating frequency space against which other pitch relationships can be generated, measured and brought into a recognisable pitch system.

Bob Gilmore sums up the nature of the octave relationship as follows: *Helmholtz (1863), Mach (1906) and Koftha (1935) shared a general tendency to conceive pitch as a one-dimensional attribute of sound... Mach wrote 'A tonal series occurs in something which is an analogue of space, but is a space of one dimension limited in both directions and exhibiting no symmetry...it more resembles a straight line'. This tendency left unsolved the psychoacoustical problem that any representation of pitch as one-dimensional does not account for the phenomenon of octave equivalence; and octaves moreover, are only one of many musically useful relationships that stand out from this continuum. Revesz (1913) had suggested that pitch be treated instead as a bidimensional attribute, the first dimension representing overall pitch level (what would become known as pitch height), and the second defining the position of tone within the octave (tone chroma).*[1]

Further light can be shed on these problems through the understanding that the recognition of the property of valency implicates a multi-dimensional model of the tonal space in which frequency changes operate. Here different dimensions of tonal space arise because the connection between musical tones can derive from any one or more of numerous partial frequencies. The ratio of 1/1 signifies the connection of kind to kind - which is a process of pitch replication that is essentially static.

Analogous to a single point in space, the monotone is theoretically dimensionless, in that it possesses no means of extension outside of itself. The ratio of 2/1 however, implicates a change of frequency (dynamic replication), and therefore a movement in a particular dimension of frequency space. It is like two such points which together form a line running in a particular direction. Because two is divisible by one twice means that a frequency connection of this

---

[1] Bob Gilmore, Changing the Metaphor: Ratio Models of Musical Pitch in the Work of Harry Partch, Ben Johnston, and James Tenney; in PNM, 33, 1, 467.

order occurs in the same mathematical dimension as 1/1. The octave thus becomes a manifestation of the paradox that is a motion in frequency space which itself remains static. 1/1 therefore signifies the static representative of the first dimension of tonal space, whilst 2/1 signifies its dynamic representative. Being dynamic, it theoretically counts as a prime number, but being divisible by two, it represents a repeat of the condition that is one. Two, it may be noted, is the only prime number that possesses this unique dual property.

Consequently, the phenomenon of 2-valency serves to define the periodic nodes of pitch recurrence at higher or lower levels of the frequency continuum. This process, as pointed out by Kirnberger, is governed by the geometric progression of numbers 1, 2, 4, 8, 16, 32, 64, etc. Therefore it is quite appropriate that all frequencies conforming to this progression are ascribed the same note letter. Further, because of the notion of recurrence implicit within this framework, each unit of frequency space delineated by that geometric progression of numbers ceases to be viewed as a linear section of frequency, and instead becomes a closed circle of frequency orientation. Therefore, the inevitable and most natural two-dimensional symbol so far as the musical octave is concerned is the circle whose linear representation of the process of cyclic rotation finds its logical counterpart in the rising or falling progression of frequencies from a given note to its reoccurrence on the next level of the pitch continuum.

Through the force of 2-valency therefore, tonal space becomes a helix of seven or eight turns, each turn representing one octave of the pitch continuum. Tonal space is thus not straight, as may be automatically assumed, but it is curved.

INTERVALS AS THE EXPLICATION OF VALENT BONDS

Having defined that quintessential property of musical tone described as the valency, the next stage is to consider the ramifications that result from the recognition of that property.

The mathematically regular configuration of partials that define a musical tone exists by order of nature and nature alone. The study of musical tones and their various combinations as occur in melodic lines and harmonic formations, thus possesses a certain degree of natural objectivity which gives the study of music a slant in a particular direction. If the unit of the tone has a natural and objective basis, then, by the same token, the property of valency by which one musical tone is capable of making an audible bond with another, has an equally natural and objective basis.

The array of musical intervals obtained through the combination of musical tones in accordance with the laws of valency are thus the natural elements of the musical language, that is to say, elements which are both ratified and sanctified by the order of nature. To say this is to take up an aesthetic position that hearkens back to the time of Rameau. Yet no apology need be made for this, because it is the property of valency itself which leads inevitably towards a reaffirmation of the place and part that the objective world of nature plays in the definition of the basic elements of the musical language.

Valency has already been defined as the capacity of musical tones to bond with others of kind. The importance of this natural property for the language of music cannot possibly be overestimated. As the invisible force that binds musical tones, it represents the natural substantive basis for those tone combinations presented under the guise of melody and harmony in general. Therefore to countenance music as a set of mathematical frequencies, or indeed, a range of co-ordinates in frequency space is pointless. Owing to the binding force of valency, when two notes are heard either simultaneously in the case of an harmonic interval, or successively in the case of a melodic movement, they are heard as a unit, in which the two notes become subsumed into a larger overriding identity which is the relationship that binds them.

At a general level this notion is well recognised. Baker for example, observes that *we have come rather a long way from the view that it is the note, which makes music. We begin to discern the real position: that notes are only supports for something that happens between them.*[1] That something, is of course the valent bond which conjoins them. Valency therefore, is a very curious property, for whilst it is possessed by each and every musical tone, it remains latent until attempts are made to combine tones together. In this sense, it provides an invisible guiding force, subtly leading and motivating the combination of tones in a particular direction.

Like the bonding patterns of molecules, musical tones bond in certain ways, and according to certain principles. The simplest unit in which the force of valency is able to work, is therefore when two tones are combined together. The unit of either a melodic (successive) or harmonic (simultaneous) combination of two pitches is an interval. *Interval is the most basic, the most essential of all pitch relationships*[2] writes Alden Ashforth, and this is essentially true. Valency, latent within the tone, only becomes manifest with the interval. Consequently, it can be seen that it is the interval that upon the next level of consideration replaces the tone as the nuclear unit of musical expression.

Comprising that nuclear unit, it is convenient that each interval used in a piece of music can be divorced from its contextual appearance and examined as a pitch relationship in its own right. The intervals thus obtained will have particular qualities and attributes which allow them to be both compared and contrasted with other intervals. These qualities and attributes, together with the methodology underlying their study will provide a particular focus for this chapter, which, it is hoped, will provide the basic grounds through which an approach to more advanced musical matters may be made.

At the first level any isolated musical interval may be viewed as a combination of two musical tones each distinguished by their own particular fundamental frequency. Theoretically the number of intervals which can be used in music is infinite since it is possible to relate any point on the frequency continuum to any other point. Running against this however, are numerous factors which effectively delimit the number of intervals which a musician or composer needs to deal with. Many of the intervals hypothetically possible would simply be transpositions of the same frequency relationship at a higher or lower register. As such, they are simply duplications of already existing

---

[1] Jurgen Baker, 'The New in Music', Tempo, 30, 1953, 12.

[2] Alden Ashforth, 'The Relationship of the Sixth in Beethoven's Piano Sonata, Opus 110', MR 32/197, 93 - 102, 93.

intervals. Although very important in music, their consideration hardly helps in the assessment of the range of different intervals encountered therein.

Then there is the notion of simple and compound intervals to be considered. Because of the principle of octave equivalence (2- valency) any interval which exceeds the bounds of the octave may be considered to be nothing but a variant of an interval already implicit within the bounds of a single octave. These are obviously important as they provide spatial and textural alternatives to a basic sonority. Yet for the moment they can be excluded as the principal concern here is intervals that are fundamentally different from one another.

Because of these two factors - transposition and octave equivalence - all intervals that can be used in music can be said to be generated within the range of a single octave. This contraction of range from the entire pitch continuum down to the range of a single octave considerably reduces the number of separate classifiable intervals.

Because, after the range of a single octave, the sphere of simple intervals starts to be replaced by the sphere of compound intervals, means that the octave itself is both a dividing point, and sphere of encompassment of the entire spectrum of simple musical intervals. The world of musical intervals thus begins with the unison and ends with the octave.

Any interval between these two points will have a particular size, or breadth, in relation to the octave. Through use of logarithms, that size can be accurately expressed as a proportion of that octave space. The proportions thus obtained allow the most accurate investigations concerning the exact sizes of intervals and the proportional differences between them. Theorists can thus investigate intervals, scales and tuning systems without being entirely dependent upon the cumbersome and often complicated domain of vibration numbers and string lengths.

Logarithms of the original frequency numbers provide the general key to the ingenious systems of intervallic measurement which have been devised over the last two centuries or so. These include the system of cyclic 'Cents' introduced by Alexander Ellis (1814 - 1890),[1] the related unit of the 'Centitone' developed by Joseph Yasser (b.1893),[2] the cycle of 301 'Heptamerides' developed and introduced by J. Saveur (1653 - 1716),[3] and the system of 'Savarts' named after their French progenitor Felix Savart (1791 - 1841).[4]

---

[1] For an account of the system of Cents as derived and used by Ellis, see Hermann Helmholtz, On the Sensations of Tone, Section C, 'Additions by the Translator', 446.

[2] As used and explained by Joseph Yasser in his 'Theory of Evolving Tonality', American Library of Musicology, New York, 1932.

[3] J. Saveur, Mémoire de l'Académie 1701, 310.

[4] As introduced and popularised by the nineteenth century French scientist Felix Savart.

As to which system is preferable, the facility itself is the most important thing, which means that any system that works will suffice. The system in common use today, Ellis's system of 'cents', divides the octave into 1200 equal units, each of which is equivalent to one-hundredth of an equally tempered semitone. To obtain the precise value for a single 'cent' the logarithm of 2 is thus divided by 1200:

$$\text{Log. } 2 = 0.301029995664 \div 1200 = 0.00025085832972$$

According to this system, the interval whose ratio is 3/2 has a measurement of 702 when expressed to the nearest cent:

$$1 \div 2 \times 3 = 1.5$$
$$\text{Log. Of } 1.5 = 0.1760912590557$$
$$0.1760912590557 \div 0.00025085832972$$
$$= 701.955000863$$

For the rest of this study, the system of cents will be used, as it is the system most commonly accepted today. Here are the sizes, expressed to the nearest cent, of some of the commonly used intervals in Western music, as conceived from the standpoint of just intonation - that is pure, as opposed to tempered intervals:

Sizes of Commonly Used Intervals Expressed in Cents

Interval	Ratio	Cents
Unison	1/1	0
Octave	2/1	1200
Perfect fifth	3/2	702
Perfect fourth	4/3	498
Major third	5/4	386
Minor third	6/5	316
Major sixth	5/3	884
Minor sixth	8/5	814
Major second	9/8	204
Minor seventh	16/9	996
Minor second	16/15	112
Major seventh	15/8	1088
Augmented fourth	45/32	590

The size of an interval is important for purposes of theoretical comparison. Far more important than the size of an interva is its valency. This is discovered by observing how two notes are actually able to make a bond with one another. Conveniently, it can be measured through the mathematical ratio between the frequencies of the two fundamental tones of the interval concerned. The ratio of 2/1 automatically signifies that the fundamental of the upper note is at the same time the second partial of the lower note. The result is a valent bond of such strength and tenacity that it is used and appreciated wherever music is found.

Similarly, the ratio of 3/2 signifies that the third partial of the lowermost note is at the same time, the second partial of the uppermost note. This too, is an exceedingly powerful bond between musical tones. So powerful in fact, that the interval of 3/2 ranks alongside the octave as one of the *universals* of the musical language, that is an interval which is used and employed wherever in the world music is practised.

Each interval represents the explication of a single valent bond. The nature of that bond is revealed through the ratio of that particular interval. In this sense, the ratio is an absolutely precise expression of the relationship between two tones. Given the ratio of a musical interval, it cannot be confused with any other. According to the story recounted by Nicomachus (late 1st. century - early 2nd. century AD) it was Pythagoras who first discovered the ratios of the octave (2/1); perfect fifth (3/2) and the perfect fourth (4/3).[1] In effect therefore, Pythagoras had already discovered the mathematical terms by which the force of valency could be clearly defined.

Unfortunately, since the general adoption of equal temperament and its subsequent standardisation of interval sizes, the use of precise note ratios has become something of an anachronism. As Partch observed *tones were therefore deliberately falsified or compromised - only a few at first; later, all. And the ancient idea of simple ratios was junked.*[2] Even the validity of simple ratios has been questioned.

As early as the fourth century BC, the Greek philosopher Aristoxenus was questioning the concept of Pythagorean note proportions, preferring instead to view pitch as a continuum which could be divided by a number of smaller equal intervals. Although one of the first theorists to conceptualise the idea of equal interval scales, Aristoxenus nonetheless retained the simple ratios for the prime (1/1), octave (2/1), perfect fifth (3/2) and fourth (4/3) by which the framework for the two tetrachords was established.

---

[1] Oliver Strunk, Source Readings in Musical History, Faber and Faber, London 1952, 13.

[2] Harry Partch, Bitter Music: Collected Journals, Essays, Introductions and Librettos, Ed. by Thomas Mc Geary, University of Illinois Press, Urbana and Chicago 1991, 162.

His equal scale divisions were thus applied not to the whole octave, but to the division of the tetrachord, in which he observed that *a whole tone is the difference in compass between the first two concords (the fifth and the fourth) and may be divided by the three lowest denominators, since melody admits half-tones, third-tones and quarter-tones.....*[1]

Between these two sides, represented by the note proportions of Pythagoras and the equal interval system of Aristoxenus exists a conflict that has long been waged in theoretical circles. Mark Lindley points out the apparent modernity of this extract: *It has not yet been demonstrated that the ratio of the fifth is 3/2 and one encounters excellent geometricians who deny all the ratios of the concords and discords which Pythagoras, Euclid, Ptolemy, Boethius, Zarlino, Salinas, et al. have given, and who believe that the ratios of all the notes and intervals are 'inexplicable' or surd and irrational. For they maintain that all the tones and semitones are equal, that three major thirds make a pure octave, that the augmented fifth is no different from a minor sixth, that the diminished fifth and augmented fourth are the same.*[2]

An excellent summary of some of today's attitudes towards musical intervals, the extract concerned comes from Mersenne's *Questions Harmonique!* (Paris, 1634). So very little has actually changed since Mersenne's time. Yet is such a conflict of interest necessary? The precise relationship between tempered and non-tempered methods of intonation would serve to indicate that it is not.

Ideally, music should be performed in respect of the simple ratios of its constituent intervals: in *just intonation.* Yet in keyboard music it is impossible to play all of the intervals accurately without using complex and cumbersome keyboards which involve at least thirty or more separate keys to the octave. To solve this problem a temperament may be used which reduces the number of tones required per octave down to the bare minimum. The division of the octave into twelve equal semitones represents one solution to this problem. But this does not mean that the ratios of the original intervals are now invalid. It simply means that the resulting tempered intervals are providing approximations of the true ratios of the intervals required. The fifths are somewhat flat, whilst the major thirds are sharper than they should be:

---

[1] Aristoxenus, the Harmonics, Trans. by Henry, S. Macran, Clarendon Press, Oxford, 1902, Extract quoted in Ruth Halle Rowen's Music Through Sources and Documents, Prentice Hall Inc., New Jersey 1979, 19.

[2] Mark Lindley, 'Mersenne on Keyboard Tuning', JMT, 24/2, 1980, 167 - 204.

Differentials Between Just and Tempered Intervals (Expressed in Cents)

	Perfect fifth (3/2)	Major Third (5/4)	Minor Third (6/5)
Just	702	386	316
Tempered	700	400	300
Difference	-2	+14	-16

Because the twelve semitones of our Western octave are equally tempered, means that the number of intervals used in European art music would appear to be only twelve. It thus appears as something of a contradiction to find that most works on musical theory recognise more than twelve intervals within the octave. In explanation of this, it is generally accepted that the neutral intervals of equal temperament act as substitutes for any number of intervals which may be used in particular contexts. As Mitchell, in his study of chromaticism (1962) states: *because equal temperament expresses musical relationships in a limited number of pitches, it might seem that it should lead to a reduction in the total number of intervals....such a conclusion would be an over-simplification of the nature of musical relationships, for whatever pair of pitches might represent an isolated sound, as soon as it participates in a continuum of musical relationships, its nature becomes completely dependent on its surroundings.*[1]

This belief is readily implicit in the way Alexander Ellis once defined the chameleonic nature of temperament: *The object of temperament is to render possible the expression of an indefinite number of intervals by means of a limited number of tones without distressing the ear too much by the imperfections of the consonances.*[2]

The word 'indefinite' provides a diagnostically accurate indication of the complexities of acoustically pure intervals. Using the interval between *C* and *Db* on the piano keyboard, this can be easily demonstrated. Taken as the respective tonics of the keys of C and Db major, the keynotes are separated by some five perfect fourths: *C F Bb Eb Ab Db*. The precise interval between the keynotes of C and Db is thus 256/243 - the interval of the Pythagorean Limma. Alternatively, the notes C and Db could be taken as the dominant and submediant degrees of the key of F Minor, in which case the interval concerned would be a major semitone of ratio 16/15. And of course the *Db* can be equally viewed as a *C#*, in which case, if viewed as two keynotes in the circle of fifths: *C - C#* - they would be linked by the ratio of 2187/2048 - the ratio of the

---

[1] Mitchell, William J., The Study of Chromaticism, JMT, 6/1, 1962, 2 - 31.
[2] Hermann Helmholtz, Op. Cit., 'Additions by the Translator', 431 - 432.

Pythagorean Apotome. Or the *C#* can be taken as a chromatic alteration of note C, in which case the interval between them would be the great limma of ratio 135/128. Yet another interpretation, is that the *C#* can be presented as the major third of the relative minor key of A, in which case the interval concerned would be a just minor semitone of ratio 25/24.

Comparison of Breadths of Tempered and Just Semitones of Different Sizes

Interval	Ratio	Cents	Deviation
Just Minor Semitone	25/24	70.67	-29.33 cents
Pythagorean Limma	256/243	90.22	- 9.78 cents
Large Limma	135/128	92.18	- 7.82 cents
Tempered Semitone	---	100.00	00.00 cents
Diatonic Semitone	16/15	111.73	+11.73 cents
Apotome	2187/2048	113.69	+13.69 cents

These few examples suffice to show that the equally tempered interval between the notes C and Db/C# can be called upon to bear an extreme interpretive load.   This is also true with all other tempered intervals. Consequently, although it may be true to say that *with the universal adoption of equal temperament, intonation theory ceased to be an active area of inquiry*[1] for those seeking to understand the precise realities underlying the network of tonal relationships which temperament does actually serve to compromise, the equally tempered scale cannot possibly be relied upon as either a guide or an indication of their possibility.

Thus may be exposed one of the blind spots of modern musical theory which although aspiring to the comprehension of musical systems which have long since transcended the limitations of Classical tonality, fails to take into account those intonational realities, and therefore misses those points where a demonstrable progression in those realities may have occurred.

Here, one of the central problems is that within the range of a single octave there are an infinite number of intervals that can be used. Yet to moderate this view, running between the restrictive range of tempered intervals and the indefinite number of possible intervals is a mean, and this is the definite number of intervals used and evoked in the system of tonality itself.

It is this more practical range of intervals that thus provides an initial topic of interest. Yet to correctly understand the intervallic fabric of that system it is not sufficient to simply calculate the precise ratio of every interval therein. It is also

---

[1] David Loeb, Mathematical Aspects of Music, MF II, 1970, 110 - 129, 116.

necessary to understand how those intervals are compromised by equal temperament, and the features and issues, both theoretical and practical, which arise as a consequence of that compromise.

A short examination of the Western tonal system reveals that there are far more than twelve intervals involved. In the first instance, defined by the number of diatonic steps which they span, there are seven intervals:

Interval Classification by Step

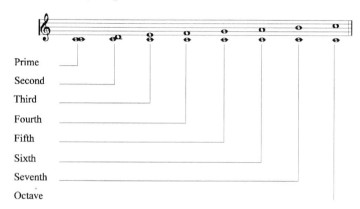

Any one of these seven can vary in terms of their modality. Differences in modality arise through the expansion or compression of a given interval by a chromatic semitone. All seven intervals can be altered in this way. When a major interval is compressed by a chromatic semitone the result is a minor interval, and visa versa. Of the seven basic intervals it is only the second, third, sixth and seventh which admit of this mutability. For this reason, these four intervals are traditionally designated as being imperfect. The other three - the octave, fourth and fifth - show no such dualistic division, and are classified as perfect. The number of perfect intervals (three) added to the number of imperfect intervals (four occurring in two positions) thus totals eleven.

The Spectrum of Major, Minor and Perfect Intervals

	Prime	Second	Third	Fourth	Fifth	Sixth	Seventh	Octave
Major		D	E			A	B	
Perfect	C			F	G			C
Minor		D♭	E♭			A♭	B♭	

The modalities of each of the seven primary interval classes can be further expanded through augmentation and diminution. The sphere of augmented and diminished intervals are classified as chromatic intervals because (aside from the diminished fifth between 'si'; and 'fa') they do not occur within the province of the diatonic scale.

An augmented interval is obtained when a major or perfect interval is expanded by a chromatic semitone, whilst a diminished interval is obtained when a minor or perfect interval is diminished by a chromatic semitone:.

The Range of Diatonic and Chromatic Intervals

	Prime	Second	Third	Fourth	Fifth	Sixth	Seventh	Octave
Augmented	C♯	D♯	E♯	F♯	G♯	A♯	B♯	C♯
Major		D	E			A	B	
Perfect	C			F	G			C
Minor		D♭	E♭			A♭	B♭	
Diminished	C♭	D♭♭	E♭♭	F♭	G♭	A♭♭	B♭♭	C♭

This means that within the confines of one particular key, there exists the possibility for considerably more intervals than there are notes in the equally tempered chromatic scale. Here there are some twenty-five intervals generated from a bass note C. And this is excluding the domain of doubly augmented (super-augmented) and doubly diminished (sub-diminished) intervals of more infrequent occurrence.

If a scale were to be devised that accommodated all of these intervals it would need to have a bare minimum of twenty-five notes to be valid for one key. This precludes those variations in micro-intervallic modality brought on by the conflicting requirements of melody and harmony.[1]

The equally tempered chromatic scale accommodates these additional chromatic intervals through the ambivalence of the equally tempered semitone. In one context it may function as a diatonic semitone, i.e. *D* to *Eb*, and in another a chromatic semitone i.e. *D* to *D#*. If the upper note of a major second is sharpened by a diatonic semitone the result is a minor third. If sharpened by a chromatic semitone, the result will be an augmented second. Both intervals will be struck on the keyboard by exactly the same notes.

---

[1] This issue will be discussed in Ch. 14: 'Valency Analysis: the Major and Minor Scales'.

Intervals sharing this relationship are described as enharmonic equivalents. Because the same keys strike enharmonically equivalent intervals, it may be mistakenly assumed that they are the same interval spelled differently. However, such an interpretation of musical intervals fails to take into account the various psycho-acoustical and psychological modifications that may be made by the perceiver.

An example of this is the augmented second occurring between the sixth and seventh degrees of the harmonic minor mode. Representing the most distinctive feature of this mode, it is an interval which combines two tendency tones - the leading note, which tends to rise upwards towards the tonic, and the minor submediant degree which tends to fall downwards to the dominant.

In just intonation this interval has a ratio of 75/64. This can be verified through subtracting the diatonic semitone between leading note and tonic (16/15), from the major third (5/4) between the submediant and tonic:

Voice leading Implications of Augmented Second Interval

Enharmonically, the interval of an augmented second is identical with a minor third, yet the folly of treating it as such will become readily evident. As a minor third, spelled either as notes B# and D# or notes C and Eb, it implies an altogether different mode of treatment to the augmented second. Within the context of E minor, the former might suggest an augmented 6/4 progression to the subdominant major chord, whilst the latter could suggest a chromatic apoggiatura chord:

Modes of Progression of Two Chromatic Intervals

A_4^6 IV   I - - -   v

The important feature concerning this category of interval is that it implies a different mode of treatment to the enharmonically equivalent diatonic interval. In the first of the above examples, there is the augmented fifth degree that forms a tendency tone up to the major submediant degree of the key of E, and in the second example, the diminished octave that forms a tendency tone down to the subtonic note D.

From this example alone it can be surmised that equal temperament is an unsatisfactory theoretical base from which to approach and understand musical intervals. Temperament has led to a standardisation of interval sizes, and a nullification of the essential differences between enharmonically equivalent intervals. As a practical musical utility this may be extremely useful. However, as a theoretical root from which to approach and understand musical intervals it can only lead to utter confusion.

How, within the framework of equal temperament is it possible to explain the difference between the major and the minor semitone, or the augmented third and perfect fourth? Within the equally tempered twelve-tone scale there is no difference. Yet to the listener, the same set of pitches operating within different contexts have entirely different meanings and connotations. These derive from the facility temperament offers to act as a substitute for any number of intervals, all of which have different ratios and sizes.

To comprehend this world of musical intervals it is necessary to abandon equal temperament as a theoretical base, and to seek knowledge of the indefinite number of intervals that Ellis mentioned in his remarks on the function of equal temperament. These are the musical realities which equal temperament compromises so well.

If equal temperament is abandoned as a base from which to understand and approach musical intervals, it becomes necessary to establish the qualities and attributes which characterises those pure intervals which lie beyond the convenience of temperament. It is easy to understand that as played on a piano a perfect fifth may be tempered. But what is the perfect fifth in its pure form?

From the fact that this interval is employed in every musical system known, it would seem that like the interval of the octave, the ear was led to it by virtue of the powerful valent bond between the notes concerned. After all, even the untrained can tell if a perfect fifth is in tune. In this sense, Aristoxenus belief that the ear should provide the sole arbiter in matters of tonal judgements makes very great sense indeed. The ear itself can perceive what is right and true without recourse to mathematical theory.

Yet it is also true that mathematical theory offers fascinating insights as to why particular combinations of tones sound right to the ear. Pythagoras's credited discovery of the ratios of the perfect consonances is a good case in point. The correlation between the aural quality of an interval and its ratio was undoubtedly a great step forward for musical theory. It enabled us to know that when a perfect fifth sounds right, true or pure, it is because the relationship between the frequencies is in conformity with the ratio of 3/2.

Here what is remarkable is that when the perfect fifth is tempered, or heard on an out-of-tune instrument, the ear is able to sense the degree of deviation and adjust itself accordingly. Therefore, after some exposure to such out-of-tune perfect fifths, there will come a point when they no longer seem to be so out-of-tune. Discussing this general point Martin Vogel observes that: *It has often been proved that an intuitively comprehended tone ratio is often different from the acoustically given ratio. In such cases the apperceived proportion is simpler than the real one...The ear is accustomed to tolerating a slight deviation from a simple numerical ratio and hearing the simpler one.*[1]

The factor that characterises untempered intervals is thus their ratio. The importance of interval ratios in the history of musical theory is largely due to this correlation between the ratio and quality of intervals. Intervals played and rendered according to their exact ratios are deemed to be pure intervals, as opposed to their tempered counterparts. In an ideal world all music would be performed using these pure intervals. Yet this is often impractical, especially on those instruments which offer only a closed range of pitches.

Here Harry Partch's achievements can only be admired. Dissatisfied with temperament he constructed his own microtonal scale of pure intervals. Because there were few instruments that could play music written in his scale, he devised his own, or asked others to make them for him. In some senses this may be regarded as an extreme reaction to the vicissitudes of temperament. Yet in others, it points the way forward for a musical language that is veritably stagnating under the imposing weight and authority of equal temperament.[2]

With the rational discovery of the harmonic series an explanation of the reasons why intervals with simple whole number ratios tended to be consonant became possible. Subsequent to initial investigations made by Esteve and Saveur on the role of shared partials,[3] Helmholtz explanation is undoubtedly the most convincing. The degree of consonance of a musical interval depended upon the relationship between the partials of the two notes concerned. Partials in close proximity produce beats, and these are heard as a roughness. The more closely crowded any or all of the partials belonging to two complex tones, the greater the sense of dissonance. The tritone, or 'diabolus in musica' is thus one of the roughest of intervals, because the partials of the two complex tones are mostly crowded to within a distance of a semitone from one another.

The results of Helmholtz's analysis of the interplay between partials in musical intervals, is that the following may be regarded to be 'consonant':

---

[1] Martin Vogel, On the Relations of Tone, 163.

[2] Harry Partch's unique scale system, and the just intonational aesthetic behind it, is fully explained and accounted for in his Genesis of a Music, Da Capo Press, New York 1974.

[3] The basis for the property of valency, but not perhaps directly for consonance

Consonant Intervals According to Helmholtz[1]

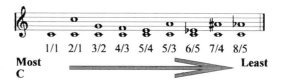

| 1/1 | 2/1 | 3/2 | 4/3 | 5/4 | 5/3 | 6/5 | 7/4 | 8/5 |

Most
C ——————————————————————→ **Least**

Despite refinements, or deeper levels of explanation as to why these intervals may be regarded to be consonant i.e. Plomp and Levelt's theory of the critical bandwidth,[2] Helmholtz work still provides the basic model for those who seek an acoustic or psycho-acoustic explanation for the phenomenon of consonance and dissonance.

The connection between the quality of an interval and the property of valency is an interesting feature. The array of partials which constitute a musical tone make it highly susceptible to bonding or uniting with other musical tones. Prime numbered partials are the most relevant factors because they offer unique connections between musical tones. There are 2-valency intervals, whose ratios involve no prime number higher than two; 3-valency intervals whose ratios involve no prime number higher than three; then there are the 5-valency, 7-valency, 11-valency intervals, etc.

In terms of 2-valency intervals these have ratios which cannot involve any prime number higher than 2. Therefore there is only one 2-valency interval, which is the octave. 3-valency intervals have ratios that cannot involve any prime number higher than three. Therefore the following are all 3-valency intervals: 3/2; 4/3; 9/8; 16/9; 27/16; 32/27; etc. Amongst this group there are only two intervals that represent a primary valent bond. These are 3/2 and 4/3. This is because the ratios of all of the others involve multiples of the prime number 2 and 3, and are therefore cannot be counted as first order bonds.

Explication of the Order of Valent Bond in the Cyclic Major Sixth of Ratio 27/16

$$27 \text{ divided by } 3 = 9 \quad 16 \text{ divided by } 2 = 8$$

---

[1] Helmholtz, On the Sensations of Tone, 179 - 211. See also Mathew Shirlaw's Theory of Harmony, (Novello & Company Ltd., London 1917, 283-284), where he shows that M. Esteve and M. Saveur had anticipated Helmholtz's discoveries by more than a century. For a general discussion of Helmholtz's theory, and other confirmatory evidence provided by C. Stumpf, see Alexander Woods Physics of Music (Methuen, London, 1962),157 - 170.

[2] Plomp & W.J.M. Levelt, Tonal Consonance and Critical Bandwidth, JASA, 38:548, 1965.

$$9 \text{ divided by } 3 = 3 \qquad 8 \text{ divided by } 2 = 4$$
$$4 \text{ divided by } 2 = 2$$

The bond between notes separated by the ratio of 27/16 is thus a tertiary or third order bond.

5-valency intervals have ratios that cannot involve any prime number higher than five. Here there are four that represent primary valent bonds: the major third of ratio 5/4, the major sixth of ratio 5/3, the minor sixth of ratio 8/5 and the minor third of ratio 6/5. It may be argued that 5/3 is the sum of 4/3 and 5/4, as 8/5 is the sum of 4/3 and 6/5, and both of these observations are true. However 5/3 cannot be viewed as a composite since it represents the first order bond between the prime numbered partials 5 and 3. Neither of the composite intervals of 4/3 or 5/4 fulfils that condition. 5/3 therefore, represents the explication of a primary bond.

Similarly 8/5 cannot be viewed as composite since it represents the first order bond between the prime numbered partials two and five. Neither of the composite intervals 4/3 or 6/5 replicates that relationship. 8/5 thus also represents a primary bond. Those intervals that do represent a primary bond are all of those intervals that may be regarded to be consonants. This means therefore, that in the absence of any objective mathematical criterion, the quality of consonance is the ears method of arriving at and deducing intervals which represent those primary bonds.

Work undertaken in the area of psycho-acoustics, an area of study which has provided a much needed bridge between the often conflicting views of psychology on the one hand, and acoustical science on the other, reveals that the ear is well equipped to perceive such bonds.

Here the relevant organ is the basilar membrane. Located within the cochlea and approximately just over one-inch long the basilar membrane is covered with thousands of receptors called hair cells. Sound, entering through the oval window of the cochlea, causes the fluid within the cochlea to vibrate. This in its turn sets the basilar membrane in motion. The hair cells then transmit these vibrations to the appropriate nervous conductors.[1]

For every frequency of audible sound exists a spatial correlate within the basilar membrane, a series of receptors sensitive to particular frequencies in a graded progression from the lowest sounds at one end of the membrane to the

---

[1] J. Roederer, Introduction to the Physics and Psychophysics of Music, 2nd. Edition, Heidelberg Science Library, Vol. 16, Springer-Verlag, New York/Heidelberg/Berlin 1975, 20.

48

highest at the other.[1] These resonance regions are not organised on a unit per unit vibration basis, but on a logarithmic basis, which means that the physical distances between the resonance regions of the basilar membrane are established not by differences in the frequency of two simple tones, but by their ratio.[2] Five frequencies connected by the ratio of 2/1 therefore, would mutually excite five more or less equidistant resonance regions:

Logarithmic Displacement of Resonance Maxima of the Basilar Membrane

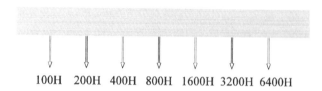

100H   200H   400H   800H   1600H   3200H   6400H

Through the provision of receptors for the entire range of audible frequencies, the basilar membrane serves to corroborate the theoretical construct of the pitch continuum. The principle underlying the regular displacement of the resonance regions of the basilar membrane also finds its correlate within the pitch continuum in the form of the invariable relationships between musical tones expressed in the form of ratios. It would thus seem that pure intervals, together with the ratios that define them, are quite natural to the auditory system. Furthermore, if for each simple tone there is a corresponding area of resonance on the basilar membrane, means that a complex tone invariably sets up a characteristic pattern of resonance on the basilar membrane. It is thought that this pattern might play a significant part in the ear's recognition of the complex set of harmonic partials as a single unified entity.[3] This occurs through what

[1] Ibid., *The remarkable fact is that for a pure sound of a given frequency, the maximum basilar membrane oscillation occurs only in a given limited region of the membrane, whose position depends on the frequency of the tone. In other words, for each frequency there is a region of maximum sensitivity, or 'resonance region', on the basilar membrane....a change in frequency of the pure tone causes a shift of the position of the activated region. 21.*

[2] Ibid., *In general, whenever the frequency f is multiplied by a given factor, the position x of the resonance region is not multiplied but simply shifted a certain amount. In other words it is frequency ratios, not their differences, that determine the displacement of the resonance region along the basilar membrane. A relationship of this kind is called 'logarithmic' 22.*

[3] Ibid., *'Natural' sounds of human and animal acoustic communications contain an important proportion of harmonic tones...In spite of its complexity this pattern does bear some invariant characteristics. One such invariance is the particular distance relationship between neighbouring resonance maxima...because of the particular relationship between resonance place and frequency, the resonance regions crowd closer and closer together as one moves up the harmonic series. p. 54.*

Roederer describes as *a spatial pattern recognition process, i.e. an auditory Gestalt perception.* He then goes on to say that: *the characteristic feature that is recognised in this process, that is common to all periodic tones regardless of their fundamental frequency and Fourier spectrum, is the nearly invariant distance relationship between resonance maxima on the basilar membrane. The pitch sensation is to be regarded as the 'final output signal' of this recognition process.*[1]

That the human ear is capable of distinguishing the fundamental frequency of a single tone in this fashion is remarkable, but even more remarkable is that it can accomplish the same feat for two, three, four or more notes at the same time. To do so, the ear must have the ability to recognise and distinguish the basic pattern of the harmonic series as presented by each of the respective musical tones, which means that it must also be able to recognise the relationship between their respective partials.

Here it is curious to note that the ear would seem to have a natural limit with regard to those valent bonds that it can or cannot detect. If an interval of an extremely complex ratio (i.e. 2013/1009) is sounded, the ear will tend to relate it to the nearest primary interval of the harmonic series (in this case an octave). Consequently, an altogether new interval will not be perceived, but only a mistuned or poor version of the octave. It would thus seem that the ear gives precedence to those intervals which, representing first or second order valent bonds, are familiar to it. Intervals with more complex ratios may thus be interpreted as variants of these primary intervals.

This explains why the harmonic major third (ratio 5/4) is much more satisfactory than the Pythagorean major third (81/64): it is because the latter is not heard as a new interval, but simply a very rough approximation of the former.

A theory that endeavours to explain the connection between musical sounds purely in terms of mathematics is thus incomplete, because within certain limits the ear will interpret the connection between two sounds according to the nearest primary bond to which it can be matched.

This process of harmonic resolution amounts to the interpretation of the fields of aural connection between musical tones according to those primary resonance patterns. Equal temperament works therefore, because although a tempered fifth is slightly out from the pure fifth – and thus an altogether different interval - the ear accepts the connection between the two notes as being a slight deviation from the pure fifth.

A truce thus becomes possible between those who support either tempered or just methods of intonation. Even within a tempered context, the ear is

---

[1] Ibid., 135.

capable of discerning the presence of a valent bond between musical tones. Logically, this is because the minute divergence between the shared partials of the lower and upper notes of the tempered interval is insufficient to activate two physically distinct areas of resonance upon the basilar membrane, and therefore by the same token insufficient to evoke the recognition of an altogether new intervallic modality.

THE PENTATONIC SCALE AS A MANIFESTATION OF THE LAWS OF VALENCY

The idea that the primary members of the harmonic series may be major influential factors upon the way in which intervallic connections between musical tones are perceived is one which has gained wide currency ever since the seventeenth century when Marin Mersenne observed that the major chord was implicit within the natural overtones of the trumpet.[1] It is an idea that strongly affected the thinking of the French composer and theorist Jean Philippe Rameau (1683 - 1764), although despite Mersenne's observations that the seventh harmonic actually produced a concordant interval,[2] Rameau felt it necessary to place an arbitrary limit on the series.[3]

Nonetheless, the concept of the harmonic series led to a shift of focus away from the neo-Pythagorean metaphysics associated with the note ratio, and towards a more rational attempt to explore pitch relationships from a purely acoustical standpoint. Here, after Rameau, one of the most notable contributions to this field perhaps, came from Hermann Helmholtz, whose *On the Sensations of Tone* endeavours to account for the entire fabric of tonal music in acoustical terms.

Not all theorists however, have been content with a purely acoustical view of tonal relations. Some have preferred to view tonal relations in psychological or even metaphysical terms. The most notable opponents of the purely acoustical theory of tonal relations were the Belgian historian François-Joseph Fétis (1784 - 1871) who believed that the mass of tonal relations both derived from and subsisted within the unity of the tonic principle,[4] and the German theorist

---

[1] Albion Gruber, Mersenne and Evolving Tonal Theory, JMT, 14, 1970, 36 - 67.

[2] Marin Mersenne, Harmonie Universelle, Book IV, Trans. by Robert F. Williams, Ph. D. diss., University of Rochester 1972, 207-19.

[3] Jean-Philippe Rameau, Treatise on Harmony, Trans. by Philip Gosset, Dover Publications Inc., New York 1986.

[4] As put forward in Féti's Traité complet de la théorie et de la pratique de l'harmonie, Paris and Brussels 1844.

Moritz Hauptmann (1792 - 1868) who endeavoured to explain the laws of tonal music through reference to Hegelian dialectics.[1]

Whilst it is true that acoustical science may not hold all the answers to the problems posed by tonality, recent work this century unfolding the functions of the basilar membrane, and the theory of the pattern matching process of pitch perception which ensues from that, points to a validation of the concept that the basis for pitch relations do lie within the resources implicit within a single musical tone. The significant difference here however, is that the concept of the harmonic series has a broader reach than was hitherto suspected.

Unfortunately, in recent times there has been a growing tendency to abstract the harmonic series from its proper context. Seen on countless times, paraded as a mathematical table in textbooks on physics and acoustics it can seem almost irrelevant to the subject of music. This is unfortunate because it fails to do justice to the fact that the harmonic series is a revelation of the innermost nature of musical tone. Imprinted as a template upon the human auditory system, its structure embodies the key to the explanation of the property of valency i.e. why one tone may bond with another.

One way of looking at this property, is to consider harmonics to be the 'hooks' through which one sound makes an audible connection with another. In simple terms tonal bonds govern tonal relationships, and tonal bonds are the partials which notes share in common with one another. The strongest of tonal bonds therefore, are those where the ratio is the simplest, as these indicate those relationships where there are most shared partials. The more hooks or points of connection between two notes, the closer the felt relationship between them. Thus notes an octave apart bear the closest possible relationship because of the great abundance of shared partials.[2]

Here it is significant that the interval of the octave has attained the status of a universal in music, in that it extends right across the entire range of the musical systems that are known to us. This, it can be asserted, is because of the special valent bond that exists between notes an octave apart.

To say however, that those musical systems with a developed sense of harmony as found in the West, are based on the harmonic series as a primary phenomenon is to go too far. They are based on the valent connections

---

[1] As explained in Moritz Hauptmann's Die Natur der Harmonik und Metrik, Leipzig 1853. Trans. by William E. Heathcote, London 1988.

[2] If the vibrating lengths are in a simple ratio, so are the frequencies (in the inverse ratio), and therefore the two notes must possess partials in common which can explain the relationship which the ear apprehends. See also: Arithmetical simplicity in the ratios of the frequencies carries with it the possession of low-order partials in common, and therefore indicates a relationship which the ear recognises and appreciates. Alexander Wood, The Physics of Music, 6th. Ed., University Paperbacks, Methuen, London 1962, 182/186.

between musical tones prompted by the mathematical structure of that series. These, connections, evident even to the untrained ear, are clearly the inviolable basis from which music has developed. It thus proves fruitful at this stage, to begin to examine those avenues of tonal connection as are presented and put forth by the harmonic series. In doing so, one of the most important principles underlying the property of valency in general will emerge.

First there are those intervals which bond through media of the first partial. That the first partial establishes the priority of pitch means that there is only one such interval which belongs at this level: the interval of the unison whose ratio is 1/1. After this there are the 2-valency intervals whose ratios involve no prime number higher than two. Here again, there is only one possibility: the interval of the octave - ratio of 2/1.

Yet it may be argued that the ratios of 3/2, 4/2, 5/2, etc., also involve the second partial. However, in the case of 3/2, this is a 3-valency interval, which therefore extends beyond the limits defined by the phenomenon of 2-valency. The same argument can be applied to the ratio 5/2, for this is a 5-valency interval. And with the interval 4/2, this is simply a repetition of the same bond designated by the ratio of 2/1.

Through this it becomes apparent that the property of valency implicates a hierarchy of intervallic values whose stratification is defined by the prime numbers of the harmonic series. This is because the relationships defined by the prime numbers are incommensurate with one another and therefore unique to their level. Where a strong cue can be taken from the harmonic series is the precise order in which those relationships are presented, which is:

Levels of Valency as Presented by the Harmonic Series

Valency	Primary Ratio	Factors	Connections	Dimensions
1- valency	1/1	1	--	None
2- valency	2/1	1,2	Monovalent.	One
3- valency	3/2	1,2,3	Bivalent	Two
5- valency	5/4	1,2,3,5	Trivalent	Three
7- valency	7/4	1,2,3,5,7	Tetravalent	Four
11- valency	11/8	1,2,3,5,7,11	Pentavalent	Five
13- valency	13/8	1,2,3,5,7,11,13	Hexavalent	Six

The phenomenon of 1-valency has already in part been discussed. Being rooted in the first partial, it carries an importance which cannot be stressed too much, for it serves to establish the three fundamental principles of the tonal universe upon which all others subsist: pitch priority, pitch replication, and the principle of the prototypical tone.

This can be understood through the observation that the force of 1-valency deals essentially in the connection of kind to kind. The channel of replication thus constitutes the first partial, which establishes the fundamental condition of all tonal structures: pitch priority, a feature shared and inherited by every single tone in the musical concourse. In this sense, all music is a pure manifestation of the fundamental principle embodied by that number one.

This informs much about the power of 1-valency, for dealing in the connection of kind to kind, it establishes that initial possibility of pitch replication, expressed harmonically in the state of the unison (1/1), and melodically in the phenomenon of pitch repetition.

Now given that music has already been defined as the replication of tone, it becomes apparent that processes of replication are not generally haphazard. They usually occur from a particular point, and generally return to it, forming as it were an arc of development whose structure is underpinned by the unifying force that this point represents.

Although psychologically this is very satisfying, and embraces within its broad sweep numerous aesthetic criteria, such as the need for balance and coherence, how much this is a natural response to the force of 1-valency is difficult to say.

Certainly, as represented by the ratio of 1/1, the unison is utterly unique amongst musical intervals for it is the only interval that has no dimensional extension. Being dimensionless, it represents the tonal relation which speaks of that dimensionless point from which, beginning with the prime number two, represents the generating power of the first dimension of tonal space.

Given the existence of such a point, the ultimate source and fountain of all valent relationships, it becomes necessary to posit a prototypical tone in which is seated the ultimate power and authority of that primeval source of tonal generation. Here it does not matter which tone, for every musical tone is capable of representing the prototypical tone, providing it is remembered that the prototypical tone represents the point from which all processes of tonal replication both arise and eventually return.

The power of 2-valency is also considerable, for it generates that all important first dimension of tonal space within which, and against which all subsequent frequency projections made possible by higher prime numbers are firmly placed. As represented by the octave, the phenomenon of 2-valency thus serves to circumscribe the natural limits of the musical cosmos. Consequently, for a pitch to extend beyond the octave is simply to enter into the bounds of yet another octave.

In this way, 2-valency offers the prototypical tone the possibility of a tangible material and audible expression within the general terms of the pitch continuum. Dealing in the phenomenon of octave equivalence, it thus also enables the manifestation of the prototypical tone, and its representatives upon all levels of that continuum. In this way, 2-valency serves to extend the power and dominion of the prototypical tone upon all levels of the tonal network.

Other levels of valency (3-valency, 5-valency, 7-valency, etc.) attach a significance to the prototypical tone each according to their own level and characteristic mode of dimensional extension, so that the tone concerned may be viewed on different levels. The theory of valency thus generates a view of pitch that is essentially multidimensional, each avenue of valent connection as arises from the harmonic series contributing yet a further dimensional perspective to the maze of possible pitch relationships present within the pitch continuum.

Therefore, after the 2-valency interval of the octave (2/1) there are the 3-valency intervals of the perfect fifth (3/2) and the perfect fourth (4/3). In looking at the way the musical tones belonging to these respective intervals bond, there is a simple principle at work which is useful for understanding the bonding patterns of intervals with more complex ratios. Here the ratio itself serves to define the bonding pattern.

In the case of the perfect fifth, ratio 3/2, tone 3 bonds with tone 2 at the second harmonic, and tone 2 bonds with tone 3 at the third harmonic:

Bonding Pattern of the Perfect Fifth

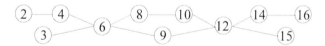

Similarly, in the case of the perfect fourth, ratio 4/3, tone 4 bonds at the third harmonic, and tone 3 the fourth harmonic.

Bonding Pattern of the Perfect Fourth (4/3)

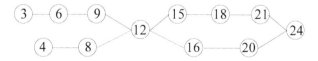

At the level of 3-valency therefore, there are two primary bonds: those represented by the ratios 3/2 and 4/3 respectively. Now as a prime number, three is incommensurate with two. Consequently, any movement in frequency space motivated by the prime number three cannot occur in the same direction as a movement controlled by the prime number two. Therefore, to represent movement in frequency space in accordance with both the prime numbers two and three means that it is necessary to posit a two-dimensional plane of projection in which both movements can occur.

Whilst therefore, the prime number two serves to generate an all important first dimension of frequency space, the prime number three serves to designate a second dimension, one which is characterised by its own particular properties and attributes. To understand these attributes it becomes necessary to ponder the nature of that two-dimensional plane of pitch projection.

The first dimension, represented by the ratio of 2/1, represents a movement in frequency space in which the prototypical tone is simply repeated on the next level of the pitch continuum. Therefore although it signifies a form of dynamic replication, it is nonetheless replication that leads to a repeat of the same pitch priority over and over again.

As the mathematical representative of the second dimension, the prime number three also signifies a form of dynamic replication. However, representing movement within another dimension, it automatically excludes the territory of pitch repetition defined by the prime number two. Thus precluding the territory of pitch repetition means that it designates the dimension of the tonal universe in which pitch classes are dynamically generated.

Consequently it is through the prime number three that the octave obtains its natural mathematical format. However because both frequency movements (2/1 and 3/2) partake of that two dimensional plane of pitch projection, means that those phenomena belonging to the second dimension of tonal space (prime three) automatically inherit certain fundamental properties belonging to the first dimension (prime two). The first of these is the intervallic polarity seen in the complimentary relationship that exists between the perfect fifth and the perfect fourth.

When a perfect fifth is subtracted from an octave it leaves the interval of the perfect fourth, and visa versa.[1] Intervals displaying this relationship are described as the inversions of one another: the perfect fifth is the same as the perfect fourth in that both utilise the same notes. The difference between them is that in the perfect fourth the lowermost note has been transposed up an octave. In this way the facility of inversion is something which the second dimension of frequency space (and all dimensions thereafter), automatically inherits from the first dimension.

---

[1] Rameau, Treatise on Harmony, 13.

Perfect Fifth and Fourth and Their Relationship by Inversion

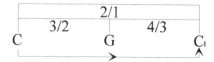

Consequently, the perfect fifth and fourth portray opposite, yet complimentary expressions of the same valent relationship. Occurring through a process of functional reciprocation, it will be seen that note G (3/2) represents the prototypical tone that has been replicated in order to obtain representation in the second dimension of frequency space (prime three). It thus constitutes the agent of the prototypical tone in that particular dimension of tonal space.

Acting as the agent of the prototypical tone, authorisation is automatically conferred upon the prototypical tone to act as its representative i.e. as the perfect fifth of F (4/3). This is why any valent bond must have two forms: a primary form and an inversion. The former confers upon the agent the power to act as its representative; the latter confers upon the prototypical tone the power to act as its agent. This interlocking of functions thus provides the diagnostic basis for the cycle of fifths, in that through the domino effect which ensues from this process, the system automatically perpetuates thereafter.

The second dimension of frequency space is thus the primary point of arrival of the phenomenon of intervallic duality, that polar opposition or tension generated by two contrasting manifestations of the same essential relationship. Tension generated between these two poles gives rise to a third or equilibrating force which serves to harness that tension in the service of a larger overriding principle. That principle is tonality: a direct result of the autogenetic powers of the prototypical tone to function as both the cause and effect of itself.

This can be clearly demonstrated when the two intervals are combined together as a unit, for together they define a third or pivotal pitch, which being locked in as a central axis between the two poles, establishes itself as a stable centre of gravity. The resulting triangular unit, hereafter referred to as the triangle of tonality, becomes an ultimate symbol of tonal strength and stability. In referring to a force of tonality however, it is not the functional tonality of Classical music that is being referred to, but a universal force of tonality of which Classical tonality constitutes but one outlet of expression.[1] That basic tonal force is present wherever musical systems base themselves on this principle of triangulation. Indeed, it cannot be avoided, since the property of valency possessed by musical tone leads inevitably to its definition.

---

[1] Joseph Yasser, A Theory of Evolving Tonality, 6.

Tonal Axis Between Fifth and Fourth

$-$	$\frac{-}{+}$	$+$
F	C	G
4/3	1/1	3/2

In this sense, tonality is that natural global force which pervades nearly all music. Being seated as a first principle in the valent powers of the octave, the perfect fifth and the perfect fourth, it is found wherever that triangular unit is employed. This is virtually everywhere. As observed by Helmholtz, the octave, perfect fifth and fourth are *found in all musical scales known.*[1] Partch agrees with this observing that they are *the most important scale degrees in nearly every musical system worthy of the name that the world has ever known.*[2]

Certainly they were the first intervals to be regarded as consonances. It was Euclid (300 BC) who in his *Introduction to the Section of a Canon* ascribed to these intervals the quality which we today describe as consonance.[3] Therefore, as early as the fourth century BC the octave, fifth and fourth were already being recognised as the fundamental manifestations of a primeval force of tonality.

Through replication, that triangular unit also serves to establish the basic grounds in which can be discerned the primeval origins of those tonal systems in which the force of tonality begins to assert itself. Since the breakdown of tonality in the West, and the search for new possibilities which ensued from that, such systems become paramount, in that they provide the basic foundations upon which a new tonality can be based, one not based on the limitations of the major and minor scales, but the entire resources of the pitch continuum, in so far as it is possible to exploit them.

Here, those approaches already made in the global history of music are all fiercely relevant to this basic quest. For example, ancient Greek theorists conducted their acoustical and harmonic experiments upon a monochord. In principle a monochord is simply a stretched string. By dividing that string into various proportions musical intervals corresponding to those present in the harmonic series can be obtained. Division of the string into halves gives the interval of the octave, into thirds the interval of the twelfth, etc.

Records inform us that Pythagoras divided the musical octave in accordance with the cycle of fifths, that is dividing the stretched string in order to produce a

---

[1] Helmholtz, Op. Cit., 253.

[2] Partch, Genesis of a Music, Da Capo Press, New York 1974, 361.

[3] Euclid, Introduction to the Section of a Canon, trans. by Charles Davy, Bury St Edmunds: J. Rackam 1787.

series of notes a perfect fifth or a fourth apart. Therefore the scale which results from this is often called Pythagorean. Even though the scale itself was not arrived at through a process of conscious selection from the wealth of relationships implicit to the harmonic series, the resultant did itself concur with that natural phenomenon in the sense that it served to isolate an interval cycle in which the prime numbers two and three are the salient features.

Whenever, and wherever such a process of arriving at scale formations ensues therefore, the result can be viewed as a phenomenon of 3-valency in that it precludes all pitch relationships which involve any prime number higher than three. In this way a tangible link is established between scales originating from highly divergent times and cultures.

Ancient Chinese musical theory is a good case in point. Acoustical experiments were conducted using not the stretched string, but bamboo pipes cut to specific lengths. A particular pipe length which, taken to represent the prototypical tone (the 'Yellow Bell'[1]) was then cut to produce a pipe the pitch of which would be a perfect fifth higher than the 'Yellow Bell'. Pipes were then further cut to produce a note either a perfect fifth higher or perfect fourth lower than the previous pipe in order to produce a musical scale.[2] In similarity with the Pythagorean method of dividing the octave both methods have a common feature: they exclude notes whose ratios involve any prime number higher than three.

The most elementary scale deriving from this process is the pentatonic scale which involves dividing the octave into five unequal steps. The universal appeal and stature of the pentatonic scale has been widely remarked upon by various authors.[3] It is found widely in the field of so-called 'primitive music',[4] and provides the background for a rich theoretical tradition originating from the far East, especially China, where, for a very long time, it was considered as the basic scale. According to the writings of Leu Buhwei, originating from about 239 BC, the first scale of Chinese music was composed of a segment of four fifths, and was arrived at by the 'music ruler' Ling Lun.[5]

---

[1] Kazu Nakaseko, Symbolism in Ancient Chinese Musical Theory, JMT1/2, Nov.

[2] Ibid.

[3] Representative examples are adequately provided for by Helmholtz (Op. Cit., 256-61).

[4] An account of this is provided for in Ruth Halle-Rowen's Music Through Sources and Documents; Faber & Faber, London 1952, 3 - 5. See also Partch's Genesis of a Music, 362, and Yasser's Theory of Evolving Tonality, 25 - 39, for various accounts of the Chinese scale system.

[5] Ruth Halle-Rowen, Op. Cit., 3-5.

Chinese Pentatonic Scale

Gong	-	Note Do	1/1
Shang	-	Note Re	9/8
Jeau	-	Note Mi	81/64
Jyy	-	Note Sol	3/2
Yeu	-	Note La	27/16

Although the story concerned probably has about as much credibility as Nichomachus's account of Pythagoras and the weighing of the hammers whereby he derived the ratios of the perfect consonances, it does indicate the important role that the pentatonic scale played in early Chinese music.

In the matter of its make up the pentatonic scale may be seen to be constructed from a segment of four perfect fifths:

The Pentatonic Scale as Defined by the First Four Fifths

Note:	C	G	D	A	E
Fifth:	Fundamental	First	Second	Third	Fourth
Ratio:	1/1	3/2	9/8	27/16	81/64

Already here can be seen three important factors in the generation of a self-sufficient tonal system: a prototypical tone which carries the ratio of 1/1, its octave which acts as a sphere of containment for the generation of pitch relationships; and a prime generating interval (or intervals in the case of more advanced scales) which divides the octave into a number of scalar steps, in this case the perfect fifth (3/2).

The pentatonic scale is comprised of two scalar intervals: the whole tone (ratio of 9/8) and the Pythagorean interval of the trihemitone (ratio 32/27). The smallest interval in the pentatonic scale being the whole tone undoubtedly contributes to the diffuse sense of tonality associated with this scale. Yasser alludes to this as a state of 'sub-tonality', what he views to be a necessary precursor to the fully-fledged 'tonality' characterised by more advanced scale systems.[1]

Be that as it may, composed of four interlocked perfect fifths, the pentatonic scale may be considered to represent the very foundations of the musical language. Daniélou sees in it a reflection of the monumental form of the

---

[1] Joseph Yasser, Op. Cit., p. 6.

pyramids of Egypt, an observation that serves as a strong reminder of the relative permanence of this scale.[1]

Employed by twentieth century composers such as Debussy and Bartok, the pentatonic scale possesses remarkable features that commended it to these composers. Partaking in the continuum of musical relationships, it has relevance that, like the prototypical tone, from which all music may be seen to arise, is capable of being forever renewed.

Practical use of the pentatonic scale brings into play a distinction between the related concepts of scale and mode. Whilst a scale may be regarded to be an arrangement of pitches spanning the octave, a mode immediately implies a definitive starting point. In the distinction between these two lies the most elementary manifestation of tonality, a note which, functioning as the focal point of a melody, brings the pitches of a scale into a relationship with that note. Because of the presence of such a note each degree of the scale acquires a functional value, an intervallic identity which is either heard, when a device such a drone bass is employed, or at least sensed mentally, by virtue of the listeners aural retention of the pitch of the tonic note.

Sometimes it can be forgotten that within this set of identities lies a very real and powerful sense of harmony, where a particular note, heard against the backdrop of a drone bass, acquires all the stature of a harmonic interval. This interval, recurring throughout a melody, can acquire a strong emotive significance that completely justifies the lack of sonority as conceived in a conventional sense. All of this depends however, on the strong projection of a tonic note of some sort.

Functional harmony, as conceived in a classical sense, is impossible within the pentatonic scale. As defined by a segment of four fifths, the pentatonic scale only offers three consonant intervals - the octave, perfect fifth and perfect fourth. To use the third, along with the perfect fifth in a common triad is uncharacteristic in that the third of the pentatonic scale is the dissonant ditone of ratio 81/64. Here however, it is interesting to see that Helmholtz tended to view the pentatonic modes from the standpoint of the harmonic series, so for him the third of the pentatonic scale would be more practically tuned as 5/4, and the sixth, 5/3.[2]

Whilst being far more expedient in terms of usage, the tuning Helmholtz offers is a retrospective one, based on modern seven note scales from which two notes have been omitted. As constructed from pure fifths, the pentatonic scale tends to suggest that type of harmony used in traditional Chinese music,

[1] Alain Daniélou, 'The Cyclic System', Introduction to the Study of Musical Scales, The India Society, London 1943.
[2] Helmholtz. Op. Cit., 259.

successions of parallel fifths and fourths, with only the occasional third or sixth. In a more modern harmonic sense such a scale is strongly implied by the practise of superimposing fifths and fourths over one another: quartal and quintal harmony.

Once the idea of a melodic centre of gravity is established, then the concept of mode comes into play - a sudden diversification of expressive possibilities made possible by taking any note of the scale as the prospective tonic note. Because of the peculiar arrangement of stepwise intervals implicit to the pentatonic scale no repetition of the same pattern occurs until the starting point is reached again: in this case note C. Hence from the one scale it is possible to obtain five distinct modalities:

The Pentatonic Modes

1	C	D	E	G	A
2	G	A	C	D	E
3	D	E	G	A	C
4	A	C	D	E	G
5	E	G	A	C	D

The intervallic constitution of the pentatonic modes can be surveyed more clearly when all five modes are transposed to begin at the same pitch. Such an action results in a nine note pitch array or transposition scale composed of a central or pivotal pitch (the common 'tonic' of each mode) from which radiate four perfect fifths and four perfect fourths.

Through the process of transposition a simple scale thus invokes a more complex one. In this lie the seeds of what Yasser referred to as the 'evolution' of tonality: the gradual appropriation of more and more complex sets of pitch relationships, and therefore, more complex scale formations. As soon as a tonic note, and therefore a force of tonality is recognised - even if only in a weak melodic sense - there is a sudden leap of expressive potentiality. A five-note scale yields five separate modes. These in their turn lead to a proliferation of intervallic relationships: mode one contains mostly major intervals, whilst mode five has a preponderance of minor intervals.

The Pentatonic Modes Transposed to a Common Keynote

Note:	Bb	F	C	G	D	A	E	B	F#
Ratio:	128/81	32/27	16/9	4/3	1/1	3/2	9/8	27/16	81/64
Mode:		5	5	5	5	5			
			4	4	4	4	4		

```
3     3     3     3     3
      2     2     2     2     2
            1     1     1     1     1
```

Viewed overall therefore the pentatonic modes offer any one of five shades of tonal brightness or colour. In the traditional music of China, where the pentatonic modes were always carefully tuned in exact fifths, these differences are interpreted both philosophically and emotively within a musical system that casts up the pentatonic modes as being reflective of what were considered to be the five elemental states of being: wood, earth, water, fire and metal.[1]

The Pentatonic Scale and its Connection with the Five Philosophical Elements

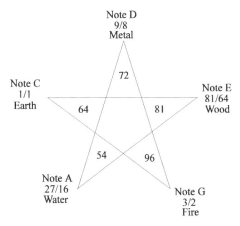

Although the consciously felt connections between music and the cosmos were long ago severed, the diagram as given above nonetheless serves as a strong reminder that the pentatonic scale represents the embryonic manifestations of tonality, in which case it should not be dismissed or discounted from any further participation within the province of more advanced tonal systems.

---

[1] Kazu Nakaseko, Op. Cit..

THE FORMATTING OF THE MUSICAL OCTAVE ACCORDING TO THE 3/2 RELATION

Musical scales as defined by the Pythagorean principle of the cycle of fifths have played an important part in the music of the West.[1] After the example provided in the sixth century by Boethius's *De Institutiones Musica* proof of the theoretical adoption of Pythagorean principles of scale construction lies in many subsequent records. The already mentioned French writer Odo of Cluny describes in his *Enchiridion Musices* a manner of division of the monochord almost exactly duplicated in the third chapter of the book *Micrologus* (1026 - 32) by the eleventh century theorist Guido d'Arezzo (c 991/2, d. after 1033).[2] Here the monochord is divided in such a way as to produce a diatonic scale in exact Pythagorean intonation.

In view of this predisposition towards cyclic methods of scale construction it is curious that the pentatonic scale never received the kind of recognition that it did in early China. This perhaps is because of the imposing influence of ancient Greek musical theory on the early development of Western music. Despite the evidence for the existence of a five tone or pentatonic stage of ancient Greek music,[3] there was a general tendency to concentrate on seven tone, as opposed to five tone scales.

Yet pentatonic influences cannot be entirely dismissed from early Western music. The pentatonic character of many Gregorian melodies has often been noticed. In his book on the polyphonic vocal style of the sixteenth century, Knud Jeppesen (1892 - 1974) observes that *a certain element of pentatonic*

---

[1] Oliver Strunk, Source Readings In Musical History: Faber & Faber 1952, 106.

[2] Hucbald, Guido and John on Music, trans. by Warren Babbit, ed. by Claude V. Palisca, New Haven and London 1978, 60.

[3] As Leichtentritt observes even before Pythagoras mythical reports tell us of a scale on a pentatonic basis...this fragmentary pentatonic system is quite universal in the infancy of music. It is found everywhere in primitive and exotic music; the Chinese, the American Indians, the Scotch, the Norse, the Celts, the Egyptians and the Siamese all based their music on a pentatonic scale of some kind...Hugo Leichentritt, 'Music, History and Ideas', Harvard University Press, Cambridge, 1966, 10. See also R.P. Winnington Ingram's The Pentatonic Tuning of the Greek Lyre, a Theory Examined in: CQ, New Series, Vol. VI 1956.

musical feeling is also characteristic of the Gregorian modes. By pentatonic music is meant of course, the musical style associated with the pentatonic (five tone) scale. [1]

Whilst the heptatonic scale was accepted and established in China as early as 40 BC. it was nonetheless viewed as a pentatonic scale to which two auxiliary notes had been added. This feature of treating the two extra fifths as auxiliary notes is not an isolated phenomenon, for as well as manifesting rather subtly in Gregorian melodies, it has also been observed in European folk music.

Yasser reported that: *in some localities where this* [pentatonic] *scale is firmly established, there has frequently been observed a tendency to extend its tonal material, and consequently its musical resources, by the sporadic application of two additional notes E and B. But from this it must not be hastily inferred that such a tonal extension inevitably transforms the pentatonic scale into the diatonic scale, for in those recorded cases where the two degrees (E and B) are added, their functions differ profoundly from the functions of the regular degrees of the pentatonic scale. In contradistinction to these regular degrees, the notes E and B merely play the role of auxiliary degrees of the pentatonic scale, serving as a basis for melodic embellishments, and they can always be omitted at will without essential detriment to the melody itself. It would thus seem that there is some kind of transition phase between pentatonicism and the full resources of the diatonic scale.* [2]

In terms of the Pythagorean method of dividing the octave, these two auxiliary notes are obtained by adding a further two fifths, to the original four responsible for the formation of the pentatonic scale:

Heptatonic Scale as Defined by Six Fifths

Fifth:		First	Second	Third	Fourth	Fifth	Sixth
Note:	C	G	D	A	E	B	F#
Ratio:	1/1	3/2	9/8	27/16	81/64	243/128	729/512

Compared to the range of mildly consonant intervals present within the pentatonic scale, the two auxiliaries yield two sharply dissonant intervals: the augmented fourth and the major seventh. They also divide the Pythagorean minor thirds of the pentatonic scale into the two smaller intervals of a whole

---

[1] Knud Jeppesen, Counterpoint; The Polyphonic Style of the Sixteenth Century, Trans. by Glen Haydon, Prentice Hall Inc., Engelwood Cliffs, N.J. 1939, 68 -
[2] Yasser, Op. Cit., 6.

tone and hemitone.[1] This fills in the minor third gaps present in the pentatonic scale, to result in a gamut consisting of five whole tones and two hemitones:

Pythagorean Seven-Toned Scale

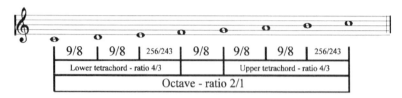

Here the significance of the hemitones needs to be pondered. In the sphere of Medieval music where, in theory at least, the Pythagorean seven toned scale predominated, the hemitones often received comment. *Ordinary singers often fall into the greatest error because they scarcely consider the force of tone and semitone...* so says Odo of Cluny (b. 878/9 - 942) in the *Enchiridion Musices*[2]. Or again: *The semitone, as Bernard said, is the sugar and spice of all song, and without it the song would be gnawed to pieces, transformed and mutilated.*[3] In many ways these hemitones are important because they create melodic leanings towards one tone or another. This in its turn allows the creation of melodic impetus, the operation of internal motive forces within the melody. In consequence, the two auxiliary notes represent a considerable leap forward in expressive potential, for they not only introduce the hemitones, but they enable the use (or avoidance) of dissonance.

This distinction between the five principal tones as belonging to the original pentatonic scale, and the two extra melodic auxiliaries has interesting ramifications for the heptatonic modes. As each note of the heptatonic scale can be taken as the tonic note of a particular heptatonic mode, means there are seven possible heptatonic modes. Of the seven there are five principal modes, whose tonic notes derive from the pentatonic scale. These are characterised by a sense of tonal stability owing to the fact that they possess a perfect prime, fourth and fifth degrees:

---

[1] Jocelyn Goodwin, Speculative Music, in: Companion to Contemporary Musical Thought; Vol. 1. Ed. by John Paynter, Tim Howell, Richard Orton and Peter Seymour; Routledge; London and New York 1992, 258.

[2] Strunk, Op. Cit., 110.

[3] Ibid., 84.

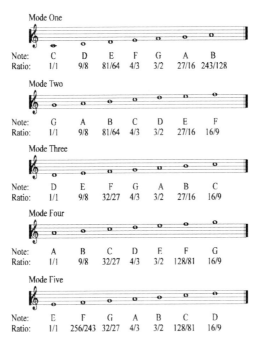

Then there are two secondary modes, which use the auxiliaries as their respective tonics. These are characterised by an intrinsic sense of tonal instability, seen in the augmented, as opposed to perfect fourth, of mode six, and the diminished fifth of mode seven:

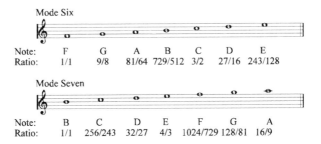

This factor of dividing up the Pythagorean seven-toned scale into five principal tones and two auxiliary degrees seems to have a strong rationale behind it. Within the Pythagorean tone system, the pentatonic scale represents a boundary of musical consonance beyond which lie intervals which bring unstable elements into the system. The two secondary modes thus epitomise this tendency as it applies to the possibilities of a complete musical scale.

The intervals peculiar to this system are Pythagorean. The most important is the minor second which, having a ratio of 256/243, is distinguished from the minor second of just intonation (16/15) by being called the hemitone (as opposed to the semitone). It is also sometimes termed the Pythagorean limma, representing the defect of the ditone of ratio 81/64 to the perfect fourth (4/3).

Then there is the Pythagorean form of minor third (32/27), which is called the trihemitone. The ditone, so called because it is the sum of two whole tones - ratio of 9/8 - is the Pythagorean form of major third, and has a ratio of 81/64. Other intervals which derive from Pythagorean intonation, such as the major sixth (27/16), major seventh (243/128), minor sixth (128/81), etc., are usually distinguished by the prefix 'Pythagorean' or else the term 'cyclic', in order to denote their specific origin. Thus the Pythagorean diminished fifth (ratio of 1024/729), may also be termed the cyclic diminished fifth.

The range of intervals evoked by the Pythagorean seven toned scale can be viewed when the heptatonic modes are transposed onto a common pitch centre. This of necessity, leads to an expanded pitch array which, when viewed from a pivotal keynote appears as six perfect fifths and six perfect fourths:

Heptatonic Modes Transposed to a Common keynote (D)

Note	Ratio	Interval	Modalities
Ab	1024/729	Cyclic Diminished Fifth	7
Eb	256/243	Hemitone	7 6
Bb	128/81	Cyclic Minor Sixth	7 6 5
F	32/27	Trihemitone	7 6 5 4
C	16/9	Minor Seventh	7 6 5 4 3
G	4/3	Perfect Fourth	7 6 5 4 3 2
D	1/1	Prime	7 6 5 4 3 2 1
A	3/2	Perfect Fifth	6 5 4 3 2 1
E	9/8	Major Second	5 4 3 2 1
B	27/16	Cyclic Major Sixth	4 3 2 1
F#	81/64	Ditone	3 2 1
C#	243/128	Cyclic Major Seventh	2 1
G#	729/512	Cyclic Augmented Fourth	1

When the modes are represented in this way, it is easier to see the different array of intervals which are brought into play against the tonic within each particular mode. It is this which serves to establish the character or 'ethos' of each mode i.e. the relative tonal darkness of mode seven with its preponderance of minor intervals, etc.

Observe that the process of transposition of the heptatonic modes to a common keynote necessitates the extension of the initial set of six fifths responsible for the formation of the heptatonic scale into an expanded set of twelve fifths. This enlarged set gives rise to a new scale structure which is appropriately designated as the Pythagorean twelve tone scale:

The Pythagorean Twelve-Tone Scale

Degree	Note	Ratio	Interval	Cents
I	C	1/1	Prime	0
II	Db	256/243	Limma	90
III	D	9/8	Whole Tone	204
IV	Eb	32/27	Trihemitone	294
V	E	81/64	Ditone	408
VI	F	4/3	Perfect Fourth	498
VII	F#	729/512	Cyclic Augmented Fourth	612
	(Gb	1024/729	Cyclic Diminished Fifth	588
VIII	G	3/2	Perfect Fifth	702
IX	Ab	128/81	Cyclic Minor sixth	792
X	A	27/16	Cyclic Major Sixth	906
XI	Bb	16/9	Cyclic Minor Seventh	996
XII	B	243/128	Cyclic Major Seventh	1110

An examination of the intervals between each of the adjacent hemitones of the Pythagorean twelve-tone scale reveals that they are not quite equal. Subtracting the value of the Pythagorean limma (90 cents) from the whole tone (204 cents), there is a difference of 114 cents, which means that the hemitones are of different sizes. The latter interval (114 cents) is the major hemitone, otherwise known as the apotome (ratio 2147/2048), in contradistinction to the minor hemitone or limma (256/243).

In terms of musical notation the difference between these intervals can be understood in the sense that the limma is the hemitonal interval that separates pitches of adjacent note classes i.e. C - Db, whilst the apotome separates hemitonal pitches of the same class i.e. C - C#. Within the scale as given above therefore, there are a total of seven limmas and five apotomes, since 7 x 90 = 630; 5 x 114 = 570; 570 + 530 = 1200 cents.

On the matter of the derivation of this scale, it proves extremely fruitful to retrace some of the steps which lead up to it, as these considerably help in the process of understanding why we use a seven-note scale, and not a scale of six, eight or nine notes (as for example).

Now it has already been observed that the first four fifths define a natural limit whose crystalline form is the pentatonic scale. To go beyond this limit is to disrupt that pattern. Therefore the fifth member of the cycle of fifths - note B - brings the intrusion of a semitone into the pentatonic pattern of whole tones. That semitone does not violate the integrity of the whole tone, for it is safely nestled within the trihemitone defined by the notes A and C. Thus occurring for the first time it divides the trihemitone into a tone and semitone respectively.

The new pattern implied by this is incomplete without the addition of a further fifth - note F# - which similarly divides the trihemitone between *E* and *G* into a tone and a semitone. The first six fifths therefore define another complete pattern, identifiable as the seven note scale.

This segment of six fifths also serves to establish a natural limitation beyond which that basic pattern becomes disrupted. Therefore the seventh fifth - note C# - is the first point at which a whole tone becomes subdivided. The note C# thus manifests as both the destroyer and the creator, for it has disrupted the pattern of notes implicit to the heptatonic scale, only to provide the basis for a new pattern belonging to an even more complex scale: the configuration of hemitones characteristic of the twelve-tone scale.

Therefore the division of the octave into 5, 7 and 12 represent three quite natural tone patterns, complete unto themselves, whose natures are fundamentally determined by the laws of valent connection as manifested through the '3/2' relationship.

In China, where all three patterns played a part in their basic tone system, a scale known as the 'luleu' was arrived at through the superimposition of eleven fifths, obtained through cutting bamboo pitch pipes according to the appropriate ratios:

The Luleu

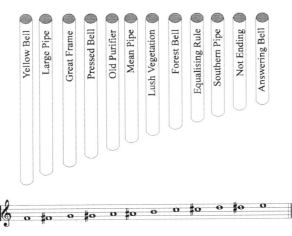

Note		Note Name	Ratio	Cents
1	C	Huang-chung (Yellow Bell)	1/1	0
2	C#	Ta-lu (Large Pipe)	2187/2048	114
3	D	T'ai-ts'u (Great Frame)	9/8	204
4	D#	Chia-chung (Pressed Bell)	19683/16384	318
5	E	Ku-hsi (Old Purifier)	81/64	408
6	E#	Cheng lu (Mean Pipe)	177147/131072	521
7	F#	Jui-pin (Lush Vegetation)	729/512	612
8	G	Lin-chung (Forest Bell)	3/2	702
9	G#	I-tse (Equalising Rule)	6561/4096	816
10	A	Nan-lu (Southern Pipe)	27/16	906
11	A#	Wu-i (Not Ending)	59049/32768	1020
12	B	Ying-chung (Answering Bell)	243/128	1110

Of these, the odd-numbered tones were considered to be male - the members of the superior generation, the even numbered tones female - the tones belonging to the inferior generation. Although this implies a division of the octave into two respective whole tone scales, there is no evidence to suggest that the twelve notes were ever used in this fashion.

The twelve Lu was not used as a chromatic scale, but in a similar sense to the Western system of keys.[1] Each of the twelve notes could serve as a keynote

---

[1] Kazu Nakaseko, Symbolism in Ancient Chinese Musical Theory, in: JMT, 1/2 Nov. 1957

upon which various scales could be constructed. From this comes the Chinese concept of the twelve *yunn*.

In terms of the number of possibilities available, the Chinese system is superior to the Western tonal system. Upon each of the twelve keys could be constructed any of five pentatonic modes, which gives 60 possibilities, and any of seven heptatonic modes, which gives a further total of 84 possibilities. From this comes the concept of the 84 *diaw* or modes, arrived at through the theoretical construction of all seven heptatonic modes on each of the twelve keynotes. Of these, sixty were considered to be principal modes, being constructed on pentatonic scale degrees, the other 24 being secondary, deriving as they did, from the two auxiliary notes of each system.

The value of the twelve-tone scale thus lay in the facility it offered both for the transposition of musical modes (heptatonic and/or pentatonic) and for the processes of establishing different keys to and from which it was possible to modulate.

When attempting to reconstruct this system a major problem arises which has strong parallels with Western musical traditions. After twelve cycles of a perfect fifth there is a very close return to the frequency of the generating tone (in this instance note F). The twelfth fifth (note E#) overshoots the octave by a microtonal interval of ratio 531441/524288 - the Pythagorean Comma. It is possible to imagine that in the case of ancient Chinese music where the pitches of the scale were standardised in accordance with a set of bamboo pipes which were cut and measured in the proportions of 3/2, or 4/3 depending upon instance, that the last pipe in the series (*E#)* must have looked conspicuously close to the size of the first pipe (*F*). It is conspicuously evident that at this point a natural cycle has been completed - a perfectly natural division of the octave into twelve hemitones.

To be able to use all five pentatonic modes from a common keynote - say note C - a nine-note segment of the circle of fifths is required. Should all five modes in all twelve keys be required an additional seven fifths need to be added to the original series of eleven. this creates a scale of twenty notes, since after the first eleven fifths, all subsequent fifths will place themselves a comma higher than the original set.

However, use of seven heptatonic modes from a common keynote is impossible, as it requires a segment of twelve fifths, or thirteen sounds in all. To be able to play any heptatonic mode in any of the twelve keys would therefore require twelve such segments, thus totaling twenty-four sounds in all:

Basic Scale for Accurate Modal Transposition in all Twelve Keys

Plus Comma:	E#	F#		G#		A#			C#		D#	
Original Set:	F	Gb	G	Ab	A	Bb	B	C	Db	D	Eb	E
Minus Comma:				Abb		Bbb		Cb	Dbb		Ebb	Fb

For practical musical purposes such a scale is very complicated, and in answer to this problem, the Chinese theorist Ho Tcheng Thyien (c. 370 - 447) advocated a form of equal temperament.[1] In so doing, Partch claims that he thereby *anticipated twelve-tone Equal temperament in Europe by about thirteen centuries.*[2]

Far from being a purely Western concept, temperament may thus be viewed as an inevitability of any pitch system which takes natural intervals as a criterion for the selection of pitch relationships. Their very incommensurability means that there is always some fraction of a tone left over at the points where intervals cycles converge. In the case of the cycle of fifths it is the Pythagorean comma which creates the major problems.

As the most primary of all musical intervals it is evident that through processes of replication, the perfect fifth sets down a series of natural scalar blueprints which provide the standards or orders of a growing tonal possibility. Within Western music, despite certain modifications due to harmonic considerations, all three of the scale structures considered so far - the pentatonic, heptatonic and dodecaphonic - have played an important part. In the main Western music seems to stop rather stubbornly with the resources of the equally tempered twelve-tone scale, despite the fact that the cycle of fifths is infinite in its extension.

In this respect it will be seen that the eleventh fifth itself defines a barrier beyond which the pattern of semitones in the chromatic scale itself starts to be disrupted. With the twelfth fifth, a new intervallic world begins to present itself: the world of microtones. The most significant microtonal interval here is the Pythagorean Comma (23.5 cents), an interval which approximates to about one-quarter of a semitone. Seen first in the difference between the twelfth fifth and the octave, the comma continually displaces subsequent fifths, leading to an ever-winding spiral progression which brings into play more and more complex scale structures.

---

[1] James Murray Barbour, Equal temperament, its history from Ramis (1482) to Rameau (1737), Ph. D. Dissertation, Cornell University 1932, 138.
[2] Partch, 'The History of Intonation', Op. Cit., 169 -170.

For those involved in microtonal composition, elementary definitions of microtonal scales as defined by the cycle of fifths are worthy of consideration, for this cycle serves to expose those natural patterns upon which such scales can be based. After the twelve-tone chromatic scale, the main staging posts are the 19-, 31- and 53-tone divisions, all three of which have been theoretically advocated at various times in the history of music. Here, the numbers involved - 19, 31 and 53 - are not in any way arbitrary, for they are significant of the points of completion of those natural patterns which also characterise the 5-, 7- and 12-tone division.[1]

In terms of the 19-tone system, the pattern involved is a very interesting one for with the twelfth fifth it is possible to see a new element coming in, in which the pattern of semitones belonging to the chromatic scale has become disrupted by the entry of the note C#, which places itself a Pythagorean comma above note Db in the chromatic scale. The next note, G#, places itself similarly above the note Ab.

Thus occurs the announcement of an altogether new scale system the characteristic feature of which is the enharmonic differentiation between the sharp and the flat. Completing itself with the eighteenth fifth, this pattern leads to a new and equally natural scale division: the nineteen note enharmonic scale.

The 19-tone Division as Defined by the Cycle of Fifths

I	C	1/1	0
II	Db	256/243	90
III	C#	2187/2048	114
IV	D	9/8	204
V	Eb	32/27	294
VI	D#	19683/16384	318
VII	Fb	8192/6561	384
VIII	E	81/64	408
IX	F	4/3	498
X	Gb	1024/729	588
XI	F#	729/512	612

---

[1] Jocelyn Godwin points out that the cycle of fifths leads to the formation of certain basic scales which have 5,7,12,19 and 31 notes. The 31 note scale is composed of 7 naturals, 7 sharps, 5 double-sharps, 7 flats, and 5 double flats. (Jocelin Godwin, Speculative Music, Op. Cit.) Here it is interesting to observe that all five of these scales have played a part in Western musical theory. It is also interesting to observe that the series of numbers which Goodwin points to - 5,7,12,19 and 31 - are all members of the type of Golden sequence called the 'Ecclesiastical sequence'. This sequence is explained in the paper Fibonacci and the Gold Mean: Rabbits, Rumbas and Rondeaux, in: JMT, 23, 2 1979.

XII	G	3/2	702
XIII	Ab	128/81	792
XIV	G#	6561/4096	816
XV	A	27/16	906
XVI	Bb	16/9	996
XVII	A#	59049/32768	1020
XVIII	Cb	4096/2187	1086
XIX	B	243/128	1110

The 31-tone division is characterised by a number of advancements upon the basic pattern implied by the 19-tone division. Whilst the existence of such a pattern is evident, its precise musical usage is not immediately apparent. Speaking of the possibilities for a tonal system even more complex than a nineteen-tone tonality, the 31-tone system represents an extremely interesting possibility. The scale pattern itself is characterised by the presence of a further note both a comma above and below the seven original 'white notes', whilst the five chromatic tones may appear as sharp or flat.

The 31-tone Division as Defined by the Cycle of Fifths

1	C	1/1	0
2	B#	531441/524288	23
3	Db	256/243	90
4	C#	2187/2048	114
5	Ebb	65536/59049	180
6	D	9/8	204
7	Cx	4782969/4194304	227
8	Eb	32/27	294
9	D#	19683/16384	318
10	Fb	8192/6561	384
11	E	81/64	408
12	Dx	43046721/33554432	431
13	Gbb	2097152/1594323	475
14	F	4/3	498
15	E#	177147/131072	522
16	Gb	1024/729	588
17	F#	729/512	612
18	Abb	262144/177147	678
19	G	3/2	702
20	Fx	1594323/1048576	725

20	Fx	1594323/1048576	725
21	Ab	128/81	792
22	G#	6561/4096	816
23	Bbb	32768/19683	882
24	A	27/16	906
25	Gx	14348907/8388608	929
26	Bb	16/9	996
27	A#	59049/32768	1020
28	Cb	4096/2187	1086
29	B	243/128	1110
30	Ax	129140163/67108864	1133
31	Dbb	1048576/531441	1177

Undoubtedly, the most complex of the practically realisable microtonal scales delivered by the cycle of fifths is the scale of fifty-three sounds, the original discovery of which is attributed to the Chinese theorist Jing Farng (40 BC), who, as Partch rightly observes, was *'a contemporary of Eratosthenes'*.[1] According to Partch: *King Fang calculated exactly the proportional numbers of liu that would give a scale based on a succession of sixty 3/2's and observed that the fifty-fourth liu was practically identical with the first (3.6 cents above). This very early discovery by King Fang is particularly noteworthy when we consider that the 'fifty-three' cycle has been the subject of much conjecture in recent decades and has been the theoretical basis for at least three new harmoniums.*[1]

Partch here is referring to the harmoniums constructed by James Paul White in the decade of 1877-87, three of which had keyboards which would enable the playing of the fifty-three cycle. Also relevant here is R.H.M. Bosanquet (1841-1912) who constructed an organ based on Mercator's equally tempered cycle of fifty-three. Mercator (1491 - 1554) himself, discovered the fifty-three cycle after having read of Jing Farng's work.[2]

The scale of 53 has often been cited as a potential successor to the equally tempered twelve-tone scale. Although based on cycles of fifths, it allows the use of fairly accurate substitutes for the intervals of just intonation. A major third of ratio 5/4 (386 cents) would be accounted for by a major third of 17 commas (384 cents), etc. Such a change is not without problems. Keyboards with 53

---

[1] Partch, Genesis of a Music, 358. For Yasser's comments on Farng's contribution see A Theory of Evolving Tonality, 31.

[2] Alexander Wood, The Physics of Music, 195.

lower the pitch of a note by one or more commas are also awkward to operate. Yet as Partch points out, such keyboards have been built. Whether such instruments will ever be brought into general practice is thus a difficult question to answer.

Beyond the cycle of fifty-three are further microtonal scales defined by the cycle of fifths. Having completed a cycle of fifty-three, the fifty-third fifth overshoots the octave by about one-seventh of a comma - the tonal degree of 3.6 cents. It is possible to continue adding further cycles of fifty-three which place themselves 3.6 cents higher each time. After nearly seven such cycles there is a further approximate return to the frequency of the fundamental at the 359th. fifth (with a difference of only 1.8 cents). This provides the basis for the cycle of 360 *lu* advocated in sixth century China.

This scale was never used for practical musical purposes, but calculated as a theoretical possibility. Part of the interest in this scale was symbolic, for it allowed a further extension of the Chinese analogy of the musical octave with the cycle of days, seasons, years, etc. Here, the twelve lu were considered analogous with the twelve months of the year. The 360 *lu* therefore offered the possibility of an individual keynote for every day of the year. Daniélou sums up this series of analogies as they are conceived within parallel Western traditions, where the octave is viewed to share correspondences with the seasons, months, signs of the zodiac, angles, etc.

Taking this point as an arbitrary limit, the cycle of fifths has yielded some seven independent scale structures, each of which leads to a complexification of the preceding structure:

> 1) The pentatonic scale (4 fifths)
> 2) The heptatonic scale (6 fifths)
> 3) The chromatic scale (11 fifths)
> 4) The enharmonic scale (18 fifths)
> 5) The double enharmonic scale (30 fifths)
> 6) The 53 tone division (52 fifths)
> 7) The 359 tone division (358 fifths)

Through a consideration of these scales it can be seen that 3-valency intervals define another dimension of the pitch continuum, one which significantly modifies the helical structure implied by the phenomenon of octave equivalence. Geometrically, this is not so easy to define, the cycle of fifths forming yet another spiral - an epicycloid - which winds its way around the spiral of octaves.

Daniélou's Scheme of Octave Correspondence Based on Chinese System of 360 Lu[1]

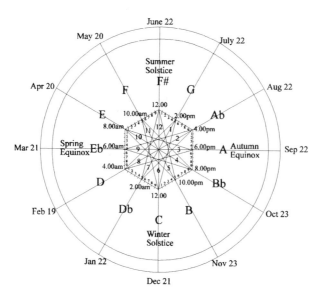

The perfect fifth is a natural interval defined both by the harmonic series, and the various nodes of connection which ensue when two notes a perfect fifth apart are combined. Scales defined by the cycle of fifths therefore cannot be considered to be the inventions of the human mind, for they are naturally ordained by the very properties of tone and tonal interactions. In this sense, they are clear and pervasive manifestations of natural acoustic laws, and in their way are akin to other phenomenon of nature in which regular mathematical structures can be seen to manifest.

This observation is of great importance, in that it shows that the way to a clear definition of a more advanced system of tonality, lies in nothing more than the observation and appropriation of what is actually ordained by the very nature of tone. Through doing so, many problems may arise, especially those resulting from our interference or modification of these natural patterns. But as long as the study cleaves to these patterns in the first place, it should be possible to unravel any problems that may arise.

---

[1] Alain Daniélou, The Cyclic System, Op. Cit..

A NEW DIMENSIONAL PERSPECTIVE - THE '5/4' RELATION

In the last chapter it was observed that the theoretical scale of the medieval world was based on a limited segment of perfect fifths.[1] Placement of the final or *finalis* upon different degrees of the resulting seven tone scale led to the generation of musical modes of diverse characters determined both by the arrangement of intervals peculiar to each mode, together with the precise axis between 'dominant' and 'final'. The particular process of modal generation and the criteria whereby different reciting tones and registers relevant to each mode were chosen had no effect whatsoever on the basic foundation scale upon which this modal superstructure was based. Similarly, the surrounding confusion concerning the nomenclature adopted for this system of modes, and especially its derivation from ancient Greek theoretical sources is also of no concern here. The most important point to observe is that the Pythagorean system of tuning envisaged for such a system necessarily excluded all pitch relationships having ratios involving any prime number higher than three.

Therefore, despite the diversification of expressive possibility enabled by that system of modes, that mathematical constraint upon the order and level of pitch relationships employed still existed. Consequently, there could only be three intervals which, having very simple ratios, may be regarded to be consonant: the octave (ratio 2/1), the perfect fifth (3/2) and the perfect fourth (4/3). All other intervals within the Pythagorean system have more complex ratios, examples of which are the ditone (81/64), the trihemitone (32/27), the cyclic major sixth (27/16) and the minor sixth (128/81). Because of the complexity of their implied ratios such intervals could never attain the status of consonance without some kind of radical change in the mathematical basis underlying the system of pitch relationships which that scale offered.

This observation certainly concurs with the observations of early theorists. Cassiodorus (c. 485 - 580 AD.), in his *Institutiones*, reports of three basic consonances: the octave, perfect fifth and the perfect fourth. Those others he

---

[1] *The basic Medieval scale consisted of the seven diatonic notes plus Bb, tuned in the 'Pythagorean' manner with all perfect fifths in the ratio 3:2.* Jan. W. Herlinger, Marchetto's Division of the Whole Tone, in: JAMS 34, 1981, 203.

mentions are simply compound forms of the same intervals.[1] Three hundred years later the Frankish treatise *Musica Enchiriadis* together with its commentary the *Scholia Enchiriadis* (ninth century) again recognises only three consonances: the octave, perfect fifth, and perfect fourth.[2] The earliest forms of polyphony as they appear in the West do seem to have favoured the simultaneities of the three perfect intervals. They are after all, the only intervals within that system, which have simple ratios. Therefore, it is perhaps inevitable; both by virtue of the aural qualities of these particular intervals, and their mathematical pedigree, those early attempts in the combination of multiple voice parts should focus upon them.[3]

Examples of this type of harmony are readily seen in the technique of 'diaphony' as described and depicted in the *Musica Enchiriadis* formerly attributed to Hucbald of St Amande (c. 840 - 930).[4] Here, an additional part - *the vox organalis* - can be added to the principal part - the *vox principalis* - at the interval of the octave, perfect fifth or perfect fourth. When in more than two parts, other voices simply doubled the first pair at the octave:

Four Part Organum[5]

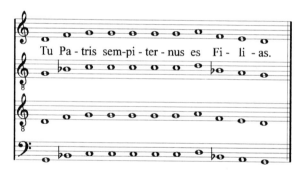

The *Musica Enchiriadis* thus alludes to a technique of parallelism at the fifth or fourth, with doubling occurring (when in more than two parts), at the octave - an essentially two-dimensional form of harmony which has long since been recognised to be prototypical amongst those races - such as the Chinese for

---

[1] Strunk, Source Readings in Musical History, 89.

[2] Ibid., 126.

[3] André Barbera, The Consonant Eleventh and the Expansion of the Musical Tetractys: A Study of Ancient Pythagoreanism, in: JMT 28/2, 1984, 191 - 224.

[4] Musica Enchiriadis, Harvard Dictionary of Music, ed. by Don Randell, 516.

[5] Example based on that given in Willi Apel's The Notation of Polyphonic Music, 5th. Ed., Cambridge 1961, 205

example - who developed their scales using only the prime numbers two and three. As far as European musical culture was concerned the theoretical adoption of the heptatonic scale seemed to have derived principally from a desire for observance of Pythagorean principles. These, as set down by Boethius (450 -520) in his text *De Institutione Musica* remained a model for subsequent theorists, even when later, it was becoming evident that it no longer retained a practical validity.

Indeed, through the Middle Ages, thirds and sixths - intervals which in the Pythagorean system are considered to be dissonances on account of their complex ratios - gradually came to be regarded as consonants too. One of the first signs of the eventual acceptance of intervals other than the fourth, fifth and octave as consonances comes from Gaudentius (2nd century AD or later) who in his *Introduction to Harmonics* recognises the ditone from the diatonic meson (G) to the paramese (B) as being *paraphonic* - that is neither consonant or dissonant.[1] Curiously he includes the tritone here as well. This view is perhaps exceptional though. In the main, it was during the beginnings of the next millennium that clear signs of a change in attitude towards consonance started to appear. In *De Musica* dating from about 1100, the author known only as John writes [it is said]: *there are just nine intervals from which melody is put together: the unison, semitone, whole tone, ditone, semiditone, diatesseron, diapente, semitone-plus-diapente, and whole-tone-plus-diapente. Six ...are called 'consonances'...being generated from those ratios called sesquioctava (8/9), sesquitertia (3/4) sesquialtera (2/3) and dupla (1/2).*[2]

Automatically precluding thirds and sixths as being consonant, from hereon in a gradual change in attitude towards thirds and sixths becomes evident. In the thirteenth century Franco of Cologne in his *Ars Cantus Mensurablis*, Chap XI (Coussemaker, *Scriptores I*) described major and minor thirds as being imperfect consonances, the minor sixth a perfect dissonance, and the major sixth an imperfect dissonance.[3] Similarly, Philip de Vitry (1291-1361) and Jehan des Murs (c1300-c1350) described thirds and sixths as imperfect consonances.[4] In the *Ars Contrapuncti Secundum Johannem de Muris* of the first half of the fourteenth century, major and minor thirds together with the major sixth are also regarded as consonances, whilst the minor sixth was still regarded as a

---

[1] Strunk, Op. Cit., 32.

[2] W. Babb. (Trans.), C.V. Palisca (Ed.), Hucbald, Guido and John on Music, Yale University Press, New Haven and London 1978, 87.

[3] Matthew Shirlaw, Theory of Harmony, Novello & Co. Ltd., London 1917, 1.

[4] Coussemaker, Histoire de l'harmonie au moyen-âge, Paris 1852, 66 - 68.

dissonance.[1] In Prosdocimus de Beldemandis's *Treatise on Counterpoint* (1412) he also excludes thirds and sixths from the province of the dissonances.[2]

Some theorists, endeavouring to find an explanation for this growing dichotomy, seemed to recognise that Pythagorean theory could no longer actually account for, or explain, current musical practice. Pythagorean thirds and sixths were rough, and difficult to sing. In practice such intervals could be made to sound considerably sweeter. Yet in so doing, the practices of musicians were beginning to impose a threat upon the established tenets of musical theory. It took an English mathematician, Walter de Odington (13th century) to point out that in practice, singers were intuitively using consonant thirds that had ratios of 5/4 for the major, and 6/5 for the minor.[3] Such an observation however, was not entirely new in the history of music. Simple ratios using the prime number five had already been recognised by ancient Greek theorists.

As early as the fourth century BC, the Alexandrian theorist Archytas recognised the ratios of 5/4, 8/5, 6/5, and 5/3 as valid scale degrees.[4] Similarly, Eratosthenes (c. 284-202 BC) had recognised the advantages of the ratio 6/5 over the Pythagorean 32/27 in the chromatic tetrachord.[5] Didymus (1st. century BC) introduced similar revisions to the diatonic tetrachord, introducing what Partch describes as the *logical 9/8 -10/9 combination in the diatonic scale*. He also, as Partch informs us, substituted 16/15 for 28/27 in the diatonic genus, and in so doing, anticipated Claudius Ptolemaes, or Ptolemy (after 83 - 161 AD).[6] Recognition of the prime number five, although in this case within the different context of monophonic ancient Greek music, was not something altogether new in the history of musical theory. It is thus not surprising to learn that in the late Middle Ages, theorists following Odington's example, began to observe the schism between a practice which admitted to consonant thirds having a ratio of 5/4, and a theory which recognised only the Pythagorean major third of 81/64.

As observed by Barbour 'the idea of consonant thirds had long been recognised in more progressive circles when Bartolomeus Ramis de Pareia

---

[1] Shirlaw, Op. Cit., 2.

[2] Strunk,Op.Cit.,

[3] J. Murray Barbour, The History of Equal Temperament from Ramis to Rameau, Ph.D. Diss., Cornell Univ. 1932, 12.

[4] Sir John Hawkins, A General History of the Science and Practice of Music, 2 Vols, Novello, Ewer & Co. Ltd., London 1875, p. 171.

[5] Eratosthenes was mentioned by Partch in 'The History of Intonation', Genesis of a Music, 367: *he was 'director of the famous library at Alexandria, was not only a musical philosopher, but an astronomer, geographer, cartographer, and inventor of astronomical instruments. In music he is generally credited with substituting ..... 6/5 for the more difficult Pythagorean 32/27 in his chromatic genus tetrachord, although this interval was implied by Archytas in his enharmonic scale*

[6] Ibid.,

(c1440; d in or after 1491) published his Musica Practica in 1482'.[1] However, it was Bartolomeus Ramis's pupil, Giovanni Spataro (? 1458 - 1541) who, in 1521, observed that 'only in practice did the major third correspond to the ratio 5/4, while theoretically it was comprised in the ratio 81/64'.[2] His teacher Ramis, in an effort to resolve that schism, had already in 1482, laid down a division of the monochord which gave ratios for a major third of 5/4, and at least implied ratios for the minor third of 6/5, the major sixth of 5/3 and the minor sixth of 8/5:[3]

Scale Derived from Ramis's 'Monochord in Just Intonation'[4]

Ratio: 1/1 135/128 10/9 32/27 5/4 4/3 45/32 3/2 128/81 27/16 16/9 15/8

However, as Barbour observes: *The striking feature about this monochord of Ramis is that it is not bound up with any new theory of tuning. To Ramis, the Pythagorean method as given by Boethius, is 'useful and pleasing to theorists, but tiresome for singers and irksome to the mind. But because we have promised to satisfy both (singers and theorists) we shall simplify the division of the monochord.*[5]

Even though it may be accepted that the note ratios Ramis gives to each note of the scale are 'not bound up with a new theory of tuning', Ramis's intonation is fascinating in that it admits in the realms of musical theory to a practice which diverges from the Pythagoreanism of Boethius. Partch mentions this in his chapter on the history of intonation: *As early as 1482 Ramis de Pareja pointed out the discrepancy between Pythagorean theory and actual practise.... The Pythagorean scale giving the highly equivocal 81/64 instead of 5/4, and 27/16 instead of 5/3, was generally theorised as the basis of music. These ratios were postulated because theorists were afraid of the number five, preferring the*

---

[1] J. Murray Barbour, Op. Cit., 13.

[2] Ibid., 29.

[3] Strunk, Op. Cit., 201 - 204. Here it states that Ramis also gives ratios for the minor third of 6/5, the major sixth of 5/3 and the minor sixth of 8/5. These, however, only seem to exist by implication. The harmonic minor third (6/5) and major sixth (5/3) is implied between notes E (5/4) and G (3/2), and notes D (10/9) and F (4/3), whilst the minor sixth (8/5) is implied between notes E (5/4) and C (2/1).

[4] In the version given by Barbour, (cited above - although here cents have been converted into note ratios) the minor third, major and minor sixth still retain Pythagorean ratios.

[5] Ibid., 28.

81/64 and 27/16 derivatives of the number three.... Yet there is not a musician, having been conditioned to the idea of more acoustic 'third' and 'sixths' who would not admit that what the ear tried to assume in the above medieval scale - if the ear ever actually heard it - was 5/4 and 5/3 instead of 81/64 and 27/16.[1]

This gradual change in attitude towards thirds and sixths, together with the recognition of their harmonic, as opposed to cyclic ratios, led to the establishment of the essential intervals which provided the fabric of a new emerging system: the harmonic major third (ratio 5/4) which provided a substitute for the Pythagorean major third (81/64); the harmonic minor third (ratio 6/5) which replaced the Pythagorean trihemitone (32/27); the harmonic major sixth (5/3) which replaced the Pythagorean or cyclic sixth (ratio 27/16) and finally the harmonic minor sixth (8/5) which replaced the cyclic minor sixth (128/81).

These came to be recognised theoretically as the imperfect consonances, imperfect because, unlike the immutability of the perfect consonances, the imperfect consonances could occur in one of two positions - major or minor. This, in the end, led to a redefinition of the ratios of the notes of the diatonic scale as follows:

Ratios of the Notes of the Diatonic Scale in Just Intonation

Here it can be seen that 5/4 comes in as a substitute for 81/64, 5/3 as a substitute for 27/16 and 15/8 as a substitute for 243/128. According to David Beach this particular tuning was first proposed as being the most desirable by Lodovico Fogliano (late 15th century -c1539) in his *Musica Theorica* (Venice, 1529).[2] The universal adoption of this particular system however, was most influenced by the Italian composer and theorist Gioseffo Zarlino (1517-90) in whose theoretical works it is cited as being the most practical and rational tuning for polyphonic music.[3] Yet Zarlino's views did not go entirely unopposed. Vincenzo Galilei (1520s-1591) *demonstrated the impracticality of*

---

[1] Partch, Op. Cit. 369. Also see footnote on this on 125.

[2] See footnote d on page 13 of Kirnberger's The Art of Strict Musical Composition, trans, by D. Beach & Jurgen Thyme, Yale University Press, New Haven and London 1982. The footnote is by David Beach.

[3] Zarlino expounds this system in ch.39-40, part II, Le Institutioni Harmoniche, Venice 1558-9.

this tuning,[1] an action which later led Zarlino, in his treatise *The Art of Counterpoint* to fiercely defend this system from any further attack.[2]

This particular type of tuning is generally described as just intonation, simply because the relationships between the intervals are as harmonically pure as possible. 'Harmonically pure' in this context means 'in as close conformity to the corresponding intervals in the harmonic series as possible'. Paradoxically therefore, Pythagorean intonation is actually just for a tonal fabric that does not extend beyond the range of the 3-valency intervals. It is not just however, for a system that utilises harmonic thirds and sixths, because the requisite intervals are not acoustically accurate renditions of their defining ratios. In other types of intonation, such as the various types of meantone temperament or equal temperament, some of the intervals retain their acoustic purity whilst others are altered to various degrees. In meantone temperament the purity of the fifths and fourths is compromised for the purity of the thirds and sixths, the very opposite of Pythagorean intonation. In equal temperament it is only the octave that retains its acoustic purity.

However, it is necessary to distinguish between an ideal of intonation where all intervals are sounded according to the ratios implied by their relationships, and the realisation of that ideal, together with the various compromises that this necessitates in the actual process of tuning. Although it may be true to say that at the level of realisation this scale is an example of just intonation, it is also a manifestation of the ideal itself. In this context, just intonation is the form of realisation that most closely approaches that ideal. In this sense, Ramis's 'Monochord' is not really an intonation, but an attempt to precisely define the ideal ratios for each note of the scale. These, as Ramis well knew, had to involve the prime number five in order to account for the consonance of the thirds and sixths.

Here therefore it is significant that together with an increase in the number of available consonances, it was also discovered that two consonant intervals with the same bass note could be combined together to form consonant triads. As to when triads were first used, this is still a matter of some contention. The twelve part round *Sumer is Icumin In* dates from the thirteenth century, yet possesses an extremely well developed sense of tertial organisation, as can be seen by looking at this extract in which the canon is realised in three parts:

---

[1] Again consult footnote d, page 13 of Kirnberger's The Art of Strict Musical Composition.

[2] Zarlino, The Art of Counterpoint, trans. by Guy A. Marco and Claude V. Palisca, The Norton Library, W.W. Norton & Company Inc., New York 1968, xiii - xviii.

Extract from Round *Sumer is Icumin In* Realised in Three Parts

It is extremely doubtful that the singers would have intoned the implied triads according to Pythagorean tuning. So it seems likely that consonant triadic combinations were in use long before any theoretical observations were made concerning their use and make-up. Consequently, it took a considerable time for the conception of the triad as an independent harmonic entity in its own right to emerge. In the fifteenth and sixteenth centuries the basic harmonic unit was considered to be the interval, which could then be combined to create what we today view as triads. As well as major and minor triads, other triadic combinations proved successful. Obtained when a major or minor third was combined with a perfect fifth, or a major or minor sixth, the spectrum of triads used in the polyphonic music of the fifteenth and sixteenth centuries were thus:

Triads Obtained Through the Combination of Two Consonant Intervals

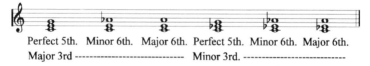

Perfect 5th.   Minor 6th.   Major 6th.   Perfect 5th.   Minor 6th.   Major 6th.
Major 3rd ---------------------------- Minor 3rd. ----------------------------

Although not conceived as independent sonorities, they were nonetheless regarded as desirable convergences of voices in the polyphonic movement of parts. It was Zarlino who encouraged the initial conception of the triad as an actual unit of harmony. As Strunk reports: *Starting from the ratios of the primary consonances, he succeeds in arriving at many of the conclusions that modern theory draws from the harmonic series, a phenomenon unknown to Zarlino and his time. He was the first to grasp the full implications of just intonation and to produce classical authority for it, the first to deal with harmony in terms of the triad rather than the interval...*[1]

---

[1] Strunk, Op. Cit., 228. But for another view see Benito V. Rivera's The Isagogue (1581) of Johannes Avianus: An early Formulation of Triadic Theory, in: JMT 22/1, 1978, 43 - 64.

In his Istituzioni armoniche of 1558 Zarlino satisfactorily defined the ratios of the notes of the major and minor triads. The ratios he gave were:

Zarlino's Definition of the Ratios of the Notes of the Major and Minor Triads

	HARMONIC			ARITHMETIC	
Ditone	Semiditone		Semiditone		Ditone

180	144	120	160	135	108
Sesquiquarta	Sesquiquinta		Sesquiquinta	Sesquiquarta	

For Zarlino therefore, the inherent parity of the major and minor triads was explained by the differential between the arithmetic and harmonic means of the perfect fifth. The spectrum of consonances recognised at the time were also derived by Zarlino from the numbers 1-6, whereby the ratios of the consonances of the octave (2/1), the perfect fifth (3/2), the major third (5/4), the minor third (6/5) and the major sixth (5/3) could be satisfactorily accounted for. Described by Zarlino as the *Senario*, this group of numbers thus offered a legitimate theoretical successor to the *Tetractys*, that group of numbers from 1 - 4 which, within ancient Greek traditions had defined the boundaries of the three perfect consonances.[1] Yet the *Senario*, although providing for Zarlino, a convenient numerical limit for the scope of consonance, did not satisfactorily account for the minor sixth (8/5) - a defect which Rameau later tried to remedy through extending the proscribed divisions of a string up to eight.[2]

The use and recognition of consonant triadic formations exerted a profound transforming effect on the original modal system which, theoretically at least, was rooted in Pythagorean principles. The complications arising from the incommensurability between cyclic and harmonic intervals led to serious considerations concerning the matter of tuning. The problems involved can be seen when the breadths of cyclic and harmonic intervals are compared. The cyclic major third and sixth are a Didymean Comma (81/80) larger than their harmonic counterparts, whilst the minor third and sixth are a Didymean Comma smaller:

---

[1] Hugo Riemann, Ideas for a Study in the Imagination of Tone, Translated by Robert W. Watson and Elizabeth West Marvin, in: JMT 36/1, 1992, 69 - 116.

[2] Robert W. Wienpahl discusses the defects of Zarlino's Senario in Zarlino, the Senario and Tonality, in: JAMS XII, 1959, 27 - 41.

Differences between Cyclic and Harmonic Intervals Measured in Cents

	Cyclic	Harmonic	Differential
Minor third	294	316	+ 22
Major third	408	386	- 22
Minor sixth	792	814	+ 22
Major sixth	906	884	- 22

The principal problem was that alternative cyclic and harmonic versions of the same interval would often be required over the same bass note. Thus for example, a triad constructed on the second degree of the Ionian Mode implies the use of a minor third between notes D and F (ratio of 6/5). This however, would result in a different ratio for the fourth degree of the scale (note F - 4/3) since 9/8 plus 6/5 equals 27/20 - the grave fourth, which is a syntonic comma smaller than the perfect fourth of ratio 4/3. The same triad would require a perfect fifth above note D, giving a ratio for note A of 27/16. Yet when that note occurred as the third of a triad constructed on the fourth degree of the scale a different ratio of 5/3 is implied. The problem is further compounded when the ratios for each note of a mode are calculated. If, in the Ionian mode, the fourth degree is given a ratio of 4/3, that same note in the Dorian mode forms with the finale a minor third of ratio 32/27. Yet in the Aeolian mode, the minor third interval between the first and third degrees has a ratio of 6/5. The 18th. century theorist Kirnberger mentions this, and he offers a list of the modes together with the implied ratios for each of their respective scale degrees:

Intervals in the Old Modes according to Kirnberger[1]

I	II	III	IV	V	VI	VII	VII	
C	1/1	9/8	5/4	4/3	3/2	5/3	15/8	2/1
D	1/1	10/9	27/32	4/3	40/27	5/3	16/9	2/1
E	1/1	16/15	6/5	4/3	3/2	8/5	9/5	2/1
F	1/1	9/8	5/4	45/32	3/2	27/16	15/8	2/1
G	1/1	10/9	5/4	4/3	3/2	5/3	16/9	2/1
A	1/1	9/8	6/5	27/20	3/2	8/5	9/5	2/1
B	1/1	16/15	6/5	4/3	64/45	8/5	16/9	2/1

Here Kirnberger takes as his basis Zarlino's tuning for the Ionian mode, and uses this to derive the ratios of the notes of the other six modes. This is accomplished by simply rotating the starting note. Therefore, in the Dorian

---

[1] Kirnberger, Op. Cit., 25-8.

mode he retains the rather illogical Pythagorean interval of the trihemitone (32/27) between the first and third degrees which, in the Ionian mode, occurs between the second and fourth degrees (*D* to *F*).

The problems surrounding this become apparent through transposition of these modes to a common tonal centre, where it will be seen that a rather complex array of intervals presents itself:

Transposition Array for the Old Modes

No.	Degree	Note	Ratio	Cents	Interval
1	Common first	C	1/1	0	Prime
2	Phrygian/Locrian 2nd.	Db	16/15	112	Major semitone
3	Dorian/Mixolydian 2nd.	D-	10/9	182	Minor tone
4	Ionian/Lydian/Aeolian 2nd.	D	9/8	204	Major tone
5	Dorian 3rd.	Eb-	32/27	294	Trihemitone
6	Phrygian/Locrian 3rd.	Eb	6/5	316	Minor third
7	Ionian/Lydian/Mixo. 3rd	E	5/4	386	Major third
8	Ion./Dor./Phry./Mix./Loc.4th	F	4/3	498	Perfect 4th
9	Aeolian 4th.	F+	27/20	520	Acute 4th
10	Lydian fourth	F#	45/32	590	Harmonic tritone
11	Locrian fifth	Gb	64/45	610	Diminished 5th
12	Ion./Phr./Lyd./Mix./Aeo. 5th.	G	3/2	702	Perfect 5th
13	Phryg./Aeolian/Locrian 6th.	Ab	8/5	814	Minor 6th
14	Ionian/Dorian/Mixo. 6th.	A	5/3	884	Major 6th
15	Lydian 6th.	A+	27/16	906	Cyclic major 6th
16	Dorian/Mixo./Locrian 7th.	Bb	16/9	996	Cyclic min. 7th
17	Phrygian/Aeolian 7th.	Bb+	9/5	1018	Minor 7th
18	Ionian/Lydian 7th.	B	15/8	1088	Major 7th

Just intonation therefore, cannot, by virtue of the incommensurability of its intervals, lead to a consistent proportional definition for each modal degree. For all intervals to be sung or played with complete accuracy such intonational complexities are unavoidable, especially for the retention of the harmonic purity of the triads, an issue not even taken into account in this interval array. Consequently, the systematic employment of triads led to a great expansion in the number of notes needed to play even a very simple piece of music.

Naturally, the problem is not so acute when dealing with unaccompanied choirs as the pitch can gradually shift a comma up or down as required. With fretted, or keyboard instruments the problems became immediately obvious. It is here that the various types of temperaments, as the provider of solutions to those problems, became a salient theoretical issue. Kirnberger also discusses this issue as follows: *The observation that B had acquired a fifth and D a major third by the introduction of F# gave composers the idea ...to give each string a major and minor third and a fifth. The four new tones C#, D#, F# and G#, tuned in such a way that they could be used as leading tones of the principal notes above them, already gave hope to the possibility of such a new system of music.... Thus one sought to tune the four semitones... in such a way that each note of the chromatic scale ... had a fifth, major third, and minor third. It was soon noticed that this is possible only if the intervals could be made a bit larger or smaller on occasion. If ...D# was adjusted so that it was the pure minor third of C, it could not at the same time, be the pure fifth of G#. Nevertheless it was found that a means could be devised for adjusting these new tones so that the intervals would still be tolerable, even though not entirely pure. This was called tempering the system...after countless temperaments were devised, a few theorists thought that the simplest means of solving the matter was to separate the notes C, C#, D, D#, etc., equally from one another. Thus the octave was divided into twelve equal parts . . . . .this was called equal temperament.*[1]

Systematic deployment of the triad also led to problems with the concise definition of the modes, as to facilitate both the harmonic and melodic sense of the music significant changes of pitch - *musica ficta* - were often made within each mode.[2] The type of changes often revolved around either avoidance of the tritone, or the felt necessity for establishing perfect triads on either the first, fourth or fifth modal degrees.

In this respect, the problems with the Lydian mode become immediately obvious, and to deal with these the fourth tended to be flattened in order both to avoid the tritone and provide a major triad upon the fourth degree. This converted the Lydian mode into a transposition of the Ionian mode. Another example is the flat seventh of the Mixolydian mode raised by a semitone to give the much favoured #VII - I   - a change which temporarily converted the Mixolydian mode into a transposed form of Ionian mode. In the Dorian mode the flat seventh was also raised to give a leading note, which converted it into a melodic minor mode in its ascending form.[3] Furthermore, when the sixth was flattened to give a minor triad on the fourth degree the Dorian mode becomes a

---

[1] Ibid., Scales and Temperament, 19.

[2] Margaret Bent, Musica Recta and Musica Ficta, in: MD 26, 1972, 73 - 100.

[3] For more information on this subject see Thomas Rive's The Dorian Origin of the Minor Mode, in: SM 2, 1968, 21 - 32.

form of transposed Aeolian mode. The Aeolian mode lent itself admirably to the use of triadic harmony, yet the sharpening of the seventh at cadences, together with the sharpening of the sixth in order to avoid the awkward and unvocal augmented second from the sixth to the sharpened seventh degree, converted the Aeolian mode into a form of melodic minor mode.[1] The Phrygian mode too, with its flat second degree, offers a diminished chord on the fifth degree. Rather than crudely raise both the seventh and second degree, a specific cadence evolved for use in this mode - the so-called Phrygian cadence.

Use of the common triad on the first and fifth degrees provided an additional factor in the transformation of the old system of modes, for it tended to negate any difference between the respective 'dominants' established for the authentic and plagal modes. Glareanus's Dodecachordon of 1557 defines some twelve modes, but here the distinction is a theoretical one.[2] Through use of triadic harmony, a definite set of principles were emerging which tended to break down the modal system, simplifying it to just two basic modes: the Ionian which later became identified as the major mode, and the Aeolian which later became identified as the minor mode.[3]

Accompanying this shift was the recognition that a more complex scale than the diatonic scale may be needed in order to account for these alterations or inflections of modal degrees - the complete chromatic scale which, possessing those 'in-between' degrees invoked through the deliberate alteration of diatonic scale degrees, offered a realistic means of achieving these effects within an instrumental context. Such a scale was strongly advocated for instrumental music by Sebastian Virdung (b1465) in his Musica Getuscht (1511) where he demonstrated that *the art of instrumental music is expanded, and is even more strictly decorated, through the use of the semitone from the chromatic genus. Accordingly, one may construct the fourth from the combination of five semitones.... and thus, according to the said chromatic genus, thirteen semitones are constructed and distributed above the main keys.*[4]

Virdung then goes on to show a diagram of a keyboard constructed along modern lines with five black and seven white notes. In this way can be seen the

---

[1] James Haar, False Relations and Chromaticism in 17th Century Music, in: JAMS 30, 391 - 417.

[2] Walter Atcherson, Key and Mode in Seventeenth-Century Music Theory Books, in: JMT 17/2, 1973, 204 - 233.

[3] On this Joel Lester states *It was a German theorist who first presented a comprehensive theory of major-minor polarity and who differentiated two types of mode, almost exclusively according to the quality of tonic triad (Johann Lippius in works from 1610-2)*, Joel Lester, The Recognition of Major and Minor Keys in German Theory: 1680 - 1730, in: JMT 22/1, 1978, 65 - 104.

[4] Strunk, Op. Cit., 101.

gradual emergence of two of the important features characteristic of the tonal system that followed: the duality of the major and minor modes, and the chromatic scale which provided a general backdrop for that system.

FROM THE SECOND TO THE THIRD DIMENSION OF TONAL SPACE

The gradual acceptance of thirds and sixths as musical consonances through the period considered so far, their combination to give various forms of triad, together with the attribution of their precise defining ratios, may be viewed as being symptomatic of a general transformational process at work in the musical language. So far as the last chapter served to highlight this process, the exact details of how the major-minor tonal system gradually coalesced from the relics of the old modal system is of no further concern here. The concern has been to show that the influence of the prime number five gradually served to displace or even supersede the time-honoured Pythagoreanism inherent in early medieval music.

In practice it is possible that the prime number five may have been regulating the intonation of singers from a very early stage. From a harmonic standpoint, it is much easier to intone a harmonic major third of ratio 5/4, than a Pythagorean third of ratio 81/64. Yet the trace of musical theory does seem to offer some support for the idea of a progressive process at work in the musical language which, beginning with the limited resources of Pythagoreanism (prime number three limit) thenceforth progressed on to an assimilation of the more advanced possibilities offered by the conscious recognition and usage of a new prime number.

As a representative example of this particular view Shirlaw observed that: *It is just the use made in modern music of these 'natural' thirds which constitutes a fundamental difference between our modern scales and early scales. The introduction of these 'natural consonances'...marks an event of the greatest theoretical importance. It led directly to the decay of the old scales, and made possible our modern tonal system.*[1]

By the term 'natural' Shirlaw evidently means those thirds present in the lower regions of the harmonic series: the major third of 5/4 and the minor third of 6/5. At first it seems that these intervals were used intuitively, and it was only later that theorists were forced to recognise and acknowledge the mathematical

---

[1] Shirlaw, Theory of Harmony, Novello & Company Ltd., London 1917, 381.

basis for this phenomena. Once this was recognised, it paved the way for the definition of an altogether new unit of harmony: the consonant triad, as opposed to the dyadic *symphonia* (perfect consonances) recognised in the Pythagorean tone system.

The recognition and practical use of common triads led to the necessity of introducing modal alterations (*musica ficta*) in order to regulate the polyphonic movement of parts in accordance with new harmonic principles. These in their turn, led to a gradual breakdown of the original modal system in three stages. First, the elimination of the distinction between the authentic and plagal modes, and the establishment of a uniform dominant degree upon the fifth degree of each mode; second, the reduction of the number of viably practical modes to just five - the Ionian, Mixolydian, Dorian, Aeolian and Phrygian; and third, the gradual fusion of these five modal forms into the two independent scale species of major and minor.

Additionally, the microtonal discrepancies between cyclic (Pythagorean) and harmonic intervals led to a great profusion in the number of notes needed for the correct performance of a piece of music. This, coupled with a gradual upsurge in the importance attributed to instrumental music, led to avid experimentation with regard to different types of temperament.

To a large extent the properties of that emergent system derived from the fact that the musical language was making increasing demands upon the possibilities represented by a prime number higher than three. Here the significance of such a move towards the recognition of the prime number five in early Western music needs to be pondered, especially in the light of the principles of valency.

The respective powers of the prime numbers two, three and five are incommensurate with one another. Any movement in frequency space controlled and motivated by the prime number five must therefore occur in a different dimension of frequency space than a frequency movement motivated by either the prime numbers two or three. In order to satisfactorily account for this movement it is thus necessary to posit a third dimension of frequency space. Tonal movement motivated by the prime number two (2/1) thus constitutes a first dimension, by the prime number three (3/2) a second, and by the prime number five (5/4) a third.

Tonal movement motivated by the number one (1/1) is a form of note repetition. Representing a single point in frequency space it is dimensionless in its aspect. Providing the fundamental defining characteristic for all three prime numbers means that the prime numbers two, three and five inherit from the number one a tangible pitch status which gives them representation on their own particular levels. In the case of the prime number five, this posits the idea of a pitch being replicated along a channel determined by the fifth harmonic of the prototypical tone. In this way can be explained the primary interval belonging to this level - the major third of 5/4:

Bonding Pattern of Two Tones Connected According to the Ratio of 5/4

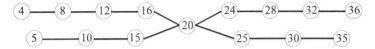

Here is the representation of an interval which is foreign to the two-dimensional fabric defined by the prime numbers two and three. Any use of this particular interval therefore automatically presupposes a third dimension of frequency space. This explains the essential difference between the Pythagorean and Western tonal systems. The former is a two-dimensional tonal system in that it only recognises the prime numbers two and three as the defining factors of tonal space. The latter, by virtue of its extrusion into the realms of a third dimension of tonal space as represented by the prime number five, represents a three-dimensional tonal possibility.

Here it is of paramount importance to understand that any use made of a third dimension of tonal possibility cannot be made independently of those other dimensions which precede it in the scale of priority. This is because each new dimension of tonal space automatically inherits certain properties and characteristics from those other dimensions. An infallible example of this is the influence of the first dimension, signified by the prime number two. Because of the principle of octave equivalence defined by that dimension, the third dimension automatically inherits the possibility of inversional polarity, where the same valent relationship is expressed in two complementary but contrasting intervals. The other interval to complete the pair in this case, is thus the minor sixth of ratio 8/5:

Inversional Polarity of the Third Dimension of Tonal Space

2/1	
5/4	8/5

From the second dimension, represented by the prime number three, certain properties are also inherited. The prime number three defines the dimension through which the octave obtains its mathematical format. Having obtained that format, it is not a simple matter to erase it, and reformat the octave according to entirely new principles. Passed on as a matter of musical inheritance from one generation to the next, it possesses considerable tenacity.

This is a vital consideration, as it affects the possibilities of all prime numbers thereafter, for these are relegated to the less imposing role of modifying the mathematical basis of a given note relationship to the prototypical tone. Principally, this happens by a process of substitution.

In the case of the interval whose ratio is 5/4, it presents itself to the ear as a more intelligible substitute for 81/64. This it would seem, happens for no other reason than the close proximity of the two intervals. Now in so doing it will be seen that the relationship from notes C to E has become transformed into a more direct one, rather than a distant one obtained through the circumnavigation of fifths. The note E, taking on the ratio of 5/4 (instead of 81/64), moves into a closer relationship with the prototypical tone C.

From the second dimension, whose basis is the prime number three, what is in effect an abstract mathematical relation thus acquires a firm identity as a tangible and functional pitch relation. Thereafter, through a process of chain progression, all other intervals which have ratios involving the prime number five, acquire a specific identity automatically after the fashion and example provided for by 5/4:

5/4	supersedes	81/64 (note E)
8/5	supersedes	128/81 (note Ab)
6/5	supersedes	32/27 (note Eb)
5/3	supersedes	27/16 (note A)
Etc.		

Properties Inherited By the Third Dimension From the First and Second Dimensions

Prime One: Pitch Status
Prime Two: Inversional Polarity
Prime Three: Identity in the Tonal Network

Through use of the prime number five European art music was thus entering into the domain of a third mathematical dimension of frequency space. Analogous perhaps, to the introduction of perspective into the visual arts, success or failure was determined by the degree of adaptation to the natural constraints imposed by the authority of that new dimension. At a three-dimensional level there are three prime numbers at play - 2, 3 and 5. Representing these by the letters A, B and C respectively, any primary valent bond would express two of these concerns. Therefore at this level there are six intervals which explicate a primary valent bond:

Primary Intervals at the Three-Dimensional (2, 3, 5) Level

A	B	4/3	B	A	3/2
A	C	8/5	C	A	5/4
B	C	6/5	C	B	5/3

The intervals whose ratios are 4/3 and 3/2 belong to the two-dimensional system, whilst the remaining four represent the primary factors of the 5-valent system. The period being referred to was thus a time of discovery and integration of these four intervals into the fabric of tonal possibility. One of the most powerful symptoms of this can be seen in the approach to matters of musical harmony. In a two-dimensional system characterised by use of the prime numbers 2 and 3, the basic harmonic unit whose reference points lie in both dimensions, is the consonant duad, in that it expresses both of the mathematical terms belonging to that system. That duad can appear either as a perfect fifth (3/2) or fourth (4/3) depending upon instance. Parallelism therefore, that age old technique which uses mostly parallel fifths, fourths and octaves, with only the occasional third or sixth, is essentially a two-dimensional harmonic practice.

At the three-dimensional level, there is a new prime number at play, and therefore an additional dimension to be both represented and taken into account. This means that the consonant harmonic unit needs to be upgraded in order to offer a satisfactory psychological reference point for all three of those dimensional influences. Hence the unit of the triad, a fusion of three valent bonds within the terms of a single unit which offers that necessary point of three-dimensional recognition. Here it became extremely interesting to see that the range of triads used at this time made full use of the six primary intervals which belong at this level. Constituting a related set of musical objects of great practical utility, these triads also serve to demonstrate how the prime number five has contributed its own unique features and attributes to the tonal concourse.

The qualities 5-valent intervals inherit from those other dimensions represented by those prime numbers which precede it in the scale of values have already been partly discussed. Yet as a prime number in its own right, and therefore a representative of a third dimension of frequency space, it contributes features which are then shared and exploited by subsequent dimensions as signified by the prime numbers seven, eleven, thirteen, etc. The most important factor can be discerned from the observation that when the major third of 5/4 is inverted, the result is the minor sixth of ratio 8/5. This represents an important distinguishing characteristic from the inversional polarity shared by the perfect fifth and fourth. In the latter case, it will be seen that inversion does not in any way affect the intervallic modality of the relationship. The perfect fifth, upon inversion gives rise to a perfect fourth. Both remaining perfect, means that they thus retain the same intervallic modality.

In the case of the major third however, inversion leads to a reversal of modality, from major to minor. Therefore, it can be seen that the principal feature which appears in strong focus at a three-dimensional level is the presence of this major and minor polarity. Viewed from the standpoint of this polarity, the four 5-valent intervals can be divided up into two groups of two, the link between them being their relationship by inversion:

Relationship of 5-valent Intervals by Inversion

| Major third | 5/4 . . . . Minor sixth | 8/5 |
| Minor third | 6/5 . . . . Major sixth | 5/3 |

The traditional theoretical designation of these intervals as being 'imperfect' is thus quite appropriate, because, they admit of this basic duality which distinguishes them from the 'perfect' intervals.

The prime number five therefore, introducing into the musical dialogue a polarization of intervals between major and minor, means that the three-dimensional harmonic unit (or triad) which belongs at this level would automatically reflect that polarization as a matter of course. The triad thus appears in two forms - major or minor. The major and minor triads are equal therefore because they each represent one side of the intrinsic duality which the prime number five introduces as its specific contribution to the tonal nexus.

Therefore the retrospective observation that the major triad occurs by implication in the first six members of the harmonic series is a useful one because it might serve to show that nature ratifies the major polarization as a first principle. But, as Riemann and others have done since, to posit an inverse harmonic series - the so-called undertone series - in support of the minor triad is to court the unnecessary.[1] The minor triad needs no ratification, and neither

---

[1] Hugo Riemann, Die objektive Existenz der Untertöne in der Schallwelle, Berlin 1877. Also see William Mickelson's Hugo Riemann's Theory of Harmony: A Study, University of Nebraska Press, Lincoln 1977.

does the major, for they are the equal and opposite sides of the same principle: the essential duality of the third dimension of tonal space.

This can be understood through further reference to the concept of the prototypical tone (1/1). Through use of 5-valent intervals the prototypical tone has grown in stature for it now represents (excluding the first dimension of octave equivalence) the point at which two dimensional strains or influences cross: a second dimension represented by the prime number three, and a third represented by the prime number five. In confirmation of its newly acquired status it is only appropriate that the prototypical tone is represented along with the two strains which have conferred upon it this more elevated position. It thus obtains its final representation in the form of the triad, the fifth (3/2) of which represents the prime number three, the third (5/4) of which represents the prime number five. Thus is the fundamental definition of the triad which provides the fundamental and substantive basis for harmony at this level.

The triad is major because 5/4 represents the primary connection which generates the 5-valency interval group. Representing the pure unmitigated relationship which exists between the prime five and its generating principle represented by the number one, it belongs on a par with 3/2 and 2/1 in that it represents the concentrated latent power of the entire dimension of frequency space which it serves to generate. For this reason, although the major and minor triads are equal, the major triad carries with it the sanction conferred upon it by that authority. I

The minor triad represents the negative reflection of the major triad. The major triad can be viewed as the prototypical tone which has replicated itself in order to obtain representation within those other dimensions of tonal space. Yet there is a reciprocal process at work, in that it results from those agencies conferring upon the prototypical tone the power to act as their representative. Therefore the minor triad is generated downwards from the uppermost tone:

The Minor Triad as Negative Reflection of the Major Triad

From this perspective the major and minor triads possess an enantiomorphic (displaying properties of mirror symmetry, or left and right handedness) relationship. However, the vitally important point is that note C is not the root of both triads. *Ab* to *C* is the same relationship as *C* to *E*, except in the former case, *Ab*, as the negative agent of prime five, is enacting the role of the prototypical tone. Similarly, *F,* as the negative agent of prime three, is also enacting the role of prototypical tone. Therefore the root of the minor triad as given above is note F. The minor triad is thus a consequential result of the exchange of functions which occurs when intervals are inverted.

Dimensional References in The Major and Minor Triads

Agent of the prototypical tone
in the second dimension of   G (3/2)
frequency space

Agent of the prototypical tone
in the third dimension of   E (5/4)
frequency space

Prototypical tone   C (1/1)

That agent (prime five) with the
power to act as prototypical tone   Ab (8/5)

That agent (prime three) with the
power to act as prototypical tone   F (4/3)

In this way the major and minor triads come to represent the positive and negative polarizations of three-dimensional frequency space. The existence of a third dimension therefore considerably modifies the perspectives to be gained, not only of tonal space itself, but the pitch continuum which occupies that space. In order to comprehend the possibilities which exist at this level therefore, these new perspectives need to be clearly defined.

First, the modified view obtained of the pitch continuum as a result of the influence of this dimension. It will be recalled that so far as 3-valent intervals are concerned, the system is essentially bivalent in that the third partial offers only two points of valent connection between musical tones. A straight line composed of two links which represents those two valent connections - a perfect fifth up, and a perfect fifth down can for the moment represent the dimension in which these connections operate.

In terms of the pitch continuum as a whole however, it needs to be remembered that this line is simply a short section of an epicycloid, a spiral of fifths which ensheaths the helical chain of octaves. Therefore the next step to consider is the way in which 5-valent intervals lead to a modification of this basic structure.

Bivalency of the Prime Number Three as Expressed in the Chain of Fifths

G (3/2)

C (1/1)

F (4/3)

The prime number five is a tetravalent bonding agent enabling four primary connections to be made from the prototypical tone. Manifesting through the intervals of the major and minor third and sixth, these divide into two groups. Group one, composed of the major third and its inversion the minor sixth, can be represented as a straight line composed of two links: a major third up and a major third down. Group two, comprising the minor third and its inversion the major sixth be similarly represented: a minor third up and a minor third down. The problem is how to accurately portray these six connections which arise from the prototypical tone in a way that accurately defines the sum of their possible interrelationships.

Thankfully, this portrayal has already been accomplished in the form of the tone lattice as discovered by Euler and presented in his paper to the St. Petersburg Academy in 1773. Later, rediscovered by Arthur Oettingen,[1] it was also used in a slightly modified form by Alexander Ellis who called it the 'harmonic cell',[2] a unit of seven notes which satisfactorily fulfils all of these requirements.

Each valent bond within the cell is represented by a consistent vectorial value: a perfect fifth represents a vertical line, the major third a diagonal line moving up from left to right, and the minor third a diagonal line moving dawn from right to left. In this way the harmonic cell embraces all of the possibilities of valent connection at this level, together with the possibilities for their replication upon each and every musical tone thus represented. It also, on reflection, embraces the six triads of sixteenth-century polyphonic music, together with the major, minor, diminished and augmented triads of the major-minor tonal system.

---

[1] Martin Vogel, On the Relations of Tone, 108

[2] Helmholtz, On the Sensations of Tone, 457-64. See also Bob Gilmore, Changing the Metaphor: Ratio Models of Musical Pitch in the Work of Harry Partch, Ben Johnston, and James Tenney, in: PNM 33/1, 1995, 458 - 503, (501).

Harmonic Cell as it Represents the Six Valent Connections Available from the Prototypical Tone

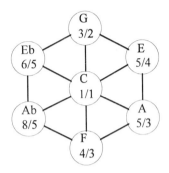

In just intonation, the harmonic cell is an extremely valuable unit for it allows the accurate calculation of each and every pitch value required. When taking all of the dimensions into account it becomes increasingly difficult to offer an accurate geometrical reflection of the pitch continuum. By virtue of the harmonic cell, each fifth within the spiral of fifths occupies a position as the central axis of each hexagonal unit. These, interlocking in chain like fashion, effectively convert that spiral into a two-dimensional lattice or ribbon composed of these interlocking hexagons. The spiral of fifths becomes like a spiral staircase, the treads of which are the bar polarities generated between the 5-valent intervals:

The Three Dimensions of the Pitch Continuum Apparent within a Prime Number Five Limit

Dimension	Harmonic	Leading Interval	Dimensional Model
None	Fundamental	Prime (1/1)	Straight line
First	Second	Octave (2/1)	Helix
Second	Third	Perfect fifth (3/2)	Epicycloid
Third	Fifth	Major third (5/4)	Spiral staircase

Through the addition of this new dimension, the force of tonality has grown and expanded to embrace a more pervasive possibility. Arising in the first place as the equilibrating principle brought into being as a result of the polarization of two dimensional frequency space, subsequent processes of polarization as they occur in each dimension thereafter, give to that tonal force a more sophisticated and subtle organ of expression.

In the case of the major and minor tonal system this becomes apparent in the first place through the construction of complete triads upon the various degrees of the diatonic scale. The successful operation of tonality depended mostly upon those triads constructed upon the three degrees by which two-dimensional frequency space becomes polarized: the tonic triad whose root is 1/1, the dominant triad whose root is 3/2 and the subdominant triad whose root is 4/3. Secondly, it brought into play the principle by which the third dimension of frequency space became polarized: the duality between major and minor expressed in the differential between the tonic major and minor triads, and their extension into the major and minor modes of Classical tonality.

Through the gradual assimilation of those relationships belonging to a higher prime number, the system of tonality has been growing. Yet this is a double edged sword, for each new level brings with it the capability of both destroying and recreating the force of tonality anew. Therefore, for tonality to expand beyond the limitations of its original two dimensions, the old system had to pass away to be replaced by a new, more sophisticated system. In this sense, tonality represents the phoenix of musical expansion which, being destroyed as it emerges into a new level, later re-emerges triumphantly from its own ashes.

The transition from the modal system of Medieval music to the system of tonality with its major and minor modes is tantamount to the destruction and recreation of that tonal phoenix upon a new level. That this particular incarnation can be linked to a progression of the musical language from a two-dimensional possibility signified by the prime numbers two and three, to a more advanced three-dimensional possibility as signified by the prime numbers two, three and five, indicates that vital clues as the nature of subsequent incarnations of the tonal phoenix may yet lie in the possibilities of those prime numbers which lie beyond five.

The remaining sections of this book will examine this particular idea in some detail, beginning in the next four chapters, with a detailed examination of the possibilities of the prime number seven as a potential bonding agent between musical tones.

THE '7/4' RELATION AS THE 'DIABOLUS IN MUSICA'

From the two previous chapters, it became exceedingly clear that over a considerable period of time, the prime number five gradually came to displace the prime number three as the salient factor of European art music. In so doing, a number of significant changes occurred, radical alterations in the fabric of pitch relationships which led to considerable advances, especially in the sphere of musical harmony. Having observed that such changes occurred, it is not the place here to offer much further comment upon them. The focus of interest here lies in the further possibilities which may, or may not as the case be, exist higher up in the harmonic series, especially in relation to the next prime number, which is of course seven.

Towards this end, it became important to show that the history of music and musical theory in general tends to vindicate the idea that a progression from the resources of a prime number three limit, through to the more advanced resources of a prime number five limit, did in fact occur. Here perhaps, it is significant that some theorists have felt that the trace of this progression so far (from a three limit up to a five limit) may point to the prime number seven as yet a further factor in the development of the musical language. The most significant contribution to this subject to date, is of course Martin Vogel's *Die Naturseptime*,[1] the only book in existence which is devoted entirely to this particularly fascinating subject.

Of course, the idea that the prime number seven may eventually supersede the prime number five, as the prime number five once superseded the prime number three is a general idea which is very easy to dismiss on account of the fact that it reduces the processes of musical transformation to a neat evolutionary pattern which does not always accord with the evidence. The Italian composer Nicola Vicentino was theoretically utilising the prime numbers seven, eleven and thirteen in a microtonal 31-toned scale as far back as the sixteenth century.[2]

---

[1] Martin Vogel, Die Naturseptime, Verlag für systematische Musikwissenschaft GmbH, Bonn 1991.

[2] Nicola Vicentino, L'antica musica ridotta alla moderna prattica, Rome 1555.

Such exceptions therefore, tend to moderate the belief that music progressed from three, as one stage, to five as the next. Yet this concept of musical progression through the prime numbers of the harmonic series does raise an extremely important issue. It implies that in a broad sense, it is feasibly possible that other higher prime numbers may contain the seeds for further processes of musical growth and expansion, as yet unsuspected or unknown.

This idea, or at least the consciousness of it on behalf of various theorists has led to detailed investigations into the possibilities of the prime numbers seven, eleven, thirteen, and even higher prime numbers, all in the hope that these agents may provide a vehicle for the enrichment and expansion of the web of tonal relationships. In the process of doing so, a lot of information has been generated, some of which is of doubtful practical value. Indeed, one of the greatest stumbling blocks which encounters any theorist endeavouring to approach these matters is the lack of any objective criterion from which such a study can be undertaken. Consequently, a lot of guesswork becomes involved, with no means of checking or verifying the information thus obtained.

Here however, the concept of valency becomes of immense value, for being based on the natural connections between musical tones ordained by the very fact and nature of the harmonic series, it provides an objective tool for the examination and assessment of tonal possibility. Indeed, from the way in which the concept of valency allowed a rather precise definition and explanation of the difference between the major and the minor triads, indicates that such a concept may yet reveal more important insights into the stable system of major and minor tonality. However, tempting though this prospect might seem, the major and minor system has received such attention, been systematised in so many different ways, and from so many different standpoints, that to do so is tantamount to flogging a dead horse.

In this study, the concept of valency will be used for the more relevant possibility of unfolding the precise nature and tonal possibilities of the prime number seven. This entails an investigation into the possibilities which the seventh member of the harmonic series offers as a bonding agent between musical tones. Here, something which the seventh harmonic shares in common with the eleventh, thirteenth, and all prime numbered partials thereafter, is that it does not quite fit in with our modern musical scales. In relation to this, Raymond Fuller observes that *all the partials from one through sixteen are used in harmony - except that the 7th, 11th and 13th partials are considered grossly out of tune with our present scales'.*[1] This of course, is an interesting attitude, for it almost gives the impression that the fault lies with nature itself for

---

[1] Ramon Fuller, A Study of Microtonal Equal Temperaments, in: JMT 35, Spring 1991, 234. It is quite sure that he also intended to include the fourteenth partial in this statement.

providing such 'grossly out of tune' intervals in the first place. Be that as it may, this is certainly true for the seventh harmonic, for it does not produce a true Bb. Whilst the tempered minor seventh has a measurement of 1000 cents, the interval 7/4, or seventh harmonic, has a measurement of 969 cents. It is thus 31 cents flat, an interval of about one-sixth of a tone. This is mentioned in the *New Grove's Dictionary of Music and Musicians* article *Harmonic Seventh* which states: *The interval between the 4th and 7th harmonic partials (i.e. between the 3rd and 6th overtones) of a note. It has a frequency ratio of 7:4 and is about 1/3 of a semitone smaller than an equal-tempered minor seventh. It was designated the letter I in the first volume of Die Kunst des reinen Satzes (1771) by Kirnberger, who attempted to introduce it into the modern system of music notation by inventing a symbol for the flattening a note by the difference between a minor seventh and a harmonic seventh.*[1]

Whilst Kirnberger's attempts to use the interval 7/4 may be viewed as being admirable in this respect, this does not conceal the fact that intervals formed using the bond of the seventh harmonic - 7-valent or septimal intervals - would seem to be incommensurate with the basic scale of Western music. Lying outside of the province of that scale it may therefore be assumed that they are of no use or value to us. This in fact, is reflective of the general position taken with regard to the seventh harmonic, and it provides one of the obvious reasons why not many composers have tried to use it.

To use it properly would require a considerable effort: it may require an altogether new method of notation, the building of entirely new musical instruments, or in terms of those instruments which can easily produce it, such as string instruments, it may require the development of new and difficult techniques of performance. For a composer struggling to earn a living therefore, it is not surprising if they choose to express themselves through media of that which is easily available i.e. instruments adapted to the twelve-tone tempered scale. In this sense, the seventh harmonic is, and always has been, a rather problematic issue.

In spite of this, it is interesting to see that intervals possessing ratios involving the prime number seven were recognised as far back as ancient Greece. Here, one of the most notable sources of information is Ptolemy's *Harmonics*[2] which as well as presenting his own views on tuning, contains numerous references to the tuning policies of other theorists with regard to the diatonic, chromatic and enharmonic tetrachords. According to Ptolemy, the

---

[1] Harmonic Seventh, The New Grove Dictionary of Music and Musicians, Mc Millan Publishers, London 1995, Vol. 8,164.

[2] Greek Musical Writings II: Harmonic and Acoustic Theory, (Ed. by Andrew Barker, Cambridge University Press 1989) contains the translation of Ptolemy's Harmonics used here.

Pythagorean theorist Archytas invoked the prime number seven in all three tetrachords. His diatonic tetrachord utilised whole tones with ratios of both 9/8 and 8/7 respectively, the semitone left over being given to the differential ratio of 28/27. The ditone according to Archytas, should thus have a ratio of 9/7. This interval of 9/7 he retained in the chromatic tetrachord, where it was divided between the Pythagorean trihemitone (32/27) and the rather remote septimal interval of ratio 243/224. In the enharmonic tetrachord, he gives a new ratio for the ditone of 5/4, the remaining semitone being divided up between the intervals of 36/35 and 28/27.

Archytas's Tuning for the Diatonic, Chromatic and Enharmonic Tetrachords[1]

Diatonic	Chromatic	Enharmonic
9/8	32/27	5/4
8/7	243/224	36/35
28/27	28/27	28/27

Ptolemy, perhaps influenced by Archytas, advocated the use of the prime number seven in four tetrachords: the tonic diatonic, the soft diatonic, the tense chromatic and the soft chromatic. His tonic diatonic is identical to Archytas's diatonic tetrachord so no more need be said about this. In the soft diatonic Ptolemy uses the larger septimal semitone of 21/20. This gives an interval of ratio 80/63 for the ditone, which is divided unequally between 10/9 and 8/7. In the tense chromatic tetrachord he also advocates the use of the prime number eleven. Here, the minor third of the chromatic tetrachord is given to the septimal interval of 7/6, which when subtracted from the perfect fourth, leaves the septimal interval of ratio 8/7. This he divides between the intervals of 12/11 and 22/21.

---

[1] Ibid., 45-52.

Tetrachords of Ptolemy which Involve the Prime Number Seven (and Eleven)[1]

Tonic Diatonic	Soft Diatonic	Tense Chromatic	Soft Chromatic
9/8	8/7	7/6	6/5
8/7	10/9	12/11	15/14
28/27	21/20	22/21	28/27

In some ways, these allusions to the prime number seven may be regarded as a purely theoretical stance aimed at replacing the extremely complex ratios encountered in Pythagorean methods of tuning with much simpler and more mathematically logical harmonic counterparts. Whether such intervals were ever used in practise is thus a matter of debate. But reference to them by these theorists, does at least show that there are clear precedents for their recognition in the history of musical theory. Despite the existence of such precedents the issue of the prime number seven has since been surrounded with a degree of prejudice which at times, can be quite disarming. This seems to start around the time that Italian Renaissance composers such as Vicentino and Fabio Colonna were starting to investigate the prime number seven as a means of revival of the ancient Greek chromatic genera.

Apparently, it is the number itself which seemed to possess negative properties. In this respect Marin Mersenne (1588 - 1648) mentions that the astronomer Kepler (1571 - 1630) was firmly opposed to the introduction of the number seven into music, on account of the geometrical properties of the heptagon.[2] In a world in which everything was seen to be interconnected, such a view was not at odds with the prevailing mood of the times. It seemed that, numerologically speaking, the number seven possessed unfortunate properties. These too, are mentioned by Mersenne, in which he observes that: *It is believed, moreover, that the number seven is fatal to music, because it arises from the two terms of the fourth, namely from three and four, which make seven, and because the fourth, being so unfortunate that some call it a*

---

[1] Ibid., 309-10.

[2] Marin Mersenne, Harmonie Universelle, Treatise Four, trans. by Robert F. Williams, Ph. D. diss., University of Rochester 1972, 207.

monstrosity when it is with the bass, produces another monstrosity, namely this
number seven, which is the fundamental enemy of music.[1]

Here, the terms 'fatal' and 'fundamental enemy' undoubtedly project an aura
of negativity over the whole idea of seven. It is thus perhaps, not that
surprising, to discover that some of the most influential theorists of European
art music have automatically excluded the prime number seven from any
consideration whatsoever.

A good case in point is Gioseffo Zarlino. Because of his derivation of all of
the 'elemental' consonances from the 'Senario' - the arithmetical series of
numbers 1, 2, 3, 4, 5 and 6 - the number seven, and any intervals which may
arise from it, is immediately excluded from the picture. Zarlino's contemporary
and chief critic Francisco Salinas (1513 - 1590) also abjured seven, observing
that *neither beyond 1:6 in the ratio 1:7 is a consonance to be found, just as not*
in 7:6 beyond 6:5.[2] Yet such attitudes of cursory dismissal do not fully conform
to logic. If, as Zarlino attested, all of the consonances can be derived from the
numbers 1 through to 6, how is the consonant minor sixth between the eighth
and the fifth harmonics to be explained? Aware of this obvious defect of the
'Senario' to fully account for the range of recognised consonant intervals,
Zarlino excuses the minor sixth as being a composite interval resulting from the
sum of two others. Yet in so doing he is obviously inventing an explanation of
the minor sixth to justify his otherwise arbitrary limit of six. The perfect fifth,
after all, can also be explained as a composite interval arising from the sum of a
major and a minor third. Consequently, the 'Senario' itself cannot possibly be
taken as a natural limit of musical consonance.

Looking at this issue from the standpoint of valency, it will be recalled that
where there are three prime numbers at play - two, three and five - that there
are thus six valent intervals. The 'Senario' only embraces five of these, leaving
the minor sixth out on its own. Admittedly, Zarlino probably never took the
principle of valency into account when devising a scheme to account for the
consonances. But he did know that the minor sixth was treated as a
consonance, in as much the same way as the major third was. It would thus
seem that to justify his scheme, and thereby automatically preclude the
problematic prime number seven, Zarlino had to modify the facts to fit in with
his numerical theory. There is thus no real logic for the exclusion of seven from
that system.

Zarlino's rejection of seven was no doubt motivated by practical, as well as
metaphysical considerations. The number seven possessed an obvious link with
the sphere of chromaticism, and in the works of composers such as Nicola

---

[1] Ibid., 207-19.
[2] Robert W. Wienpahl, Zarlino, the Senario and Tonality, in: JAMS XII, 1959, 35.

Vicentino, Anthoine de Bertrand (ca. 1535 - ca. 1580), Cipriano de Rore and the young Lassus, chromatic elements were playing an increasingly important part, a trend which Zarlino both distrusted and disliked. As attested by his attack on the use of chromaticism (at the end of his treatise *The Art of Counterpoint*,[1]) Zarlino believed utterly in the purity and simplicity of the diatonic genus. Towards this end, his formulation of the 'Senario' was extremely useful, for it not only precluded the prime number seven, but it favoured the diatonic genus as well.

In the seventeenth century, the tendency towards the use of metaphysics to justify or denigrate musical practice was not so evident. Instead, theorists tended to justify their judgements with reason. A good case in point is the philosopher René Descartes (1596 - 1650) who overall tended to agree with the limit provided by Zarlino's senary division of a musical string. Unlike Zarlino, who endeavoured to justify the senary division of a string through reference to the mystical significance of the number six, Descartes at least tries to offer a tangible reason for the exclusion of seven.

For Descartes, six was the natural limit of musical consonance provided for by the very nature of our aural perception. As stated in his *Compendium Musicae* of 1618 *I can still further divide the line A-B into four, five or six parts, but not more, because the capacity of the ear does not extend beyond this point*. According to Descartes therefore, the ear simply cannot perceive the relationship between tones beyond the sixth division. For Descartes the intervals which provided the substantive basis for musical harmony were the perfect fifth of 3/2, and the major third of 5/4. These together made up the perfect triad which was the corner stone of the whole system of harmony. For a 5-valent system Descartes observations are clearly very sound, but his justification for excluding the participation of any higher prime number seems slightly contrived.

On the whole Rameau, in his *Treatise on Harmony*, tended to agree with Zarlino and Descartes. Unlike Descartes, however, Rameau recognises that the ear can apprehend the relationship between tones connected according to the ratio of 7/4. He however, excludes it from consideration on the grounds of nothing more than artistic taste. In the chapter 'On the Origins of Consonances and on their Relationships' he states *notice that number seven* '[a division of the string into seven parts] *which cannot give a pleasant interval (as is evident to connoisseurs) has been replaced by number eight'*.[2] In an attempt to provide

---

[1] Gioseffo Zarlino, The Art of Counterpoint, trans. Guy A. Marco and Claude V. Palisca New York 1976.

[2] Rameau, On the Origin of Consonances and on their Relationships - Harmonic Ratios, Treatise on Harmony, 5.

some kind of justification for his aesthetic judgement of the interval 7/4 he makes an appeal upon the reader to either join him or be damned as somebody who is evidently not a connoisseur. On the positive side though, Rameau manages to remedy the defects implicit in the 'Senario' by extending the number of divisions of the musical string up to a full complement of eight. In this way Rameau can account for the consonance of the minor sixth in a way that Zarlino's scheme could not.

Yet in extending the series of numbers from six to eight, Rameau exposes himself to a theoretical dilemma: how to deal with the problem of seven. To leave it alone is obviously to imply that his system of harmony is incomplete. Therefore, to remedy this, and least make some attempt to fill the gaping hole left where seven should be, he implies that intervals involving the number seven are not worth considering because of their intrinsic 'unpleasantness'. It is thus interesting to see that Rameau, in trying to set down what he saw to be the natural and ineffable laws of musical harmony, leaves out a deeply significant prime number on the grounds of personal feeling and opinion.

The prejudices of Descartes and Rameau with regard to the number seven found a keen disciple in the twentieth century through the work of Heinrich Schenker (1868-1935). In his treatise on harmony he states that: *The human ear can follow Nature as manifested to us in the overtone series only up to the major third as the ultimate limit; in other words, up to that overtone which results from the fifth division. This means that those overtones resulting from higher subdivisions are too complicated to be perceived by our ear, except in those cases where the number of divisions is a composite which can be reduced to a number representing the lowest, perceivable, order of division by two, three, or five...whereas the overtones 7, 11, 13, 14, etc., remain totally extraneous to our ear.*[1]

The justification he gives for this statement is not only questionable, but hints at knowledge which he may not have possessed. The reasons that the ear cannot comprehend the seventh harmonic (he mistakenly calls it the seventh 'overtone') are taken straight from Descartes. He observes that they rest entirely on the 'physiological organisation of the ear' and how it is 'capable of reacting only to the first five simple divisions while rejecting the others'. Conveniently, he says that this is all too complicated to explain, and we are requested to accept it on faith. He does, however, point out as evidence for his observations that a musical stave has five lines, the human being has five senses, and other such

---

[1] Heinrich Schenker, The Natural Tonal System (Major), 11. No Overtone Beyond the Fifth in the Series Has Any Application to Our tonal System, Harmony, Trans. by Elisabeth Mann Borgese, The Mit Press, London 1973, 25.

112

numerological analogies that may seem to support the limit of five which he is trying to impose.

As if this were not enough, having made such a series of sweeping statements he then states the complete opposite: *We can derive, furthermore, the fourth F of the C-scale and, finally, the seventh of our system as indicated by the seventh overtone.*[1] At first sight this statement seems rather confusing. It seems that he has again mixed up two separate systems of the classification of harmonics. In terms of partials it is the seventh he is referring to, but in terms of overtones it is the sixth. Also, he has not expressed himself very clearly. The seventh of our system - the leading note - has a ratio of 15/8, and can in no sense be equated with the seventh partial. Schenker is evidently referring to the minor seventh interval present in the chord of the dominant seventh, which is why he indicates that it is note F that is governed by the seventh partial:

Harmonics Four, Five, Six and Seven as Defining a Chord of the Dominant Seventh

Note:	G	B	D	F
Frequency:	384	480	576	672
Ratio:	4	5	6	7

This belief that the configuration of the fourth, fifth, sixth and seventh harmonics forms a purely tuned chord of the dominant seventh is an issue which will be examined shortly. The point being made here is that he has entirely contradicted himself, for according to his earlier statement, the seventh partial is too complicated to be perceived by our ear and thus remains extraneous to it. If this is so, then how could the ear perceive the implication of harmonics 4,5,6 and 7 in the chord of the dominant seventh? His explanations just do not make sense. Another statement he makes is just as confusing: *such an interpretation' [with regard to the seventh partial] 'on the one hand, would violate Nature by the teleological assumption of a design with regard to our system in general and to the seventh in particular. It would rest, on the other hand, on a misconception of the seventh overtone, which under any circumstances must be smaller than the minor third 5:6, as is evident even from the foregoing scheme. Since the seventh of our tonal system and the seventh overtone do not coincide in reality, this interpretation must thus be satisfied with an 'approximate' coincidence between the two.*[2]

---

[1] Ibid., 22.
[2] Ibid., 25.

This statement needs to be unpacked in order to find out exactly what he is saying. First, how can the seventh 'overtone' (really partial), which in itself, is a simple tone belonging to the harmonic series, be smaller than an interval, in this case 6/5? Evidently, what he means by this is that the interval of ratio 7/6 is smaller than the minor third of 6/5. This statement is undoubtedly true since the interval whose ratio is 7/6 (267 cents) is some 49 cents or a quarter of a tone smaller than the minor third of ratio 6/5 (316 cents). The central problem with this statement is that he has already said that the seventh of our system can be derived from the seventh 'overtone'. Now he is saying that they do not coincide in reality. It would thus seem that although on the whole, Schenker tends to reject the interval 7/4 as a legitimate musical resource, he is nonetheless quite unsure of his position with regard to it. He thus presents us with his own conflicting ideas on the subject.

Of course, viewed in the light of the theory of valency, the positions of Descartes, Rameau and Schenker with regard to the prime number seven do make some sense. Valency shows us that within the constraints of three-dimensional frequency space there are only eight primary bonds possible between musical tones: those signified by the ratios of 1/1, 2/1, 3/2, 4/3, 5/4, 8/5, 6/5 and 5/3. It also shows why seven is, or can be excluded from the scheme. It is because it falls outside of the terms of that three-dimensional constraint. The problems which these theorists encountered endeavouring to justify their positions, thus arose simply because the harmonic series itself was taken as the defining criterion, rather than the property of valency which arises from that series.

When logic is applied to the problem of seven the vagaries of prejudice, taste and opinion do not stand up. Thankfully, some relief from these is provided for us by Hermann Helmholtz, who, with his scientific background and meticulous approach to musical matters, would never allow himself to be swayed by such unscientific observations as have been put forth by the likes of Descartes, Rameau or Schenker. Indeed, Helmholtz the scientist, contributes some extremely interesting insights into the subject of the seventh harmonic, and why it is, or apparently should be excluded from participation in the accepted language of music. Helmholtz's work on the qualities of musical intervals has already been mentioned. Having no personal reason to exclude the seventh harmonic from his investigations, he applied the same rigorous spirit of investigation to the interval whose ratio is 7/4, as to any other musical interval being investigated. His conclusions seem to run opposite to the beliefs of Rameau, Descartes and Schenker, in that he finds it to be an interval with readily apprehended qualities. Indeed, he states: *The subminor seventh 4:7 or C - Bb is very often more harmonious than the minor sixth 5:8 or C - Ab, in fact it is always so when the third partial tone of the note is strong as compared with the second, because then the fifth has a more powerfully disturbing effect on the intervals distant from it by a semitone, than the octave on the sub-minor seventh, which is rather more than a whole tone removed from it. But this subminor seventh when combined with other consonances in chords produces intervals which are all worse than itself, as 6:7, 5:7, 7:8, etc., and it is consequently not used as a consonance in modern music.*[1]

His statement on the harmoniousness of the interval whose ratio is 7/4 neatly fills the gap left by the omission of seven from Rameau's octonarian division of the string. His comments upon the other septimal intervals also invite interesting conclusions for they imply that if the seventh partial was used in any significant way as a bonding agent between musical tones, that some of the intervals involved, such as 7/6, 7/5 and 8/7 would not be considered to be consonant. Here it is significant that this does not preclude the possible participation of the number seven, but simply explains the lack of its usage as a recognized consonance.

Perhaps one of the most salient points concerning the exclusion of the prime number seven was made by Joseph Yasser who observed that: *The use or perception of the natural, minor seventh (7/4) on the plane of the diatonic system errs against aesthetic truth, as is confirmed by the age long practise of composers who, when unambiguously using this system invariably resolved the minor seventh....It is then immediately evident that these composers, in as much as they did resolve the minor seventh, never had this interval in view in its acoustically pure form which demands no resolution. Such are the facts of musical creation which have to be taken into consideration besides those of musical acoustics in order to remain on a strictly scientific basis. And that is why, starting from these facts, we may say that the interval of a natural minor seventh (7/4) being absolutely true from the acoustic point of view, nevertheless is musically false in the diatonic system and, therefore, inadmissible in music which does not go beyond the limits of this system.*[2]

Here Yasser observes that a pure minor seventh tuned to the ratio of 7/4 would demand no resolution. That composers did invariably resolve the minor seventh thus indicated to Yasser that the intended interval was actually the dissonant minor seventh of 16/9 (or 9/5) which is found in the diatonic scale. As such, he concludes, the seventh partial is not actually endemic to the diatonic system.

---

[1] Hermann Helmholtz, Degree of Harmoniousness of Consonances, On the Sensations of Tone, 195.

[2] Joseph Yasser, A Theory of Evolving Tonality, 193.

This is an observation which is clearly supported by the work of Zarlino, Descartes, Rameau and others: the diatonic system, together with the triads which can be constructed upon the various degrees of the scale, is quite convincingly defined by the parameters of the prime numbers 2, 3 and 5, and there are no defects present within that system which would call for the introduction of the prime number seven. This does not mean that there is no place for the seventh harmonic, but simply that Yasser feels that it is foreign to the diatonic system as defined by conventional musical theory.

Another theorist who tended to aver the seventh harmonic was the German composer Paul Hindemith (1895 - 1963). Observing that: *The seventh overtone in the series based upon C (-Bb) does not make the triad into a dominant seventh chord such as we know in practise. It is flatter than the Bb that we are used to hearing as the seventh of C*[1] he goes on to state that *The seventh overtone' [like Schenker, he means harmonic here] 'of C - Bb (448) cannot be used.*[2] The reason he gives is that the seventh harmonic has no real place in the tonal system: *Like the seventh overtone, the higher prime numbered members of the series.....do not fit into our tonal system....our tonal system, which strives to bring incomprehensible multiplicity within our grasp, cannot find a simple and clear place for them.*[3]

The observation that the seventh harmonic is 'out of tune with our current scales' subtly implies that the seventh harmonic is defective in some way. Hindemith rightly observes that it is not the seventh harmonic that is to blame, but the system that cannot find a clear and recognisable place for it. The futility which Hindemith feels towards this task has a mystical edge too, as can be seen in his statement: *Is it not remarkable that musical mankind, after thousands of years of musical practice, should not have arrived at mastery of the characteristics of the seventh overtone?...the secret of the number 7 was well known; to conquer it was to become master or destroyer of the world. it is understandable that such a mystic and unfathomable number should have been looked upon as holy. And in the world of tone too, we must acknowledge the holy circle to be inaccessible.*[4]

This might go some way towards explaining why the prime number seven has often borne the brunt of theorists' prejudices. Seven, the sacred number of the ancient world, has such a considerable archetypal status that it tends to evoke a certain element of fear. The epitome of this view becomes readily apparent in

---

[1] Paul Hindemith, A Craft of Musical Composition, Vol. 1 (Theory), Schott & Co., Ltd., London 1945, 24.

[2] Ibid., 37.

[3] Ibid., 39.

[4] Ibid., 39.

the writings of Alain Daniélou (b. 1907) on the subject who stated that: *In this world, limited to five elements in which we live, no prime number higher than 5 can enter into the composition of the substance from which a melodic or an harmonic relation is made....the introduction of any higher prime number would take us beyond this reality into dangerous regions which are not within the scope of our normal perception and understanding. 7 is the number of the heavenly worlds, as well as that of the infernal regions, and we have usually no means of knowing to which side it may lead us. The intervals which contain the element 7 cannot be psychically pleasant, being, by definition, beyond the limits of physical harmony: their musical effect also is normally beyond our control. Consequently their utilisation in music and its theory serves no useful purpose.*[1]

Seven therefore, is both the devil and the angel of musical expansion, and the consequences of its introduction are, to the mystic, too horrendous to even contemplate!

On a more practical note, Harry Partch, one of the keenest twentieth century investigators into the use of harmonically 'pure' intervals, was well aware of those theorists who sought to exclude the prime number seven, and he covered this subject well in the section *The Problem of Seven* in his *The Genesis of a Music.* He states that *the number seven is not represented in our current theory and seldom in our current practice, and the issue is still sky high.*[2] The first reason he gives for this is that the five limit was *expedient in the building and tuning of fretted and keyboard instruments.*[3] However, this statement, could be challenged on the grounds that it was the introduction of five that led to those problems of intonation that made necessary the development of some kind of temperament. Such a situation was far from expedient. However, perhaps he meant that to extend beyond the limit of five would make matters even more complicated, which it undoubtedly would.

The second reason he gives is that *its demands on notation were less complex.*[4] The number seven was therefore never taken up because, according to Partch: *By the time the value of the harmonies that seven involves had been theoretically recognised the patterns of both instruments and notation, with their five limit, had fixed themselves too definitely in the education and theoretical thinking of the army of musicians to be dislodged.*[5]

---

[1] Alain Danielou, Introduction to the Study of Musical Scales and Modes, 230-1.
[2] Partch, Op. Cit., 93.
[3] Ibid., The Problem of Seven, 119.
[4] Ibid. 119.
[5] Ibid., 119.

However, during the period Partch is referring to, the 'harmonies that seven involves' had already been identified with chords of dominant function such as the dominant seventh, ninth, etc. Here, the participation of the seventh harmonic was taken to be something of an intonational ideal, that is a chordal correspondence with a configuration of pure harmonics which served to naturally define the chord of the dominant seventh.

Guiseppe Tartini sought to perform music directly in fulfillment of that ideal.[1] However, at no point is a change of notation required, simply an adjustment of intonation on the part of the performer. And for those performers using tempered instruments, the issue did not matter anyway, because they could not change the intonation of the chords being played.

Certainly, some attempts were made by theorists to provide notation to indicate when such a change was required. A good example is Kirnberger who proposed using the letter I to indicate the seventh partial:

Kirnberger's Designation of the Seventh Partial[2]

Partial:	Fundamental	Fifth	Third	Seventh
Ratio:	1/1	5/4	3/2	7/4
Note Name:	C	E	G	I

In an age, however, when ideals of intonation were being heavily compromised through meantone tuning and equal temperament, such an idea never really caught on. Chladni ridiculed Kirnberger's attempts, retorting that *If one wanted to joke about the designation 'I', one could say it comes from the Latin and that it means 'Go away because we can't use you.*[3]

Yet even without a proper means of notation and played on tempered instruments, the implication was still there, as Partch certainly recognised: *On the basis of numerous tests there can be little doubt that the number seven is implied - though very badly implied- throughout today's musical thinking. The ratios of 6/5 and 5/4 are implied in all our triads, and the ear - though it prefers fact to implication - quickly realises the implication, despite the fact that these intervals are one-sixth and one-seventh of a semitone out of tune, respectively, in Equal Temperament. Likewise, but to a lesser degree, the ear tends to realise the implication of 4/5/6/7 in the 'dominant seventh' chord even though the 7 ingredient is a third of a semitone too sharp in equal*

---

[1] Wilfrid Perret, Some Questions of Musical Theory, W. Heffer and Sons Ltd., Cambridge 1926, 4.

[2] Kirnberger, The Art of Strict Musical Composition, 38.

[3] Martin Vogel, On the Relations of Tone, 116-7.

temperament. This explanation of the chord - positing the consonant seven, and avoiding the dissonant 9/5 - has been advanced by a long line of important men in science and theory, beginning at least as early as Euler (eighteenth century).[1]

Here he effectively disarms his previous observations concerning the rejection of seven because he says the ear recognises the implication anyway. If this *is* so, then no new notation would be required for the seventh harmonic. Despite the inconsistencies in Partch's logic, his statements do serve to summarise some three hundred years of resistance to the idea of the prime number seven in music. Yet as Partch's music itself has shown, the prime number seven can and has been used with some measure of success.

This brings the discussion to the other side of the coin: those figures who, during the period just considered, have tended to support the idea of the prime number seven. This is where the study starts to become particularly interesting, because when attempts are made to recognise the seventh harmonic as a legitimate bonding agent between musical tones, various unique problems come to the forefront. It is these, and their potential solutions, which represent the real crux of the matter, for they lead directly to the very cutting edge of the further development of the musical language.

---

[1] Partch, The Problem of Seven, Genesis of a Music, 120.

THE '7/4' RELATION AND THE 'EULERIAN' DOMINANT

Whilst some theorists have been opposed to the introduction and use of the prime number seven, others have both supported and positively encouraged its introduction, either for practical purposes, or for the purposes of the theoretical recognition of its implicit properties. Harry Partch identifies a group of important figures who have recognised the value of the prime number seven amongst which are Mersenne, Tartini, Euler, Serre and Perret.[1] Here an assessment of their contribution will be made, together with other significant figures encountered along the way. These contributions have led to the prevailing view of the prime number seven as it is positively understood today. However, despite the existence of such an impressive lineage in the study of the subject, all such contributions will be treated as assumptions until tested against the weight of evidence which the prime number seven presents.

One of the earliest contributions to the subject of the prime number seven stems from the seventeenth-century mathematician and physicist, Marin Mersenne. Mersenne saw in the natural harmonic series of the trumpet a reflection of the basic intervals, which provided the very fabric of music:

Table 5 of the Fourth Treatise of Mersenne's *Harmonie Universelle*[2]

I	II	III	IV
		15	8
		20	6
		24	5
		30	4
		40	3
		60	2
		120	1

---

[1] Harry Partch, The Problem of Seven, Genesis of a Music, 120.
[2] Marin Mersenne, Table 5, Treatise Four, Harmonie Universelle, trans. by Robert F. Williams, Ph. D. diss., University of Rochester 1972, p. 30.

Here the harmonic intervals are placed in an order which corresponds to their placing in the harmonic series. The deliberate omission of seven brings to the forefront the obvious presence of the perfect triad in the harmonic series. In pointing these features out, Mersenne created a precedent which was eagerly followed by subsequent theorists, such as Rameau, who saw in the harmonic series a possible means for explaining the fundamental grounds for musical harmony. Here it is interesting to observe that the scheme which Rameau was later to use in his octonarian division of a musical string, and from which he derived the spectrum of musical consonances, exactly duplicates Mersenne's table. Yet perhaps it is equally significant that unlike Rameau, who excluded the prime number seven for aesthetic reasons, Mersenne himself asks *For why are not the two sounds whose ratio is ... 7 to 6, or ...8 to 7, agreeable?*[1]

He then observes that the exclusion of seven seems rather illogical, and that septimal intervals should logically be included in the spectrum of recognised musical consonances. He also fails to find any justifiable reason for the exclusion of seven in the arguments of others, especially those arguments justified on numerological grounds. Four is the number of the body, he observes, and three is the number of the soul; there being a contrariness between body and soul, three and four cannot possibly unite in an agreeable sound. Seven as the sum of three and four is thus not to be utilised. Yet despite these arguments, Mersenne observes that the combination of sounds it produces are agreeable to the ear. Faced with a conflict between practical observation and metaphysical implication, it is interesting to see that Mersenne opts for the former, and concludes that the prime number seven should be included in the scheme, as it gives rise to intervals which serve to enrich the spectrum of musical consonance.[2]

In keeping with Mersenne's entirely logical observations concerning the prime number seven, there is evidence to show that in the next century serious attempts were being made both to recognise and exploit the charm of septimal intervals. A good example is Kirnberger who observed that the septimal interval whose ratio is 7/6 could just be considered to be consonant: *The minor third (6/5) is universally considered as a consonance, while the major second (8/9) is always considered as a dissonance. Since one also finds that this minor third can be made noticeably smaller without losing its consonant nature, it follows that the ratio 6/7 is the last one that can be comprehended by the ear.*[3]

---

[1] Ibid., p. 30.

[2] Ibid., p. 207. For Mersenne's complete discussion on the subject, which makes very interesting reading, read pages 207-19, Proposition XXXIII: Why there are only eight simple consonances?

[3] Kirnberger, The Art of Strict Musical Composition, 37-8.

Kirnberger evidently felt that the interval of ratio 8/7, occupied a position somewhere between the recognised consonances and dissonances. Thus he observes: *Since 8/9 is already difficult, but 5/6 can still be made smaller, this leaves the two proportions 6/7 and 7/8 between the clearly perceived consonances and dissonances. The first is somewhat more difficult to perceive than 5/6, the other somewhat easier than 8/9. Since 5/6 is still strongly consonant (because the minor third can be made smaller), but 8/9 is certainly already dissonant, the proportion 7/8 appears to be the dividing point between the consonances and the dissonances. To be sure the interval 6/7, which could be called a diminished third, cannot be found on our organ or clavier; however it is produced by trumpets.*[1]

Here again, are a series of important observations on the essential nature of septimal intervals which tend to neatly fill the gap left by Rameau's omission of seven from the octenary. Here it is noticeable that Kirnberger does not mention the primary septimal interval whose ratio is 7/4. That he did regard it to be consonant becomes apparent in a statement elsewhere in his work where he observes that: *there would be good reason to include at least 1/7 in our system. When transposed down to the first octave, this note is in the ratio 4/7 to the fundamental. For the fundamental C, it would fall between A (3/5) and B (8/15); we shall label it 'I'. It is really consonant, and this chord:*

C	E	G	I
4	5	6	7

is not a dissonant seventh chord but a four-part chord.[2]

Here Kirnberger gives the note corresponding to the seventh harmonic its own symbol. This is quite apt for a prime number which designates an altogether new dimension of frequency space. Yet Kirnberger's adoption of the symbol of the letter 'I' for the interval 7/4 is evasive, in that it fails to express the relationship of that interval to the environment in which it finds itself. Is 7/4 a sixth, or a seventh? If a seventh, of what type? Is it chromatic or diatonic, natural or altered? Carrying the letter 'I' it simply stands on its own, with no immediately discernible connection to the notes that surround it. Kirnberger, it would seem, was either unable to place the interval of 7/4 in a readily identifiable tonal context, or else he was more interested in the specific qualities of septimal intervals, than any function that they might perform within a given tonal context. This factor of finding a proper harmonic function for septimal intervals has an important bearing on the subject, for without a definable

---

[1] Ibid., 38.
[2] Ibid., 38, f. 24.

function, it is difficult to justify their use in a tonal context. Therefore, whilst it may have been accepted in some quarters that the number seven produced a range of musically viable intervals, the definition of a practical musical function for the interval 7/4 proved wanting.

One theory which seemed to fill this gap devolved around the close association of 7/4 with the minor seventh. Before the advent of valve trumpets and horns composers were limited to the harmonic series of the note at which the instrument was pitched. On the trumpets used in Bach's time the seventh, eleventh, thirteenth, seventeenth and nineteenth harmonics were often called upon to produce the notes Bb, F#, Ab, C# and D# (assuming a fundamental tone of C) as and when they were required. In Bach's Cantata 31 for example, he invokes the entire range of the harmonic series up to the 20th harmonic.[1]

Here, the technique of lipping gave players more versatility, for this allowed slight alterations of the pitch of these harmonics in order to bring them closer to the pitch which they approximated. Instances thus occurred where composers, requiring a note a minor seventh above the keynote of the instrument concerned, used the seventh partial as a substitute. Walter Piston mentions this in his treatise Orchestration observing that, in terms of the trumpet notes available to late eighteenth-century composers, *among these tones, the seventh was too flat, but it was nevertheless occasionally written.*[2]

In terms of brass instruments in particular, there is another type of usage to be taken into consideration which also invokes the resources of harmonics beyond the fifth, and this is where composers specifically call for the natural harmonics which those instruments can offer. Here it is curious to observe that the very notes which are considered 'out-of-tune' with our current scales, are those which have the most striking and aurally vivid effect. In the case of the slow movement of Vaughan Williams's Pastoral Symphony, the composer chooses to exploit the natural rustic associations of these notes.

Here, the seventh harmonic of the *Eb* fundamental - written as the note Db - stands at the epicentre of a melodic line which delicately traces the natural configuration of harmonics 4,6,7,8,9 and 10. Heard against the pedal chord of Eb major the effect is one of natural beauty and grace.

---

[1] Guy Oldham, Harmonics, The New Grove Dictionary of Music and Musicians, Vol. 8, Mc Millan Publishers 1995, 165 - 166.
[2] Walter Piston, Orchestration, Victor Gollancz Ltd., London 1978, 248.

Excerpt from Vaughan Williams's, *Pastoral Symphony*, Movement II.

Reproduced by permission of J. Curwen and Sons Ltd

Here, the seventh harmonic of the *Eb* fundamental - written as *Db* - stands as the epicentre of a melodic line which delicately traces the natural configuration of harmonics 4-10. Heard against the sustained chord of Eb major the effect is one of natural beauty and grace.

Benjamin Britten's *Serenade for Tenor, Horn and Strings* provides another example. For the Prologue Britten (1913 - 1976) asks for the notes be played on natural harmonics. Here the 'odd notes' to our ears are *Bb*, corresponding to the 7th harmonic, *F* corresponding to the 11th harmonic, and note A which corresponds with the 13th harmonic. That these produce such a striking effect upon the ear, indicates that they should be recognised as a legitimate part of the musical language. Yet in both of these cases the use of natural harmonics series may be regarded not as a conscious progression towards the resources of a higher interval nexus, but simply a reversion to a previous mode of instrumental limitation as an expressive gesture.

A general exception to this type of usage is when the Jazz cornet or trumpet player deliberately overblows to produce the seventh harmonic, in order to give the characteristic 'blue seventh'. In this case it the seventh harmonic is being allied to a particular expressive function.[1] Here the connection between the interval of 7/4 and the minor seventh becomes self evident. Indeed, it is through this perceived association between the two intervals that the interval of ratio 7/4

---

[1] Intervals, The New Grove Dictionary of Music and Musicians, Vol. 9, 1995, 277.

has acquired its most commonly known epithet in musical theory - the 'natural seventh' known otherwise as the 'harmonic seventh'. Not that either of these names are strictly logical. The interval of 7/4 is no more 'natural' than either the cyclic minor seventh (16/9), or the harmonic minor seventh (9/5) for which, in certain musical contexts, it is often viewed to be the better substitute. The term 'harmonic seventh' is perhaps more apt, because it intimates that the seventh concerned is the one apparently found in the harmonic series. But then again, here it is liable to be confused with the 'harmonic minor seventh' of ratio 9/5.

Whatever the problems surrounding the descriptive terms used for the interval of ratio 7/4, its perceived link with the interval of the minor seventh is a factor which has enabled theorists to proffer an acoustical explanation of one of the most powerful sonorities of tonal harmony. The chord being referred to is of course the dominant seventh, which being the one sonority upon which the absolutely precise and unmistakable definition of tonality depends, is thus elevated over and above all others - both in terms of its function and nomenclature. In musical theory it is described as the primary seventh chord in the diatonic complex, all other seventh chords being relegated to the less imposing function of secondary sevenths.

The perspicuity of the resolution of the V7 - I progression has been well charted in works on musical harmony, and there is no need to discuss this point here. Certainly it would be difficult to deny that the dominant seventh chord performs a crucial role in tonal music. Indeed, its function is so important for the maintenance and upkeep of tonality in general, and for the purposes of modulation, that it does indeed tend to stand out alone as a quite unique sonority. It is thus rather tempting to see in this chord the outward signs of the influence of a higher mathematical dimension of tone connection - the dimension of seven.

One of the most convincing explanations of how the interval of ratio 7/4 might participate in the dominant seventh chord was put forward by Euler (1707-1783). In his *Tentamen novae theoriae musicae* of 1739 he had already observed that the 'natural seventh' (7/4) could be considered to be a primary consonance because of its rather simple ratio.[1] From there it was but a short step to connect the great significance of the chord of the dominant seventh in tonal music with the primary nature of the seventh harmonic. After all, if the major chord conforms to harmonics four, five and six, and the minor seventh conforms to the seventh harmonic, then the dominant seventh chord could thus be defined by harmonics four, five, six and seven. Working on this theory in general, Euler arrived at a scheme in which it was possible to show how the ear may substitute 7/4, for the conventional minor seventh of 16/9.

---

[1] Leonard Euler, Tentamen Novae Theoriae Musicae, St Petersburg 1739.

In his *Conjecture sur la raison de quelques dissonances généralement reçues dans la musique* of 1764, Euler observed that *the character of the chord sol-si-re-fa consists in the relationship of si, expressed by the number 45, with fa, represented by the number 64*.[1] He then postulates that the number 64 undergoes a modification, in which the ear substitutes 63 for 64, so that all of the numbers of the chord are thereby divisible by 9. In other words, when listening to the sounds sol-si-re-fa, represented by the numbers 36-45-54-64, the ear really understands 36-45-54-63, which, reduced to their simplest terms, gives 4-5-6-7.[2] That the human ear is capable of reducing 36-45-54-64 to a much simpler 4-5-6-7 is of course entirely reasonable. The faculty of the inner ear, particularly the basilar membrane to interpret complex or irrational ratios to their nearest equivalent in the harmonic series has already been commented upon.[3] Viewed in this context, the chord of the dominant major ninth (*G B D F A*) would also be readily implied by harmonics 4, 5, 6, 7 and 9.

Yet if such a process does occur, would it not apply to other chords in which the minor seventh occurred.? And if so, why is the minor seventh of the dominant seventh chord usually perceived to be a dissonance? Perhaps Euler felt that it was the presence of the major chord and its conformity to the harmonic numbers 4, 5 and 6 that gave the minor seventh the presentiment of the seventh harmonic. Offering a progressive slant on Euler's theory, it indicates the continuation of a trend already implied by the history of music, where the prime number five was introduced because it offered a simpler and more consonant major third than was present in the Pythagorean scale complex. Could not the prime number seven make its influence felt through a similar process of substitution of a simple intervallic relationship (7/4) for a more complex one (16/9)?

In this way, it could be said that through the chord of the dominant seventh, and its determining ratio of seven, music had thus progressed to a new level, as significant perhaps as the stage where five gradually became accepted as an additional agent to three. Through five (5/4), the consonant duad of the perfect fifth had become a triad. Now, through seven (7/4), the consonant triad of the major chord had become a tetrad. Here it is to be noted that other theorists, aside from Euler, had observed the closeness of the minor seventh to the seventh harmonic, and come to similar, although not always identical

---

[1] Leonard Euler, Conjecture sur la raison de quelques dissonances généralement reçues dans la musique (1764), Opera Omnie, Serie III, Band 1, Leipzig and Berlin 1926.

[2] See F.J. Fétis' article on Euler in his Esquisse de l'histoire de l'harmonie, Paris 1840. Also see Shirlaw, Theory of Harmony, 348

[3] Ch. 3.

conclusions. Euler's contribution no doubt impresses because of its mathematical logic and flair.

In 1747, Georg Andreas Sorge (1703 - 1778) published his *Vorgemach der Musikalischen Composition*[1] where he observed that the configuration of the fourth, fifth, sixth and seventh harmonics gave a very close approximation of the chord of the dominant seventh. However, Sorge was rather atypical in that he believed the seventh harmonic to be a dissonance. This idea was perhaps necessary for the justification of Sorge's theories, for he believed that the natural force of tension emanating from the 'natural seventh' was the factor that gave the dominant seventh chord such a compelling resolution to the tonic triad.[2] Yet there is something very worrying in this argument. It depends for its success on the attribution of a degree of tension to the interval of 7/4 which may not actually be apparent.

It has long since been established that the interval 7/4 may, in certain contexts, be considered more consonant than the minor sixth of 8/5.[3] Therefore the minor sevenths of ratio 16/9, or 9/5, may both be regarded to be much more dissonant than the natural seventh of 7/4. Consequently, if it is the quality of tension that goes to enhance the effectiveness of the resolution of the dominant seventh to the tonic triad, then the more dissonant 9/5 or even 16/9 would provide the better prospects. To change the ratio to 7/4, would thus be to weaken, not strengthen, the dissonant qualities of the dominant seventh.

Furthermore, Sorge's belief that the natural seventh was also implied in the half-diminished seventh chord (*B D F A* in the key of C major) and the supertonic seventh chord (*D F A C* in the key of C major) is also rather problematic. The central problem is that each new septimal 'seventh' that is introduced leads, like a chain reaction, to a considerable escalation in the complexities of the intonation. Indeed, it is necessary to ask where the extent of the influence of the seventh harmonic is seen to stop. If the notes G to F, B to A, and D to C are seen to be natural sevenths then why not *E* to *D* as well?. In the end this prospect leads to such a radical change in the otherwise simple tuning of the major mode that the very value of that change becomes questionable: the septimal dominant has grown out of all proportion to its significance and taken unto itself the principle by which the entire scale is deduced.

In this way, Sorge's theory seems to create more problems than it actually solves. And tonally speaking, such a scale construction is extremely weak. This

[1] Georg Andreas Sorge, Vorgemach der Musikalischen Composition, Lobenstein 1745.

[2] Shirlaw, Theory of Harmony, 307.

[3] Helmholtz, Op. Cit., 179 - 211.

is because the complex septimal ratios offer several conflicting definitions of the degrees of the diatonic scale, and in so doing, serve to undermine the strength of connection with the tonic note that actually characterises those tonal degrees.

A very good example is the close correspondence of the seventh of the dominant seventh chord with the subdominant degree of the scale - ratio of 4/3. The function of this degree, as the note of which the tonic itself is the dominant, is severely compromised by the complex septimal ratio of 21/16. But there again, in support of Sorge's basic idea, it can be seen that in musical matters context is the final arbiter, and any competent performer, who having been made aware of such intonational complexities, would be able to switch between one or the other types of second, third, or whatever, depending upon the context in which it occurred.

Sorge no doubt intended that the subdominant degree thus has a different ratio depending upon the context in which it was presented. As the root of the subdominant triad it would have a ratio of 4/3, whilst as the 'natural seventh' of the dominant it would have a ratio of 21/16. This perhaps is quite feasible, because one of the principal defects of Zarlino's tuning for the major mode lies in its very inability to offer a consistent ratio for the subdominant degree. This is because between notes D (9/8) and F (4/3) exists the Pythagorean interval of the trihemitone - ratio of 32/27. Therefore to enable a pure minor triad to be constructed upon the supertonic degree, the third of that triad (note F in the key of C) needs to be raised by a syntonic comma (81/80) in order that it may concur with the ratio of 6/5. This effectively alters the ratio of the subdominant degree from 4/3 to 27/20, the ratio of the acute perfect fourth.

Similarly, the fifth between notes D (9/8) and A (5/3) is a syntonic comma short of a perfect fifth. Forming the interval of a grave fifth which has a ratio of 40/27, the upper note A needs to be raised by a syntonic comma to give note A+ (27/16). In this respect, the precise ratios for both the subdominant and submediant degrees are far from consistent. However, applying this inconsistency to the minor seventh of the dominant it will be seen that a subdominant degree of ratio 4/3 gives a seventh of the dominant which has a ratio of 16/9, whilst a subdominant degree of ratio 27/20 gives a dominant seventh interval of 9/5. The former it will be noted, is a syntonic comma smaller than the latter.

The 'natural seventh' (7/4) is smaller still: the difference between the seventh harmonic (7/4) and the cyclic minor seventh (16/9) is the septimal comma of ratio 64/63. A fractional interval resulting from the incommensurability of the third, fifth and seventh partials, it is one of those small intervals which, like the Pythagorean or Didymean commas, tends to cause problems for tuners:

Comparison of the Breadths (in Cents) of the Cyclic (16/9) and Harmonic Minor Seventh (9/5) to the Interval Whose Ratio is 7/4

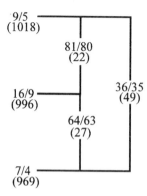

Any system which did introduce the prime number seven, but was not a purely theoretical one, would need to take into account this proliferation of micro-intervallic modality prompted by its introduction. The resulting system would be considerably richer simply because of the added intonational possibilities introduced by the septimal intervals. Differences between these respective types of seventh (7/4, 16/9 and 9/5) are however, quite significant, and would give to the chord of the dominant seventh different qualities depending upon which one was used. The sweetest chord is clearly that defined by harmonics 4,5,6 and 7.

Although focusing the discussion on the interval of the seventh, it might also be worth mentioning that the dominant seventh chord can be obtained through the addition of a minor third to a major triad. In this respect, Cornu and Mercadier's study of the intonation of the dominant seventh chord proves interesting, for this showed that in practice, the minor third of the dominant seventh chord tended to follow a harmonic (6/5), rather than a septimal (7/6) or Pythagorean (32/27) ratio.[1] In this case the ratio of the seventh above the dominant would undoubtedly be 9/5. This, it will be recalled, is the larger minor seventh, which as can be seen in the diagram given above, is bigger than the interval whose ratio is 7/4 by a not inconsiderable interval of 36/35, which approximates to about a quarter of a tone.

A further element of uncertainty appears when 7/4 is compared with the harmonic form of diminished seventh, an interval obtained when three minor

[1] Andrew G. Pikler, History of Experiments on the Musical Interval Sense, in: JMT 10/1, 1966, 54 - 95.

thirds are stacked one upon the other to produce a pure chord of the diminished seventh. If all three of the minor thirds are deemed to be pure, that is tuned according to the ratio of 6/5, the resulting diminished seventh will have a ratio of 216/125 (947 cents). Comparing this to the interval 7/4 (969 cents) it can be seen that it is actually closer than the cyclic minor seventh (16/9 - 996 cents), for it is only some 22 cents flatter, whilst the cyclic minor seventh is 27 cents sharper.

This might be the reason why Kirnberger considers the interval of 7/6 to be a diminished third - G to Bbb as opposed to G to Bb.[1] So, assuming that the fundamental tone is note C, it is difficult to decide at first, as to whether the seventh harmonic should be spelled as a Bb (the minor seventh), Bbb (the diminished seventh), or neither of these at all. Perhaps it does not matter. The important issue might be the introduction of the septimal intervals in order that they may enrich the system.

One of the most productive efforts towards the enrichment of the system of tonality using septimal intervals was made by the Italian violinist and theorist Guiseppe Tartini (1692 - 1770). Well aware of those micro-modal differences between intervals, he sought an avenue for the exploitation of 7/4 which, rather than being angled towards a merger of intervallic identities, was actually consistent with those differences. In his *Trattado de Musica* (1754) he discusses the interval of 7/4 observing that: *This interval is....produced naturally on marine and 'da fiato' trumpets and also on hunting horns - instruments which are not subject to human reason but function according to the laws of physics and harmony. To the diatonic scale one may therefore add in the form of a musical note the term 1/7 representing the above mentioned interval, and this added note should be given the sign* ♭, *as distinct from the b used for B fa............*[2]

Tartini thus believed the diatonic and natural sevenths were different from one another. To distinguish the former from the latter the sign ♭, was used to indicate that note should be flattened by that requisite amount. The quarter tone interval between these two sevenths could then be exploited in melodic contexts to give effects reminiscent of the ancient Greek enharmonic genera. For Tartini therefore, the prime number seven did not belong at a diatonic level, but on an enharmonic level, where its effects were most easily visible. Thus he states: *Although the sextuple harmonic extension does not in its integral unity go beyond 1/6 to 1/7, 1/6 being its limit, it is not the case that the harmonic system cannot by nature progress to 1/7, 1/8, etc. Indeed, it follows from this*

---

[1] Kirnberger, Op. Cit., 37-8.

[2] Guiseppi Tartini, Trattado di Musica, Padua 1754, 126, (quoted extract trans. by Laura Davey).

that if the extension is restricted to 1/6, then we have the diatonic genus; if the extension exceeds 1/6, then we have the enharmonic genus.[1]

Tartini's interest in the prime number seven was largely bound up with a desire to reintroduce a tangible basis for chromatic and enharmonic tetrachords. Hence his extremely lucid demonstrations of how this interval can be used, either for the purposes of utilising an enharmonic tetrachord, or to give a consonant seventh, that is one which need not be prepared. That being said, Tartini's ideas did not gain a very wide following, despite their knock-on effect upon string intonation. Perhaps this was because of the obscure and often extremely complex way in which he expressed his ideas. His preoccupation in the *Trattado di Musica* with difference tones, which are used to prove virtually every point he makes, does tend to verge on the obsessive.

Despite Tartini's claims concerning the application of the prime number seven in the realisation of the enharmonic genera, the prevailing view passed on to the nineteenth century concerning the interval of ratio 7/4 was after the fashion of Euler and Sorge i.e. that it provided the seventh of the dominant seventh chord. One of the major sources for the propagation of this view was the historian Francois-Joseph Fétis (1784 - 1871), who, in his two main works *Esquisse de L'histoire de l'Harmonie* of 1840,[2] and the *Trait complet de la theorie et de la pratique de l'harmonie* of 1844,[3] espoused views of the prime number seven which were basically a fusion of what he had read about both Euler's and Sorge's ideas. This was rather curious, because Fetis was one of those figures who, in general tended to scorn acoustical theories concerning the origins and functions of chords.

Shirlaw points out the contradiction inherent to this: *Fétis, then, after having ostentatiously rejected all acoustical phenomena, not only follows Rameau in deriving harmony from the sounds of the harmonic series, but goes one better, in making use of the number 7, with which Rameau would have nothing to do. He has defined the chord of the dominant seventh as 'the only natural dissonant chord' and as the chord which has determined our tonality. It is the only natural dissonant chord because it alone, of all dissonant chords, admits of being taken without preparation. Fétis considers it for this, and the explanation he gives is that this chord is derived from those sounds of the harmonic series represented by the numbers 4/5/6/7. Yet he knows quite well*

---

[1] Ibid., 128, (quoted extract trans. by Laura Davey).

[2] Francois-Joseph Fetis, Esquisse de L'histoire de l'Harmonie, Paris 1840. (Trans. by Mary Irene Arlin, Ph.D. diss. Indiana University 1971)

[3] Francois-Joseph Fétis, Trait complet de la theorie et de la pratique de l'harmonie, Paris and Brussels 1844.

that this 'natural 7' is not the real fourth degree of the scale, and he constantly ridicules other theorists who make use of it.[1]

Rather than serving as a point of origination of any new ideas about the prime number seven, Fétis was thus content to propagate the prevailing views of the subject at that time. Thus entering the domain of popular musical theory, the theory of the natural dominant seventh tetrad was later to become an unshakable article of faith amongst musicians.

As a continuation of this thread of belief concerning the interval of ratio 7/4, the contribution of Helmholtz is also worthy of mention. In the main, Helmholtz tended to support those beliefs as propagated by Euler, Sorge and Fétis. He does however, make a theoretical distinction between the diatonic and 'natural seventh' intervals in that he called 7/4 the 'sub-minor seventh': *The sub-minor seventh 4:7 or C Bb- is very often more harmonious than the minor sixth........* writes Helmholtz.[2]

The musicologist Alexander Ellis, a firm follower of Helmholtz, thoroughly upheld this view of the interval 7/4. In fact, because 7/4 is the primary septimal interval, means that the identities of all other septimal intervals are established accordingly. As Ellis believed wholeheartedly in the theory of the 'natural seventh', meant that those other septimal intervals which he classifies were categorised according to that theory. The chief septimal intervals were thus categorised by Ellis as follows:

Ellis's System of Identifying Septimal Intervals After the Fashion of Helmholtz[3]

Ratio	Interval
7/4	Sub-minor seventh
7/5	Sub-fifth
7/6	Sub-minor third
9/7	Super-major third
8/7	Super-major second
10/7	Super-fourth
12/7	Super-major sixth
14/9	Sub-minor sixth

This particular set of identities for septimal intervals has inspired the creation of numerous musical instruments specifically designed to produce such pure septimal intervals. One such instrument was designed by the Reverend Henry

---

[1] Shirlaw, Op. Cit., 348.

[2] Helmholtz, Op. Cit., 195.

[3] Ibid., 454-55.

Ward Poole (1826-1890). Taking the form of a keyboard instrument which not allowed the playing of music in just intonation in the keys of Db to B (along the line of fifths) it also allowed use of the 'sub-minor seventh' in dominant seventh chords within each of those keys. To be able to accomplish this a scale of over 100 separate tones to the octave were required, all feasibly provided for by the use of a complex set of pedals and a rather complicated, cumbersome keyboard.[1] Here it is a shame that Mr. Poole never got beyond the stage of constructing a cardboard model of his keyboard!

Since then numerous keyboards and organs have been constructed along similar lines, the major intention being to provide pure septimal intervals, and therefore ostensibly a purer, more natural dominant seventh chord. One of the most explicit accounts of such instruments as have been developed for this purpose is Martin Vogel's *Denkschrift zum Bau von Tasteninstrumenten in Reiner Stimmung* of 1986. Within, accounts are given of keyboard instruments which have any number of notes ranging from 17, 19, 31, 48, 72 and 171 tones to the octave. For its lucid explanation and summary of some of the acoustical principles involved in the construction of such instruments, the book is essential reading. Unfortunately it has not been translated into English yet.[2]

Generally, such instruments are not often very popular with performers. One of the factors which no doubt contributes to their lack of popularity, is their complexity, often comprising rows upon rows of keys and pedals which presents a daunting prospect even to the most seasoned and expert performers. If such instruments are to become more popular, undoubtedly the element of simplicity will provide the key to success.

Two examples are extremely promising. The first is the 'Archiphone'.[3] Roughly based on the five-manual keyboard of Nicola Vicentino's Arcicembalo (which was tuned in 31 tone meantone tuning), the Archiphone is a keyboard instrument tuned to 31 tone equal temperament, a method of tuning which gives an excellent rendition of septimal intervals. Another instrument, this time not of the keyboard variety, is Martin Vogel's 'Enharmonic Guitar',[4] which possesses frets which allow the performer to distinguish between notes which, in twelve tone equal temperament, are taken to be enharmonically equivalent i.e. the notes E# and F as for example. This too, gives very good approximations of septimal intervals.

---

[1] Ibid., 474.

[2] Martin Vogel, Denkschrift zum Bau von Tasteninstrumenten in Reiner Stimuung, Verlag für systematische Musikwissenschaft GmbH, Bonn 1986.

[3] Joel Mandelbaum, Toward the Expansion of our Concepts of Intonation, in: PNM 13/1, 1974.

[4] Martin Vogel, Die enharmonische Gitarre, Verlag für systematische Musikwissenschaft GmbH, Bonn 1982.

The chief advantage of such instruments is that chords of the dominant seventh can be rendered 'pure'. Consequently, a more clear and harmonically logical chord is obtained, configured quite naturally by the fourth, fifth, sixth and seventh harmonics. Whilst respecting this relatively new found facility, it is nonetheless necessary to question whether a smoother form of minor seventh chord is actually required to enhance the resolution of the dominant seventh chord to its prospective tonic. The essential nature of the chord of the dominant seventh devolved around its perception as a primary dissonance. Consequently, the more this dissonant factor could be loaded, through the addition of the ninth, and then the eleventh, thirteenth, fifteenth, etc., the more satisfactory the ultimate resolution of that dominant chord to the tonic triad.

In this context, the more complex ratio of the just minor seventh (9/5) is perhaps more in keeping with the function of a chord which depended upon the presence of harmonic tension, than the relatively mild and extremely tame 'natural seventh' (7/4). Although in keeping with the natural order of the intervals in the harmonic series, this tuning would render it rather ineffective as a primary dissonance - an observation which has been made numerous times by various theorists. As a representative example, Van der Pol observes that *the Eulerian dominant seventh is too consonant, and so looses the character of the diatonic dominant seventh chord.*[1]

But there again, this argument could equally be reversed, in that it could be said that by accepting the compromise that is the mild consonance of the septimal dominant, harmony is considerably enriched through the participation of that new and aurally stimulating septimal element.

This argument applies equally to the diminished triad. In the articles 'Falsch' and 'Verminderter Dreyklang' in Sulzer's *Allgemeine Theorie der schönen Künste*, Kirnberger explains that the closer the proportion is to 5/7, the more usable is the small fifth as a consonance in the diminished triad[2] - an opinion echoed again a few years later by Sorge in his *Vorgemach der musikalischen Composition.*[3] Partch mentions this subject too, observing that: *In the 'pure scale era' of sixteenth century Italy the diminished triad was frankly called consonant by theorists. To anyone who has taken the trouble to make the tests it is inconceivable that a human ear could react to the Pythagorean 1/1-32/27-1024/729, or to 1/1-6/5-36/25, or to 1/1-6/5-45/32 as consonant. The ear could jump the distance between what it heard and what it wanted to hear, or -*

---

[1] Balth van der Pol, Music and Elementary Theory of Numbers, in: MR7, 1946, 1 - 25.

[2] Kirnberger, Op. Cit., Footnote c,. (David Beach), 47.

[3] Andreas Sorge, Op. Cit., 18-19.

at least a part of the time - voices and viols intoned unconsciously the consonance 5/6/7 and the ear found it infinitely pleasing.[1]

So the issue depends to a certain extent upon priorities. The interval 7/4 seems to offer a consonant dominant seventh, the interval 7/5 a consonant diminished triad, and through their use the harmonic palette is considerably enriched. If priority is given to dissonance in order to exacerbate the effectiveness of the resolution of those chords to their respective tonics, then the conventional diatonic dominants are clearly much more desirable.

During the beginning of this century one of the most convincing champions of the cause of the prime number seven was the writer Matthew Shirlaw, still remembered for his lucid and perceptive work *The Theory of Harmony* (1917). Throughout this interesting book he makes numerous comments upon the possibilities which the prime number seven may offer, as well as exposing some of the fallacies and illogicalities of those theorists such as Rameau who sought to evade the problems which it presents. As Shirlaw himself states: *Rameau is unable to explain why in the generation of the consonances by the first six numbers the next number, that is 7, should introduce, as he tells us, a dissonance. The reason alleged by Rameau, which he borrows from Descartes, namely that the comparison of the consonances produced by the senary division gives the smallest intervals which the ear is capable of appreciating is not adequate. Consonance is not determined by the extent to which the ear can appreciate minute differences of tone....It is quite evident however, that in deciding that the number seven introduces a dissonance, Rameau is influenced less by theoretical considerations than by the judgement of his ear. Yet even by allowing the ear to become the sole arbiter, the matter could not thus be placed beyond the range of controversy or of individual opinion. On the other hand Rameau might have maintained that it was time enough to treat of this 'natural seventh' and to give it a place in the musical system, when musicians actually begin to make use of it. This is by no means the most serious of the difficulties with which Rameau is soon to find himself confronted.*[2]

Rameau comes under attack again, later in the book: *Descartes had already remarked that we hardly ever hear a musical sound without at the same time hearing its octave. This octave indeed, forms part of the resonance of the fundamental sound. But what is true of the octave is true also of the fifth and fourth, as well as of the natural thirds. As Helmholtz himself informs us, all sounds suitable for musical purposes are richly endowed with upper partial tones. In every musical sound then, produced by the human voice, these consonances were to be heard..... First the octave, fifth and fourth (1:2:3:4)*

[1] Harry Partch, The Problem of Seven, Genesis of a Music, 120.

[2] Shirlaw, Op. Cit., 78-9.

were apprehended, and later the natural thirds (4:5:6). Rameau therefore, might well claim, not only that 'harmony arises from a definite principle' but that 'this principle resides in musical sound itself'. But these are, in fact points for which Rameau has all along been contending. What then, of the seventh upper partial tone, the 'natural seventh' which may also be distinguished, though with greater difficulty, in the resonance of musical sound?. Is it consonant or dissonant? But in as much as this 'natural seventh' has no place in our harmonic system, the solution of the many problems connected with our system of harmony does not depend on the answer to this question. It is very improbable that there exists any consensus of opinion among musicians themselves as to whether this interval (4:7) is consonant. Those who have been accustomed to regard the chord of the dominant seventh as a 'fundamental discord' formed by means of the 'natural seventh' would probably tell us that this interval is dissonant. Others, again would be of opinion that in itself it is a consonance. One thing however, is certain: its employment in harmony and in the art of music would necessitate a change in our harmonic system.[1]

Here Shirlaw intimates an implied three-stage progression of music as determined by the range of intervals used in the harmonic series. First, the perfect consonances were apprehended, to be followed later by the imperfect consonances. The next stage, distinguished logically by the use of prime number seven is all of a haze, and Shirlaw is unsure as to its nature. He feels that 7/4 has no place in our harmonic system, and that its use in musical harmony would necessitate a change to that system. It is strange, therefore, that he persists in calling 7/4 the 'natural seventh' for it is this view that leads to the concept of the septimal dominant.

Overall, Shirlaw tends to disagree with this view of the seventh harmonic, and he blames Fétis for promulgating the idea in the first place: *The widely disseminated doctrine of Fétis that our modern harmonic system has been brought about by the introduction into harmonic music of the natural chord of the dominant seventh has become almost an article of faith among musicians. Nothing has tended more to obscure the true nature of harmony and of our harmonic system.*[2]

To Shirlaw, therefore, the answers to the questions posed by the number seven do not lie in an alliance with the chord of the dominant seventh. For him that alliance serves merely to obscure the very thing which it is meant to fortify.

---

[1] Ibid., 179 - 80.

[2] Wilfrid Perret, Some Questions of Musical Theory, W. Heffer and Sons Ltd, Cambridge 1926.

To be consistent in that logic, however, he could have dropped the tag of 'natural seventh' which provides the basis for such theories in the first place.

A somewhat different approach to the problems of the number seven was taken by Shirlaw's contemporary Wilfrid Perret, author of *Some Questions of Musical Theory* (1926). A lucid account of his own personal endeavour to come to terms with the problem of seven, it is a small book which is written in two parts.[1] The first part is largely conjectural, in that it speculates on the precise derivation of the scale devised and used by the Greek musician Olympus (c. 660-620 BC), as a consequence of his rediscovery of the enharmonic genus of antiquity, a discovery originally attributed to Olympus by the Greek author Plutarch (before AD 50 - after AD 120) in his treatise *De Musica*.

Perret speculates that Olympus rediscovered those intervals which use the prime number seven, and used them in order to revive the enharmonic genera. The value of his speculation in terms of current theories concerning ancient Greek music is beyond the bounds of this book. It can be observed though, that Perret's work shares an affinity with work undertaken by the Renaissance composer Nicola Vicentino, who also endeavoured to revive the ancient Greek enharmonic genera through the use of harmonic prime numbers beyond five. In a smaller measure, it also bears resemblances to Tartini's approach in the Trattado di Musica, in that it concerns itself with the microtonal distinction between the 'natural' and harmonic minor sevenths.

In the second part of his book, he refers to the 'Olympion', a keyboard which he had developed in order to be able to play music which uses the enharmonic genera. For Perret, the way forward from what he felt to be the retrogressive and pernicious influence of equal temperament was a return to the sophistication of ancient Greek music, i.e. a revival of the chromatic and enharmonic genus. To be able to do this, Perret felt, like Tartini before him, and Vicentino before him, that the introduction of the prime number seven was undoubtedly necessary.

As such it is an interesting book, particularly for the references it makes to the prime number seven. Perret himself made a keen study of septimal intervals. Through his studies he developed a feeling for their particular qualities. This becomes apparent in the following statement, where Perret talks of the intervals of ratios 7/4, 7/5 and 7/6 respectively: *I discovered it [the interval of 7/5] myself a good many years ago in a new way, by singing the chromatic scale very softly, falsetto, with a C = 256 v.s. tuning fork sustaining my keynote very gently close to the left ear, while I listened enraptured to the two resultant tones which are clearly audible under these conditions. I was at that time immensely puzzled, having read in Pole's Philosophy of Music that the tritone,*

---

[1] Ibid., 2-3.

the semitone between the fourth and the fifth of the diatonic scale, is called the diabolic interval. I wondered porquoi diable it should sound so sweet to me. The fact that the two lower tones which may be heard filling up the accord 2/3/5/7 are precisely the same as when the minor sixth is sung to the tuning fork in the same way (5/8, resultants 3 and 2) also suggested fascinating problems. Becoming acquainted further, with the interval 7/4 by failing to find Bb (16/9) in the key of the tuning fork, the smaller harmonic numbers (7/4 followed by 9/5) substituting themselves for the larger ones; and having .....admired 7/6 on a toy concertina, which in spite of its penny trumpet quality of tone produces a not unpleasant effect by reason of its loud difference-tone when these two reeds are sounded together (1/6/7), the idea presented itself that by raising or lowering C by a very small interval it might be possible to construct a new chromatic scale which would displace the tritone in favour of 7/5 and bring in 7/6 and 7/4.[1]

Perret then describes how he went on to develop a twelve-note chromatic scale that utilised these intervals. For Perret, there is no question but that the intervals mentioned are to be regarded as consonant. Using the judgement of his own ear, he realised, as Mersenne had felt some three hundred years back, that such intervals should indeed be included in the list of musical consonances. From his original twelve-note scale, he then went on to develop a nineteen-note scale, which uses most of the primary septimal intervals.

Perret's scale is based loosely upon the harmonic form of the chromatic scale. Modifications to the chromatic scale are the substitution of the 'subminor second' (21/20) for the minor second (16/15) and the 'subminor fifth' (7/5) for the diminished fifth of 64/45. To this chromatic core he has then added seven septimal intervals: the 'submajor second' (35/32), the 'subminor third' (7/6), the 'subfourth' (21/16), the 'subfifth' (35/24), the 'subminor sixth' (63/40), the 'subminor seventh' (7/4), and the 'suboctave' (63/32).

Curiously, he omits a number of important primary septimal intervals for reasons which he does not offer: these are the septimal intervals of 8/7; 9/7; 10/7; 12/7 and 14/9. From an examination of the scale the reason can be surmised. There is a distinct preponderance of subminor intervals, whilst there is a complete lack of supermajor intervals, i.e. the inversions of the sub-minor intervals. As such the scale is rather imbalanced, or an incomplete realisation of what may in fact be a larger and more complex scale. Despite this slight lapse, Perret's intended use of septimal tones is an admirable achievement, and the harmonisations of the melodies based on enharmonic formulae which he develops from the scale, are interesting examples of chords which conspicuously utilise septimal tones.

---

[1] Ibid., 3.

Wilfrid Perret's Nineteen-Note Scale.[1]

Degree	Note	Ratio	Interval	Cents
1	C	1/1	Prime	0
2	7Db	21/20	Sub-minor second	84
3	7D	35/32	Sub-major second	155
4	D	9/8	Major second	204
5	7Eb	7/6	Sub-minor third	267
6	Eb	6/5	Minor third	316
7	E	5/4	Major third	386
8	7F	21/16	Sub-fourth	471
9	F	4/3	Perfect fourth	498
10	7Gb	7/5	Sub-minor fifth	583
11	7G	35/24	Sub-fifth	653
12	G	3/2	Perfect fifth	702
13	7Ab	63/40	Sub-minor sixth	786
14	Ab	8/5	Minor sixth	814
15	A	5/3	Major sixth	884
16	7Bb	7/4	Sub-minor seventh	969
17	Bb	9/5	Minor seventh	1018
18	B	15/8	Major seventh	1088
19	7C	63/32	Sub-octave	1173
1	C	2/1	Octave	1200

Harry Partch, keenly aware of Perret's work, as a reading of his The Genesis of a Music will show, tended to concur with the belief that the interval 7/4 was implied in the dominant seventh chord. He states: *there can be little doubt that the number seven is implied..... throughout todays musical thinking.....the ear tends to realise the implication of 4/5/6/7 in the 'dominant seventh' chord even though the 7 ingredient is a third of a semitone too sharp in equal temperament. This explanation of the chord - positing the consonant seven, and avoiding the dissonant 9/5 - has been advanced by a long line of important men in science and theory, beginning at least as early as Euler (eighteenth century). Also, the ear tends to recognise the 'diminished triad' as 5/6/7 even though the seven ingredient is again too sharp in Equal temperament, this time a sixth of a semitone.*[2]

---

[1] As explained in Part 1 of Perret's Some Questions of Musical Theory.

[2] Harry Partch, Op. Cit., 120.

From the content of this statement, there can be no doubt that Partch agrees with the theory that the dominant seventh chord is a septimal sonority, and that despite the limitations of our musical instruments, the implication is there, even if the actual sound is not. Partch of course, was well qualified to speak with authority on such matters, having spent many years of persistent endeavour developing his own idiomatic tone system which uses both the prime numbers seven and eleven.

Whilst Partch upheld the cause of seven across the Atlantic, in Europe it was the Dutch theorist Adriaan Fokker (1887 - 1972) who championed the interests of the prime number seven. Like Partch, Fokker felt that the resources of equal temperament had been exhausted, and that it was time to expand the nexus of pitch relations to embrace higher prime numbers in the harmonic series. To do this the scale would of course have to be expanded to accommodate these new relations. Fokker believed that, as he himself puts it: *there is a great need for using a novel variety of harmonic intervals and chords, and to expand the realm of harmony. It goes without saying that the very first thing to do will be adding the seventh to the common chord so as to use the primary tetrad with harmonic numbers 4:5:6:7. That was a demand of Belà Bartók.*[1]

Observing that the agents of this expansion will be prime numbered harmonics, the intervals he implicates in this process of expansion of the network of tonal relations are: the 'perfect fifth' (3/2); the 'perfect major third' (5/4), the 'perfect seventh' (7/4), the 'perfect eleventh' (11/8), and finally the 'perfect thirteenth' (13/8). Here the interval of 7/4 is termed the 'perfect seventh', a name which although stemming from an obvious misappropriation of conventional intervallic nomenclature, nonetheless embodies the very essence of what Fokker was trying to accomplish: to break the iron grip of twelve-tone equal temperament, and introduce those natural relationships present in the harmonic series, and implied by the prime numbers thereof. To describe the seventh as 'perfect' therefore, is to stand heavily braced against that branch of thinking which casts up 7/4 as being 'out-of-tune'. To Fokker's way of thought it is obviously the other way around: 7/4 provides the model seventh to which the musical language should graciously aspire.

Whilst discussing the general subject of the 'harmonic seventh' it should be noted that as a result of the combined influence of both Partch and Fokker, recent decades have seen a considerable upsurge of interest in the possibilities of the prime number seven. In the 1970's, the British composer Brian Dennis (1941-1998), known chiefly for his educational musical projects, developed a compositional system utilised in his six *Chinese Song Cycles* composed between

---

[1] Adriaan Fokker, On the Expansion of the Musicians Realm of Harmony, in: AMXXXVIII, 1966, 197 - 201.

1973 and 1975, where the first seven harmonics are reflected in a subharmonic series, so establishing a species of harmonic dualism analogous to the differential between the major and minor chords or modes.[1] The durations of the pitches are determined quasi-serially by their place in the harmonic/subharmonic series. Therefore, if the fundamental is given a value of a quaver, the seventh harmonic is given a value of seven quavers, etc. However, given that he puts no requirement upon his performers to actually intone the seventh harmonic accurately, being content to operate within the domain of equal temperament, his system may be regarded to be a referential, rather than an intonational or functional system.

Some composers today though are requesting that the seventh harmonic should be intoned as accurately as possible. A good example is the American composer, La Monte Young (b. 1935), who in his improvisatory piano piece *The Well Tuned Piano* (1964), required the piano be retuned in just intonation. In this and subsequent works, La Monte Young tends to place emphasis on pure fifths and natural sevenths at the expense of the thirds, given their association with the triads of Classical harmony.[2]

Another composer engaged in independent experimentation with regard to the seventh, and often other higher prime numbered harmonics, is Ben Johnston. For him the twelve note equally tempered scale does nothing but to anchor musical practice and thinking in what to him is tantamount to an acoustical deception which we are all more or less guilty of perpetuating. This notion is succinctly expressed in his notes to the recording of his fourth string quartet: *Over the whole of the historical period of instrumental music Western music has based itself upon an acoustical lie. In our time this lie - that the normal musical ear hears twelve equal intervals within the span of an octave - has led to the impoverishment of pitch usage in our music.*[3]

In his *Mass* of 1972, Johnston endeavours to expand the framework of intervallic reference by deliberately incorporating septimal intervals. His system of pitch organisation he calls *proportional organisation of pitch*.[4] Intuitively based on the principle of valency, such an approach to pitch organisation can only be described as deeply perceptive. Other works in which he deliberately

[1] Peter Hill,'The Chinese Song-Cycles of Brian Dennis, Tempo, June 1981, 137.

[2] Edward Strickland, Minimalism: Origins, Indiana University Press, Bloomington and Indianapolis 1993, 167-73.

[3] Paul Rapoport, Towards the Infinite Expansion of Tonal Resources, in: Tempo 144, March 1983, 7 - 11.

[4] Randall Shinn, Ben Johnston's Fourth String Quartet, in: PNM 15/2, 1975, 145 - 173.

employs the seventh harmonic include *One Man* (1967) for trombone, *Rose* (1971), the *Fourth String Quartet*, and *Innocence* (1975).[1]

For Johnston, the prime number seven is an important contributory dimension to the network of musical relations. As he himself so succinctly puts it: *Each prime number used in deriving a harmonic scale contributes to a characteristic psychoacoustical meaning. One to one is the relationship of identity; two to one, of recurrence or repetition. Three to one (or three to two) contributes polarity, a sense of gravity, of right side up and upside down (e.g. the root/fifth relationship, and the tonic dominant relationship). Five, in combination with the other prime relationships, contributes major-minor coloration. In a manner analogous to the scale derivations given above, other prime numbers can be introduced into rational pitch scales. There would be no point in introducing a new prime into harmonic usage unless its psychoacoustic meaning were quite distinct. To hazard a guess based on consonant use of the dominant 7th chord (tuned in the ratio 4:5:6:7) prime number seven may be said to contribute a sense of centralised instability, suspending the dominant-tonic (3 to 2) polarity.*[2]

Here it is interesting to see that Johnston is not only recognising the various mathematical dimensions of musical tone as determined by the prime numbers of the harmonic series, but he is also endeavouring to attribute particular qualities and functions to the phenomenon which fall under their respective domain. The functions of septimal intervals it will be seen, he views after the fashion of Euler, that is as dominant agents.

Another composer deliberately exploring the intonational possibilities of the seventh harmonic is the Canadian composer James Tenney (b.1934). In his pieces *Bridge* of 1984, and *Changes*, composed a year later, he explores the possibilities of the septimal interval whose ratio is 8/7. Gayle Young describes his attitudes to this type of exploration, observing that *he is concerned with the attempt to allow sounds to be heard as phenomena. Combinations of sounds are not intended to form expressive gestures or to illustrate extra-musical ideas, but to be perceived simply as structures of sound for their interest.*[3]

For Tenney the value of the prime number seven does not lie in its alliance with particular musical functions, but as a generator of intervals which possess their own unique and innate aural qualities. Seduced by the charm of septimal intervals, his music aims specifically at breaking down our conventional listening

---

[1] John Fonville, Ben Johnston's Extended Just Intonation: A Guide for Interpreters, in: PNM 29, No. 2, 1991, 106 - 137.

[2] Ben Johnston, Scalar Order as a Compositional Resource, in: PNM 2/2, 1964, 74.

[3] Gayle Young, The Pitch Organization of Harmonium for James Tenney, PNM 26/2, 1988, 210.

patterns in an attempt to open up new avenues of aural awareness. The importance of his music thus seems to lie in this, rather than in the conventional notion of 'self-expression' as it is ordinarily understood Here can be seen a different fundamental approach to the theoretical problems posed by the number seven. By concentrating on the aural qualities of septimal intervals, rather than their function within a tonal scheme, composers such as Tenney are availing themselves of a new mathematical dimension of tonal connection, one which, perhaps, is highly necessary for the further development of the already impoverished musical language of the late twentieth century.

FUNCTIONAL INTONATION AND ITS INFLUENCE ON THE PERCEPTION OF THE '7/4' RELATION

From the trend discussed in the last chapter it would seem that a keen interest in the possibilities of the prime number seven seems to be growing. In this respect it is possible that history might be repeating itself. As once there existed a schism between a theory which admitted only to the prime number three limit of Pythagoreanism, and a practice which admitted to consonant thirds and sixths deriving from the prime number five, so perhaps such a schism has been occurring in more recent times in relation to the prime numbers five and seven. Although considerably complicated by the issue of temperament,[1] conventional harmonic theory is still rooted in the prime numbers two, three and five that Descartes had recognised hundreds of years back. Yet musical practice from at least the eighteenth century onwards, points towards an increasing participation of the prime number seven.

Conflict Between Theory and Practice as it Appears on Two Levels

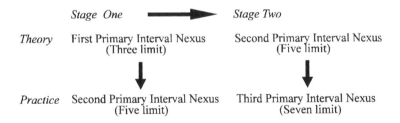

One way in which the prime number seven seems to have found a niche is through the characteristic media of vocal and string intonation. Not being fretted, the stringed instruments have always possessed that marvelous

---

[1] See chapter 12 - 'Chromatic relations and temperament' - for a relevant discussion of the issue of temperament.

flexibility of intonation which, allowing the players to use intervals of different sizes as are characteristic of just intonation, is second perhaps only to the human voice. In string music therefore, there are first rate opportunities to exploit the charm of septimal intervals.

The virtuoso violinist and composer Tartini showed a very keen interest in the 7/4 relation, observing that: *This interval is very easily produced on the violin, and arises from the natural harmonic series: it is produced naturally on marine and 'da fiato' trumpets and also on hunting horns - instruments which are not subject to human reason but function according to the laws of physics and harmony.*[1]

Considering the relative ease by which this relationship can be produced on string instruments, it is interesting to observe that from about the nineteenth century onwards, attempts seem to have been made to bring the seventh of the dominant into a closer relationship with the ratio of 7/4.[2] This practice greatly contrasts with previous centuries where the stringed instruments tended to employ just intonation. As Barbour observes *as early as 1588 Zarlino had stated that voices, violins and trombones intone justly, in contrast to the meantone temperament of the keyboard and the equal temperament of the fretted instruments.*[3] Now according to Barbour, this predisposition towards the rendering of pure intervals lasted until about the middle of the eighteenth century. He states: *violinists of all schools, at least until the middle of the 18th century played in just or in meantone intonation.*[4] In contrast to equal temperament, the consequences of this type of intonation, is that it respects the differences between enharmonically equivalent notes such as *F#* and *Gb*.

Here the relationship between the sharps and flats becomes a salient feature. In just (and meantone) intonation, the flats are higher in pitch than the enharmonically equivalent sharps. This means that *C#*, in a chord of the augmented sixth - *Eb G C#* - would be intoned lower than *Db* of the dominant seventh chord *Eb G Db*.

In the popular tuning lore of the eighteenth-century, this difference between *C#* and *Db* (for example) was accounted for as the differential between the minor semitone: *C - C#*, and the major semitone: *C - Db*. This view is implicit in the way the singer and musical theorist Pier Francesco Tosi writes in 1723: *Everyone knows there is a semitone Major and Minor because the Difference*

---

[1] Guissepe Tartini, Trattato di Musica, Padua 1754, 126. Extract kindly translated for the purposes of this study by Laura Davey.

[2] For a study of the various issues surrounding this see Jutta Stüber's Die Intonation des Geigers, Bonn 1989.

[3] James Murray Barbour, Violin Intonation in the 18th. Century, in: JAMS 5/3, 1952, 224 – 235.

[4] Ibid.

cannot be known by an Organ or Harpsichord if the Keys of the Instrument are not split. A tone...is divided into nine almost imperceptible intervals, five of which constitute the Semitone Major and four the Minor. [1]

Table of Intervals Measured in Cents in Just, Meantone and Pythagorean Tuning

Note (from C)	Just	Meantone	Pythagorean
C	0	0	0
C#	92	76	114
Db	112	117	90
D	204	193	204
D#	275	269	318
Eb	316	310	294
E	386	386	408
F	498	503	498
F#	590	579	611
Gb	610	621	588
G	702	697	702
G#	772	772	816
Ab	814	814	792
A	884	890	906
A#	977	966	1020
Bb	1018	1007	996
B	1088	1083	1110
C	1200	1200	1200

Here Tosi is expressing the difference between the major and minor semitones in terms of the 'Musicians Cycle' - a division of the octave into fifty-five equal units which approximate in size to a syntonic comma. The major semitone has five commas, and thus corresponds to the diatonic semitone of 16/15, the semitone which occurs between adjacent pitch classes. The semitone minor has four commas and is thus the chromatic semitone (135/128), which occurs when a given pitch class is sharpened or flattened.

In this system the flats are higher than enharmonically equivalent sharps. However, at some time during the late eighteenth and early nineteenth century a change in policy with regard to melodic intonation is evident. Principally, this

---

[1] Bruce Haynes, Beyond Temperament: Non-keyboard Intonation in the 17th. and 18th. Centuries, in: EM XIX/3, 1991, 357.

revolved around the felt necessity for raising or lowering tendency tones such as the leading note or seventh of the dominant, towards the direction of their inclination i.e. the leading note would be sharpened, whilst the seventh of the dominant would be flattened. The result of this is that flats were played lower than sharps - as found in Pythagorean intonation. As explained by Chesuit: *Several nineteenth century violin teachers...explicitly recommended shading pitches in the direction of their 'attachment' as defined by harmonic context, in order to achieve an 'animated' performance....we might call such a tuning system 'functional intonation'. In such a system tendency tones, such as the leading tone and the seventh of the dominant seventh chord are inflected in the direction of their tendency to resolve, diatonic steps are smaller than chromatic half steps, and sharped notes are higher than enharmonically equivalent flatted notes. Present day string intonation seems to follow this 19th century practice.*[1]

Although the tuning of stringed instruments in fifths (and basses in fourths) may have something to do with this predisposition towards Pythagorean intervals in melodic voice leading, it cannot explain similar tendencies observed in unaccompanied choirs - a raising or lowering of pitches in the 'direction of their attachment'. Because we have become accustomed to this performance practice, the leading note and dominant seventh used in both meantone and just intonation are sometimes adjudged to be too flat and sharp respectively.[2] However, when the leading note is thus sharpened, the major third between the dominant and leading note is thus distorted, and brought away from its perceptible ratio of 5/4 with the dominant.

Kraehenbuehl and Schmidt (1962) see a positive advantage to this. Viewing it as one of the last vestiges of Pythagorean tuning, they argue that the complexity this gives to the intonation of the chord of the dominant enhances its effective resolution to the tonic triad as the point of harmonic repose.[3] In this way, this particular feature of voice leading may not be so injurious to the harmonic relations between the different parts. On the contrary, it gives the dominant chord a degree of tension which the authors feel is quite apt.

Similarly, when the seventh of the dominant, which in just intonation has a ratio of 9/5, is flattened in the 'direction of its attachment' it is also brought closer to the septimal interval of 7/4. Consequently, 'functional intonation' with its characteristic use of the *notes sensibles* seems to favour the Eulerian theory of the dominant seventh. Here, Barbieri observes that: *In the eighteenth*

---

[1] John Hind Chesuit, Mozart's Teaching of Intonation, in: JAMS 30, 1977, 254 - 271, 256.

[2] Helmholtz, On the Sensations of Tone, 315.

[3] David Kraehenbuehl and Christopher Schmidt, On the Development of Musical Systems, in: JMT6, 1962, 32 - 65.

century the natural tendency to lower the tuning of the flats was probably one of the factors that favoured attempts to introduce in practise the seventh harmonic, until then considered the diabolus in musica.....the minor seventh generated by the seventh harmonic (whose ratio is 7/4) is in fact, from the melodic point of view 'compassionable' almost to the point of caricature. Its character is derived from the fact that it lies only a little more than half a semitone from the note to which it must resolve.[1]

Yet Barbieri's observations are not strictly correct. The seventh harmonic of the dominant (21/16 - 471 cents) lies some 85 cents (21/20) above the major third degree (5/4 - 386 cents) of the scale to which it would 'resolve', so making it much more than half a semitone, since half a semitone would be only about 50 cents. Between is an interval which is more akin to a complete minor semitone.

Barbieri's general observation however, is extremely interesting. The result of intoning the seventh flatter, as he suggests, and therefore by the same token the sixth of an augmented sixth chord sharper, is a complete reversal of the intonational polarity between the two intervals: the dominant seventh would correspond more closely with the interval of 7/4, and the augmented sixth would correspond more closely to a justly intoned minor seventh. Harmonics 4:5:6:7 according to this view, would thus indeed give a chord of the dominant seventh.

But there again, the issue is not as simple as it might appear. According to the principles of functional intonation, the third of the dominant seventh is closer to the Pythagorean than the justly intoned norm, which would give an approximate ratio for the third of 81/64. If the seventh is taken as 7/4, means that the diminished fifth between B and F would have a ratio of 112/81 (561 cents). This is a rather small diminished fifth, a syntonic comma short of 7/5 which the Eulerian dominant requires.

The result is a scrambling of harmonic theory in favour of a melodic intonation which doesn't quite make logical sense. To endeavour to cite 'functional intonation' in support of the Eulerian theory of the dominant seventh therefore, is not without its dangers. Functional intonation after all, is not, and never was intended to be, a new theory of harmonic relations, but a performance practice designed to enhance the expressivity of melodic lines.

Solo work offers performers great flexibility with regard to their expressive use of intonation. Ensemble work however, tends to be moderated by harmonic considerations. This was pointed out as far back as the second half of the nineteenth century by the physicists Cornu and Mercadier (1869), who found that a major third, when sung as a melodic interval, was intoned slightly sharp.

---

[1] Patrizio Barbieri, Violin Intonation: A Historical Survey, in: EM XIX/1, 1991, 83-4.

Sung as a harmonic interval however, it corresponded more to the ideal harmonic ratio of 5/4.[1] Trained musicians it was found, employed either functional or just intonation depending upon the context. For the melodic setting of an interval, functional intonation was used, whilst for its harmonic setting, just intonation.[2] Observing these tendencies, Cornu and Mercadier came to the conclusion that *the Pythagorean and the syntonic mean-tone scales, in theory mutually exclusive, were compatible: the former was preferred in melodic contexts, the latter in harmonic ones.*[3]

Music performed in this apparently inconsistent fashion seems to be more interesting to the ear. Endless successions of pure consonant intervals have only a limited appeal, for after a while they can strike the ear as being rather bland. When some of those intervals are stretched through the action of expressive melodic forces the result is a peculiar and enjoyable tension generated between the conflicting requirements of the horizontal and vertical orientations of the music.

Here the very idea of stretching an interval, rather as if it was like a piece of material which possessed elastic properties, is something which also needs to be pondered. If a perfect fifth, whose ratio is 3/2 is stretched, does this not mean that in effect, another interval has been put in its place? Objectively speaking, the answer would have to be yes, for the slight raising of the upper note may alter the ratio from say 3/2, to 76/50. Mathematically speaking, these are two quite different intervals. However, as Martin Vogel has already observed: *It has often been proved that an intuitively comprehended tone ratio is often different from the acoustically given ratio. In such cases the apperceived proportion is simpler than the real one ....The ear is accustomed to tolerating a light deviation from a simple numerical ratio and hearing the simpler one.*[4]

Practically speaking therefore, the interval of ratio 76/50 would present itself to the ear as a perfect fifth which is slightly sharp. The pure consonant intervals with their simple ratios, are thus providing the basic aural percepts which allow us to enjoy and appreciate this particular type of tension in the first place. Offering the basic standards against which deviations are measured and compared, it would thus be foolish to reject these in favour of some kind of regressive Pythagorean tuning.

Endeavouring to contextualise the practice of functional intonation therefore, it is clearly necessary to view the matter on two levels. First there are the

---

[1] Andrew G. Pikler, History of Experiments on the Musical Interval Sense, in: JMT10/1, 1966, 77.
[2] Ibid., 78.
[3] Ibid., 84.
[4] Martin Vogel, On The Relations of Tone, 163.

defining characteristics of the harmonic relations implied within a piece of music, for which purpose the standards and values of just intonation i.e. intervals as defined by their natural valent bonds, as expressed by whole number ratios would seem to be valid. Secondly, there is the factor of the variability of particular pitches introduced either for expressive and functional purposes, or through the facility of temperament.

Here, our tolerance for deviations from the acoustical norms prescribed for musical intervals, obviously varies depending upon the interval. Here Dirk de Klerk observes that *Since the human ear is most sensitive to deviations in the intervals with the simplest frequency ratios, the latter must fulfil the highest requirements of perfection. So for the minor third and seventh harmonic, we can tolerate somewhat larger deviations than for the fifth and major third.*[1]

Consequently, it may be argued that it is just intonation that defines the basic standard of a given interval, against which the magnitudes of its variability can be measured and charted. Cazden suggested this solution to the problem as far back as 1958, observing that: *the Pythagorean norms for intonation' (i.e. simple whole number ratios) 'describe correctly objective standards for the measurement and psycho-acoustic identification of the terms of musical relations' but that these are not necessarily valid for the 'variable magnitudes dependent upon collocation and function.*[2]

In effect therefore, this means that it might be wholly inappropriate to use functional intonation as a support for the theory of the Eulerian dominant, or indeed, as a general signpost of the further development or evolution of harmonic relations into the realms of the next prime number - seven. Indeed, considering the conflicting opinions which have been presented so far concerning the possibilities of the prime number seven, it is extremely doubtful that the problem of seven has, yet, received a satisfactory solution.

---

[1] Dirk de Klerk, Equal Temperament, in: AcM LI, 1979, 140-141.
[2] Norman Cazden, Pythagoras and Aristoxenus Reconciled, in: JAMS XI, 1958, 97–105.

THE '7/4' RELATION AS CHROMATIC INTERVAL OF THE AUGMENTED SIXTH

If the way in which functional intonation favours the Eulerian dominant is secondary to its intended effect i.e. to enhance the suggestion of voice leading within the music, then where does this leave the 7/4 relation? Here it may come as a surprise when it is said that this leaves it in a very strong position, for the interval whose ratio is 7/4 may yet prove to be indicative of a further or more refined tonal capability than has hitherto been attributed to it.

Simple common sense indicates that if music did enter into a new domain of intervallic generation using the seventh partial as a bond of connection between musical tones, it is probable that such intervals would participate in a full and uninhibited fashion. One of the problems with the Eulerian dominant is that, excluding secondary or applied dominants, there is only one dominant seventh chord in a particular key. Therefore, the participation of septimal intervals is kept to a bare minimum.

The principle of valency points to the full and balanced participation of the entire range of intervals which belong to a particular level or dimension of tonal space. In corroboration of this, the interval of 5/4 which represents the principal generator of the third dimension of frequency space, generates a number of important intervals, all of which participate within that three-dimensional continuum of relationships in a full and convincing fashion.

7/4 is only one of a number of primary intervals which belong at the next level up from the prime number five. Representing the four prime numbers at play (2,3,5 and 7) by the letters A, B, C and D, where A represents the second, B the third, C the fifth and D the seventh, it will be seen that all of the following count as intervals which represent a primary valent bond between musical tones.

There are thus twelve primary intervals at this level, of which the first two are 3-valent intervals, and the four after this the 5-valent intervals. Therefore, there are six primary intervals in which the prime number seven is a direct participant. Dividing into two groups of three, those in the first column are the inversions of those in the second column. So the most important septimal intervals are the three in the second column, which have ratios of 7/4, 7/5 and 7/6 respectively. In accordance with the basic principles of valency, these present themselves as the principal players of the septimal complex of intervals.

Primary Intervals at the Level of Four Dimensional Frequency Space

A	B	4/3	B	A	3/2
A	C	8/5	C	A	5/4
B	C	6/5	C	B	5/3
A	D	8/7	D	A	7/4
B	D	12/7	D	B	7/6
C	D	10/7	D	C	7/5

In the chord of the dominant seventh these do appear in the relations between the internal components of the chord, and are brought into focus within the respective inversions of the dominant seventh. But the whole point of valency, is that it generates a web of relations which surround and encompass a given tone, and which give that tone the possibility of movement or replication along predefined pathways. To fix these possibilities within the provenance of the chord of the dominant seventh is a severe curtailment and limitation of septimal possibilities.

Therefore the distinction made by Helmholtz between the minor seventh and the sub-minor seventh is one which identifies the seventh harmonic by proxy, and therefore gives it a recognised name for the purposes of classification. However, the name itself automatically makes two assumptions: first, that the interval whose ratio is 7/4 is categorically perceived by the listener as a form of minor seventh, and second, that there is actually a place in the system of tonality for such a 'sub-minor' intervallic modality. If there is, then it would seem to have no recognisable function within the tonal system aside from assisting in the realisation of a rather bland rendition of the chord of the dominant seventh. Furthermore, not only is the rendition itself bland, but there would seem to be no actual necessity for it within the tonal system.

Yet, as a prime number, and therefore an original connective pathway between musical tones, it follows that the ratio 7/4 may signify a musical interval which is not only new to the diatonic system, but also the bearer of new tonal functions. Indeed, it is probably only this which might eventually justify the full recognition of the prime number seven: the fact that its usage either explains or supports new functional territories of tonal relationship and design. The 'sub-minor seventh' brings nothing new to the system of tonality, aside from a preferential intonation of a particular chord. To pass the prime number seven off as the progenitor of dominant harmony, may thus be to curtail any further possibilities for the enrichment and reinvigoration of the matrix of tonal functions. Consequently, the terms 'sub-minor seventh' and 'natural seventh', although providing a convenient tag for the seventh harmonic, may in fact provide a barrier against any further progress in this area.

It is clear that intervals deriving from the prime number seven do have very specific and recognisable qualities. It is equally clear that such intervals may be usable within a tonal context. However, as long as such terms as 'sub-minor seventh' persist, it is difficult to see any further progress can be made beyond this point. Yet if usage of the terms 'sub-minor seventh' and 'natural seventh' is avoided, one is faced with a nameless interval, and therefore an empty theoretical void where before there was at least a name, a label, or a functional tag that meant something. Perhaps this is the best place from which to approach the prime number seven: without the baggage of a descriptive nomenclature that assumes for itself a function which is not fully apparent in composed Western music.

On the other hand, it may be possible to devise an alternative name for this interval. The association between the seventh partial and the minor seventh is one which is prompted more than anything else by association, i.e. the fact that the minor seventh is the nearest interval to 7/4 in the tonal system. But is it? Looking more closely at those intervals which lie more or less within close proximity to the interval whose ratio is 7/4 an extremely interesting observation can be made. Here, there are a number of candidates for association with 7/4, of which the minor seventh is just one. One of these, already mentioned in the last chapter, is the diminished seventh resulting from the sum of three minor thirds of ratio 6/5. Then there is the interval of the augmented sixth: a chromatic interval obtained by sharpening the upper note or flattening the lower note of a major sixth. This has a ratio of 225/128.

An examination of the differences between these intervals shows that neither of the two forms of minor seventh are actually the closest intervals to the seventh harmonic. Indeed, the diminished seventh (216/225) is nearer to the seventh harmonic than both forms of minor seventh. But the nearest interval of all is the augmented sixth (ratio of 225/128), which is only 7 cents larger than 7/4, an interval of some 1/26th. of a tone. If, therefore, the identity of the seventh harmonic was decided on the grounds of how close it was to a particular interval within the tonal system, it could not possibly be the minor seventh. The only feasible candidate would the interval of the augmented sixth. Indeed, since the augmented sixth is only some 1/26th. of a tone larger than the seventh harmonic it is extremely doubtful that the ear could detect any difference between them.

Sizes of Intervals in Close Proximity to 7/4 (969 Cents)

Interval:	Dim. 7th.	Aug. 6th.	Min. 7th.	Min. 7th.
Ratio:	216/125	225/128	16/9	9/5
Cents:	947	976	996	1018
Diff.:	- 22	+7	+27	+49

Recalling for a moment the functioning of the basilar membrane, it became apparent that those intervals which represented primary valent bonds were key factors in the aural interpretation of pitch relationships. Intervals of extremely complex ratios, or the irrational ratios of equal temperament, were found to be interpreted according to the nearest familiar resonance patterns to which they could be matched. Consequently, the augmented sixth of ratio 225/128, being almost exactly the same breadth, would be perceived by the ear as the interval whose ratio is 7/4. This would occur because the resonance patterns elicited by the former, would correspond almost exactly with the resonance patterns elicited by the latter. In simple terms this would mean that the ear would perceive the two intervals as being identical.

The major third in equal temperament is some 14 cents larger than the just major third of 5/4, but the ear has no difficulty whatsoever in recognising the implied third of 5/4: the difference between them is simply not large enough to evoke the recognition of a new intervallic modality. It can thus be appreciated that with a difference of only 7 cents between the augmented sixth and the seventh harmonic, the ear will give deference to the interval of the simplest ratio. Consequently, the augmented sixth will be heard as having a ratio of 7/4. Accordingly, the interval formed by the seventh and fourth harmonics should rightly be described not as a form of minor seventh but as an augmented sixth. Of course it may reasonably be objected that in the Western scale of tempered semitones such a distinction is purely academic, since the minor seventh and augmented sixth are struck by the same notes. This means that they could be viewed to be the same interval which is simply spelled differently.

But this type of thinking is extremely crude, and does not do any justice to the sensible realities which underlie the fabric of musical intervals. The realities being referred to are of course those valent connections between musical tones prompted by the harmonic series, and by which the ear establishes the relationship between musical tones. Viewed from the standpoint of these bonds the augmented sixth and minor seventh intervals are quite different from one another and have different functions and implications. Viewed within the terms of three-dimensional frequency space, the augmented sixth is a rather remote interval when compared with the minor seventh, as can be easily discerned by looking at the number of valent connections which separate the prototypical tone C (1/1) from the augmented sixth, note A# (225/128):

Valent Connections Involved in the Derivation of the Interval of the Augmented Sixth

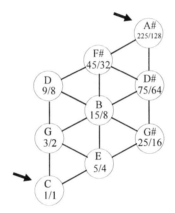

Here it is quite problematic to try to equate the augmented sixth with the interval of the minor seventh. They are fundamentally different from one another, and derive from different areas of the tonal network. But even accepting first, that there is a difference between the minor seventh and the augmented sixth, and second that the ear may take the interval of the augmented sixth to be 7/4, then what possible significance can this have? Is it not just quibbling over identities which in an equal tempered context do not matter anyway? The augmented sixth would seem to be a relatively unimportant chromatic interval that cannot possibly match the importance or magnitude of an interval of the order of the minor seventh. So even if 7/4 is viewed as an augmented sixth, what possible advantage can this have over the view that is a minor seventh?

Before these questions can be satisfactorily answered, the first task is to see whether this basic observation obtains any corroboration in the history of musical theory. It would be very surprising if such a close correspondence between the augmented sixth and the interval 7/4 has not been observed before. It is a quite remarkable correspondence, one which could lead not only to a more accurate prognosis of the possibilities of the prime number seven, but even to the possibility of a precise exposition of the musical possibilities which it embraces.

Here investigation shows that theorists from as far back as the sixteenth century supposed that the seventh harmonic gave an interval of an augmented sixth. A very good example, is the Italian composer and theorist Nicola Vicentino (1511-75). A pupil of Adrian Willaert (1490-1562), Vicentino is best known for his uncompromising attempts to revive the ancient Greek chromatic and enharmonic genera within a perspective where they could be viewed as a valuable addition to the Western musical resource.[1]

His 31-toned archicembalo ostensibly allowed the accurate rendition of the microtones which a realisation of the enharmonic genera required. In his *L'antica Musica Ridotta alla Moderna Prattica* (Rome, 1555) Vicentino describes the derivation of his thirty-one note scale. For tuning purposes, he employs a form of meantone tuning. Yet, as Barbour is at pains to point out, each interval is also conceived to have a specific ratio, that is, in just intonation.[2]

Vicentino's Harmonic Intervals[3]

Partial: 1 2   3   4   5   6   7   8   9   10 11 12 13 14 15 16 18 20 21 22

Because he omits the nineteenth and seventeenth harmonics, means that Vicentino has evolved a scale which operates within a prime number thirteen limit. Fascinating though this may seem, Vicentino's precise use of these intervals, and the identities he ascribes to prime numbers higher than seven, extend beyond the bounds of this present chapter. Although it would be interesting to focus more specifically on Vicentino's work, at this stage it will be

---

[1] For a discussion of Vicentino's work, and its perspective within the Italian chromatic repertory, see Karol Berger's Theories of Chromatic and Enharmonic Music in Late 16th Century Italy, UMI Research Press 1980.

[2] J. Murray Barbour, The History of Equal Temperament from Ramis (1482) to Rameau (1737), Ph. D. Dissertation, Cornell University 1932, 62.

[3] Ibid., 63.

sufficient to focus upon the one really relevant piece of information: the identity he ascribes to tone number seven - *A#*.

Vicentino regards tone number seven to be *A#*, and not *Bb*. Therefore the interval whose ratio is 7/4 is being viewed as an augmented sixth, not a minor seventh. That this is not an accidental or careless position can be gauged from his identification of the 21st. harmonic. Lying a perfect fifth above the fourteenth harmonic it should be represented as an *E#* rather than an *F*. The scheme above does indeed represent 21/16 as an augmented third - *C* to *E#*. In this sense, his representation of 7/4 by the note A# is a result of the application of a musical logic which is consistent with this premise. Is, however, Vicentino's position an isolated one, or have other theorists had similar views?

To answer these questions it is necessary to observe that when tone number seven is identified as A#, a number of significant features arise which seem to have some kind of bearing on the issue of ancient Greek musical scales. Lying between the numbers 6 and 8, tone number 7 presents itself somewhere between the perfect fourth from notes G to C (assuming a fundamental of *C*). Taken together they form a three note figure which utilises the pitch classes *G A# C*. Here, there is a pitch missing which is the note corresponding to the fifteenth harmonic - note B. Identifying tone 7 as *A#* thus immediately implicates it in a chromatic tetrachord.

Chromatic Tetrachord Implicated by Harmonics Six, Seven and Eight

Ratio: 3/2 7/4 15/8 2/1

Through implicating a chromatic tetrachord in this fashion, it also implicates, through duplication of the same tetrachord in the lower segment of the octave a complete seven note septimal scale:

Septimal Scale Derived from Two Chromatic Tetrachords

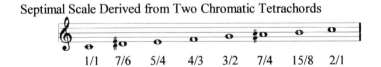

1/1 7/6 5/4 4/3 3/2 7/4 15/8 2/1

Now whilst no claims are being made for this scale, it does serve to demonstrate the way possibilities begin to open up when tone seven is identified as *A#;* possibilities which are essentially new, or different to the diatonic complex defined and operable within the prime number five limit. In the sixteenth and seventeenth centuries such structures automatically suggested ancient Greek scales to theorists. This is self evident in the foregoing statement by John Wallis (1616 - 1703), and cited by Wilfrid Perret in *Some Questions of Musical Theory*: *How does it come about that with so many men writing on Greek music nobody seems to have noticed that one of our earliest and best workers in this field, the learned and ingenious Dr. Wallis, clearly pointed to the seventh harmonic as a clue?   In his 'Remarks' appended to Thomas Salmon's 'Proposal to perform Musick in Perfect and Mathematical Proportions' (London, 1688, p. 40) Wallis wrote, 'If I would divide the proportion of 3 to 4, or 6 to 8, into two near equals, those are to be 6 to 7, and 7 to 8: and therefore C D# as 6 to 7, and D# F as 7 to 8.....And such arts we must make use of, if we would revive the Greeks Chromatick and Enharmonick Musick. But the speculation is too nice for most of our present practisers.*[1]

The theory that the prime number seven provided firm leads into the precise nature of ancient Greek musical scales persisted into the next century and beyond. It is probable that such theories aimed more at trying to revive the ancient Greek chromatic and enharmonic genera within a context that would be applicable to the modern harmonic system, than to explain actual ancient Greek musical practice. It is in this sense that the theorist Jean Adam Serre (1704 - 1788) wrote in 1753: *It is not surprising that the theory which, so to speak, drowns the commas and the quartertones in the modern temperament, and moreover banishes from harmony, without any modification, without any reservation, the sound.....expressed by the ratio 4/7, as a false and non-harmonic sound - it is not surprising, I say, that this theory gives us no enlightenment as to the origin and the possibility of the enharmonic of the ancients.*[2]

Here the important issue does seem to be the precise identity ascribed to the interval whose ratio is 7/4.   Rather than being a minor seventh, it is an augmented sixth. This becomes apparent in Serre's statement: *if C is to E as 4 to 5, and C to G as 2 to 3, and G to E# as 4 to 7, then E is to E# as 5/4 is to 3/2 x 7/4 (21/16) or 21/20.*[3] Here Serre overtly identifies the seventh harmonic as tone A#, and this deduction then leads him to define the ratio of a septimal chromatic semitone: *E* to *E#* of ratio 21/20. Curiously, it is this statement that

---

[1] Wilfrid Perret, Some Questions of Musical Theory, Preface, vii.

[2] Jean Adam Serre, Essais sur les Principes de l'Harmonie, Paris 1753. Also see Wilfrid Perret's Some Questions of Musical Theory, 62, where he acknowledges the strong influence of this essay upon his own thinking.

[3] Ibid.

inspired Wilfrid Perret to design his nineteen-tone septimal scale, although it is something of a mystery as to why Perret switches the identity of the seventh harmonic to a sub-minor seventh.[1]

One of the most cogent attempts at an exposition of the possibilities of the prime number seven to renew the ancient Greek chromatic and enharmonic genera came from Tartini in his *Trattado di Musica*. His reasoning was that harmonic number six gave a limit which was sufficient for the definition of the diatonic system, but not for the chromatic and the enharmonic. To proceed from six to seven, was thus to pass from the sphere of the diatonic to the sphere of the enharmonic.[2] In his treatise Tartini goes on to demonstrate both enharmonic and chromatic species of tetrachords harmonised in two parts. Integral to the design of such tetrachords is the number seven. It is not the place here to try to prove or disprove Tartini's demonstrations, or even to comment upon their validity. The important thing which this chapter is focusing upon is the precise identity ascribed to the seventh harmonic.

Tartini himself approached the seventh harmonic with the same ambiguity as other theorists. Early on in his thesis he speaks of 7/4 as a form of minor seventh,[3] whilst later he demonstrates that really the interval whose ratio is 7/4 would be better understood as a form of augmented sixth: *it now remains for us to look at the fourth term ('termine'), that is, the musical note D#.... The three musical notes (F A C) are 1/4:1/5:1/6. Thus, because the fourth term, the musical note D#, is in harmonic proportion with the three previous notes, it must be 1/7. C - 675, and D - 576, may therefore be compared to the ratio 6:7, or 1/6:1/7. Here there is a minimal rational difference of the ratio 224:225, which is missing from D#. But this differential ratio is much smaller than the ratio 81:80, by which 675 exceeds the true 'sesquiquinta' form, and yet this is admitted to the harmonic system. Thus the much smaller ratio 224:225 should also be admitted to the system, particularly in view of the fact that the difference 80:81 is physically perceptible in terms of the third sound, through which it is physically possible to distinguish between the minor tone and the major. Whereas the difference 224:225 is not physically perceptible, since 1/6:1/7 in the musical notes will give rise to the third sound F. Equally, given (F A C D#) the third sound will also be F, because when the player's finger presses the string it does not differentiate the physical point of a single term of the difference 224:225, but presses on the physical points of both of the above mentioned terms - indeed, it presses on even more than that, and this is a*

---

[1] Perret, Op. Cit., 62.

[2] Tartini, Trattado di Musica, Padua 1754, 126. Excerpt translated by Laura Davey.

[3] Ibid, 126-33.

defect. And in this case, the third sound may be proved physically to be F. Thus the true form is (F A C D#) and it is consonant.[1]

The septimal degree (224/225) which differentiates the seventh harmonic and the augmented sixth intervals, is such a small interval that, as Tartini says, it cannot be physically realised by the player's fingers. To all intents and purposes therefore, the augmented sixth of ratio 225/128 is indistinguishable from the interval 7/4. Those theorists who did identify the seventh harmonic of fundamental tone C, with tone A#, sensed fresh possibilities therein, yet tended to view those possibilities through a revivalist framework which never really bore fruit. The reason for this is that they were probably just too early to witness the maturation of the tonal system to the point where septimal structures, as will be later shown, could be used and assimilated.

Ironically, a more tangible and practicable connection between 7/4 and the interval of the augmented sixth was making itself felt as an automatic consequence of tuning policies adopted in the sixteenth and seventeenth centuries. Church organs tuned according to meantone temperament suffered a deficiency of enharmonic pitches. The notes Gb, Db and Ab had to be played by the notes F#, C# and G# respectively.[2] This meant that the minor sevenths between *Eb-Db* and *Bb-Ab* were really augmented sixths. In meantone temperament, the augmented sixth (966 cents) is almost identical to the seventh harmonic (7/4 = 969 cents). This observation leads Lindley and Smith to assert that in the following example *The Db as VII ..was tuned as C#' - so making it into a septimal sonority.*[3]

Extract from a Frescobaldi's 'Passacagli' of 1673.

Frescobaldi was probably attracted to this chord on account of the peculiar charm arising from its septimal derivation. The chord concerned however, is an augmented sixth chord parading itself as a minor seventh, for no other reason than the fact that the instruments concerned offered no other option.

---

[1] Ibid., 162.

[2] Owen H. Jorgensen, Tuning, Michigan State University Press, East Lansing 1991, 28.

[3] Mark Lindley & Ronald Turner Smith, Mathematical Models of Musical Scales: A New Approach, Verlag systematische Musikwisseschaft GmbH, Bonn 1993, 174.

This type of constraint contributed to the origination of augmented sixth chords. Alexander Ellis observed: *in meantone intonation, the extreme sharp sixth has only 966 cents, and is therefore still closer to the subminor seventh 7/4 = 969 cents. As a matter of fact, on my meantone concertina I find F D# (966 cents) much smoother than F Eb (1007 cents). The chord introducing this interval occurs in three forms. The Italian (Db F B), and the German (Db F Ab B), are simply imitations of the true chord of the dominant seventh (Db F Ab Cb). The French form (Db F G B) is the harshest of all. The G seems merely to be an anticipation of the note of the chord C Eb G on which it resolves.*[1]

Here Ellis comes to some very interesting conclusions. First, he sees that 7/4 provides the acoustic interval which comprises the core of the various forms of augmented sixth chord. Second, he observes that in meantone temperament, which prevailed in England until about 1850, the difference between the augmented sixth and seventh harmonic is only some 3 cents. Meantone temperament strongly favours other important septimal intervals, as can be easily verified in the following table:

Septimal Identities and their Meantone Equivalents

Ratio	Cents	Meantone Interval	Cents	Difference
8/7	231	Diminished third	234	+3
7/6	267	Augmented second	271	+4
9/7	435	Diminished fourth	427	−8
7/5	583	Augmented fourth	580	−3
10/7	617	Diminished fifth	614	+3
14/9	765	Augmented fifth	773	+8
12/7	933	Diminished seventh	931	−2
7/4	969	Augmented sixth	966	−3

The difference between the septimal and equivalent meantone interval is so small as to be almost negligible. An obvious correlation between meantone tempered augmented and diminished intervals and septimal intervals helps Ellis to rationalize how the various chords of the augmented sixth actually arose. He states: *These last three chords... [Ellis is talking of the French, German and Italian sixth chords]... arose in the days of meantone temperament. The chord of the dominant seventh omitting the fifth (Eb G Db) had then to be played with tempered notes (Eb G C#), because there was no Db on the instrument,*

---

[1] Helmholtz, Op. Cit., 337.

and as the seventh harmonic would have been (Eb   G   Db)   the effect was so good that the chord was adopted in writing and distinguished from the chord of the dominant seventh by resolving upwards instead of downwards.[1]

Here Ellis is ascribing chords of the augmented sixth to the influence of the seventh harmonic. He observes that composers, although having an unsatisfactory dominant seventh chord, found the effect of its substitute *Eb G C#* so good, that it itself became a new chord. The effect was so good, moreover, because of the closeness of that chord to the seventh harmonic.

In just intonation the interval 7/4 is extremely close to the augmented sixth. Kirnberger, who also noticed this, said: *there would be good reason to include at least 1/7 in our system. When transposed down to the first octave, this note is in the ratio 4/7 to the fundamental. For the fundamental C, it would fall between A (3/5) and B (8/15); we shall label it 'I'. It is really consonant, and this chord: [C E G I] is not a dissonant seventh chord but a four part chord. This is evident from the fact that in certain cases the best harmonists treat the minor seventh as well as the augmented sixth as consonances, examples of which are well known. The reason for this lies without doubt in the fact that these intervals sound like 4/7. In fact, the augmented sixth (128/225) is only 1/225 larger than 4/7, which is not perceptible; and the minor seventh is only 1/64 larger than 4/7.*[2]

Although he is hesitant to ascribe a precise identity to the seventh harmonic here, his statement that the interval 7/4 is so close to the augmented sixth as not to be perceptible, agrees with Tartini's summing up of the situation. It is thus rather odd that Kirnberger does not ascribe the seventh harmonic the note A#, especially as he tended to use the 7/4 relation in his own compositions as an augmented sixth which resolved outwardly to the octave.[3] Instead he gives it its own symbol of 'I'.

Let us assume that both Tartini and Kirnberger are correct: the seventh harmonic may be an ambivalent interval. Consequently, the configuration of harmonics 4:5:6:7 might have led composers' ears to both dominant seventh and the augmented sixth chords. The problem with this view is that although struck by the same notes (on a tempered instrument), these two chords have such contrasting functions that it is difficult to see how the harmonic configuration 4:5:6:7 lies behind both.

The behaviour of the minor seventh of the dominant chord is completely opposite to the augmented sixth, the one resolving inwardly and down to the next scale step, the other resolving outwardly to the octave:

---

[1] Ibid. 337.

[2] Kirnberger, The Art of Strict Musical Composition, 38.

[3] Martin Vogel, On The Relations of Tone, 117.

Contrasting Resolutions of Minor Seventh and Augmented Sixth

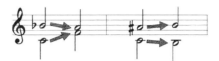

It is patently clear from this that the minor seventh and augmented sixth are different intervals. To imply that the seventh harmonic provides the valent bond behind both intervals is surely to confuse the issue. If this is so, then where do their completely opposite modes of resolution stem from? They can only stem from the fact that the ear perceives the two intervals to be different. The one is a seventh and contracts in upon itself, the other is a sixth, expanded by augmentation, which then continues outwards in the direction of that augmentation. If the seventh harmonic were the natural percept behind both intervals, it is extremely unlikely that they would manifest such contrasting tendencies to the ear. Indeed, it seems more likely that 7/4 is the natural percept behind one of them, but not the other.

Perhaps the positions in the scale in which these chords occur need to be taken into account. In the harmonic form of the chromatic scale there are only two intervals which almost exactly correspond to the interval 7/4. These are the augmented sixth intervals which lie between the notes Db and B, and Ab and F#. Nowhere else in the scale are there any intervals which come as close to the seventh harmonic.[1]

If, therefore, the configuration of harmonics 4:5:6:7 led the ear to any chord, it would probably be the type of augmented sixth chord known as the German Sixth which, for harmonic purposes occurs most commonly in these two positions. These are the two points in the scale where there is an almost exact correspondence with that configuration. The inexactitude is the interval of 224/225, which, as both Tartini and Kirnberger point out, is a difference which is imperceptible. As such, the two augmented sixth chords implied by that scale are the two places where there is the closest mathematical correspondence to the configuration of harmonics 4:5:6:7.

The acoustician Helmholtz observed this, although his thinking is not that clear on account of his classification of the seventh harmonic as the 'natural seventh'. Indeed, speaking of the interval of the minor seventh (16/9) he observes that *this closer minor seventh is the interval of a seventh in the scale nearest to the natural seventh or seventh harmonic, 7/4....although not so close*

---

[1] Martin Vogel, On The Relations of Tone, 117.

as the extreme sharp sixth.[1] Ellis, the translator, has added cents measurements to facilitate the comparison:

Closer minor seventh (16/9)	996
Extreme sharp sixth (225/128)	976
Seventh harmonic (7/4)	969

Clearly, therefore, the seventh harmonic ought to be equated with the latter. On the next page, Helmholtz unwittingly affirms this. Discussing the consonant properties of the augmented sixth, he makes an extremely interesting observation: *The numerical ratio [of the superfluous sixth] is 225/128, so that it is about a comma less than the closer minor seventh of the chord of the dominant seventh......The superfluous sixth may be conceived as composed of two just major thirds and one just major tone....Its harmoniousness is equal to that of the minor sixth, because it is almost exactly the natural seventh 7/4.....When it is inverted into the diminished third 256/225 or nearly 8/7, it is, as already observed considerably damaged, but it is improved by taking the upper tone B an octave higher, in which case it is nearly 7/2. Its near agreement with the natural seventh and its comparative harmoniousness seem to have preserved this remarkable interval in certain cadences, although it is quite foreign to our present tonal system. It is characteristic that musicians forbid its inversion into the diminished third (which lessens its harmoniousness) but allow its extension into the corresponding thirteenth (which improves its harmoniousness).*[2]

It is surprising that he persists with the term 'natural seventh' when he has just implied that the ear takes the augmented sixth to be the seventh harmonic, and it is from this that the interval of the augmented sixth derives its consonant properties. Shirlaw was rather unfair to Helmholtz when he accuses him of not noticing the closeness of the augmented sixth to the seventh harmonic. Shirlaw himself states that: *It appears to have escaped the attention of Helmholtz that the ratio of the augmented sixth F-D# (F = fourth degree of the scale of C major; D# = chromatically raised second degree) approximates more nearly to the ratio of the 'natural' seventh than does the minor seventh G-F = 9:16. Here are the respective ratios:*

Natural seventh 4:7	=	*128:224*
Augmented sixth	=	*128:225*
Minor seventh (9:16)	=	126:224

---

[1] Helmholtz, Op. Cit., 336.

[2] Ibid., 337.

While the difference between the augmented sixth and natural seventh is represented by the extremely small interval 224:225, the difference between the minor seventh g-f and the natural seventh is that of the much larger interval 63:64, an interval larger than the syntonic comma (80:81). It would be more reasonable, therefore, to identify the chord of the augmented sixth with the natural seventh, rather than with the chord of the dominant seventh, as does Helmholtz.[1]

Yet even Shirlaw cannot write on the subject without contradiction, because to identify the chord of the augmented sixth with the natural seventh is to call the natural seventh the augmented sixth! Yet he still persists in calling it the 'natural seventh'.

The confusion which can surround this issue of the identity of the interval 7/4 becomes well apparent in Fokker's summing up of the situation. In his *New Music with 31 Notes* he states that: *the pure seventh, the natural seventh 4/7 can be included in the tonal system. The sum of a second 8/9 and two major thirds has the resultant 8/9 x 4/5 x 4/5 = 128/225. The pure seventh has the resultant 4/7 = 128/224. The difference consists of only 224/225, very little more than 1 in 240 (1/3 in 80), that is, one third of a comma. Logically one can equate these two intervals.....* [2]

With impeccable logic, he points out one of the possible derivations of the augmented sixth interval within the domain of tonal music. The intervals which he adds together to obtain the harmonic augmented sixth of ratio 225/128 form part of a well known form of augmented sixth chord, in which the fifth of the chord of the dominant seventh in third inversion is chromatically raised to give a tendency tone up to the major mediant degree i.e. the third of the tonic major triad:

Chord Implicated in Fokker's Derivation of the Interval of the Augmented Sixth

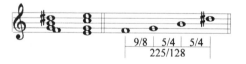

He then points out that the resultant interval 225/128 is extremely close to the interval whose ratio is 7/4 - a difference of only 1 in 240. His summary of the size difference is not quite accurate since it is nearer 1/140. This notwithstanding, he indicates that the breadths of these intervals are so close,

---

[1] Mathew Shirlaw, Theory of Harmony, 376.
[2] Adriaan Fokker, New Music with 31 Notes, 39.

that they can be considered to be interchangeable. In support of this, he points out that in meantone intonation there is even less of a difference between them: *This equation is more easily justified in the meantone system, as here the second is a half comma too small, and therefore the sum of a second and two major thirds approaches the pure seventh more nearly; it is now not more than a third of a comma too large, but rather a sixth of a comma smaller than the seventh 4/7.*[1]

Logically one would have thought that Fokker would arrive at the obvious conclusion to be drawn from this: that the interval 7/4 gives rise to a true harmonic form of the interval of the augmented sixth. However, he presents a twist in the argument which at first seems difficult to fathom: *A glance at the table shows us that intervals such as C to A#, G to E#, D to B#, Ab to F#, Eb to C#, etc., can be viewed as pure sevenths.....Musicians schooled in conventional music theory will object that G to E# is no seventh, but rather an altered sixth, strongly dissonant in the bargain, as the tonal relationship 128/225 shows. This objection we can negate if we furnish the pure seventh with its own form of notation. For that purpose we will use the little hook designed by TARTINI, which indicates a small amount of flattening - a semiflat.*[2]

He describes the resultant augmented sixth intervals rather illogically as 'pure sevenths', and considers that by using Tartini's hook to notate that relationship, he has thereby negated the objection that they are not actually 'sevenths' but augmented sixths. Yet this does not negate the objection, it simply side-steps it by the transference of the 7/4 relation on to a notational plane all of its own. Like Kirnberger's letter 'I', this isolates the 7/4 relation, rather than integrating it clearly and simply into the tonal scheme. To achieve that integration, no such symbols are needed, for as Fokker has pointed out, 7/4 is virtually identical to the augmented sixth.

To notate the 7/4 relation as it is generated from note C therefore, all that is needed is a note A#. Here, however, there is no intention to try to undermine Fokker's contribution to this subject, for it is mostly his work that opened up the subject in the first place. In bringing attention to the possibilities of the 7/4 relation, he has provided a key which, as will be gradually shown through the course of this book, serves to open up the possibilities of an altogether new tonal system: the chromatic system of tonality. In this sense, Fokker was a pioneer whose work represents a great step forward in both the furtherance and understanding of the musical language.

---

[1] Ibid., 39.

[2] Ibid., 40.

The difficulties which theorists have in ascribing a precise intervallic identity to the seventh harmonic are well summed up by Eric Regener (1975): *Since the acceptance of the senario of Zarlino, the number 7 has been the stepchild of intonation theory. In theory textbooks the seventh partial of the fundamental C is usually indicated as Bb, with the disapproving footnote 'out of tune' or 'slightly flat'. The best known theorists are not sure what names to use for ratios involving the number 7. Hindemith (1940, p. 105) suggests that the augmented fourth can be either of the ratios 7:5, or 10:7, implying that the former ratio could be either an augmented fourth or a diminished fifth. Barbour (1953, p. 129) speaks similarly of 'the augmented sixth (that is, the minor seventh, 7/4)'....* [1]

Regener then goes on to discuss what he sees to be the major problem involved: *One source of the theorists difficulties is a failure to dissociate pitch notation from its now standard interpretation in twelve-tone tempered intonation. The enharmonic equivalence of the diminished second and the perfect prime is a unique feature of this particular intonation system, and is not inherent in the notation. In talking about intonation systems in general, the assumption that enharmonically equivalent notes are the same is therefore bound to cause confusion.* [2]

This state of confusion has led some theorists to assert that the minor seventh is the same interval as the augmented sixth, the difference being in the way they are spelled. Regener nonetheless sympathises with the difficulties that the number seven does present to the theorist: *Even in a consistent system, the number 7 poses a real dilemma. Given any ratio including 7 as a prime factor (and no other prime factors other than 2,3 and 5), the corresponding interval will be uniquely determined, providing we can assign an interval with any certainty to any one ratio involving the number 7, say the ratio 7/4. The hesitancy of theorists is based here on the real uncertainty, not necessarily due to the confusion engendered by enharmonic equivalence: it is not clear, as it is with the more fundamental ratios 3/2 and 5/4, what interval is 'meant' by the ratio 7/4.* [3]

Regener's answer is to apply pure mathematics to the problem. [4] Although the processes involved extend beyond the bounds of this book, his conclusion is nonetheless entirely reasonable in the light of the evidence presented in this

---

[1] Eric Regener, The Number Seven in the Theory of Intonation, in: JMT 19/1, 1975, 140-54.

[2] Ibid., 141.

[3] Ibid., 142.

[4] Regener's methodical application of mathematics to the problems posed by intervals and temperament is expounded in his Pitch Notation and Equal Temperament: A Formal Study, University of California Press, Berkeley, Los Angeles, London 1973.

chapter so far. He concludes that *it seems reasonable therefore, to consider 'the augmented sixth as the best interval to represent the ratio 7/4 in an extended system of just intonation.*[1]

Perhaps the last word on the subject should be left to one of the most knowledgeable musicologists in this particular field, Martin Vogel, in both whose works *The Natural Seventh* (1991) and *On The Relations of Tone* (1993) can be found a very serious attempt to come to terms with the dilemma that the prime number seven presents to the theorist. For Vogel, as for other significant figures already mentioned so far in this chapter, the issue is not so clear as it is for Regener. Pure mathematics are only one facet of that larger musical problem which Vogel so well exposes.

Whilst generally upholding the idea that the prime number seven offers a potential source of great enrichment for the language of tone, Vogel feels that every prime number after five *can no longer be represented and described with the letters and signs of our conventional tone system.*[2] This of course, is a very reasonable observation, for our notational system has been developed from a three-dimensional standpoint, which means that its terms derive from the constraints imposed by the thirds, fifths and octaves which serve to define the intricate latticework of tone relations already discussed.

In relation to this constraint Vogel observes that: *Even though we speak of sevenths, we should note that the fundamental interval 7/4 is neither a seventh nor an augmented sixth...but is an independent interval in its own right, which cannot be derived using fifths or thirds. It thus deserves its own nomenclature and its own compositional rules.*[3]

This is true, for the 7/4 relation represents an incipient movement into the terms of an altogether new and relatively unfamiliar fourth dimension of frequency space. It is thus quite befitting that the possibilities of that fourth dimension are not viewed and interpreted from a lesser three-dimensional standpoint. Instead, an effort should be made to accept the 7/4 relation as the pure relationship that it represents. Yet looking back at the course of musical history, an exactly similar argument could be applied to the 5/4 relation. This too is a pure harmonic relation, and there is no divine edict which states that harmonic 5 represents the *E* of the fundamental tone C. The reason that it was assigned the note E is that in a harmonic context it offered a more consonant and therefore easier to sing substitute for the Pythagorean major third of ratio 81/64.

---

[1] Regener, The Number Seven in the Theory of Intonation, 152.

[2] Martin Vogel, On The Relations of Tone, 117.

[3] Ibid..

In this way, a tonal relation which belongs to an altogether new dimension of frequency space managed to obtain a purchase on the network of musical relations, despite the fact that the mathematical terms of the original Pythagorean network precluded its participation. In this respect, the closeness of the augmented sixth of 225/128 to the interval whose ratio is 7/4 is deeply significant, for the ear, seeking the most direct pathway of connection between the two tones concerned, will perceive the latter. The 7/4 relation therefore, offers a pure harmonic form of augmented sixth.

But of course this argument cannot be settled either by mathematics or logic alone. It can only be settled through observation of actual musical practice. This brings the discussion on to the next part of this study where it will be systematically demonstrated that by taking 7/4 to be an interval of the augmented sixth, a key is provided which allows the precise and systematic explanation of many of the important developments of musical harmony belonging to the 18th, 19th and early 20th centuries.

CHROMATIC RELATIONS AND TEMPERAMENT

From the information reviewed so far, there is no universally recognised theoretical approach that satisfactorily answers all of the questions posed by the prime number seven. Is, or is it not a part of the Western system of tonality? Does, or does it not correspond to the interval of the minor seventh? Is it consonant or dissonant? Should it be regarded as an augmented sixth or a minor seventh? Such are some of the perplexing questions that present themselves when the problem of seven is tackled.

There is however, a way of answering most of these questions in such a way as to reconcile many of the conflicting points of view which surround the issue of the prime number seven. The quarter tone difference between the 'natural seventh' of ratio 7/4 and the diatonic minor seventh of the dominant seventh chord is one which seems to be fairly unobtrusive. When compared with the 1/26th. tone difference that separates the augmented sixth (225/128) and the interval whose ratio is 7/4 however, it takes on a different perspective, looming up as a discrepancy which it becomes harder to ignore.

To offer the 7/4 relation its own particular note symbol, as Kirnberger, Tartini and Fokker have done, is one way of dealing with this discrepancy, for then the issue of the precise identity of 7/4 in the tonal complex is not so crucial: the 7/4 relation is what it is, and that is all there is to it. Yet in many ways this is an evasive approach to the problem, for it does not satisfactorily define either the identity or function of that intervallic relation within the tonal scheme. Instead it sets it apart from other tonal relationships, whereas in point of fact the motive is surely to integrate that relationship into the tonal scheme. This is much more problematic because of the changes which have to be made to the original tonal scheme itself as a result of the intrusion of the potent fertilising powers of the seventh harmonic.

Therefore to satisfactorily solve the problem of seven it is necessary to tackle the issue head on, and recognise that whilst the theory of the 'natural seventh' is highly attractive, that most of the evidence indicates the interval whose ratio is 7/4 gives rise to a natural harmonic form of the interval of the augmented sixth.

Having demonstrated that the interval of ratio 7/4 implies the interval of the ugmented sixth more than any other interval, it becomes expedient at this stage to consider the significance of this idea, and what it might mean for the musical language. Solutions to the various problems which surround the consideration of the prime number seven will then start to be cleared up.

Irrespective of the ratio which might be ascribed to the augmented sixth it plays a definite part within the network of tonal relations. Because of the participation of the interval of the augmented sixth within that system, it could reasonably be argued that the prime number seven (that provides the sensible and rational basis for that interval) is offering an important natural signpost to it. The question has to be 'why'?

A major problem which prevents an immediate answer to this question is the perceived conflict between pure intervals as conceived in just intonation (and extended systems of just intonation), and the system of twelve-tone equal temperament. This problem is compounded by the fact that, because of the importance of the piano and the organ in the Western repertoire, those instruments which are not limited to the constraints of equal temperament are often required to accommodate this particular type of tuning.

Consequently there arises the general theoretical axiom that the equally tempered twelve-tone scale is *the* scale of Western music. With this axiom comes the assumption of various theoretical values and proscriptions which directly affect the way in which the interval of ratio 7/4 is viewed. The first is that the interval of ratio 7/4 is 'out-of-tune' with the notes of the equally tempered twelve note scale.

How serious this problem is seen to be, entirely depends upon the standpoint from which it viewed. Similar arguments could be levied upon the intervals of 5/4 and 3/2, both of which are also 'out-of-tune' with twelve-tone equal temperament, the former being 14 cents out from a tempered major third, the latter 2 cents out from a perfect fifth. The only interval in twelve-tone equal temperament which is completely pure is the octave. Admittedly, compared to a discrepancy of 31 cents for the interval of 7/4, the interval of the major third, and especially the interval of the perfect fifth are significantly more 'in-tune' in twelve tone equal temperament.

Here it needs to be recognised that twelve-tone equal temperament was never devised with the interval 7/4 in mind. Originally it was devised for the purposes of a three-dimensional reference system operating within the mathematical constraints of the prime numbers 2, 3 and 5. Because it was originally devised with this limitation in mind, does not necessarily mean that it is a constraint which determines what the composer is able to imagine, or the listener able to hear. A good example of this is the interval of the augmented sixth itself, which may be accorded an initial definition within that three-dimensional format as the interval between the second and eleventh degrees of the chromatic scale (*Db* to *B* in the key of C). Possessing a ratio of 225/128, it too is out of tune with the equal tempered scale, being 24 cents smaller than the tempered minor seventh.

Significantly, this basic fact has not prevented either the participation or usage of this particular interval within the musical language. That the ear in all probability takes 225/128 to be 7/4 does not affect this basic argument, because to assert that 7/4 is 'out-of-tune' with the tempered system, is as irrelevant as saying that the augmented sixth of 225/128 is 'out-of-tune' with the tempered system. The fact is that 7/4 gives an exceedingly 'in-tune' augmented sixth, and the fault lies with the tempered system for not representing that relation more accurately.

This is an important observation, for it serves as a timely reminder that equal temperament is a practical solution to problems posed by the conflict between an ideal realisation of the mathematical relationships inherent between musical tones on the one hand, and the physical limitations of a musical instrument designed with a closed pitch system on the other.

A piano or organ with a separate key for every pure tone implied within the music of the Western repertoire is not only extremely difficult to construct, but it will also be excessively cumbersome to play. Without recourse to electronic musical instruments,[1] and their superior capabilities in this respect, there exists the option of severely limiting the range of mathematical relationships used.[2] Yet this leads to such constraints on the part of the composer that as a general option, it too becomes impractical.

Equal temperament is a necessary compromise between all of these positions. As a result of that compromise, and its universally agreed to availability for all concerned, an unnerving degree of complacency has gradually developed towards those natural tonal relations which equal temperament served to compromise in the first place. Indeed, the horror of the situation lies in the fact that the compromise is now often accepted as the fundamental reality, whilst the natural relations themselves are either ignored, or made folly of.

Consequently, the body of knowledge concerning those note ratios and harmonic proportions which do comprise the fundamental reality of the musical language have now become relegated to the domain of acoustics and the

---

[1] Martin Vogel, Denkschrift zum Bau von Tasteninstrumenten in Reiner Stimuung, 8 - 12.

[2] La Monte Young (b. 1935) tried this with some success in his improvisatory piano piece The Well Tuned Piano (1964) which uses numerous septimal intervals. For more information on this see Edward Strickland's Minimalism: Origins, Indiana University Press, Bloomington and Indianapolis 1993, 167-73.

understanding of the finer points of historical tuning. In some ways it may be supposed that this is advantageous, or even clever. There is no need to worry over ratios and proportions any longer, because equal temperament takes greatly simplifies the network of tonal relations. Through the context in which a pitch or interval is presented, the pure mathematical relationship of which it is an expression can be grasped by the listener.

Yet in simplifying those relations it does not mean that temperament then serves to *replace* those relations. As the twentieth century German composer Paul Hindemith once quite humorously remarked, temperament *is a compromise which is presented to us by the keyboard as an aid in mastering the tonal world, and then pretends to be that world itself.*[1] Aside from the way it obscures those natural relations by which the tonal world is defined, there is another fundamental problem which arises, and that is the enharmonic equivalence of the interval of the augmented sixth and the minor seventh in twelve-tone equal temperament. Sounded by the same notes it seems reasonable to consider that enharmonically contrasting intervals such as the augmented sixth and minor seventh are therefore in fact the same interval.

This position starts to establish itself as early as the nineteenth century. Shirlaw cites an article entitled *'Fundamental'* (author not stated) from the *Encyclopedie ou dictionaire raisonne des sciences, des arts, et des Metiers* (Paris, 1751 - 80) where it observes of the chord of the augmented sixth that *this chord is not in reality a chord of the sixth; for from Fa to Re~ there is really a seventh. It is only custom which makes us persist in giving this chord the name augmented sixth.*[2] Shirlaw quite rightly points out that *The writer here considers that Eb may be substituted at pleasure for D# without in any way altering the tonal significance of the chord, and, like not a few other theorists, is of the opinion that temperament simplifies and reconciles all things.*[3]

Yet there is a grain of truth in this, because the enharmonic equivalence of the German Sixth and dominant seventh chord has been used to good effect by composers for the purposes of enharmonic modulation. Discussing this point in his *Theory of Harmony*, Prout observes that: *This enharmonic change of an augmented sixth to a dominant seventh, and vice versa, is mostly used when a modulation is desired to a key a semitone up or down. If, for instance, in C, the chord of the augmented sixth on Ab is taken, and the F# changed to Gb, the chord becomes the dominant seventh in Db, and can be resolved in that key. It*

---

[1] Paul Hindemith, Craft of Musical Composition, Vol. 1 (Theory), Schott & Co. Ltd., London 1945, 155. See also Partch's comments on this statement in his Genesis of a Music, 422.

[2] Matthew Shirlaw's Theory of Harmony, 279.

[3] Ibid., 279.

might also be quitted as the supertonic seventh of Gb, or the tonic seventh of Ab, but these resolutions, the latter especially, are seldom, if ever to be met with. Conversely, if we take the dominant seventh in the key of C, and change the F to E#, the chord becomes an augmented sixth in B major or minor - possible even in F# major or minor.[1]

Equal temperament makes such a modulation extremely easy. Yet the process of enharmonic modulation depends upon the facility which equal temperament offers of being able to deceive the listener into believing that the note F is in fact an *E#*.

Functionally the two notes are different, but because they are represented by the same pitch in equal temperament such a deception is readily possible. Because that deception has been used so often by composers, does not mean that it has now become a truth. Perspective in painting is a technique of deceiving the eye into accepting that a flat image possesses depth. To start to accept, in the realms of theory, that the note E# is therefore the same as *F* is as preposterous as starting to believe that the image on the canvass really does possess depth.

Despite the illogicality of the view that the note E# is the same as the note F, this is the view often taken today, and taught quite willingly in the study of music at university or academy level. Yet this view of what are obviously two quite different notes or intervals as being the same, is the cause of numerous problems.

Leading to a complete nullification of the distinctions between notes which are considered to be enharmonic equivalents - notes E# and F as mentioned above for example - this occurs in two stages. First, the difference is passed over to one of pure spelling, in which the pitch is the same, but the way in which that pitch is spelled is different. Differences in the spelling of a particular pitch, in their turn, become the prime vehicle of expression for the precise harmonic or melodic function ascribed to that pitch: as the *Eb* of a minor seventh there exists a tendency to resolve stepwise to the tone below; but as the *D#* of an augmented sixth there is a contrary tendency to rise a semitone to the note above. Bearing in mind the behaviour of that pitch, as determined by the direction in which it is moving, it is thus quite appropriate to notate the former as an *Eb*, and the latter as a *D#*. Yet this assumes that the composer is respecting the tendencies of those intervals. At times, the *Eb* may rise, and the *D#* fall, but of course these are exceptions, understood in the context of irregular or unusual modes of intervallic resolution.

The second stage is that because both functions are performed by the same pitch, then it becomes irrelevant how the note is spelled. As long as the

---

[1] Ebenezer Prout, Harmony: Its Theory and Practice, Augener Ltd., London 1903, 282.

performer is aware of the composers intention, the note could be spelled as an *Eb* or a *D#*. On a tempered instrument it makes no difference. Certainly, the listener is not going to worry about this. It is only the perplexed analyst or even the editor, trying later to make sense of an ambiguous chord progression who is going to care about this.

This increasingly deteriorating position is epitomized by Schoenberg in his *Theory of Harmony* who states: *It goes without saying, there is not much point in cracking one's skull over the question whether, because of the harmonic meaning, we should write C# or Db, G# or Ab. We write what is most simple. The shortcoming lies in our imperfect system of notation. In nothing else.*[1] But surely there is no need to 'crack one's skull' simply because all that is being talked about is a simple choice between two options: sharp or flat.

Harmonic meaning is the essence of the tonal language, and should never be compromised in any way. Otherwise the language of harmony can only deteriorate into a set of vaguely understood formulae that might or might not progress in a particularly appropriate fashion.

Any imperfection that might exist in this sphere obviously does not lie in the system of notation, for it has the necessary symbols by which the sharp and the flat may be clearly distinguished. The shortcoming lies in the failure of equal temperament to distinguish between notes such as *C#* and *Db*. Temperament has led to the standardisation of a completely uniform twelve-note octave which denies the finer enharmonic differences and distinctions between musical intervals. Yet these distinctions are the essence of chromatic harmony. The proof of this lies in the observation of the divergence of function between the dominant seventh and German Sixth chords.

As Aldwell & Schachter state *these two chords - so divergent in function but so similar in sonority - provide wonderful opportunities for composers...*[2] This divergence of function hinges upon whether the upper note, assuming the note Ab to be the common generator, is considered to be either an *F#* or a *Gb*. To understand the chromatic harmonic environment in which the interval of the augmented sixth occurs, twelve-tone equal temperament cannot be taken as an indication or guide as to its possibilities.

The way to understand the chromatic world to which the augmented sixth belongs is to look at the precise mathematical relationships underlying the intervals involved.[3] Once these have been understood, the correct functional

---

[1] Schoenberg, Theory of Harmony, 225.

[2] Edward Aldwell & Carl Schachter, Harmony and Voice Leading, Harcourt Brace Jovanovich Ltd., London 1989, 497.

[3] As Harry Partch has stated 'tones were therefore deliberately falsified, or compromised - only a few at first; later, all. And the ancient idea of simple ratios was junked'., Harry Partch,

notation for a particular chord or chromatic note will become readily apparent, as will the precise role which equal temperament is performing in each of these examples.

As a chromatic interval the augmented sixth belongs to a specific group of intervals which are well recognised in the sphere of European art music: the sphere of augmented and diminished intervals. When a perfect or major interval is enlarged by a semitone an augmented interval. results. Processes of augmentation can be applied to any of the seven intervals, but because the augmented seventh is enharmonically equivalent to the octave, means that its participation in the continuum of musical relationships as represented through twelve tone equal temperament is perhaps minimal.

The main augmented intervals recognised in Western music are thus the augmented prime, second, third, fourth, fifth and sixth. When a perfect or minor interval is compressed by a semitone a diminished interval results. The diminished second is coequal with the augmented seventh in that, resulting in the unison as conceived from an equally tempered base it has only limited application. So there are six main diminished intervals as well: the diminished third, fourth, fifth, sixth, seventh and octave. As a group there are thus twelve eminently usable intervals which belong to this category.

Augmented and Diminished Intervals

An important feature of these intervals is that they are enharmonically equivalent to either a perfect or an imperfect interval. For the theorist, this schizophrenic scheme can make the study of chromatic harmony extremely perplexing. This also applies to the composer too. For a composer with a fondness for chromatic harmony like Wagner, composing at the piano must have caused numerous problems, not least of which was how to interpret the chord structures he used, and to set them in a proper and meaningful context.

Bitter Music: Collected Journals, Essays, Introductions and Librettos, Ed. by Thomas Mc Georg, University of Illinois Press, Urbana and Chicago 1991, 162.

Enharmonic Equivalence of Diatonic and Chromatic Intervals

Perfect/Imperfect Interval	Augmented/Diminished Interval
Minor second	Augmented prime
Major second	Diminished third
Minor third	Augmented second
Major third	Diminished fourth
Perfect fourth	Augmented third
Perfect fifth	Diminished sixth
Minor sixth	Augmented fifth
Major sixth	Diminished seventh
Minor seventh	Augmented sixth
Major seventh	Diminished octave

Although enharmonically equivalent to one another, each pair of intervals possess highly divergent properties and characteristics. A good example are the intervals of the augmented fifth and minor sixth. When the fifth of the dominant triad is sharpened to give an inclining tone up to the major mediant of the key of C, it would be inappropriate to represent it as *Eb*. Functionally speaking, the supertonic degree - note D - has been raised to give *D#,* which then performs the chromatic function of leading up to the semitone above: the mediant note E. To represent the note D# as an *Eb* fulfils the requirements of pitch notation in a tempered context, but it does not fulfil the more exact requirements of functional pitch notation. They are spelled differently in order to accord recognition to the difference between their function.

Contrasting Behaviour and Functions of Enharmonically Equivalent Intervals of the Minor Sixth and Augmented Fifth

In terms of pure intervals it is well understood that these two intervals are different to one another. They not only derive from a different combination of intervals, but the notes D# and Eb imply different pitches. Just like the difference between the keynotes of F# and Gb in the cycle of fifths, the keynote of Gb has a ratio of 1024/729 and is therefore a Pythagorean comma lower than the keynote of F#, whose ratio is 729/512. Similarly the *Eb* in the first chord is a minor sixth (8/5) above the bass note G. It thus has an ideal measurement of

814 cents. The *D#* in the second chord however, is an augmented fifth above the bass note. Looking at the example, it can be seen that this augmented fifth is obtained as the sum of two major thirds of ratio 5/4: *G* to *B*, and *B* to *D#*. It thus has a ratio of 25/16 and a measurement of 773 cents.

The real difference between *D#* and *Eb* is an interval of 41 cents, the *greater diesis* of ratio 128/125, which is equivalent to almost a full quarter of a tone. This difference, it will be discovered is the mean distance that separates intervals which display this enharmonic parity. Here, note C is taken to represent the interval of the prime, note Db the minor second, etc.

Mean Differences Between Intervals Sharing Parity in Just Intonation

	C#		D#		E#		G#		A#		
	(25/24)		(75/64)		(125/96)		(25/16)		(225/128)		⟵
											+128/125
C	Db	D	Eb	E	F	G	Ab	A	Bb	B	⟵
(1/1)	(16/15)	(10/9)	(6/5)	(5/4)	(4/3)	(3/2)	(8/5)	(5/3)	(9/5)	(15/8)	−128/125
	Ebb		Fb		Abb		Bbb		Cb		⟵
	(256/225)		(32/25)		(192/125)		(128/75)		(48/25)		

Observe that all of the diminished intervals are a diesis smaller than their respective enharmonic equivalents, whilst all of the augmented intervals are a diesis larger. The diesis, amounting almost to a quartertone, represents an audible difference between intervals. Ideally music should be performed in respect of these basic differences. Equal temperament equalises, but does not invalidate them.

Reducing the number of intervals to twelve to concur with equal temperament is a sad loss to both music and its appreciation. This applies especially to understanding the role that is played by the prime number seven in tonal music, because every one of the chromatic intervals represented in the above scheme, are septimal intervals, and recognisable by the ear as such.

Indeed, when the matrix of septimal intervals is examined in relation to the above scheme it shows that the synchronicity of the augmented sixth of ratio 225/124 and the interval of 7/4 is much more than a chance meeting of intervallic identities. This can be seen in the following table where the precise breadths of all of the primary septimal intervals (those which display primary valent bonds) are compared to the breadths of the chromatic intervals presented in the enharmonic equivalence table above. Here it will be infallibly seen that septimal equivalents exist for every one of these chromatic intervals, and that the degree of difference between them is a constant septimal degree (225/224):

Septimal Definitions of Chromatic Intervals

Interval Name:	Aug. 6th.	Aug. 4th.	Aug. 2nd.	Dim. 4th.
Septimal ratio:	7/4	7/5	7/6	9/7
Cents:	969	583	267	435
Just ratio:	225/128	45/32	75/64	32/25
Cents:	976	590	275	427
Difference:	+7 cents	+7 cents	+7 cents	−7 cents

Interval Name:	Dim. 3rd.	Dim. 5th.	Dim. 7th.	Aug. 5th.
Septimal Ratio:	8/7	10/7	12/7	14/9
Cents:	231	617	933	765
Just Ratio:	256/225	64/45	128/75	25/16
Cents:	223	610	925	773
Difference:	−7 cents	−7 cents	−7 cents	+7 cents

Where there appears to be an 8 cents difference this is because the cents have been rounded off: the unit of difference at play is always 225/224, or approx. 1/26th of a tone. A clear pattern is at work here, for there is a common unit of difference between the conventional chromatic intervals and their septimal counterparts. This difference, a measurement of + or - 7 cents corresponds exactly with that between the interval 7/4 and the augmented sixth. Therefore to each of the intervals presented above the same argument may thus be applied as to the seventh harmonic and augmented sixth. With only some 1/26th. of a tone difference between each pair, the difference between them is aurally negligible. Thus the diminished fourth, with ratio 32/25, will be indistinguishable to the ear from the septimal diminished fourth of 9/7, and so on. Accordingly, the precise identities of septimal intervals, as signified by their respective ratios can now be further confirmed as follows:

Table of Septimal Identities

Ratio	Identity	Ratio	Identity
7/4	Augmented sixth	8/7	Diminished third
7/5	Augmented fourth	10/7	Diminished fifth
7/6	Augmented second	12/7	Diminished seventh
14/9	Augmented fifth	9/7	Diminished fourth

The reason for this excursion into the undervalued domain of note ratios is now quite clear: to be able to unfold the precise identities of septimal intervals within the tonal scheme. Considering that these all play a part in the system of tonality, means that no special notation is required for septimal intervals. Taking note C to be the generator, note A# signifies 7/4, note F#: 7/5 and note D#: 7/6; etc.

Reducing the number of intervals used in music to the twelve of equal temperament is to abnegate any possibility which the prime number seven may offer for the further enrichment of tonality. Significantly, the figure who most encouraged this, was Arnold Schoenberg, who in his *Theory of Harmony* observed that *the raw material of all forms produced by the connecting of tones is a series of twelve tones.*[1] Thereby automatically excluding the participation of the prime number seven, and the great wealth of chromatic intervals which it both generates and supports, Schoenberg effectively cut himself off from a new fourth dimension of tonal possibility. It is no wonder that he encouraged the abandonment of tonality: it is because he did not perceive those new possibilities already implicit within that system, which admitted of continuance and development.

As offering the ideal ratio for the interval of the augmented sixth, the ratio of 7/4 tends to suggest a certain type of musical logic, peculiar to its own domain. This logic can be further understood through pondering the nature of the augmented sixth interval itself. Obtained by sharpening the upper note, or flattening the lower note of a major sixth by a chromatic semitone (135/128), it does not participate at a diatonic level. It is a chromatic interval, and as Schenker points out in his treatise on harmony *the diminished third and the augmented sixth always indicate that we are dealing with a state of alteration.*[2]

Thus signifying a state of chromatic alteration, the augmented sixth interval both signifies and belongs to a sphere of musical influence which transcends the constraints of the diatonic scale. Lying outside of the diatonic system it satisfies the intuitions of those theorists such as Zarlino, Descartes, Rameau, Schenker and Yasser who felt that a prime number five limit was sufficient for that system. But it does not mean the interval whose ratio is 7/4 is not part of a more complex encompassing system of which the diatonic sphere itself is a part. This observation satisfies the beliefs of those theorists and composers who, like Kirnberger and Tartini, have felt that the prime number seven may have an important function to perform in the language of music.

Here it is important to note that the principle objections to the prime number seven have always been made from a diatonic perspective. Viewing 7/4 as an

---

[1] Schoenberg, Theory of Harmony, 386.

[2] Heinrich Schenker, Harmony, A Modification of Tonicalisation, 279.

augmented sixth means that such objections are entirely founded. The prime number seven would seem to have no place in music when conceived from a purely diatonic basis. So where does this leave the 7/4 relation, and its place in the musical language?

In answer to this question it may be observed that over the last hundred years or so, the diatonic system has gradually been transcended, and superseded as the prime focus of compositional interest by much more complex pitch structures. In the main, the trend of historical musicology has been to view the development of these structures from a reactionary standpoint, that is from an expressed desire on the behalf of composers to break down the barriers of the major and minor tonal system. The trend of analysis has performed a complimentary function in this respect, in that it has served to show how and in what way, composers have departed from the constraints of the diatonic tonal system.

Although highly informative, this approach has tended to foster a negative view of the last 150 years or so of musical history. Whilst it is true that the language of European art music has been characterised by a process of transformation from age to age, it is also true that any process of transformation possesses two essential elements: a negative element through which the established system gradually gets broken down, and a positive element in which something new is built up to take the place of the old system.

The factor not often mentioned is that in breaking free of the limits of one system of musical orientation, the composers concerned automatically fall subject to the natural constraints provided by another. A clear precedent for this is the emergence of the major and minor system of tonality from the relics of the old modal system, a change which occurred ever so gradually, and probably imperceptibly to those composers directly involved in such a process of transformation.

In this respect, a large portion of modern theory is capable of improvement, for it has only tended to offer a one sided view of that process of transformation as it proves relevant to the last hundred and fifty years: the negative or destructive side, the picture obtained of a system in a continual state of decay, with nothing to replace it except further processes of destructive activity.

Considering that composers often look towards the domain of musical theory in order to gain a firm perspective of their own work in relation to the trace of musical history so far, it is not that surprising that in the 1960's composers were eventually driven to the absurdities epitomised by the piece of music in which two dead fish were slapped together by one performer, whilst another was banging rocks in the background. This highly acute state of self-consciousness is itself a strong symptom of the fact that to progress, the musical language clearly needs a positive as well as a negative input.

To obtain such an input, it is necessary to ponder the reasons why the tonal system started to become destabilised in the first place. This can be explained to be a result of a search for new possibilities. Seeking something more, something new which the diatonic scale could not provide, composers started to look beyond the terms of the diatonic scale, and towards those relations contained in the chromatic scale. Now what is a chromatic relation? It is a diatonic relation chromatically altered to produce an interval not present in that diatonic scale. Through seeking to use such alternative resources to the diatonic scale therefore, it can be seen that the system of tonality was being laid open to invasion by altogether new influences.

Superficially this manifested as the gradual breakdown of syntactical patterns used and established over some considerable period of time. Yet one of the most striking of such invasive influences was the prime number seven as represented by the sphere of chromatic intervals, especially the chromatic relation of the augmented sixth. The word invasion, as used in this context would seem to be quite appropriate, for the prime number seven entered into music like a virus which imitates a bodily cell so it cannot be spotted by the antibodies: it entered subtly and unobtrusively concealed under the mask of its enharmonically equivalent interval of the minor seventh. Once it entered into the musical language, a process of transformation occurred. The chromatic virus had started to spread. Operating invisibly and imperceptibly behind the screen of equal temperament, it multiplied, and in doing so, placed the very stability and constitution of the diatonic tonal system under threat.

Viewed from a negative standpoint, such a process represented the gradual demise and death of the system of tonality. Yet from a positive standpoint, it can be seen that through dying, the possibility existed for the birth of a new tonal system arising from the ashes of the old one. Here it is important to see that the very principle which caused the death of that original system, was the same principle by which a new system became capable of being built up: the chromatic relation.

In order to understand how this occurred, and the possibilities which existed for the formation of an altogether new system of tonality it is necessary to recognise that the augmented sixth interval, as providing a primary vehicle for the manifestation of the prime number seven within the terms of tonal music, represents the basis for an altogether new dimension of frequency space: a fourth dimension which is as significantly different to the third, as the third was found to be to the second:

Dimensions of Frequency Space Defined Within a Seven Limit

Dimension	Prime	Interval	Primary Intervals	Harmonic Unit
First	Two	2/1	One	Monad
Second	Three	3/2	Two	Dyad
Third	Five	5/4	Four	Triad
Fourth	Seven	7/4	Eight	Tetrad

THE '7/4' RELATION AS ENTERING INTO TONAL MUSIC THROUGH THE VEHICLE OF THE CHORDS OF THE ITALIAN, FRENCH AND GERMAN SIXTH

The augmented sixth is an interval which has been in use in Western music for a very long time now. Given that this interval implies the ratio 7/4 more than any other interval, means that, aside from preferential intonations of the chord of the dominant seventh, the prime number seven and its influence has been gradually filtering through into the fabric of Western tonal music through the various chords of the augmented sixth. It is noticeable in this respect that the theorist Rameau, who endeavoured to deny the prime number seven as a legitimate musical resource, omitted to discuss the interval of the augmented sixth, and the various chords which involve its use in his *Treatise on Harmony*. Whether this is a coincidence or not, it is difficult to answer. That such chords were a relevant feature of contemporary harmonic practice can be gauged from Heinichen (1683 - 1729) who in his *der General-Bass in der Composition* of 1728 discusses all of the chromatic intervals - the augmented second, fourth, fifth and sixth, and the diminished intervals of the fourth, fifth and seventh, and the three forms of augmented sixth chord.

Certainly, the crux, so far as musical harmony that typifies and embodies septimal intervals is concerned, seems to be this key interval of the augmented sixth. It possesses very unique properties. As Aldwell & Schachter observe: *The presence of an augmented sixth chord is a sure indication of chromaticism, for the augmented sixth cannot occur diatonically; no diatonic scale contains for example, both F natural and D♯. The resolution of an augmented sixth to an octave sounds like nothing else in tonal music. With its half-step progressions by contrary motion, it intensifies the following chord in a unique way. As a consequence augmented sixth chords often occur just before important structural points; composers can use them to signal the beginning or end of a phrase in the tonal movement or the form.*[1]

---

[1] Edward Aldwell & Carl Schachter, Harmony and Voice Leading, Harcourt Brace Jovanovich Ltd., London 1989, 478.

Here the authors highlight three elements characteristic of chords of the augmented sixth. First they point out that no diatonic scale contains both *F* and *D#*. This is an essential observation for the terms of this study because it further corroborates the idea that the ratio of 7/4 is providing the underlying acoustic link responsible for forging an intervallic connection between musical tones which is unique to the sphere in which it operates. Second, they talk about the uniqueness of chords of the augmented sixth and how, quite rightly, they sound like nothing else in tonal music. This quality of uniqueness it may be asserted, is itself symptomatic of the influence of that fourth dimension of frequency space which itself can only be characterised by properties which are unique to those dimensions which precede it in the scale of priority. Third, they talk about the importance of these chords in terms of the overall structural detail of a musical work. This in itself imparts to those chords an importance which belies their humble origins: they are the paupers, or, as Schoenberg terms them, the *vagrants*[1] which, signaling the entry of tonality into the province of a new mathematical dimension, become in fact the princes of the new realm.

As the entry port into a new dimension of frequency space the various chords of the augmented sixth deserve serious consideration. The three most common forms of appearance of augmented sixth chords are those sonorities known respectively as the Italian, German and French Sixth chords:

The Three Most Common Forms of Appearance of the Chord of the Augmented Sixth

$$I_6 \qquad G_6 \qquad F_6$$

Involving the characteristic interval of the augmented sixth, all three of these chords are classified as chromatic chords, obtained through the chromatic alteration of one or more diatonic scale degrees. This can be demonstrated through the consideration of the simplest of all of the chords of the augmented sixth: the Italian Sixth which, unlike the other two which are tetrads, is itself a triad.

To obtain that triad in the minor mode (a), the root of the subdominant triad in first inversion needs to be chromatically raised to give a leading note up to the dominant degree. Within the major mode (b) it is also necessary to flatten the third of the otherwise major subdominant triad:

---

[1] Arnold Schoenberg, Theory of Harmony, 246.

The Italian Sixth Chord

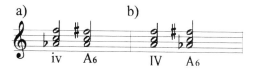

The chromatic derivation of the Italian Sixth chord is quite straightforward. It originates from a simple iv - V progression, the root of the minor subdominant triad of which has been sharpened to create a chromatic passing note up to the dominant degree of the scale. Kirnberger quite rightly said of this chord that it was *purely a melodic ornamentation carried over into a harmony*.[1]

This linear mode of interpretation of the chord however, is not a direct contradiction of its essential status as a vertical aggregation. The chord of the dominant seventh originated in a similar fashion, the seventh arising as a passing note between the dominant and mediant degrees of the scale. Through a process of elision, 7 then came in to replace 8, to establish the chord of the dominant seventh as an independent sonority in its own right. Highlighting the question 'when is a chord a chord?', exactly the same argument can be levied to explain the Italian Sixth chord.

Conceived as iv - #iv, it is a 'melodic ornamentation carried over into a harmony', but when, through a similar process of elision, #iv came in to *replace* iv, the Italian sixth attained the status of an independent triad. In this context a chord becomes a chord when its melodic tendencies become transferred onto the plane of the vertical. Thus being transferred, it attains a degree of independence which allows it to function as a self-sufficient harmonic entity.

Now generally speaking, the Italian Sixth is used as a chord of dominant preparation, progressing either to the tonic 6/4 and thence to the dominant (a) or simply straight to the dominant (b):

Treatment of Italian Sixth Chord

---

[1] Kirnberger, The True Principles for the Practise of Harmony, a translation by David W. Beach and Jurgen Thym, in: JMT 23/2, 197, 164 - 226.

However, at times, it is noticeable that the Italian Sixth triad progresses straight to the tonic triad. An example of this can be seen in Schumann's Humoresque, Opus 20 where he uses the Italian Sixth chord as a direct tonicising agent:

Excerpt from Schumann's 'Humoreske', Opus 20.

Reprint with permission of C.F. Peters, Frankfurt/M., Leipzig, London and New York.

Here the Italian Sixth does not occur on the minor submediant degree as is more usual for augmented sixth chords. Instead it occurs on the flat supertonic degree. These two are the points in the chromatic scale where there is an almost direct correlation with the interval 7/4. Viewed in this context, the interval 7/4 would appear to possess its *own tonicising properties*. Schumann enables it to function in this fashion by transferring the leading note implications of the chord to the tonic - as opposed to the dominant degree - and the bass note, being a diatonic semitone above the tonic, acts as a falling leading note, or a declining tone. In this case the chord has a different horizontal derivation. It derives from a chromatic passing note being introduced between the supertonic and tonic degrees in the chord of VII:

Derivation of the Italian Sixth Constructed Upon the Flat Supertonic Degree

Its capability in this respect can be explained from the fact that the Cb (as seen in the Schumann example above) may be viewed to be a chromatically lowered third of a diminished triad in first inversion. Adding the dominant root a major third below, the Italian Sixth has all of the hallmarks of a chromatically altered dominant sonority:

Relationship of Italian Sixth to Dominant Seventh Chord

Bb: V₇   V♭⁵₇

With the *A* in the bass, the augmented sixth appears inverted as a diminished third, and the seventh of the dominant harmony appears as a diminished fifth over the bass note A. As such it presents a rather awkward sonority, with equally awkward voice leading implications. When the *Cb* is in the bass, as per usual, the seventh of the dominant forms a major third with the bass, and the *A* an augmented sixth. This results in a much more smooth sonority, with more effective voice leading. Consequently the Italian Sixth is mostly used in this position.

It is thus perhaps mistaken to view the Italian Sixth as an altered subdominant harmony. A problem with this view is that it necessitates the concept of an altered root. To sharpen the root of the tonic major tonic triad *C E G* to *C# E G* results in a chord which cannot be viewed as a tonic triad anymore. The chord resulting from this alteration is vii of ii, or alternatively V7 of ii (with omitted root).

Similarly, the chromatic sharpening of the root of the minor subdominant triad needed to effect the Italian Sixth invalidates the subdominant root to create a chord of dominant leanings whose true root lies elsewhere. Otherwise, how is the Italian Sixth constructed upon the flat second degree to be explained? Here is the same chord, but arriving from a different contrapuntal path. Consequently, the derivation cannot be regarded as a statement concerning the origins of the chord.

Which note is the true root of the Italian Sixth chord? This is an extremely difficult question to answer. The ratios of the notes of the chord, conforming to harmonic numbers 4, 5 and 7 seem to implicate tone 4. So in the chord used by Schumann in the above example note Cb would be the implied root. However, viewing the Italian Sixth as a chromatically altered form of dominant harmony implicates another root altogether: note F as the root of the dominant seventh which has thus been altered. Therefore, the Italian Sixth constructed upon the flat supertonic degree may be viewed as chord V₇ with a flattened fifth (and omitted root), whilst the chord constructed upon the minor submediant degree may be viewed as V₇b₅ of V. There would thus seem to be a conflict of roots present in this particular chord.

The view of the Italian Sixth chord as a chromatically altered dominant seventh chord highlights one of the most interesting features of this particular sonority. It is not implied within either the major or minor modes, and, additionally, it is not composed of major and/or minor thirds - as are all other triads. The diminished third between notes F# and Ab makes it an interesting chord. Being the inversion of the augmented sixth, the diminished third may be taken to have a theoretical ratio of 8/7. In this way, the presence of a diminished third in a chord becomes a direct signal of the presence and participation of the prime number seven.

The Italian Sixth chord would thus seem to be inexplicable from a three-dimensional standpoint. As Helmholtz observes: *This chord cannot be deduced from the major and minor modes, and hence appears very enigmatical and inexplicable to many modern theoreticians......But it is easily explained as a remnant . . . in which the major seventh D#, which belongs to the old dominant chord B D# F#, is combined with the tones F & A, which are taken from the subdominant side.*[1]

Here Helmholtz is erring towards a modal derivation of the chord which links it to the old Phrygian cadence formula. Here, instead of having the usual flat seventh (the root of the D minor triad when in the tonality of E) the seventh is sharpened to provide a leading note up to the E:

Connection of Italian Sixth Chord to Phrygian Cadence Formula

The result is a chord which combines both dominant and subdominant ingredients in the one sonority. The dominant leading tone ingredients serve to highlight the tone above as a prospective tonic, whilst the subdominant ingredients act as a counterbalance which works the other way.

On a keyboard instrument, the Italian Sixth shares an enharmonic relationship with a dominant seventh chord the fifth of which has been omitted. One of the essential differences between the two chords (aside from their spelling, derivation and behaviour) is that the former is often treated as a consonant triad. Kirnberger alludes to this, observing that *This false (diminished) third, like the false fifth, is dissonant, although the augmented sixth resulting from its inversion is sometimes used as a consonance.*[2]

---

[1] Helmholtz, On the Sensations of Tone, Remnants of Old Tonal Modes, 308.
[2] Kirnberger, The Art of Strict Musical Composition, 35.

This felt quality of consonance cannot be explained by the complex harmonic ratio of 225/128 possessed by the interval of the augmented sixth. It can only be explained through the notion already discussed - that the ear takes 225/128 to be the much simpler 224/128 (7/4). Now given that the consonant augmented sixth conforms to the ratio of 7/4 means that the ratios of the other notes of the Italian Sixth chord can be defined accordingly:

Ratios of the Notes of the Italian Sixth

$$
\begin{array}{ccc}
\text{Ab} & \text{C} & \text{F\#} \\
\end{array}
$$

Ab		C		F#
	5/4		7/5	
		7/4		

The Italian sixth is thus a septimal triad which utilises three primary valent bonds combined within the one consonant unit. As its usage does not affect the tonality of the music shows that the harmonic purpose of the chord, aside from its local tendencies of inflection to or from particular degrees of the scale, is to support the presence of the septimal note F# (7/5) within the province of the tonality of C.

This represents a radical departure from the sphere of diatonic music in that the note F# belongs to the diatonic territory of the key of G, and not of the key of C. Its usage within a diatonic context therefore automatically implicates the key of G even if only for a fleeting moment. The Italian Sixth chord however, does not belong to the diatonic field of the key of G, or even of the key of C: it belongs to no diatonic field whatsoever. In this way can it be viewed to offer the unique imprint or signature of a new mathematical dimension of musical logic: the fourth dimension, for which the Italian Sixth provides the simplest entry point.

That being said, in practical terms the function of the Italian Sixth chord is fairly clearly defined. Aldwell & Schachter define its function in the following way: *Like applied V and VII chords, augmented sixths exemplify a fundamental type of chromaticism: leading-tone chromaticism....However, the augmented 6ths. differ from applied chords in at least one crucial respect. The temporary leading tone, taken by itself, is an agent of tonicisation, but the chord as a whole does not belong to the 'key' of the chord to which it resolves.....Unless there is strong evidence to the contrary, therefore, the resolution of an augmented sixth will not sound like a tonic, one reason why augmented 6ths. function so well as preparations for important dominant chords.*[1]

---

[1] Aldwell & Schachter, Op. Cit., 478.

In proffering an explanation of the function of augmented sixth chords in general, Aldwell & Schachter allude to a sphere of influence which extends beyond the realms of the diatonic: the chromatic world; a world which, from a diatonic standpoint is simply described by two words: altered state. Chromaticism, that is the affected practice of the chromatically altered state, appears whenever one or more diatonic scale degrees are altered in the accompanying harmony. The possibilities of alteration lie to the right and the left, to sharpen or to flatten, to raise or depress. In doing so, a note or notes foreign to the diatonic territory of the key in question are being introduced. Therefore in the key of C major, *Db*, *Eb*, *F#*, *Ab* and *Bb* are all chromatic notes.

Now when that state of alteration conforms to the diatonic territory of another key, the integrity of the diatonic sphere has not been compromised. It therefore speaks of a level of chromaticism which is diatonically supported. This is the world of secondary dominant harmony. However, when that state of alteration does not conform to the diatonic territory of another key i.e. as in the case of the Italian Sixth, a new sphere of tonal influence is being implied: the chromatic sphere.

In this way, the Italian Sixth chord implies a new level of tonality - a four-dimensional chromatic level of tonality, which although much more diffused than the three-dimensional diatonic level, is nonetheless richer in its colouristic possibility. Because the defining principle of the relationships between the notes of the chord of the Italian Sixth is the prime number seven, means that the chromatic sphere of tonality is therefore governed by a new valent principle: the principle of seven, which replaces five as the next cogent factor in the development of tonality.

Whilst the Italian Sixth chord is a triad, the other two chord forms to which it is related by association - the German and French Sixths - are tetrads. The German Sixth is identical to the Italian Sixth except that in the former there is an additional note which lies a perfect fifth above the bass note. The derivation of the German Sixth is very similar to the Italian Sixth, except that here root of the subdominant minor seventh chord in first inversion is raised by a semitone. In the major mode there are three alterations that need to be made to the subdominant seventh chord: the third and seventh need to be flattened, whilst the root needs to be sharpened.

In essence the German sixth may be regarded to be nothing more than an Italian Sixth with added perfect fifth. Their functions within a tonal context are very similar, both being employed as chords of dominant preparation. This function is exemplified in the following example from the slow movement of Beethoven's Piano Sonata in F Minor, Op. 57:

Excerpt from Beethoven's Pianoforte Sonata in F minor, Op. 57.

BEETHOVEN: Pianoforte Sonata in F Minor, Op. 57, 'Appassionata'
@ 1932 by The Associated Board of the R.A.M. and the R.C.M. Used by
permission.

In this example two features are noteworthy. Beethoven has spelled the note
Fb as an *E*. That it should be an *Fb*, can be gauged not only from the correct
spelling of the German Sixth (*Bbb Db Fb G*), but also because note E appears
incorrectly as a falling chromatic passing note between the mediant and
supertonic scale degrees: *F-E-Eb*. Logically, expressing a chromatic
enhancement of the mediant scale degree the figure concerned should be spelled
as *F-Fb-Eb*. His resolution is also slightly different from the norm in that the
note G, which would ordinarily rise upwards to the *Ab*, instead falls to the *Gb* -
the seventh of the dominant chord. Although not unusual, it demonstrates a
different type of progression of the augmented sixth interval than is the norm.

Instead of opening out to the octave, the sharp sixth falls to the semitone
below, perhaps bringing to mind Tartini's observation that the 7/4 relation can
equally rise or fall: *This interval is very easily produced on the violin, and
arises from the natural harmonic series: it is produced naturally on marine
and 'da fiato' trumpets and also on hunting horns - instruments which are not
subject to human reason but function according to the laws of physics and
harmony. To the diatonic scale one may therefore add in the form of a musical
note the term 1/7 representing the above-mentioned interval, and this added
note should be given the sign , as distinct from the b used for B fa...such a 7th
is consonant, not dissonant. And thus, there is no need for it to be either
prepared or resolved. It may ascend or descend. And it will sound equally
well in just intonation.*[1]

The question is whether making it fall turns it into a minor seventh, or
whether it is to be viewed as an augmented sixth interval resolving irregularly.
If viewed as a minor seventh this creates another problem, for the chord
concerned (*Bbb Db Fb Abb*) can only be construed to be the dominant seventh

---

[1] Tartini, Trattado di Musica, 126. Excerpt translated by Laura Davey.

of the Neapolitan triad (*Ebb Gb Bbb*) which is chromatically shifted down by a semitone to land up on the proper dominant for that key. If construed in this way of course, then the 7/4 relation is conspicuously absent.

Thankfully, not all manifestations of the German sixth chord are so problematic in their mode of treatment. Yet because, within the context of equal temperament, the German Sixth chord is enharmonically identical to the chord of the dominant seventh it is sometimes spelled as such. The nature of the chord is thus determined by its behaviour. In this example, raised by Prout (1835 - 1909) Beethoven spells a German sixth chord as V7 of Eb major (in the key of D):

Extract from Beethoven's 'Symphony in D Major'.

Prout comments on this example observing that *Its resolution shows it to be the last inversion of the German sixth on the minor sixth of the key of D. In this key Ab is not a note; its true notation is G#.*[1] The presence of the German Sixth chord is thus revealed by virtue of its characteristic mode of resolution. The shock of the sudden arrival of chord V7 of bII played *ff*, is thus assuaged with the listeners retrospective realisation that it is in fact an augmented sixth chord.

When another of the four tones of the German Sixth lie in the bass it would seem reasonable to assume that these are in fact the inversions of the German Sixth. However, to regard these chords in this way is problematic. The German Sixth is usually seen to derive from the subdominant minor seventh chord whose the root has been chromatically raised. In his *Theory of Harmony* Schoenberg comments on the problems which this type of thinking creates: *In the derivation of the augmented six-five chord...we find again the assumption of a raised root. I regard this assumption as incorrect in a system that considers roots (that can only be unraised ones) its unit of measure.*[2] Indeed, later he observes that this would mean that the 'root position' of the German

---

[1] Ebeneezer Prout, Harmony, Its Theory and Practice, Augener Ltd., London 1903, 278.

[2] Arnold Schoenberg, Theory of Harmony, 246.

Sixth chord would necessitate the sharpened tone being in the bass - a very unnatural and awkward position for the German Sixth.[1]

In terms of definition and usage, the augmented six-five chord appears to be the root position, yet this would imply that the note Ab (key of C) is the true root. Schoenberg, along with other later theorists endeavours to solve these problems of root identity by pointing out that the German Sixth chord can feasibly be considered to be a chromatically altered dominant ninth chord with omitted root.[2]

In this way the function of the German Sixth chord can be explained in terms of chromatically altered dominant harmony: *Therefore I find it more appropriate to derive the augmented six-five chord from the ninth chord on II in major or minor, by way of secondary dominants, that is, from the diminished seventh chord.* In this context the German Sixth appears without the root:

Theoretical Root of German Sixth Chord

This notion presents no problems as the diminished seventh chord may in certain contexts be regarded to be a dominant ninth chord in which the root is implied but absent. In this example from the second movement of Rimsky-Korskov's *Capriccio Espagnol*, the composer includes the implied chordal generator - note A:

Extract from Rimsky-Korsakov's *Capriccio Espagnol* (2nd Movement)

---

[1] Ibid., 248.
[2] Ibid., 246.

Roger Sessions observes that it is the tendencies of the augmented sixth interval which gives the chord its characteristic function, a factor which may override the sense of root progression. Speaking of augmented sixth chords in general he writes *that their very definition as such runs counter to the idea of root progression, since it accentuates the fact that it is the characteristic augmented interval with its tendency to resolve outward rather than a 'root' which gives the chord its character and its reason for existence. It is the position of the sixth therefore, and not the 'root' which is fundamental.*[1]

This goes some way towards the solving the problem of ascribing 'roots' to chords of the augmented sixth. Augmented sixth chords may possess more than one root depending upon how they are viewed: a natural root determined by the placement of the augmented sixth, and a diatonic or functional root determined by the chords chromatic derivation.

Another common form of augmented sixth chord is the French Sixth, in which, instead of the perfect fifth present in the German Sixth, there is an augmented fourth. The presence of this interval means that the French Sixth chord is more dissonant than the German Sixth, especially in its inversions. Dissonant qualities of the French Sixth help to explain why, in the eighteenth century, it was used less often than the Italian or German forms, although examples can be found. In this controversial example by Mozart[2] the simultaneous presence of the augmented fourth ($G - C\#$) and diminished fifth ($A - Eb$) which gives the French Sixth such a powerful capacity for resolution can be seen at work. Here Mozart uses the French Sixth as a dominant substitute, in that it progresses straight to the tonic chord:

Excerpt from Mozart's Symphony in G Minor

Cecil Hill however, feels that *this chord arises more from the contrary motion of the outer parts than from a deliberate use of it as a secondary dominant.*[3]

---

[1] Roger Sessions, Harmonic Practice, Harcourt, Brace and Company, New York 1951, 335.

[2] Prout, Op. Cit., 274.

[3] Cecil Hill, Mozart's French Sixth Chord in the Symphony in G Minor, in: MR 46, 1985, 162.

In the nineteenth century the French Sixth chord tended to be used much more often. Possessing a certain vagueness and tonal instability suggestive of the whole tone scale, it had a particular expressive appeal for Romantic composers. In this example, by Grieg, two such chords are employed in quick succession. The first is constructed upon the minor submediant degree (*Gb Bb C E*) whilst the second is a chromatically altered form of dominant major ninth chord which is used as a substitute for the conventional dominant sonority (*F A C# Eb G*):

Excerpt from Grieg's *Scherzo-Impromptu*, Op. 73, no. 2.

Reprint with permission of C.F. Peters, Frankfurt/M., Leipzig, London and New York.

The origin of the French Sixth chord has been variously explained. Like other septimal chords it is problematic to classify within diatonic terms. Theorists therefore often struggle to explain it. A good example is Schenker who devotes about two pages of his *Harmony* to a discussion of this chord. Schenker sees in it a combination of two sonorities, each belonging to their own particular key.

First of all he views it as a dominant seventh chord with the fifth flattened: *G B Db F*. Secondly, he views it as chord ii7 of the subdominant minor tonality, the third of which has been chromatically raised. To Schenker therefore, it is a chord characterised by a multiple function as is evident from the following statement: *in this harmony three elements are engaged in a struggle against three other elements - whereby it does not matter that two of the three elements are identical in either case - and while one of the litigating parties constitutes a V7 in C Major, the other forms a II7b5b3 in F Minor. Thus two different effects combine in a surprising unit: first of all, the effects of two different scale steps, a V and a II, and, in addition, the effects of two different diatonic systems, the major and the minor, as the V refers us to a major, the II to a minor, system.*[1]

---

[1] Schenker, Harmony, 277/8.

If Schenker is fully convinced at this type of interpretation, it is surprising he does not mention that it could also be interpreted as an altered vii7 of the flat submediant key. This derivation of the chord is made highly explicit in the following example, where the chromatic alteration made to the original chord (vii7) is plainly evident:

Excerpt from Granados's *Twelve Spanish Dances for the Piano*, (Dance 9).

Schoenberg offers a much simpler explanation of the French Sixth chord viewing it as a chromatic alteration of the supertonic seventh chord. The French Sixth *is best derived from the IInd. degree in major or minor, by raising the third and lowering the fifth. By raising the third we create an ascending leading tone, by lowering the fifth, a descending. The resulting chord combines dominant (and secondary dominant) possibilities with the minor-subdominant relationships.*[1] According to Schoenberg therefore, the French Sixth grew out of the use of a chromatic passing note being applied to the third, and, in the major mode the fifth of the supertonic seventh tetrad. Yet there is another pathway to the French Sixth which is the application of a chromatic passing note to the bass note of the dominant seventh chord in second inversion:

Two Pathways to the French Sixth Chord

Whichever way the French Sixth chord is viewed it is extremely difficult to pin it down with one explanation. Like the Italian or German Sixth chords, it derives from numerous points along the chain of dominant harmony. Bearing in mind observations made by these theorists all three forms of augmented sixth chord discussed so far - the Italian, French and German Sixth chords - may be regarded to be chromatically altered forms of chords of dominant function. This is the functional feature which they all seem to share in common. The factor that tends to corroborate this, is that when viewed together as a group,

---

[1] Schoenberg, Op. Cit.,

only one alteration needs to be made to the original dominant harmony, in order to be able to obtain all three of the chords:

Alterations Required to Produce all Three Forms of Augmented Sixth Chord

C: V$_{b9}$ A$_6$ A$_6$ A$_6$

The fifth of the dominant needs to be flattened, an alteration which brings into play that curious interval of the diminished third between the third and fifth of the resulting dominant triad. The presence of this interval is clearly of monumentous importance. Chords constructed from major and minor thirds can all be accounted for by the prime numbers three and five, the ratio of the major third being 5/4, the ratio of the minor third 6/5. This embraces all chords used in tonal music, bar the various forms of augmented sixth chords. Involving a diminished third in their make-up means that they are quite unique, for they automatically fall outside of the provenance of the diatonic system of tonality, as circumscribed by the three-dimensional constraints of Euler's tone lattice. This may be held to be the case even within a tempered context, for as Riemann observes *it appears at first glance, to be sure, that temperament is a white lie - that the absolutely pure intoned fifths (3/2) and the thirds intoned 5/4 are what our natural tonal sense requires.*[1]

From the standpoint of the three-dimensional diatonic system augmented sixth chords are thus quite inexplicable. Coupled with the observation that the ratio 8/7 offers a clear valent pathway between musical tones a diminished third apart, indicates that such chords represent the direct manifestation of the influence of that fourth dimension of frequency connection whose ruling prime number is seven. If therefore, a chord is used which possesses a diminished third, this may be seen to be symptomatic of the influence of the prime number seven, and therefore, the entry into tonal music of a new mathematical dimension of tonal connection.

Septimal harmony therefore, implies the application of an altogether new principle in the process of chordal generation. This principle is that conventional

---

[1] Ideas for a Study on the Imagination of Tone, by Hugo Riemann, Trans. by Robert Watson and Elizabeth West Marvin, in: JMT 36/1, 1992, 99.

diatonic chords (composed only of major and/or minor thirds) may be altered in such a way as to incorporate diminished thirds as well. Such a principle has to be countenanced in order to account for the three forms of augmented sixth chord so far considered. Otherwise, theoretically speaking, such chords cannot exist.

Now given that the ratio of the diminished third may be considered to be 8/7, means that the ratios of the pitches of the three augmented sixth chords discussed so far can be defined accordingly:

Ratios of the Notes of the Italian, German and French Sixth Chords

The Italian Sixth

Note:	Ab	C		F#
Ratio:	1/1	5/4		7/4

The German Sixth

Note:	Ab	C	Eb	F#
Ratio:	1/1	5/4	6/5	7/4

The French Sixth

Note:	Ab	C	D	F#
Ratio:	1/1	5/4	45/32	7/4

Of the three, the German Sixth has the most mathematically clear resonance, being defined by the configuration of the fourth, fifth, sixth and seventh harmonics. The Italian Sixth also has a strong resonance having behind it the full force of harmonics four, five and seven. It is only the French Sixth that has a quite complex pattern of resonance. Despite this, the presence of the augmented sixth gives this chord its compelling power.

Viewing the German Sixth as being defined by the harmonic numbers 4, 5, 6, and 7 offers interesting leads and clues about the essential nature of the fourth dimension of tonal space. Embracing within its domain the three primary 7-valent intervals of 7/4, 7/5, and 7/6, it serves to precisely define their identities within the tonal complex, and thus also, the identities of their respective inversions:

Septimal Identities Defined by the Chord of the German Sixth

Ratio	Interval	Ratio	Inversion
7/4	Augmented sixth	8/7	Diminished third
7/5	Augmented fourth	10/7	Diminished fifth
7/6	Augmented second	12/7	Diminished seventh

Looking at this range of intervals, it will be seen that the German Sixth informs us of one of the exact features which the fourth dimension of tonal space contributes to the continuum of musical relationships.

The second dimension, governed by the prime number three, contributes a sense of diatonic tonal polarity as defined by the differential between the perfect fifth and perfect fourth. The importance of this has already been discussed, for it is the principle which, manifesting through the all-important functions of the dominant and subdominant, establishes the prototypical tone as the being the very seat of the tonic principle. Matching this contribution, the third dimension whose ruling principle is the prime number five, contributes a sense of major-minor polarity, as infallibly demonstrated by the polar opposition of the major third (5/4) and its inversion, the minor sixth (8/5).

Compared to the unchanging world of the second dimension, in which polarisation led to the retention of the same intervallic modality, the third dimension thus led to a significant change of perspective through the arrival of that dual distinction between major and minor. In this observation lies the essential difference between the perfect and the imperfect intervals. The perfect intervals, not being characterised by that duality, constitute a direct expression of the unity of the first principle whose ratio is 1/1. It is thus quite appropriate that they represent the triangular seat of tonality: that applied force of unity which pervades all levels of the musical continuum. Imperfect intervals, demonstrating that division, are therefore one step removed from that unity, embodying as they do a chromatic polarization in which that unity has divided into two contrasting states: major and minor.

Now looking on to the particular dimension governed by the prime number seven, processes of polarization of the fourth dimension of tonal space can be seen at work. Here however, polarization leads to a further split, as seen in the differential between the augmented sixth (7/4) and its inversion the diminished third (8/7). This in its turn leads to an equivalent proliferation of tonal possibilities, in that the polar axis whose dual terms are major and minor, has become subdivided by a further axis whose dual terms are simply augmented and diminished. In this way, the chord of the German Sixth informs us that at a four dimensional level, tonality is the quintessential force which offers the promise of unity to those four interconnected states or conditions.

Tonality as Quintessential Force

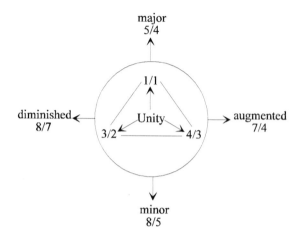

The constitution of this tonal system, it will be seen, depends upon the aggregated effect of some four levels of intervallic constitution:

Four Levels of Intervallic Constitution

Dimension	Prime Limit	Intervallic Level
First dimension	Two	Prime unity
Second dimension	Three	Perfect intervals
Third dimension	Five	Major and minor
Fourth dimension	Seven	Augmented and diminished

In this sense the German Sixth represents a neat and concise summary of that possibility. Hence it is a chord which possesses four notes, for each one of these, when the chord is considered to be generated from a state of unity, offer a direct reference point to the four dimensions of frequency space as signified by the prime numbers two, three, five and seven. In this way the German Sixth, or 4:5:6:7 tetrad, represents a radical new departure point in the ongoing development of tonality, for it represents the basic tetradic unit which offers the possibility for ejection into an altogether new tonal domain.

German Sixth as Four Dimensional Reference Point

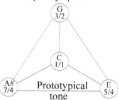

Represents the prototypical
tone in the second dimension
of frequency space

Represents the prototypical
tone in the fourth dimension
of frequency space

Represents the prototypical
tone in the third dimension
of frequency space

A clear symptom of the arrival of this possibility can be found in Chopin's *Prelude in F Major*, where the composer ends the piece on what to all extents and purposes, appears as a F dominant seventh chord.

Excerpt from Chopin's F Major Prelude

CHOPIN: Prelude in F Major, Op. 28, No. 23.
@ 1955 by The Associated Board of the Royal Schools of Music. Used by permission.

Looking at the behaviour of the chord however, this must be denied. Even Schenker, who rejected the prime number seven as a legitimate musical resource could not but help to go back on his own principles to observe that: *In the concluding passage of Chopin's Prelude No. 23, on the other hand, almost at the end, a seventh-chord is built on the tonic by the addition of the seventh Eb. Instead of hearing in this chord a true seventh chord, I feel inclined to*

*interpret it as a poetic-visionary attempt to offer the association of the seventh
overtone - the only attempt, to the best of my knowledge.*[1]

Chopin spells the tetrad defined by the harmonic numbers 4, 5, 6 and 7 as a
dominant seventh chord, but not as a German Sixth. Yet this spelling of what is
really a consonant septimal tetrad is extremely common in music which assumes
for itself the convenience of equal temperament. What is important to observe is
that Chopin uses it as a stable entity, in which the seventh harmonic is
introduced in order to add colour. The chord concerned therefore, is being
treated as a consonant tetrad.

In order to demonstrate that this is not an isolated occurrence, another fine
example of the consonant 4:5:6:7 tetrad can be found in Chopin's *Nocturne in
Bb Minor*, Op. 9, No. 1. There, for a span of some eight bars occurs a passage
in which a prolongation of the dominant seventh chord of the key of Gb major
seems to be apparent:

Excerpt from Chopin's *Nocturne in Bb Minor*, Op. 9, No. 1.

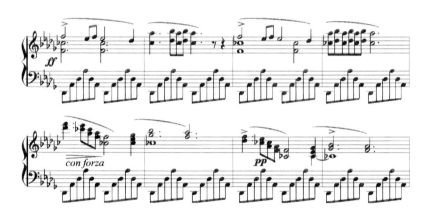

CHOPIN: Nocturne in B flat minor, Op. 9 No.1.
@ by The Associated Board of the Royal Schools of Music. Used by permission.

Yet there is something curious about this passage, for there is no sense
within it of the impending tonicisation of the Gb major triad that represents the
implied chord of resolution of this particular dominant. Instead, the music
continues its course quite unaffected in the key of Db major, in which the
melodic subject just presented is repeated, except that this time, the 'seventh' is
conspicuously absent. The curiosity of this passage thus lies in the highly

---

[1]Schenker, Theory of Harmony, 25.

unconventional treatment offered to the dominant seventh chord. Never resolving to its implied tonic, it is presented as a consonant tetrad. This chord, it may thus be asserted, is another prime example of the use of the 4:5:6:7 consonant tetrad.

Confirmation of this lies in the observation of the profile of the melodic line that Chopin employs. Suggestive of the harmonic series of the fundamental tone Db, the upper parts of the music almost suggest a duet between a pair of natural piccolo trumpets tuned to the pitch of *Db*. It is this factor which indicates that the *Cb* which occurs in all eight bars of the extract, is a manifestation of the seventh harmonic of that fundamental.

Here it may be objected that the seventh harmonic of the fundamental would give note B according to the indications presented so far in this study. And so it should. But the important point is that the seventh harmonic is being presented in a consonant relationship to the fundamental. As such it does not actually go anywhere. It appears in bar 51 to add its colour to the harmony, and as mysteriously as it appears, it disappears in bar 59. Within this particular context therefore, it doesn't actually matter whether it is spelled as a *Cb* or a *B*. The important point is that such a chord is certainly not a dominant seventh chord, but a rather magnificent prolongation of the 4:5:6:7 tetrad.

VALENCY ANALYSIS: THE MAJOR AND MINOR TONALITIES

Whatever the reasons behind the titles ascribed to the three most popular forms of augmented sixth chord - Italian, German and French Sixth - they still count as three of the most intriguing chords to be encountered in the study of conventional harmony. Their defiance of inversional theory sets them apart from most other tertially organised chordal sonorities, in that the root position of all three chords seems to be where the sixth occurs in relation to the bass. In terms of the Italian Sixth, this means that a 6-3 chord is being tendered as the root position, whilst for the German and French sixth chords, an equivalent role is being performed by a 6-5 and 4-3 chord respectively. It is no wonder that Rameau chose to omit them from his treatise on harmony, for their classification must have troubled him immensely. Indeed, they hardly help either to support or demonstrate his otherwise sound theory of root movement.

Chords of the augmented sixth are also quite mysterious in the sense that they do not originate from the diatonic scale. Neither for that matter, does the augmented triad, but being a chord which is present in the harmonic minor mode, its origins are at least diatonically traceable. So far as chords of the augmented sixth are concerned their scalar origin is as much a mystery as their curious national names. Somehow, they have managed to invade the tonal system, so bringing with them a rather curious and enigmatic brand of musical logic. Indeed, their very consideration tends to evince a particular type of curiosity about their exact nature and origins. From where do they stem? What led the ear to them? Why in fact, are they so attractive to the ear? How is it that the German Sixth, so close in sound to the dominant seventh, performs such a different and contrasting function?

Such are the type of questions which tend to arise in relation to chords of the augmented sixth. A compelling answer to some of these questions was provided in the last chapter, where it was observed that, against the fabric and substance of three-dimensional tonal space, augmented sixth chords can be viewed as the manifestations of a fourth dimension of tonal space defined by the prime number seven. As the manifestations of a new prime number it is perhaps not that surprising to discover that such chords present features and attributes which defy that branch of theoretical logic which recognises no prime number higher than five. The existence of such logic is still widespread today, for as Ian Morton observes: *Pitch organisation as we have known it in Western culture is a result of frequency multiplication and division on a 1 - 3 - 5 base. The fact that these relations have been rounded off in equal temperament does not invalidate the notion, since the mind seeks constantly to resolve the complex tempered ratios into simple terms.*[1]

Clearly therefore, there is a fundamental problem to be solved before this study can proceed any further, for the general theory of music is still anchored within the three dimensional possibility represented by the prime number five limit, whilst musical practice, as evidenced by the usage of the various forms of augmented sixth chord, brings into play an enigmatic and mostly misapprehended fourth dimension as represented by the prime number seven. Consequently, there is a chasm between what is, and could be, given a clearer understanding of the actual implications of that fourth dimension.

Despite Morton's imposition of a prime number limit on Western music which may not be valid any longer, within the basic point of his statement can be discerned one of the more enlightened positions of modern musical theory. Equal temperament clearly represents a triumph of human resourcefulness over the infinitely complex web of tonal relations which exists by order of nature, and the natural property of tonal valency. Being brought forth on the wake of that triumph, it might be mistaken to assume that as the tempered scale. has twelve pitches, then so does the tonal music imperfectly realised by that system. To believe this is to assume the imperfection of equal temperament onto the level of musical theory itself. This is extremely dangerous, because it is to lose touch with the reality of that network of valent bonds by which the musical language has always been informed and nourished. The result of this can only be a mathematically sterile and expressive void in which tonal realities can no longer find a place.

In order to be able to unfold the more advanced possibilities which the prime number seven presents as a major but mostly unrecognised participant in the musical language, it is thus necessary to deal with two basic problems. The first is to re-establish the basic grounds by which the network of tonal relations may be more realistically understood, and the second is to trace how that network has been extended through the unconscious utilisation of the resources of the prime number seven. To solve the first problem it becomes necessary at some point to return to the simple basics of the musical language: the fundamental property of valency, that quintessential element by which the most elementary bonding between musical tones occurs. Automatically, the expression which

---

[1] Ian A. Morton, Numerical Orders in Triadic Harmony, in: JMT 4/2, 1960, 153.

both indicates and allows a precise detection of the valency of a particular musical interval is the time honoured note ratio. In order to begin to unlock exactly what is, and has been going on in music over the last few centuries, it is thus necessary to go against the grain of current musicological study, and reclaim this ancient tool of musical theory from the theorists' junkyard.[1] The process by which this is accomplished may be called valency analysis, in that it seeks to explicate those valent bonds between musical tones of which a given piece or passage of music may be seen to be the demonstrable sum.

The importance of the application of valency analysis to tonal structures derives from the observation that if chords of the augmented sixth are the entry ports into tonal music of the influence of the prime number seven, then in some subtle way, the network of pitch relations used by composers has expanded beyond the limits proscribed by the prime numbers two, three and five. Consequently, even the basic scale of tonal music has been subtly expanded through the participation of those septimal influences. To understand how it has changed, and the need which existed for such changes, it is necessary to delve into the precise network of relations used and employed within tonal music, in order to see how and where that network departs from the theoretical format usually proscribed for it. Initially, this will involve a short examination of the basic scales used in Western tonal music.

As *the* scale of Western music, it might be appropriate to begin this examination with a consideration of the equally tempered twelve-tone scale. Each of the twelve notes may carry a precise meaning or signification which will be determined by their precise contextual setting. An example of this is the obvious differential between the external and internal representatives of tonality as embodied in the scheme of keynotes belonging to the tonal system on the one hand, and the major and minor scales which can be built upon each of these keynotes on the other.

Despite the presence of intonational conflicts brought about by the requirements of fulfilling both concerns simultaneously, it will be seen that twelve-tone equal temperament does an admirable job in reconciling these conflicts within the limited terms of its own specific pitch array. Therefore at one particular level, the twelve notes of the tempered scale may be viewed as an ordered representation of the various independent tonal centres or keynotes which lie at the very heart of the Western tonal system. That there are twelve tempered semitones means therefore that there are twelve keynotes, and therefore twelve keys. Because each key may be either major or minor depending upon instance, means that there are thus a total of 24 keys recognised in tonal music.

---

[1] Harry Partch, Bitter Music: Collected Journals, Essays, Introductions and Librettos, 162.

However, this view is something of an over-simplification; the result of a convenient rounding off, which having behind it, the full authority of Bach's 'Well-Tempered Clavier', gives to the twelve-tone tempered scale a greater sense of theoretical weight and aura of determinacy which it may not actually possess. The evidence of practical usage, as demonstrated by the range of key signatures used in the history of tonal music, shows that there are more than twenty-four recognisable keys. This fact can be simply demonstrated through a purview of that well-known scheme which has come to be known as the circle of fifths:

The Circle of Fifths (As it Applies to the Major Keys)

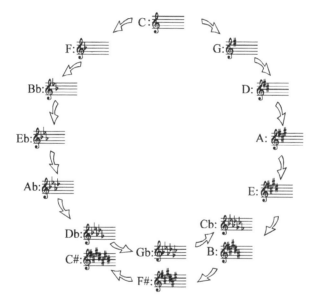

Taking key signature as evidence of tonal recognition, some fifteen tonal centres are implicated. Recognising these as being integral to the system of tonality, another theoretical 'white lie' is exposed, the concept of the *circle* of fifths. Exposing that fallacy as a construct which is unique only to equal temperament represents a perfectly viable application of the process of valency analysis. Successive keynotes in the cycle are related according to the ratio of 3/2. Tracing the ratios of each fifth it is easily demonstrated (as seen in chapter 5) that the keynotes of C#, F# and B are all one Pythagorean comma higher in pitch than their respective equivalents in the circle of fifths. As such, it is well known that the so-called 'circle' of fifths is a tangible section of what to all extents and purposes is an infinite winding spiral from which the composer selects the keys required for a musical composition.

Given the necessities of practical realisation, it is not always possible to embrace an infinitude of possibility, attractive though the idea may seem. In an improvisation between pieces of music in different keys, an organist wishing to modulate via the shortest route from the key of B major to Db major, would no doubt do so through the submediant triad which, being chromatically altered to give the dominant of C# major, would thenceforth be treated as the enharmonic dominant of Db major. A lengthy alternative to this would be to modulate through a seemingly endless chain of subdominant keys which would be both tedious to maintain and monotonous in its effect.

The organist would no doubt do this because practically speaking, within the limitations of twelve-tone temperament, there is no difference between the keys of Db and C# major. Yet within the sphere of tonal relations which subsists upon the reality of the valent bonds between musical tones, there is an immense difference between them, to which the minute scrap of a tone named in honour of Pythagoras that separates them does not do justice. Therefore, to say, for the sake of practical expediency that the key of Db major is the same as C# major, is to take the compromise that is temperament as the defining factor of tonal relations, when it is quite clear that it is not, and never can be.

As the concern here lies in the valent principles which temperament serves to compromise so well, each keynote needs to be identified properly by a ratio which accurately defines its relationship to adjacent keys within the spiral of fifths. Assigning the ratio of 1/1 to the keynote of C as the basic standard, the ratios of the keynotes of the other major keys can be defined as follows:

Ratios of the Keynotes of the Major Keys as Defined by a Valency Factor of Three

Key	Ratio
Cb major	4096/2187
Gb major	1024/729
Db major	256/243
Ab major	128/81
Eb major	32/27
Bb major	16/9
F major	4/3
C major	1/1
G major	3/2

D major	9/8
A major	27/16
E major	81/64
B major	243/128
F# major	729/512
C# major	2187/2048

This however, only accounts for the major keys. The different tonal circuit traversed by the minor keys is a factor which, because of equal temperament, is also sometimes conveniently forgotten. Whilst for major keys the closest relative lies a perfect fifth up or down, for major-minor key relationships the closest relative is a key a minor third below the tonic of the corresponding major key. This is for two immediately obvious reasons. First, the relative minor key utilises the same diatonic note set as the relative major key, and consequently has the same key signature, and second, the diminished triad of C major - *B D F* - has a latent ambivalence in which it also may be interpreted as the supertonic triad of A minor, in which case it participates as a dominant element with tonicising properties in both keys.

Effectively, this means that the ratio of the tonic of the relative minor key is defined by the ratio of the submediant of the major key. Yet a glance at the scheme of keynotes for the major keys will show that the keynote of A major has a ratio of 27/16, whilst the keynote of A minor, as the submediant of C major, has a ratio of 5/3. Therefore whilst in the major keys the circle of fifths starts with the ratio of 1/1, the circle of fifths as it applies to the minor keys, starts with a ratio of 5/3:

Ratios of the Keynotes of the Minor Keys

Major Key	Ratio	Relative Minor	Ratio
Cb major	4096/2187	Ab minor	10240/6561
Gb major	1024/729	Eb minor	2560/2187
Db major	256/243	Bb minor	1280/729
Ab major	128/81	F minor	320/243
Eb major	32/27	C minor	160/81
Bb major	16/9	G minor	40/27
F major	4/3	D minor	10/9
C major	1/1	A minor	5/3
G major	3/2	E minor	5/4
D major	9/8	B minor	15/8

A major	27/16	F# minor	45/32
E major	81/64	C# minor	135/128
B major	243/128	G# minor	405/256
F# major	729/512	D# minor	1215/1024
C# major	2187/2048	A# minor	3645/2048

The connection between major keys as defined by the cycle of fifths may thus be seen to represent a dimensional movement of interconnected tonic axes through the second dimension of tonal space. A similar observation may also be made with regard to the circuit of minor keys, which also have their residing point within the defining terms of the cycle of fifths. However, through the link between a major key and its relative minor key, and visa versa, a connection between tonic axes is occurring which belongs to the order of a different dimension of tonal space - the third dimension whose ruling prime is five.

The scheme of keynotes implicit to the system of tonality thus implies a two-dimensional projection which appears as two quintal chains connected to one another by virtue of a tertial link established through the relationship of relative major and minor keys. This imparts to the key system an important purchase upon both of the dimensions of tonal space represented in such a scheme.

Through the link between relative keys, what was originally conceived to be a spiral of fifths thus becomes a double helix; a spiral staircase in which every key belonging to the system of tonality has its authenticated place and point of origination. One of the consequences of this is that each particular key is now surrounded by those keys to which it has the closest relationship. Therefore, in terms of the key of C major, these are the keys of G major, F major, A minor and E minor; whilst in terms of the key of A minor, these are the keys of E minor, D minor, F major and C major. All of these, it will be noted, are based on primary valent bonds generated between tonic axes.

Here it is interesting to observe that the keynote of the subdominant key of A minor viz. D minor, is not the same as the supertonic key of the relative major mode, for whilst the former has a ratio of 10/9, the latter has a ratio of 9/8. Therefore within the auspices of this particular scheme, the connection between the parallel major and minor keys, is a rather remote one. Whilst the former possesses a tonic axis which lies in the second dimension, the latter possesses a tonic axis which, relative to the first, lies in the third dimension. To move between one and the other therefore, is a significant step, for it represents an addition to the possibilities of the original defining system.

The ratios of the major and minor scales are readily definable through the service of both practical usage and theoretical conventions as they incline towards the interest of valency. Representing the pure bond between musical tones mediated by their respective partials, it will be seen that the implications of practical usage within the format of the major scale necessitates the provision of a pure triad upon each degree thereof. The ratios of the major scale as viewed according to the theoretical convention formulated and handed down by Zarlino[1] are only good for those triads constructed upon the tonic, subdominant, and dominant degrees:

Valency Diagram of the Major Scale

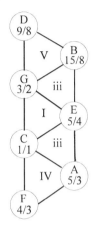

The vertical lines signify a valent bond between musical tones expressed by the ratio of 3/2, whilst the diagonal lines moving upwards towards the right signify a similar connection, but this time expressed by the ratio of 5/4. The diagonal lines moving upwards from left to right, are thus significant of the connection between musical tones according to the ratio of 6/5. The total of lines present within this diagram thus represents a summary of the valent pathways between musical tones as recognised by Zarlino's original scheme.

The diagram itself readily demonstrates the role of valency, not only in defining the major pathways of harmonic connection between musical tones, but also in the generation of basic tonal functions. In so doing it serves to reconcile the apparent conflict between those interests which place relevance upon the harmonic series as the principal matrix of interpretation (Helmholtz), and those which lend their emphasis to the dynamics of function as revealed, for example, in the philosophical processes of Hegelian dialectics (Hauptmann).

---

[1] Zarlino expounds this system in Le Institutioni Harmoniche, Venice 1558-9, part II, ch. 39 - 40.

Principally, this reconciliation lies in the observation that the septenaric constitution of the major mode results from the interunion of a functional tetrad and a functional triad of influences. The tetrad, defined by the left hand column, comprises those degrees of the scale whose ratios involve no prime number higher than three. Therefore, constituting the tonal representatives of the second dimension of frequency space, these scale degrees are automatically implicated as being the most important tonal functionaries of the scale. In traditional tonal parlance they are thus designated as the four tonal degrees, which, irrespective of the mode (major or minor) embrace the fundamental principle of tonality as it is embodied in the tonic or prototypical tone (1/1), and its three agents of expression i.e. the triangle of tonality as manifested through the respective functions of the tonic (1/1), dominant (3/2) and subdominant (4/3). The supertonic (9/8), lying a perfect fifth above the dominant, obviously accords the dominant the possibility of a full triadic expression as befits its role as the positive agent of the force of tonality. As the dominant of the dominant, the supertonic also performs an important function as external assistant to the core triangle of tonality, in that it is the principle which gives that triangle the possibility of movement or replication along the cycle of fifths (modulation).

The remaining three notes, E, A and B of the C major scale, comprise those scale degrees which have ratios involving the prime number five. Accordingly, they are the sole representatives within the major mode of the third dimension of frequency space. The role of the third dimension is the binding of the second dimension into the terms of an oscillation between two apparently opposite poles: the positive and negative polarisations of third dimensional frequency space as defined and referred to by the conventional terms major and minor. Accordingly, they are designated as the three modal degrees, in that they are the primary points of manifestation of this polarisation.

Unlike the minor mode, which will be considered shortly, the major mode thus represents a truly independent scale system for it successfully offers a complete triangular expression (tonic, dominant and subdominant) of the positive polarisation of three dimensional frequency space. A glance at the valency diagram will show that it satisfactorily accounts for the ratios of the submediant and mediant triads too. These are of course minor, the necessary manifestation within the major mode of the principle of equipolarity, in which the negative polarisation of three-dimensional frequency space, is theoretically the equal of the positive polarisation. In this way, minor may be regarded to be a part of major as major is a part of minor, the two together bespeaking of a state of fundamental tonal unity.

Positive and Negative Polarisations of Three-dimensional Frequency Space:

Minor (-)   *Major (+)*

D

(Bb)← →B

G

(Eb)← →E

C

(Ab)← →A

F

    Problems of intonation arise when the leading note and supertonic triads are brought into consideration. These problems arise principally because of the Pythagorean trihemitone of 32/27 present between the supertonic and subdominant degrees. Because the leading note triad is composed of two superimposed minor thirds of ratio 6/5, means that in theory at least, the Pythagorean minor third between the supertonic and subdominant degrees needs to be augmented by a Didymean comma (81/80). This effectively raises the subdominant degree of the scale from a ratio of 4/3 to 27/20 as defined by that particular harmonic context. This raising of the subdominant degree by a syntonic comma also brings the supertonic triad into line, in that it gives the requisite pure minor third between notes D and F (as conceived from the standpoint of the key of C).

    The supertonic triad is still somewhat problematic, in that its root relates to the dominant, as the dominant relates to the tonic. Thus having a ratio of 9/8 means that the note A required for the supertonic triad is a syntonic comma short. In other words, the interval between the supertonic note D (9/8) and the submediant note A (5/3) is not a perfect fifth of ratio 3/2, but what Ellis describes as a 'grave fifth',[1] an interval which has a ratio of 40/27. To obtain the requisite perfect fifth, the submediant note A (5/3) must be raised by a syntonic comma to give note A+ - ratio of 27/16. These two micro-modal alterations of the original scale- note F (4/3) being raised to *F+* (27/20) and note A (5/3) being raised to *A+* (27/16) are indisputably necessary in the major mode in order to give a pure triad on every degree of the scale:

---

[1] Hermann Helmholtz, Op. Cit., 455.

Extended Valency Diagram for the Major Mode

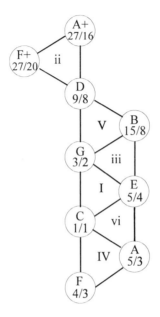

Here it is interesting to look at the way in which the dominant seventh chord is configured according to this tuning. Invoking the note F (27/20), its dominant function serves to compromise the otherwise clear subdominant relation. By taking the seventh slightly flatter than it should be, as found in the practice of functional intonation, the note F is brought into line with its proper ratio of 4/3. The result is that the fifth and seventh of the dominant form a Pythagorean third of 32/27 - a rather rough minor third which is perhaps in keeping with the nature of the dominant seventh chord. Whether such slight alterations to the ideal pitch of the notes are justified, it is difficult to say, but as long as such practices are understood in the light of the firm principles of valency, it is hard to see that there is anything wrong with it. Indeed, such alterations, sensitively introduced, can only go to enhance the performance of a piece of music.

The effects of such slight alterations, are easily seen in twelve-tone equal temperament, which possesses a subtle leaning towards Pythagorean intonational principles. This can be demonstrated through a short examination of the major mode as it is configured according to equal temperament. In just intonation, the perfect fifth (3/2) has a value of 702 cents, the perfect fourth (4/3) a value of 498 cents. Equal temperament (which offers values of 700 and

500 respectively) thus gives an excellent rendition of the perfect fifth and fourth. Its rendition of thirds and sixths however, is far from satisfactory. The major third (5/4) in just intonation has a value of 384 cents, as against 400 cents for the tempered major third. The tempered major third is therefore closer to the Pythagorean ditone (81/64), which has a value of 408 cents, than the just major third. Similarly, the minor third (6/5) in just intonation has a value of 316 cents, against 300 cents for the tempered minor third. Consequently, the tempered minor third is closer to the Pythagorean equivalent - the trihemitone of ratio 32/27 which has a value of 294 cents.

Equal temperament also represents the seventh of the dominant as being a trihemitone above the supertonic, rather than a pure minor third. As such, it serves to line up that seventh with the subdominant degree, whilst just intonation causes the subdominant to be fractured between the acute and perfect fourth. The leading note of equal temperament also has a closer affinity with the Pythagorean third of the dominant, rather than the pure major third. Sharper than it should be according to just intonation, it can be seen that by favouring Pythagorean intonation, equal temperament actually serves as a model for the functional intonation practised on string instruments and voices since about the beginnings of the nineteenth century. As such, functional intonation may itself derive from a desire to modify string and vocal intonation in accordance with the peculiarities of equal temperament.

From the considerations presented above it is certainly important to look at the situation as it is presented from both tempered and non-tempered viewpoints, for a complete picture lies not with one or the other, but the simultaneous comprehension of both levels as they apply to a particular musical problem. Because of the great complexities involved, the comprehension of the major and minor system of tonality from the standpoint of just intonation is the most challenging, especially for those not used to the values of just intonation. These complexities can be readily gauged when attempts are made to construct a major scale within the province of all fifteen keynotes referred to above.

Indeed, the table below shows how useful temperament is, for it manages to reduce this great multiplicity to a simple array of twelve pitches. This does not mean that tonal music uses only twelve pitches, it simply means that through temperament, the microtonal differences between certain pitches has been eliminated, so leading to a great simplification of the range of pitches in practical use. In this sense, the facility of temperament places the onus for the precise interpretation of pitch upon the aural faculties of the listener, who must learn to discern, through evaluation of the precise contextual setting of a given pitch, its precise place and function in the tonal network

Ratios of the Notes of the Major Mode in all Fifteen Keys

	I	II	III	IV	IV+	V	VI	VI+	VII
Cb	$\frac{4096}{2187}$	$\frac{256}{243}$	$\frac{2560}{2187}$	$\frac{8192}{6561}$	$\frac{512}{405}$	$\frac{1024}{729}$	$\frac{10240}{6561}$	$\frac{128}{81}$	$\frac{1280}{729}$
Gb	$\frac{1024}{729}$	$\frac{128}{81}$	$\frac{1280}{729}$	$\frac{4096}{2187}$	$\frac{256}{135}$	$\frac{256}{243}$	$\frac{2560}{2187}$	$\frac{32}{27}$	$\frac{320}{243}$
Db	$\frac{256}{243}$	$\frac{32}{27}$	$\frac{320}{243}$	$\frac{1024}{729}$	$\frac{64}{45}$	$\frac{128}{81}$	$\frac{1280}{729}$	$\frac{16}{9}$	$\frac{160}{81}$
Ab	$\frac{128}{81}$	$\frac{16}{9}$	$\frac{160}{81}$	$\frac{256}{243}$	$\frac{16}{15}$	$\frac{32}{27}$	$\frac{320}{243}$	$\frac{4}{3}$	$\frac{40}{27}$
Eb	$\frac{32}{27}$	$\frac{4}{3}$	$\frac{40}{27}$	$\frac{128}{81}$	$\frac{8}{5}$	$\frac{16}{9}$	$\frac{160}{81}$	$\frac{1}{1}$	$\frac{10}{9}$
Bb	$\frac{16}{9}$	$\frac{1}{1}$	$\frac{10}{9}$	$\frac{32}{27}$	$\frac{6}{5}$	$\frac{4}{3}$	$\frac{40}{27}$	$\frac{3}{2}$	$\frac{5}{3}$
F	$\frac{4}{3}$	$\frac{3}{2}$	$\frac{5}{3}$	$\frac{16}{9}$	$\frac{9}{5}$	$\frac{1}{1}$	$\frac{10}{9}$	$\frac{9}{8}$	$\frac{5}{4}$
C	$\frac{1}{1}$	$\frac{9}{8}$	$\frac{5}{4}$	$\frac{4}{3}$	$\frac{27}{20}$	$\frac{3}{2}$	$\frac{5}{3}$	$\frac{27}{16}$	$\frac{15}{8}$
G	$\frac{3}{2}$	$\frac{27}{16}$	$\frac{15}{8}$	$\frac{1}{1}$	$\frac{81}{80}$	$\frac{9}{8}$	$\frac{5}{4}$	$\frac{81}{64}$	$\frac{45}{32}$
D	$\frac{9}{8}$	$\frac{81}{64}$	$\frac{45}{32}$	$\frac{3}{2}$	$\frac{243}{160}$	$\frac{27}{16}$	$\frac{15}{8}$	$\frac{243}{128}$	$\frac{135}{128}$
A	$\frac{27}{16}$	$\frac{243}{128}$	$\frac{135}{128}$	$\frac{9}{8}$	$\frac{729}{640}$	$\frac{81}{64}$	$\frac{45}{32}$	$\frac{729}{512}$	$\frac{405}{256}$
E	$\frac{81}{64}$	$\frac{729}{512}$	$\frac{405}{256}$	$\frac{27}{16}$	$\frac{2187}{1280}$	$\frac{243}{128}$	$\frac{135}{128}$	$\frac{2187}{2048}$	$\frac{1215}{1024}$
B	$\frac{243}{128}$	$\frac{2187}{2048}$	$\frac{1215}{1024}$	$\frac{81}{64}$	$\frac{6561}{5120}$	$\frac{729}{512}$	$\frac{405}{256}$	$\frac{6561}{4096}$	$\frac{3645}{2048}$
F#	$\frac{729}{512}$	$\frac{6561}{4096}$	$\frac{3645}{2048}$	$\frac{243}{128}$	$\frac{19683}{10240}$	$\frac{2187}{2048}$	$\frac{1215}{1024}$	$\frac{19683}{16384}$	$\frac{10935}{8192}$
C#	$\frac{2187}{2048}$	$\frac{19683}{16384}$	$\frac{10935}{8192}$	$\frac{729}{512}$	$\frac{59049}{40960}$	$\frac{6561}{4096}$	$\frac{3645}{2048}$	$\frac{59049}{32768}$	$\frac{32805}{32768}$

The complexities of just intonation are further exacerbated when the minor mode is brought into consideration. The minor mode is more complex than the major mode, for although it aspires to the tonal perfection of the major tonality, it lacks the essential ingredients by which this may be achieved. Constituting a kaleidoscopic mixture of ingredients which endeavours to satisfy both the conflicting requirements of tonality and modal purity, it thus occurs in multiple forms, each of which represent one side of its plural nature: the natural minor mode, which is the same as the melodic form of the minor mode as it descends, the harmonic minor mode, and the ascending form of the melodic minor mode. In terms of the natural minor mode, this is its purest modal form. Here it is self-evident that it inherits its ratios from the major mode.

Ratios of the Notes of the Natural Minor Mode (as Prescribed by the Relative Major Mode)

| C: | 5/3 | 15/8 | 1/1 | 9/8 | 5/4 | 4/3 | 3/2 | 5/3 |
| A: | 1/1 | 9/8 | 6/5 | 27/20 | 3/2 | 6/5 | 16/9 | 2/1 |

However, the issue is not as simple as it might at first appear:. Here, everything is in order except for the ratio of the subdominant degree of the natural minor mode - note D. Bearing a ratio to the minor tonic of 27/20, it is a syntonic comma sharp of the 4/3 ratio needed to give a pure subdominant. The subdominant of the minor mode is thus shortened by a syntonic comma in order to concur with the requirements of that particular context. This results in a comparative ratio of 10/9 when compared with the supertonic of the relative major mode which has a ratio of 9/8. This alteration gives a pure minor third (6/5) between the notes D and F in order to provide a pure minor triad on the subdominant degree.

The natural minor mode thus represents the perfect counterpart to the major mode in that it displays the mutually opposite polarization of three-dimensional frequency space. Therefore, in contrast to the major mode the tonic, dominant and subdominant triads are all minor, whilst the mediant and submediant triads are major. Major is therefore dependent upon minor, as minor is dependent upon major, in that both polarizations are indisputably necessary for a complete representation of the influence of that particular dimension. In theory therefore, the major and minor modes are thus of equal standing in that they serve as the diatonic representatives of their respective polarizations.

Valency Diagram of the Natural Minor Mode

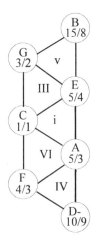

However, by ascribing the ratio of 10/9 to the subdominant of the relative minor mode, it means that the third between B and D, as present in the supertonic triad of the minor mode, is now a trihemitone of ratio 27/16, which means that it is a syntonic comma short of the intonation ideal for the minor third as expressed by the ratio of 6/5. Therefore, for the correct representation of the supertonic triad the original fourth of 27/20 needs to be retained. Being retained, the submediant degree of the scale needs to be altered to give the requisite pure minor third between D and F, which means raising note F by a syntonic comma to 81/50. The natural minor mode is thus similar to the major: various micro-modal alterations are necessary to give the required pure triads upon each degree of the scale.

An important factor which provides a tangible tonal link between the major and relative minor tonalities is thus the diminished triad - *B D F* - which carries dominant implications for both keys. In the major mode it represents the upper three notes of the chord of the dominant seventh - *G B D F* - , whilst in the relative minor mode it represents the upper three notes of the dominant minor ninth - *E G# B D F*. Although representing the perfect counterpart to the major mode, the natural minor mode is not tonally self-sufficient, for by virtue of its flat seventh, it does not possess the essential ingredients for the successful tonicisation of its own tonic triad. For the tonic triad to be successfully tonicised, the seventh needs to be sharpened in order to create both a leading tone up to the tonic, and a chord of the dominant seventh which may impart to that leading tone its effective capacity to define the tonic note that follows.

Extended Valency Diagram of the Natural Minor Mode

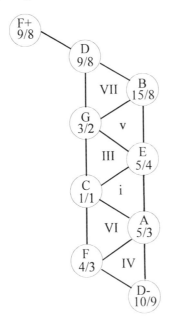

Therefore, to the array of notes required for the minor tonality, the note G#
also needs to be added. Lying a pure major third above note E (5/4 in the major
mode) it thus has a ratio of 25/16. Hence can be explained the harmonic minor
mode, with its characteristic augmented second between the sixth and the
seventh degree. The presence of this chromatic interval, although necessary for
tonal considerations, has often been felt to provide for rather awkward voice
leading. To a large degree, this problem is solved in the melodic form of the
minor mode, in which the submediant degree is sharpened upon ascent. As a
result of this borrowing from the major mode, the ascending form of the
melodic minor mode is a hybrid scale, in that it possesses a minor lower
tetrachord and a major upper tetrachord. To counteract the otherwise
disrupting influence caused by this intrusion of major elements in the other wise
minor tonality, the mode is altered upon descent, a process which cancels out
those original alterations.

In order to allow for these alterations, to the list of notes given above, an
extra note is required which is a pure major sixth above the tonic of the minor
mode. To the original major tonic, note C, this has a ratio of 25/18. The
complete minor scale complex would thus appears as follows:

Extended Valency Diagram for the Minor Modal Complex

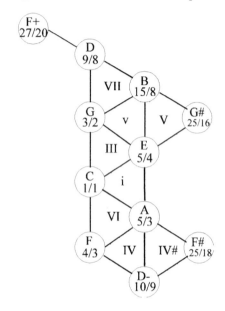

Being dependent upon a process of borrowing from the parallel major mode means in that the minor modal complex constitutes a mixture of those diatonic elements belonging to the natural minor mode, and chromatic elements imported from the major key. Because these chromatic elements have been historically assumed unto the constitution and make-up of the minor modal complex, means that the minor mode thus possesses a quality of inherent chromaticism not present in the major mode. The existence of this chromatic element gives to the minor mode one its advantage over the major mode. This is the possibilities which it presents for chromatic harmony.

Deriving mainly through the alteration of the seventh degree of the natural minor mode to give a leading note up to the tonic, this brings into play two particular chords which, in themselves, are not actually endemic to the diatonic territory of that key. In the key of A minor these are the diminished seventh tetrad, generated between notes G#, B, D and F (key of A minor) and the augmented triad generated between notes C, E and G#.

Lying outside of the diatonic territory of that key, these two chords are classifiable as chromatic chords, for their use depends upon the chromatic alteration of a diatonic scale degree. As chromatic chords they belong to a certain type. The chromatic element belonging to the harmonic minor mode is itself a constitutional element. They are therefore both examples of inherent chromatic harmony, which means that their usage in any particular harmonic context is still suggestive of, and dependent upon, the pre-established diatonic territory of a given key.

Other elements characteristic of the minor tonality, which have also been borrowed from other keys, have tended to enhance the possibilities which the minor mode presents for the use of chromatic harmony. Therefore, whilst for example, it is unheard of to end a piece in the major key with the minor triad, the reverse, known as the 'Tierce de Picardy' cadence is extremely common. Another chord which is extremely common in the minor key (as well as the major) is the chord of the Neapolitan sixth derived through chromatically flattening the supertonic degree.

Both of these chords involve chromatic alterations being made to the lower tetrachord of the minor scale. Coupled with the complete chromatic filling out of the upper tetrachord induced by the various forms of the minor mode, it will be seen that the minor modal complex soon breaks down into what is in effect a complete chromatic scale. Therefore, although the minor mode lacks tonal strength and certainty, it makes up for this in the richness and diversity of the possibilities for chromatic harmony which it presents.

To construct a minor mode upon each of the relatives of the fifteen keynotes, is a process which is thus considerably complexified by the inconsistent and often highly chromatic definition of the minor tonality. That, in the process of valency analysis, reference may need to be made to any one of these elements of the minor mode, in any key, means that no efforts should be spared in exactly calculating these possibilities. For those interested in this, a chart of ratios for the construction of the natural, harmonic and melodic minor modes in each of the relatives of the original fifteen keys is given below.

Also given is a table outlining the scale required in order to be able to play in all keys with complete accuracy. Merely a glance at the range of intervals required brings home some of the distinct advantages that equal temperament has over just intonation. Theoretical quibbling over the exact sizes of intervals and their micro-modal distinctions are no longer necessary, as all intervals are of a standard size, and everything is neatly systematised and rounded off to mathematical perfection. Yet if temperament is not to insidiously devalue the valent realities which it serves to compromise, it needs to placed into a proper perspective. It is after all, simply a system of keyboard tuning. To project that system upon to the fabric of musical reality, and insist that those realities must be modified to accommodate that system, is unrealistic. Musical reality is much more complex:

Ratios of the Notes of the Minor Scale Complex in all Fifteen Keys

	I	II	III	IV-	IV	V	VI	VI+	#VI	VII	#VII
Ab	$\frac{10240}{6561}$	$\frac{1280}{729}$	$\frac{4096}{2187}$	$\frac{20480}{19683}$	$\frac{256}{243}$	$\frac{2560}{2187}$	$\frac{8192}{6561}$	$\frac{512}{405}$	$\frac{25600}{19683}$	$\frac{1024}{729}$	$\frac{3200}{2187}$
Eb	$\frac{2560}{2187}$	$\frac{320}{243}$	$\frac{1024}{729}$	$\frac{10240}{6561}$	$\frac{128}{81}$	$\frac{1280}{729}$	$\frac{4096}{2187}$	$\frac{256}{135}$	$\frac{12800}{6561}$	$\frac{256}{243}$	$\frac{800}{729}$
Bb	$\frac{1280}{729}$	$\frac{160}{81}$	$\frac{256}{243}$	$\frac{2560}{2187}$	$\frac{32}{27}$	$\frac{320}{243}$	$\frac{1024}{729}$	$\frac{64}{45}$	$\frac{3200}{2187}$	$\frac{128}{81}$	$\frac{400}{243}$
F	$\frac{320}{243}$	$\frac{40}{27}$	$\frac{128}{81}$	$\frac{1280}{729}$	$\frac{16}{9}$	$\frac{160}{81}$	$\frac{256}{243}$	$\frac{16}{15}$	$\frac{800}{729}$	$\frac{32}{27}$	$\frac{100}{81}$
C	$\frac{160}{81}$	$\frac{10}{9}$	$\frac{32}{27}$	$\frac{320}{243}$	$\frac{4}{3}$	$\frac{40}{27}$	$\frac{128}{81}$	$\frac{8}{5}$	$\frac{400}{243}$	$\frac{16}{9}$	$\frac{50}{27}$
G	$\frac{40}{27}$	$\frac{5}{3}$	$\frac{16}{9}$	$\frac{160}{81}$	$\frac{1}{1}$	$\frac{10}{9}$	$\frac{32}{27}$	$\frac{6}{5}$	$\frac{100}{81}$	$\frac{4}{3}$	$\frac{25}{18}$
D	$\frac{10}{9}$	$\frac{5}{4}$	$\frac{4}{3}$	$\frac{40}{27}$	$\frac{3}{2}$	$\frac{5}{3}$	$\frac{16}{9}$	$\frac{9}{5}$	$\frac{50}{27}$	$\frac{1}{1}$	$\frac{25}{24}$
A	$\frac{5}{3}$	$\frac{15}{8}$	$\frac{1}{1}$	$\frac{10}{9}$	$\frac{9}{8}$	$\frac{5}{4}$	$\frac{4}{3}$	$\frac{27}{20}$	$\frac{25}{18}$	$\frac{3}{2}$	$\frac{25}{16}$
E	$\frac{5}{4}$	$\frac{45}{32}$	$\frac{3}{2}$	$\frac{5}{3}$	$\frac{27}{16}$	$\frac{15}{8}$	$\frac{1}{1}$	$\frac{81}{80}$	$\frac{25}{24}$	$\frac{9}{8}$	$\frac{75}{64}$
B	$\frac{15}{8}$	$\frac{135}{128}$	$\frac{9}{8}$	$\frac{5}{4}$	$\frac{81}{64}$	$\frac{45}{32}$	$\frac{3}{2}$	$\frac{243}{160}$	$\frac{25}{16}$	$\frac{27}{16}$	$\frac{225}{128}$
F#	$\frac{45}{32}$	$\frac{405}{256}$	$\frac{27}{16}$	$\frac{15}{8}$	$\frac{243}{128}$	$\frac{135}{128}$	$\frac{9}{8}$	$\frac{729}{640}$	$\frac{75}{64}$	$\frac{81}{64}$	$\frac{675}{512}$
C#	$\frac{135}{128}$	$\frac{1215}{1024}$	$\frac{81}{64}$	$\frac{45}{32}$	$\frac{729}{512}$	$\frac{405}{256}$	$\frac{27}{16}$	$\frac{2187}{1280}$	$\frac{225}{128}$	$\frac{243}{128}$	$\frac{2025}{1024}$
G#	$\frac{405}{256}$	$\frac{3645}{2048}$	$\frac{243}{128}$	$\frac{135}{128}$	$\frac{2187}{2048}$	$\frac{1215}{1024}$	$\frac{81}{64}$	$\frac{6561}{5120}$	$\frac{675}{512}$	$\frac{729}{512}$	$\frac{6075}{4096}$
D#	$\frac{1215}{1024}$	$\frac{10935}{8192}$	$\frac{729}{512}$	$\frac{405}{256}$	$\frac{6561}{4096}$	$\frac{3645}{2048}$	$\frac{243}{128}$	$\frac{19683}{10240}$	$\frac{2025}{1024}$	$\frac{2187}{2048}$	$\frac{16225}{16384}$
A#	$\frac{3645}{2048}$	$\frac{32805}{32768}$	$\frac{2187}{2048}$	$\frac{1215}{1024}$	$\frac{19683}{16384}$	$\frac{10935}{8192}$	$\frac{729}{512}$	$\frac{59049}{40960}$	$\frac{6075}{4096}$	$\frac{6561}{4096}$	$\frac{54675}{32768}$

Scale Required for the Just Intonation of the Major-Minor System

	Note	Ratio	Cents		Note	Ratio	Cents
1	C	1/1	0	37	F#+	729/512	612
2	B#+	32805/32768	2	38	F#++	59049/40960	633
3	C+	81/80	22	39	G--	3200/2187	659
4	Db	20480/19683	69	40	G-	40/27	680
5	C#	25/24	71	41	Fx-	6075/4096	682
6	Db-	256/243	90	42	G	3/2	702
7	C#	135/128	92	43	G+	243/160	723
8	Db	16/15	112	44	Ab--	10240/6561	771
9	C#+	2187/2048	114	45	G#-	25/16	773
10	D--	800/729	161	46	Ab-	128/81	792
11	D-	10/9	182	47	G#	405/256	794
12	Cx	18225/16384	184	48	Ab	8/5	814
13	D	9/8	204	49	G#+	6561/4096	816
14	D+	729/640	225	50	A-	400/243	863
15	Eb--	2560/2187	273	51	A	5/3	884
16	D#	75/64	275	52	Gx	54675/32768	886
17	Eb-	32/27	294	53	A+	27/16	906
18	D#+	1215/1024	296	54	A++	2187/1280	927
19	Eb	6/5	316	55	Bb--	1280/729	975
20	D#++	19683/16384	318	56	A#	225/128	977
21	E-	100/81	365	57	Bb	16/9	996
22	Fb-	8192/6561	384	58	A#+	3645/2048	998
23	E	5/4	386	59	B-	50/27	1067
24	Fb	512/405	406	60	Cb-	4096/2187	1086
25	E+	81/64	408	61	B	15/8	1088
26	E++	6561/5120	429	62	Bb+	9/5	1018
27	F--	25600/19683	455	63	A#+	59049/32768	1020
28	F-	320/243	477	64	Cb	256/135	1108
29	E#-	675/512	478	65	B+	243/128	1110
30	F	4/3	498	66	B++	19683/10240	1131
31	E#	10935/8192	500	67	C--	12800/6561	1157
32	F+	27/20	520	68	C-	160/81	1178
33	F#-	25/18	569	69	B#	2025/1024	1180
34	Gb-	1024/729	588	1	C	2/1	1200
35	F#	45/32	590				
36	Gb	64/45	610				

Here there are some 25 points where adjacent notes are separated by about 2 cents. This minute shaving of a tone is the interval of the Skhisma (ratio 32805/32768 - 1.954 cents), which represents the deficiency of the octave to a cycle of eight perfect fifths of ratio 3/2 plus a major third of 5/4. It thus also occurs as the fractional difference between note Fb taken as the eighth perfect fourth up from C (8192/6561), and note E - the harmonic major third of ratio fourth up from C (8192/6561), and note E - the harmonic major third of ratio 5/4. Because the difference between E and Fb as derived in this sense is so small, it means that to provide for it can be a source of great problems.

On keyboard instruments, to provide a separate key for each single note that may be required is problematic in itself, problems admirably overcome by the likes of R. Bosanquet, with his harmonium of 84 keys to the octave, or John White's harmonium with 56 keys to the octave.[1] To accommodate skhismatic intervals as well is to greatly increase the number of keys that would be required to play music in any key with absolute accuracy. By eliminating schismatic intervals a reduction of some 25 notes is possible to result in a much more practicable 44-note scale.

However, it is not being suggested that such a scale should take over from twelve-tone equal temperament, for there are far superior alternatives already developed for this purpose, some of which will be considered in subsequent chapters. It is suggested that the possibilities for such scales need to be taken into account if a valency analysis is to prove successful. Each note of the above scale possesses a relevance at some point in the tonal complex, a relevance which will only emerge through a consideration of the precise context in which a given pitch is being presented. In this sense, such scales are simply a more practical view of the complexities with which the human ear is faced within the context of equal temperament, where it must sort out and interpret the significance of a given pitch as defined by the context in which it is presented. Valency analysis from this perspective, is therefore nothing more than an observation of the way in which the ear relates musical tones one to the other: through the audible connections or valent bonds that occur between them.

---

[1] Hermann Helmholtz, Op. Cit., 482-3.

THE ENIGMA OF THE CHROMATIC MIXING CRUCIBLE

The dualistic distinction between the major and minor tonalities provided an important tool for the creation of both formal contrast and thematic conflict within the terms of the diatonic tonal system. Although it is not the place here to comment upon the aesthetic appreciation of the essential differences between the major and minor tonalities, it is nonetheless worthy of comment that within the terms of that stable tonal system, the contrast between the major and minor scale systems offered a useful platform for the portrayal of the terms of that intrinsic duality of forces so popular to eighteenth and nineteenth century beliefs, folklore and legend. The dynamics of light and shadow, tragedy and joy, love and hate are just a few of the manifestations of this essential duality which the major-minor tonal system served so well.

However, in common with the other arts in general, the terms of the musical language could not remain unchanged for very long. Processes of transformation were taking place in which the ingredients of music were being subtly tested, stretched, and called upon to bear an ever-increasing weight of expressive requirement. Here the major and minor tonal system was no such exception. Although founded upon the possibilities of the diatonic scale, like the germinating shoot which draws upon the nourishment of the dicotyledons displaced either side, the tonal system started to display a thrust upwards towards the exploitation of those chromatic relations which, not being present in the diatonic scale, involved an unknowing but necessary projection into the fourth dimension of frequency space:

Thrust of Tonality Towards Fourth Dimension of Tonal Space

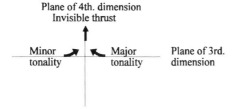

Appearing in one through the usage of such chords as the Italian, German and French Sixth, that thrust towards a more refined and sophisticated chromatic sphere is evident in many fine examples of music. A good example is the *Introduzione* to the finalé of Beethoven's Pianoforte Sonata in C, Op. 53 - the *'Waldstein Sonata'*:

Extract from the *Introduzione* (*Adagio Molto*) of Beethoven's *Waldstein Sonata*, Op. 53:

BEETHOVEN: Pianoforte Sonata in C, Op. 53, 'Waldstein'.
@ 1932 by the Associated Board of the R.A.M. and the R.C.M. Used by permission.

Beginning rather unobtrusively with an F major tonic triad, its transformation to an Italian Sixth chord in the second half of the first bar is just the first of the many surprises which Beethoven has to offer in this tonally enigmatic introduction. Looking at this extract it is not immediately evident what key it is in. Both the key signature and the first and last chords suggest F major. What happens between these two points of tonal clarity however, certainly does not belong to an F major tonality. Indeed, this music cannot be placed into the clear perspective of a diatonic tonality, for it is music which operates upon its own logic determined by the chromatic constituents present within it. This becomes evident in the chromatically descending base line, and the cadence to the B major triad at the centre of the sentence. The triad of B major is of course related to the root of F major by the interval of the tritone - a purely chromatic relationship between the chordal roots of common triads.

A further examination of this music reveals that it is not as enigmatic as it first seems. Endeavouring to make sense of this passage, it becomes apparent that the two points where the chromatic chord of the Italian Sixth occur are quite crucial, as these tend to underpin the few points of tonal stability that are present within it. Indeed, as a result of the conversion of the F major tonic triad to an Italian Sixth it soon becomes apparent that the F major key signature and opening tonic triad is in fact a very clever deception. Really Beethoven has opened this introduction in the key of E - the subsemitonal key for which the F major triad in bar one is simply the Neapolitan triad. Using the Italian Sixth as a chromatic dominant substitute, the tonic chord of E major arrives in the second bar. What follows is easy to appreciate when viewed in E major, especially the half-close on the dominant, seen in the triad of B major in first inversion. Then, through chromatic use of the diminished triad, a progression to the Italian Sixth constructed upon the flat submediant of the key of F, leads us to the dominant of the tonality of F major.

Yet even understanding the tonal deception which Beethoven has employed, does not help to resolve the music into a purely diatonic format. Indeed, it cannot be properly identified as being in a major or a minor key, for it is purely chromatic music, and to create that effect Beethoven has been compelled to draw upon the resources of both the major and the minor tonalities as and when required. This example therefore, only goes to show that in order to develop that thrust towards the usage of those chromatic relations characteristic of the fourth dimension, it became necessary to draw upon the possibilities of both major and minor tonal polarisations as required.

Faced with a general lack of knowledge concerning the direction of this thrust, it may have appeared that the major and minor polarisations were being gradually drawn together towards a state of tonal unity: a synthesis of forces in which major and minor were being slowly and inexorably merged under the terms of one grand unified system of tonality. Here it proves very instructive to trace the terms of that merger and to observe how, without precise knowledge concerning the nature of the fourth dimension, tonality was instead brought to the brink of near extinction. This trace can begin with a consideration of that very important statement made by Busoni (1866 - 1924) in his Sketch of a New Esthetic of Music: *when we recognise that major and minor form one whole....we arrive unconstrainedly at a perception of the unity of our system of keys.*[1]

By the year in which Busoni had made this statement (1911) it had become well apparent that composers from at least as early as Beethoven, had been starting to treat the major and minor modes not as two separate tonalities, but rather as two expressions of a singular force of tonality. In practise therefore, composers often moved freely between one and the other. Referring again to

---

[1] Feruccio Busoni, Sketch of a New Esthetic of Music, Trans. by Dr. Th. Baker, Schirmer Inc., New York 1911, 27.

the example given above, the Rondo that follows the displays a clear exchange between the parallel major and minor tonalities:

Major and Minor Interchange in Beethoven's *Pianoforte Sonata in C Major*, Op. 53.

BEETHOVEN: Pianoforte Sonata in C, Op. 53, 'Waldstein'.
@ 1932 by the Associated Board of the R.A.M. and the R.C.M. Used by permission.

This process of exchange, as exemplified in the above example, may be regarded as a significant step towards the unification of the resources of the major and minor keys, for it meant that the major key was being enriched through the absorption of elements belonging to the minor key, and visa versa. At that stage perhaps, the immanent dangers of such a practice were unsuspected, for like the twin pillars of Joachin and Boaz that supported the Temple of Solomon, if the major and minor tonalities were brought too close together, the entire tonal edifice might topple to yield what in potential could only amount to a state of tonal chaos. Yet underlying this exchange between the major and minor tonalities was an important third element which tended to mediate between the processes of major and minor interchange. This is the element of chromaticism.

Evidence for this lies in the simple observation that when in the C major tonality (for example), the C minor tonality cannot be approached or referred to without the use of the tones of Eb, Ab, and possibly Bb, all of which are chromatic tones for the key of C major. Similarly, the C major tonality cannot be approached from the C minor key, without due reference to the tones of E and A, both of which are chromatic tones for the key of C minor. With this observation comes a very important point. Any exchange that may occur between the major and minor tonalities, automatically contributes to the growth of that third chromatic element. In this sense, the chromatic sphere becomes much more than simply a mediating principle between the major and minor tonalities: it is also a product of their interchange, and the more that it is used the more it acquires the stature of an independent sphere in its own right. The unity of which Busoni speaks may thus be regarded to be the product of an interunion between three spheres: the major modal sphere, the minor modal sphere, and the chromatic sphere which provides the bridge by which one may connect with and pass through to the other.

Tonality as a Unification of Three Factors

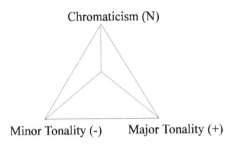

Here it is significant that the resources of a complete key at this level are no longer embraced by the diatonic scale. Representing a combination of both major and minor modal elements, a more appropriate scale needs to be devised which accommodates the full range of these possibilities. To obtain this scale it is necessary to combine the resources of the major mode, and the various forms of minor mode together:

Sub-chromatic Scale Resulting from the Combined Resources of the Major and Minor Modes

Major:	C	D	E		F	G		A		B
Harmonic Minor:	C	D	Eb		F	G	Ab			B
Melodic Minor:	C	D	Eb		F	G		A		B
	C	D	Eb		F	G	Ab		Bb	
Sub-chromatic:	C	D	Eb	E	F	G	Ab	A	Bb	B

Being predicated by the terms of that merger between the major and minor tonalities, the sub-chromatic scale embraces within its confines a dual representation of the note functions of the mediant and submediant: those modal degrees which characterise the major and minor forms of tonality.   The supertonic degree is the same in both modes, as indeed, are the tonic, subdominant and dominant degrees, which means that there is no need for these to be represented in diverse forms. The seventh degree is curious, for there the leading note is undoubtedly necessary for the maintenance of tonality in both modal polarizations. Consequently, the flat seventh degree, although implying a duality in the differential between a major and minor seventh, nonetheless has a purely local modal function in relation to the minor mode only.

Therefore it cannot be said that there is the same degree of functional equality between the flat seventh, and the leading note, as there is say, between the major and minor forms of the mediant. As such, in terms of purely tonal functions, the flat seventh degree relates more to the supertonic than the leading note, in that it constitutes the subdominant of the subdominant, as the supertonic constitutes the dominant of the dominant.   Hence the logical justification for the term subtonic, sometimes applied to the flat seventh. That however, the subtonic also offers the third for the dominant minor triad, means that it is more appropriate in this case to represent it by the ratio of 9/5 rather than 16/9. These observations are fully encapsulated in the valency diagram of the sub-chromatic scale:

Valency Diagram of the Sub-chromatic Scale

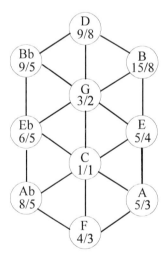

The sub-chromatic scale embraces the four tonal degrees of the middle column, which are flanked either side by the three modal degrees in each of their two polarised forms. Representing itself as a balanced pattern, the sub-chromatic scale possesses the hallmarks of a scale structure in which both major and minor possibilities are combined into the one scalar unit. Offering a clearer picture of that very real state of tonal unity to which Busoni refers, it can now be seen that his original statement conceals a remarkably profound observation. In treating the major and minor modes as the two expressions of a singular tonality, seen practically in their interchangeability within the framework of a common tonal centre, a radical and far reaching shift of musical consciousness is implied, one which is more at home, not particularly in the diatonic scale as a first principle, but within the more expansive range of the entire chromatic scale. The major, through absorption of the minor, and the minor through absorption of the major, have gradually giving birth to a state of tonality that is neither major nor minor, yet encompasses them both. This therefore is the *chromatic*, as opposed to the diatonic level of tonality.

The fundamental distinction between these two systems lies in the fact that at a diatonic level of tonality, the chromatic scale may be regarded to be a product of the merger of the major and minor modes. Having given rise to and created that product, a subtle reversal of emphasis occurs, in which the product itself takes on the status of host system to the two modal strains that created it. From this point on the chromatic scale thus provides the basis for a tonality of which the major and minor are but two polarised forms of self-expression. The first level, in which the chromatic scale is regarded as product, may be termed dualistic or diatonic tonality. The second level, in which the chromatic scale becomes the host system, monistic, monotonal or chromatic tonality:

Fundamental Distinction Between Diatonic and Chromatic Tonal Systems

The Diatonic Tonal System

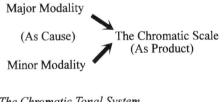

The Chromatic Tonal System

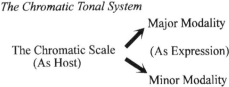

The necessity for a distinction between a diatonic and a chromatic level of tonality is well recognised in theoretical circles. This becomes especially apparent where methods of analysis applicable to the diatonic level of tonality start to break down, or prove unsatisfactory when applied to chromatic music. Recently, the inadequacy of Schenkerian methods of analysis for this type of music has been noticed. As Mitchell states: *Since many Schenkerians assume that background and middleground structures are basically diatonic, they tend to treat chromatic elements as products of surface voice leading. As William Benjamin has noted, some writers 'over-simplify' much highly chromatic music by 'explaining away large swathes of non-scale tones as substitutes for diatonic scale-degree representatives or as linear interpolations'. Other theorists such as Gregory Proctor and Patrick McCreless, claim that Schenker's methods must be expanded by new theories of chromatic tonality in order to cope with this repertory. Proctor, for example has suggested that tonal music should be divided into two main types: 'Classical diatonic tonality' as described by Schenker, and 'nineteenth century chromatic tonality' as derived from the chromatic scale.*[1]

Yet one of the central problems with the chromatic level of tonality, is the lack of effective analytical strategies with which to explain it. Smith, for example observes that *many of our analytical excursions through the harmony of complicated nineteenth century pieces are aimless expeditions through a foreign land, guided only by an ancient, untranslated map.*[2] The central problem, he sees, is the failure to understand and identify the chordal detail of chromatic works. He states: *surely most late nineteenth century chromatic masterpieces manifest a tonality that is still intimately related to, perhaps even derived from particular chordal sonorities. Unfortunately, we have had little success in characterising the chordal detail of these works. Few of us are familiar with analytical strategies that lead either to fluency with, or to insight about chromatic chords. Even the two strategies that seem to promise the most detailed attention to harmony, namely, chordal (Roman numeral) and linear analysis, have failed us in this regard.*[3]

Whilst therefore, the existence of a chromatic level of tonality may be recognised, the most severe problem, which has still not been satisfactorily resolved, is the precise nature of the chromatic sphere itself. With an appreciation of this problem, comes a particular type of anxiety, for at the point at which tonality should have taken a considerable leap forward from a diatonic

---

[1] William J. Mitchell, A Study of Chromaticism, in: JMT 6/1, 1962, p. 2.

[2] Charles J. Smith, The Functional Extravagance of Chromatic Chords, in: MTS 8, 1986, 94.

[3] Ibid., 94.

to a more advanced chromatic base, the whole system seems to collapse, leaving nothing but a state of tonal chaos in its wake.

To further appreciate this very difficult problem it is important to observe that when the resources of the major and minor modes are combined together the result is not a complete chromatic scale, for there are gaps present between the tonic and supertonic, dominant and subdominant degrees. Conventional harmony shows us that these gaps are filled in by the flat supertonic degree, which provides the root of the Neapolitan Sixth chromatic triad, and the leading note of the dominant, as found in the major supertonic triad which performs the important function as the dominant triad of the dominant itself. The scale which results from the filling in of these two gaps is aptly termed the harmonic form of the chromatic scale:

The Harmonic Form of the Chromatic Scale[1]

Note	Ratio	Cents	Interval with Tonic	Function
C	1/1	0	Prime	Tonic
Db	16/15	112	Minor second	Flat supertonic
D	9/8	204	Major second	Supertonic
Eb	6/5	316	Minor third	Minor mediant
E	5/4	386	Major third	Major mediant
F	4/3	498	Perfect fourth	Subdominant
F#	45/32	590	Augmented fourth	Dominant leading note
G	3/2	702	Perfect fifth	Dominant
Ab	8/5	814	Minor sixth	Minor Submediant
A	5/3	884	Major sixth	Major Submediant
Bb	9/5	1018	Minor seventh	Subtonic
B	15/8	1088	Major seventh	Leading note

Here it is important to make a brief reassessment of the way in which equal temperament accommodates this scale. It has already been observed that at one level, the tempered scale represents the array of keynotes or tonal centres available to the composer within the terms of the diatonic tonal system. That, within the chromatic tonal system, deference is still being offered to a central keynote, means that this array retains a validity within the terms of that new system. The essential difference is that each key is now defined by the more

---

[1] See interval table on pages 233-4 of Ramon Fuller's A Study of Microtonal Equal Temperaments, in: JMT 35, Spring 1991.

complex criterion of the harmonic form of the chromatic scale, in which the twelve notes of the tempered scale act as its imperfect representatives as they apply to and originate from each key.

The recognition of a complete chromatic scale within the province of a particular key is undoubtedly a significant step towards the development of a self-contained chromatic system of tonality, for it signifies that diatonic constraints are no longer the primary consideration. Being forcefully implied by the marriage of the major and minor modes, the harmonic form of the chromatic scale would seem to offer a great deal of promise in this respect. Indeed, an examination of this scale from the standpoint of valency shows that it has remarkable properties of balance and symmetry which do indeed tend to commend it as a potential successor to the major and minor modes as the basis for a more advanced chromatic system of tonality. Here the first observation which can be made is that it is composed of three segments of four perfect fifths:

The Harmonic Form of the Chromatic Scale as Composed of Three Segments of Four Perfect Fifths

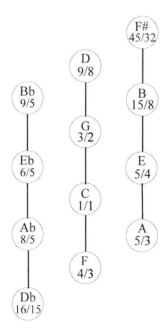

This diagram presents another angle of balance and symmetry, in that each member of the central column is flanked either side by a super-major pole (a major third up), and a sub-major pole (a major third down), the three together forming a strong triangular unit defined by the augmented triad. The scale as a whole thus appears as four interlocking triangles held together by the central column of fifths. Each triangle, being possessed of an autonomy, speaks of chordal movement or progression outside of the terms of the diatonic scale, the relationship between successive chordal axes being governed purely by these internal dynamics. A succession of four augmented triads whose axes lie a perfect fifth apart thus possesses a coherence and logic which is purely chromatic in its origins. In this respect, the opening theme to Liszt's *Faust Symphony*, rather than being some kind of anticipation of twelve-note procedures, appears more appropriately as a definitive exposition of this new found chromatically based harmonic logic.

Opening Theme to Liszt's *Faust Symphony*.

Because the augmented triad is not found in the diatonic scale, aside from the minor mode where it may be regarded as an inherent chromatic element, means that it offers prime opportunities for experiment with modes of harmonic logic which are purely chromatic in their origins. The whole tone scale, represented as the sum of two such triads a whole tone apart, is clearly a prime resultant of such experiments with purely chromatic harmonic logic.

The harmonic form of the chromatic scale offers two transpositions of such a scale. Deriving from a format which is essentially non-diatonic in its orientation means that such phenomena readily present themselves as clear evidence for the existence of a chromatic system of tonality, despite the fact that the logic of that system is not yet properly understood. Yet this by no means exhausts the chromatic possibilities of the scale. Looking at the chromatic scale from the standpoint of the other diagonal, quite a different perspective will be seen, based this time on the diminished triad.

Here the implication exists of a chain of replicated diminished triads whose axes lie a perfect fifth apart. That the diminished triad is present in the diatonic scale, means that those avenues of purely chromatic usage based on it generally devolve around the properties of the diminished seventh chord, obtained as the sum of two diminished triads, or alternatively, a diminished triad to which has been added another minor third. The chromatic scale readily breaks down into a sum of three such tetrads.

Patterns of Coherence in the Chromatic Scale Based on the Diminished Triad

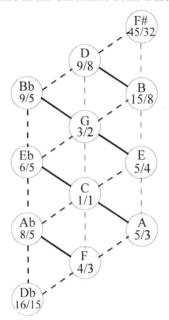

Through the enharmonic reinterpretation of each note of a given tetrad, a diminished seventh chord can be obtained which is valid for any one of four keys. Suppression of the tendencies of such chords for resolution has the effect of temporarily suspending tonality, and promoting a state of dominant prolongation whose effects are so widespread in the music of the nineteenth century that this point is hardly worth any further discussion. One point worth mentioning is that two of these diminished seventh chords combine to give rise to the octatonic scale, an essentially non-diatonic pitch collection which, like the whole tone scale, is also based on purely chromatic avenues of harmonic logic.

The harmonic form of the chromatic scale possesses truly remarkable properties, crystalline attributes of mathematical regularity and precision which have made it extremely attractive to composers. Above all, it has those extra notes which has allowed composers to escape from the constraints of the diatonic scale, and eventually attain a degree of freedom from conventional harmonic practice which has been most liberating. However, there is still a fundamental problem to be solved. As the foundation for a chromatic system of tonality it might be assumed that the chromatic scale thereby offers a completely adequate summary of the tonal resources available within a given key. An examination of this prospect shows that it is rather deficient in this respect.

Compared to the original sub-chromatic scale the chromatic scale has two extra notes. In the key of C these are the notes Db - the flat supertonic degree - and the note F# obtained when the subdominant is raised to give a leading note to the dominant. As well as serving to fill in the gaps to complete the chromatic scale, the notes Db and F# represent the first order of manifestation of a particular type of chromaticism. This arises from the fact that the notes F# and Db are chromatic notes for both the keys of C major and C minor. Not being present in either of these keys means that in effect they represent a direct reference point to an outside tonality or tonalities. Although theoretically originating from another key, the use of such chromatic notes, together with the chromatic chords used to accompany them, has considerably enriched both the harmonic palette and colouristic range of expression available within the confines of a particular key.

The note F# partakes in the major common triad constructed upon the supertonic degree. To both C major and C minor, it is a chromatic chord, in that it offers harmonic support to a note which does not belong to either key. Yet this chord belongs to the closely related dominant key, where it itself is the dominant triad. Its usage as a secondary dominant in this respect, fully justifies this observation. The appearance of the note F# in the tonality of C, either as a chromatic passing note between the subdominant and dominant, or as a substitute for the subdominant, hardly implies a modulation. On the contrary, it gives a concision to the voice leading, and a quite natural emphasis to those triads which are the important functionaries of the tonality.

The note Db too, partakes in a common triad of which itself is the root: the Neapolitan triad. This commonly used triad offers a strong harmonic support to the chromatic note Db in the keys of C major or minor. Yet it too, can be viewed to be simply a borrowing from another key. In this case the key concerned is the closely related subdominant minor key where the Neapolitan triad being referred to appears as chord VI.

In addition to the resources of the diatonic scale, tonal composers have made great use of this additional resource. Here, one of the fundamental problems which arises is that the chromatic scale, assumed to provide the underlying basis for this phenomenon, does not actually embrace or support the entire range of practices which it is purported to represent. It has already been clearly demonstrated that the chromatic scale itself is the logical consequence of the merger of the major and minor tonalities. However, that merger has only been envisaged from a purely diatonic standpoint. Therefore, for that merger to be complete, it must also include the particular chromatic procedures possible within the major and minor tonalities. When these are considered, it will soon become apparent that a single chromatic scale is quite inadequate either as a summary or encapsulation of those procedures.

Now whilst it is not possible within this space to consider every chromatic procedure used in tonal music, it certainly is possible to chart the various chromatic notes which such procedures necessarily employ. Chromatic tones all perform a definite function within the tonality, and that their precise identity will be determined by the way in which it performs that function. Therefore, in the key of C, the note F# will perform a quite different function to the note Gb. This is because to use a chromatic tone one of the notes of the diatonic scale must be flattened or sharpened. Having thus altered a note, a tendency or leaning is created towards the note above or below as the case may be. Because chromatic tones have this directionality, means that a sharp has different implications to a flat. A sharp chromatic note has a tendency to rise, whilst a flat chromatic note has a tendency to fall.

In equal temperament, these two contradictory tendencies are represented by the same pitch. Therefore the note Ab is represented by the same key as *G#*: the phenomenon of enharmonic equivalence. Now in terms of the network of tonal relations as defined by the latticework ensuing from the collective action of the valent bonds of which a given tonality is the sum, the sharp and the flat, of necessity, imply different pitches. Consequently, it can be seen that between each whole tone of a diatonic scale there should actually be two chromatic notes, not one. The first would be the result of the sharpening of the lowermost note, the second a result of the flattening of the uppermost note.

When the tone of destination is brought into the picture, the result is one of the most elementary manifestations of chromaticism - the chromatic passing note. All possible chromatic notes can be placed into a context where they occur as passing notes. In the case of a rising chromatic passing note the original note is sharpened, and thence proceeds upwards to the tone above. Therefore in the key of C Major there are five of these:

Rising Chromatic Passing Notes in the Key of C Major

With a descending chromatic passing note the reverse process occurs, for the note affected by the alteration is flattened by a minor semitone, and thence proceeds onwards to the adjacent note below. Similarly, there are five of these:

Falling Chromatic Passing Notes in the Key of C Major

Now as, at the chromatic level of tonality, a single key may be considered to result from the unification of the resources of both the major and minor modes, it follows that those chromatic passing notes originating from the minor mode, also need to be brought into consideration. These are:

Chromatic Passing Notes in the Key of C Minor

As the use of a chromatic passing note does not signify a change of key, it follows that to the original chromatic scale, all tones implicated through the use of chromatic passing notes need to be considered in order to obtain a scale which represents the true chromatic resources of that unified tonality. This uses the same logic that included the notes Db and F# within the domain of the key of C.

Therefore, to the original twelve notes, a further eight need to be added. These are the notes C#, D#, G#, A#, Cb, Fb, Gb, and Bbb. The result will then be a scale which accurately portrays and reflects the chromatic possibilities available within the province of a single key. This scale, it will be observed, will have at least nineteen notes to the octave.

Extended Chromatic Scale to Account for Chromatic Procedures

Note	Interval	Function
C	Prime	Tonic
C#	Augmented Prime	#I
Db	Minor Second	bII
D	Major Second	Supertonic
D#	Augmented Second	#II
Eb	Minor Third	Minor Mediant
E	Major Third	Major Mediant
Fb	Diminished Fourth	bIV
F	Perfect Fourth	Subdominant
F#	Augmented Fourth	#IV
Gb	Diminished Fifth	bV
G	Perfect Fifth	Dominant
G#	Augmented Fifth	#V
Ab	Minor Sixth	Minor Submediant
A	Major Sixth	Major Submediant
Bbb	Diminished Seventh	bVII
A#	Augmented Sixth	#VI
Bb	Minor seventh	Subtonic
B	Major Seventh	Leading Tone
Cb	Diminished Octave	bVIII

Now it has already been mentioned that these extra chromatic notes may be tentatively viewed as being borrowed from other keys. The chords which impart to such tones their direction and tonal purpose are also usually viewed to be likewise. In conventional harmony, aside from the use of such tones for purely melodic decorative purposes, their functions are thus obtained as an outgrowth of the principle of secondary dominant harmony. In this way can be explained the functions of those chromatic notes obtained by sharpening a scale step such as *C#, D#, G#,* etc. in the key of C.

Sharp Chromatic Tones Resulting from the Application of Secondary Dominant Harmony

C: I V ii   V vii iii   V V vi
        ii   iii   vi

Similarly, those chromatic tones resulting from the flattening of a scale step also implicate secondary dominant harmony, the chromatic note generally being the seventh, or sometimes the ninth of the dominant of the note that follows. In this way can be explained the functions of such notes as Db, Bb and Gb in the key of C:

Flat Chromatic Notes Resulting from the Application of Secondary Dominant Harmony

The network of diatonic tonal relations is considerably stretched through the use of such tones, although of course, with the push and pull of so many dominants, together with the rather hazy definition of the scale step that chromaticism brings, there was always the risk of obscuring the overall sense of tonality. The important point however, is that the harmonic form of the chromatic scale is not in itself an adequate summary of the resources of the phenomenon of chromaticism, even as it occurs from a diatonic perspective. Equal temperament, because it only has twelve notes, tends to foster this mistaken impression.

However, the matter gets worse, because even given recognition of a more complex enharmonic scale implied by the phenomenon of chromaticism, all that this points to is a sphere in which diatonic notes and chords are being borrowed from other keys in order to support processes of linear chromaticism. This therefore begs the question: where is the fundamental basis for a chromatic system of tonality as is actually implied by the harmonic form of the chromatic scale? An extended range of basic triads, the augmented triad and diminished seventh tetrad, together with a range of secondary dominants and other relatively minor chromatic discords may provide the basis for a system of chromatically enriched diatonic tonality, but they certainly do not provide a clear and tangible basis for a complete tonal system in its own right. In this sense, in the absence of any clearer knowledge concerning the fourth dimension of tonal space, the promise of a chromatic system of tonality collapses, and with it, the further possibilities of the system of tonality itself.

THE SEPTIMAL MATRIX AS THE THEORETICAL KEY TO THE CHROMATIC TONAL SYSTEM

As the underlying agent of the synthesis of the major and minor modes, the chromatic scale would seem to represent a quite natural and logical successor to the modal polarity which provided the basis for the diatonic tonal system. Born of the union of the major and minor modes, it speaks of a more diffuse and elevated tonal realm, free of the conventions and stock formulae which had become the crystallised essence of the diatonic tonal system.

Yet to advocate the chromatic scale as the basis for a new level of tonality is also extremely problematic, for it has already been shown that it does not embrace the phenomenon which it purports to represent. Here, the directional properties of chromatic elements, whereby one note gravitates either up or down to another are deeply significant. To accommodate these it is necessary to bring in extra chromatic notes, a sharp and a flat between each whole tone of the diatonic scale. This process, it has been shown, increases the chromatic scale from twelve to nineteen notes at the very minimum.

To a certain extent, some of the practical problems arising from this are lessened, because in equal temperament, the sharp and flat being referred to are represented by the same note. Yet to assert, because of this, that G# is therefore the same as Ab, is to confuse function with the imperfect means being offered for the expression of that function. The facility which equal temperament offers for the reduction of the number of notes needed to represent these differences of function is extremely felicitous. Having attained that reduction, the matrix of functions upon which the operation of tonality depends are not similarly reduced. The number of functions remains exactly the same.

To understand the phenomenon of chromaticism it is thus vitally necessary to recognise that from a functional standpoint, the note G# is significantly different from an Ab. However, even given that recognition this does not mean that the problems of a chromatic level of tonality are thereby solved. Such a step seems to make the matter worse than it was before. This is because those extra chromatic notes which are used in a particular key are simply a borrowing from other keys, the manifestation of secondary leading notes and their accompanying dominant sevenths or ninths which represent the tonicising agents of the note to which a given chromatic tone progresses. In this sense, there would seem to be no chromatic level of tonality, simply a diatonic tonality enriched by the use of chromatic elements deriving from other keys.

From this standpoint the very idea of a chromatic system of tonality would seem to be a falsehood, a chimera based on the mistaken assumption that the death throes of tonality were in fact the signs of new life. Yet there is surely more to it than that. The force of tonality arises as a result of that natural property of tone called the valency. Stemming from the autogenetic powers of the prototypical tone, tonality is, more than anything else a deep-seated recognition of that fundamental principle from which all tonal relations arise in the first place. To destroy tonality therefore, is quite impossible, because to attempt to do so is to remove the principle which generates tonal relations. To do this, is to leave nothing but the tempered scale as a substitute for those original relations. The empty husk which is left, admittedly offers interesting opportunities to composers, as it is a material over which it is possible to exert an absolute intellectual control. But control at what price?

All that this means is that musical compositions are being organised without the co-operation of the natural force of valency, in which case the musical material itself is akin to dead matter. Although expedient for a time, such a solution to the problems posed by the musical cosmos can only be a short term one, a temporary respite or adjournment whilst a new assault is being planned.

Because the force of tonality is rooted in the property of valency, means that any problems which do arise in respect of that system can only be solved at source, that is by returning to the point of origin of that system: the valency of tone. In respect of this observation, it immediately becomes apparent that an important factor which has not yet been systematically and productively applied to the problem of a chromatic tonal system is the prime number seven as it provides the basis for the various chords of the augmented sixth.

This may seem rather curious, in that such chords do not seem to be that important to musical harmony. Rameau's *Treatise on Harmony* got by without even mentioning them. Examination however, shows that such chords are more important than at first may become apparent from a study of conventional musical harmony. This is because, representing the prime entry point into tonal music of the 7/4 relation, they represent the media of expansion and upgrading of the tonal system from a three-dimensional to a four-dimensional format. Looking for example, at the harmonic form of the chromatic scale, it will be seen that there are only two possible points where there is an extremely close match to the interval whose ratio is 7/4 (969 cents): between the notes Db & B, and Ab & F#:

Table of Interval Sizes Compared to the Seventh Harmonic (7/4) in the Chromatic Scale

Pitches	Ratio	Cents	Difference (to 7/4)
C - Bb	16/9	996	27
Db - B	225/128	976	7
D - C	16/9	996	27
Eb - Db	16/9	996	27
E - D	9/5	1018	49
F - Eb	9/5	1018	49
F# - E	16/9	996	27
G - F	16/9	996	27
Ab - F#	225/128	976	7
A - G	9/5	1018	49
Bb - Ab	9/5	1018	49
B - A	16/9	996	27

Looking more closely at these augmented sixth intervals it will be seen that the note Db is a diatonic semitone (16/15) above the tonic note C, whilst the note B is a diatonic semitone below. Consequently, the augmented sixth is the interval left over when two diatonic semitones are subtracted from the octave:

Derivation of Augmented Sixth Interval

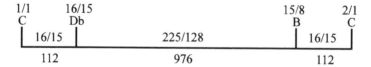

If, as has been asserted, the ear takes this sharp sixth relation to be the interval whose ratio is 7/4, then one of the semitones must be ascribed a different ratio. This is the note Db, lying as it does, outside of the range of the diatonic (major and minor scales) territory of the key of C. To bring this note in line with the proper septimal ratio needed, it must be raised slightly by a septimal degree (225/224) from 16/15 to 15/14:

Implied Septimal Ratio for the Flat Supertonic Degree

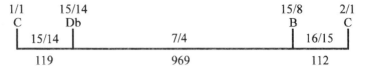

In terms of the other augmented sixth between the notes Ab and F#, the conventional three-dimensional tuning for the chromatic scale assigns the ratio of 8/5 to the minor submediant degree, and 45/32 to the sharp fourth degree. This also results in an augmented sixth of ratio 225/128:

Augmented Sixth Between Minor Submediant and Sharp Fourth Degrees

Substituting 7/4 for the more complex ratio 225/128 means that one of the two notes will also need to be ascribed a different tuning. This is the chromatic note F# which needs to be flattened by a septimal degree (225/224) from 45/32 to 7/5:

Septimal Augmented Sixth Between the Minor Submediant and Sharp Fourth Degrees

```
3/2        8/5                               7/5      (3/2)
G          Ab                                F#         G
   | 16/15 |              7/4              | 15/14 |
```

In this way, the mathematics underlying the tuning of these particular intervals have been upgraded in accordance with the mechanics of the audible process which, within the liminal margins of a particular interval always tends to offer deference to the nearest simple ratio, in this case 7/4. Here there is something very special to be seen about this particular interval. Aldwell & Shachter, for example, observe that: *The presence of an augmented sixth chord is a sure indication of chromaticism.... No diatonic scale contains for example, both F natural and D#. The resolution of an augmented sixth to an octave sounds like nothing else in tonal music. With its half-step progressions by contrary motion, it intensifies the following chord in a unique way. As a consequence augmented sixth chords often occur just before important structural points; composers can use them to signal the beginning or end of a phrase in the tonal movement or the form.*[1]

Here the authors make a vitally important point. The notes F and D# belong to no diatonic scale. Unlike other chromatic chords, such as the augmented triad and diminished seventh chord therefore, chords of the augmented sixth are not diatonically referable. They work and operate within a sphere all of their own. In this sense the various chords of the augmented sixth acquire an increasingly important theoretical status in that, not originating from the diatonic sphere, they are therefore the functionaries or emissaries of a larger chromatic sphere which lies outside of the terms of the diatonic scale.

Arranging for convenience the notes of the chromatic scale in fifths it can be easily demonstrated that the augmented sixth interval cannot actually belong to the diatonic sphere as defined by the ten note chromatic mode. Beginning with the note Db it will be seen that the note B required to give an augmented sixth lies outside of that ten note limit:

Interval of the Augmented Sixth as it Exceeds the Range of the Sub-chromatic Scale

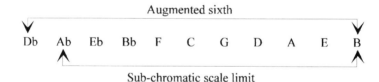

Sub-chromatic scale limit

This means therefore, that wherever and whenever the interval of the augmented sixth occurs, it cannot be viewed as a borrowing from a closely related key simply because there is no single key in which such an interval occurs. Consequently, the notes Db and F# have a dual signification. On the one hand they are borrowed chromatic notes belonging to other diatonic keys, yet on the other, through the augmented sixth intervals that they bring into the key, they represent the entry port into an altogether larger encompassing sphere - a chromatic sphere of tonality which necessarily precludes the participation of all diatonic elements.

As the points of entry into the sphere of tonality of the 7/4 relation, the notes Db and F# constitute a vital link between the diatonic sphere as defined by a prime number five limit, and the more advanced chromatic sphere as defined by a prime number seven limit. This is why the location of the chromatic sphere

---

[1] Aldwell and Schachter, Augmented Sixth Chords, Harmony and Voice Leading, 478.

has proved to be so elusive. It lies in a *different dimension* to the diatonic sphere.

Within this observation there is a strong feature which points to the fundamental grounds and basis for the chromatic system of tonality. Because augmented sixth chords do not belong to any particular diatonic key, means that their usage does not therefore suggest any other key. This means that through chords of the augmented sixth harmonic support is being offered for a chromatic note or notes which in conventional terms would not be construed as belonging to the tonality in question. However, because of the harmonic context in which that chromatic note occurs it cannot be construed as a borrowing from another key either. Both the chromatic note and the augmented sixth chord which accompanies it, originates from outside of the diatonic sphere of operation of tonality. It is thus a foreign element which belongs to and originates from the sphere of purely chromatic tonal relations.

This has a very important bearing on the notion that the chord of the augmented sixth has a septimal basis. Possessing intervals whose ratios involve the prime number seven, its component intervals are introducing new elements which cannot be explained through reference to the prime numbers three and five alone. Here the ratio 7/4 provides an interesting case. As occurring in an augmented sixth chord constructed upon the minor submediant degree, it invokes the note F# which, in relation to the tonic note C, has a ratio of 7/5. This note possesses a simple, clear and easily perceptible ratio to that tonic note - a direct valent relationship which serves to accomplish an important task. It claims that note F# into the domain of the key of C, and in so doing provides it with a firm contextual place and function therein.

In other words, possessing a ratio of 7/5 to the tonic note, the note F# cannot be viewed as a borrowing from the dominant key. It is a diatonically detached note which, by virtue of its strong relationship to the tonic note, can only be construed as belonging to the tonal field in which it occurs. In this way, through the support offered to such chromatic notes by the prime number seven, the limits of the diatonic sphere are being subtly breached. Thus breached, another sphere is beginning to form in its place: the more complex sphere of operation of a chromatic system of tonality.

Therefore the first question that needs to be answered is how to recognise that sphere. In answer to this question it may be observed that the chromatic scale delineates twelve pitch points within the octave. Now when a minor triad is constructed on the dominant degree, the harmonic minor third (6/5) required above the dominant would bring into play a different version of the minor seventh, a comma of Didymus (81/80) larger than the cyclic minor seventh implied by two superimposed fourths. The former would have a ratio of 9/5, the latter a ratio of 16/9.

However, this does not delineate a new pitch point within the octave since both pitches perform the same essential function - as a minor seventh relationship to the tonic degree. There is thus no change of macro-intervallic modality, simply an implied shift of micro-intervallic modality made to facilitate accuracy and clarity of intonation. If, however, it could be shown that through the use of septimal harmony, a proliferation of macro-intervallic modalities which extended beyond the twelve-point chromatic system occurred, it would no longer be true to say that the chromatic scale was the governing intervallic matrix so far as those practices were concerned. On the contrary, a new expanded scalar matrix would have to be recognised which at least theoretically supported such practices, showed their precise point of origination, and at the same time offered an explanation of how and why divergences from the original twelve-point chromatic system occurred.

However, is it true to say that there has been a proliferation of intervallic modalities beyond the scope of the twelve-point chromatic system? To be able to establish this, the first task is to recognise the usage of a range of intervallic modalities which breaches the limitations of the chromatic scale. This is assisted by the observation that the imperfect degrees of the scale - the second, third, sixth and seventh - occur in two positions each: major and minor, whilst the three perfect degrees are, in the main immutable, except for the sharpening of the fourth. The chromatic scale thus consists of eight points within the octave arising from the mutable positions of the imperfect degrees, three points arising from the immutability of the perfect degrees, and an additional point arising from the sharpening of the fourth degree - thus making a total of twelve.

Intervallic Layout of the Twelve Point Octave

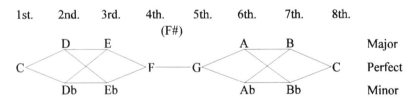

If therefore, a scale degree was used which formed an interval of an augmented second with the tonic, then it could be asserted that the usage of this particular note implied an immanent expansion of intervallic modalities which breached the limits of the chromatic scale. This is extremely well recognised in the process of modulation, where, for example, beginning in the key of C major the composer modulates say, to E minor, and introduces the note D# as the required leading note to the newly established keynote.

However, in this case the note D# automatically falls outside of the terms of any possible expansion of intervallic modalities, simply because the note D# belongs to the province of a new tonality, and therefore cannot be interpreted as performing a primary tonal function within the tonality of C major. On the contrary, it is a note the presence of which tends to temporarily contradict the tonality of C major through the implied tonicisation of a new tonic triad, in this case E minor. Therefore the note D#, although alien to the twelve-point chromatic system of the key of C, is an integral part of the twelve-point chromatic system of the key of E - i.e. the major modality of the interval of the seventh (15/8).

If, however, it could be shown that the note D# was being used in the key of C without any implied change or alteration of tonal centre, and without any primary reference to the twelve point chromatic system of another key, then it could be asserted that at least in this case, an interval was being used which exceeded the bounds of the twelve-point chromatic octave.

Evidence to support this lies in the further consideration of chords of the augmented sixth. The already discussed Italian, German and French Sixth chords by no means exhaust the range of augmented sixth chords commonly used within the sphere of tonal music. There are quite a large number which were in general use throughout the course of the nineteenth and twentieth centuries.

A systematic key to the understanding of such chords lies in the existence of a constructive principle which can be both observed and derived from the Italian, French and German sixth chords. First, as a collective group of chords, they derive from a tertial chain of dominant harmony which extends up to the ninth. Second, all three chords share a common feature, which is the possession of a diminished third. Third, it becomes apparent that these diminished thirds all arise from the chromatic alteration of a minor third.

Derivation of Septimal-Chord Types

From this it can be seen that any minor third belonging to a dominant seventh or ninth chord can feasibly be chromatically altered to form a diminished third.

Application of this principle leads to a dual result since it is possible to either flatten the upper note, or sharpen the lower note:

Results of Application of the Principle of Septimal Alteration

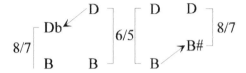

In this way chromatically altered septimal chords may be obtained, many of which have been used by composers in one form or another. Moreover, the chords arrived at through the application of that principle are different from all other chords. Sonorities used within the constraints of the three-dimensional diatonic system of tonality are composed of an admixture of major and/or minor thirds. Septimal chords however may be composed of an admixture of major, minor, diminished and/or augmented thirds. The latter interval arises when the third of a major chord is sharpened to produce a diminished third between the third and fifth, which means that the interval between the root and the third will be an augmented third of ratio 21/16.

The existence of such a principle can be observed with the augmented sixth chord types discussed earlier. Moreover, having discovered such a principle, it is now possible to approach the matter of septimal sonorities from the other direction. Having looked at examples to discover the principle, the principle itself can now be used to see how many, and of what kind, are the septimal sonorities which can be generated through its conscious application. Confining this to chords belonging to the dominant pillar it can be seen that there are numerous minor thirds which fall subject to this principle:

Septimal Chords Resulting from Alteration of Dominant Sonorities

Examples of Septimal Alterations of the Chord of the Dominant Seventh

	1a	1b	1c	1d	1e	1f
Seventh:	F	F	F	Fb	Fb	F
Fifth:	D	Db	D#	D	Db	D
Third:	B	B	B	B	B	B#
Root:	G	G	G	G	G	G

Examples of Septimal Alterations of the Diminished Seventh

	2a	2b	2c	2d	2e	2f
Ninth:	Ab	Ab	Ab	Ab	Ab	Ab
Seventh:	F	F	Fb	F#	Fb	F#
Fifth:	Db	D#	D	D	Db	D#
Third:	B	B	B	B	B	B

Examples of Septimal Alterations of Half-diminished Seventh

	3a	3b	3c	3d
Ninth:	A	A	A	A
Seventh:	F	F	Fb	F
Fifth:	D	Db	D	D#
Third:	B	B	B	B

Examples of the use of these septimal chords provide proof that the twelve-point octave has been breached. One such sonority is the augmented 6-4-3 chord (chord 2c): a chord enharmonically equivalent to both the chords of the dominant seventh and the German Sixth. In a tempered context the features that distinguish it are the way in which it is spelled, and/or treated. Here the fifth of the German Sixth chord is spelled as a doubly-augmented fourth:

The Augmented 6-4-3 Chord

$$A_3^6$$
(Ger. Sixth) $$A_4^6$$ 3

The other major distinction is the manner of its resolution. Because, in equal temperament, the *Eb* is spelled as a *D#* it automatically precludes the minor mode, in that it implies stepwise progression upwards to the note E. It thus progresses most appropriately to the tonic major 6/4 chord. Progressing thus, it can be seen to originate from a pair of chromatic passing notes being applied to the root and third of the minor supertonic seventh:

Origination and Resolution of the Augmented 6-4-3 Chord

C: ii$_4^{6\flat5}$ A$_4^6$ I V

Because the equally tempered chromatic scale is the medium through which most composers have chosen to express their ideas, the augmented 6-4-3 chord is often spelled as a German Sixth chord. The presence of the augmented 6-4-3 chord is always betrayed by the apparently irregular mode of resolution of the German Sixth, the fifth rising up to the major mediant degree of the scale:

Irregular Mode of Resolution of German Sixth Chord Betraying Presence of Augmented 6-4-3 Chord

$$\text{C: } A^{6}_{5(4)} \quad I^{6}_{4} \quad V$$

The progression of the augmented 6-4-3 chord to the tonic major chord somewhat quashes the notion that it is a chord of dominant preparation. Yet because it progresses to the tonic 6/4 the dominant is never far behind. In one sense then, chords of the augmented sixth can be explained through a process of goal orientation. The composer is heading the chord progression towards the dominant, and because the arrival of the dominant is structurally important, it is intensified through the use of a chord of the augmented sixth. The different types of chords of the augmented sixth thus perform similar functions, but imply different types of voice leading.

Therefore, in the case of the augmented 6-4-3 chord, the note D# acts as an inclining tone up to the third of the tonic triad. However, it is extremely difficult to explain this chord as a chromatic alteration of chord V of V. This is easy with the Italian, French and German Sixth chords, but the presence of the D# in the case of the augmented 6-4-3 chord means that chord V of V would have a sharp root. Similarly, although this chord can be brought into play through chromatic alteration of the supertonic seventh chord, does not necessarily mean therefore, that it is a form of manifestation of the supertonic seventh. The root of the augmented 6-4-3 chord must thus lie elsewhere.

One way of discovering the absent root is to see where it occurs in the dominant pillar of V. Here, an augmented 6-4-3 chord is implied by flattening the diminished fifth of the chord of the diminished seventh:

Derivation of the Augmented 6-4-3 Chord

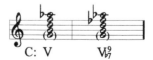

$$\text{C: } V \qquad V^{9}_{\flat 7}$$

The augmented 6-4-3 chord may thus be regarded to be a chromatically altered form of the diminished seventh chord. This explains the characteristic modes of resolution of this chord. By virtue of its intervallic tendencies, it generally implies a resolution to two functional triads:

Chords of Resolution of the Augmented 6-4-3 Chord

In this example by Schumann an augmented 6-4-3 chord constructed upon the flat supertonic degree progresses to chord vi of the key of A:

Extract from Schumann's *Novelette*, Opus 21, No. 7.

Discussing this chord in *Harmony: Its Theory and Practice*, Prout asserts that: *The notation is evidently inaccurate as Bb and E# cannot possibly belong to the same key. The E# is really F natural and the resolution of the chord is unusual, being on the first inversion of the submediant triad.*[1] Yet as one of the well recognised forms of augmented sixth chord it would be spelled *Bb D E# G#*.

The important point is that the note E# does not belong to the chromatic scale of the key of A, which is probably the reason why Prout chooses to reject it. Not generally being recognised, four-dimensional phenomena arising from the intuitive use of the prime number seven are often dismissed as being inaccurate, or interpreted from a theoretical foundation which stops with the limitations of the third dimension of tonal space. As Partch has so well observed concerning this theoretical limitation: *In another way the men whose work is widely recognised as the heart of 'Western Golden Age of music' - Bach, Mozart, Haydn, Beethoven and many more - were also daring men, who simply*

---

[1] Ebenezer Prout, Harmony, Its Theory and Practice, 280.

appropriated as a medium of expression whatever was at hand, which happened to be instruments and notation based on the five limit.[1]

Operating within the five limit, Prout chooses to dismiss the note E#. Yet from a septimal standpoint it can quite easily be accounted for. The interval from *Bb* to *G#* has a ratio of 7/4, which means that the ratio of the interval from *D* to *G#* will be 7/5, whilst the interval between *E#* and *G#* is a minor third of ratio 6/5. Therefore the ratio of note E# to D is 7/5 minus 6/5 which equals 7/6.

Ratios of the Intervals of the Augmented 6-4-3 Chord

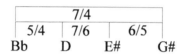

That the usage of this chord serves to breach the confines of the chromatic scale can be easily demonstrated by considering the various notes belonging to this chord in relation to the chromatic scale itself:

Placing of the Augmented 6-4-3 Chord in the Chromatic Scale

Note	Ratio	Interval	Chordal Tones			
C	1/1	Prime		C		
Db	16/15	Minor Second	Db			
D	9/8	Major Second				D
D#	7/6	Augmented Second			**D#**	
Eb	6/5	Minor Third				
E	5/4	Major Third				
F	4/3	Perfect Fourth	F			
Fb	9/7	Diminished Fourth				**Fb**
F#	7/5	Augmented Fourth			F#	
G	3/2	Perfect Fifth				
G#	14/9	Augmented Fifth	**G#**			
Ab	8/5	Minor Sixth			Ab	Ab
A	5/3	Major Sixth				
Bb	16/9	Minor seventh				
B	15/8	Major Seventh	B (28/15)			B

---

[1] Harry Partch, Application of the 11 Limit, Genesis of a Music, 119.

The augmented 6-4-3 chord in its most commonly used positions, thus invokes some four points in the octave which are not considered in theory to comprise a part of the recognised scale. These points are represented by the notes D# (ratio 7/6), Fb (ratio 9/7), F# (ratio 7/5) and G# (ratio 14/9) and are represented in bold.

Another commonly used septimal chord is the augmented six-four-two chord (chord Ic of the above list). This is related to the French Sixth chord, the difference being that instead of a major third there is a whole tone above the bass. The resulting sonority is very easily perceptible as a chromatically altered dominant seventh chord::

Constitution, Derivation and Progression of the Augmented Six-Four-Two Chord

Whilst being enharmonically equivalent to a dominant minor thirteenth (*F G B Eb*), the augmented six-four-two is distinguishable from it by virtue of its characteristic mode of resolution, in which the *D#* tends to rise to the mediant. Within an equally tempered context, it is only this, and possibly the way the chord is spelled within the score, that informs the listener of the precise distinction between the two chords. In this example by Beethoven, the augmented six-four-two chord is used as a colouristic variant of the chord of the dominant seventh:

Excerpt from Beethoven's *Diabelli Variations*, Opus 120, Var. 28.

BEETHOVEN: Diabelli Variations, Op. 120, @ G. Henle Verlag, Munchen. Used with permission.

One of the interesting features of this chord is that the augmented sixth interval occurs on the subdominant degree of the scale, as opposed to the flat supertonic or minor submediant degree. The significance of this becomes clear when the septimal constitution of the chord is analysed. Here, there is only one septimal tone, note G#, which has a ratio of 7/4 with the bass note Bb, and therefore a ratio of 7/6 with the tonic note F. As a colouristic variant of the chord of the dominant seventh, it can obviously be used wherever secondary dominant harmony is used within the key. This therefore, implies the construction of the augmented sixth interval (7/4) or its inversion the diminished third (8/7), upon different degrees of the scale. In this example it is the subdominant degree which provides the relevant foundation.

Judging by this chord, espying the exact septimal tones used within a particular key is not difficult. Septimal tones are those which, lying outside of the harmonic form of the chromatic scale, are used as if they were a part of the key. This automatically means that they will be the enharmonic equivalents of notes already present in the scale. Examples of this in the key of C are note D# (7/6) which is enharmonically equivalent to note Eb (6/5); note Fb (9/7) - the enharmonic equivalent of note E (5/4); note F# (7/5) the enharmonic equivalent of note Gb (10/7); note G# (14/9) - the enharmonic equivalent of note Ab (8/5); note Bbb (12/7) - the enharmonic equivalent of note A (5/3), and of course, note A# (7/4) - the enharmonic equivalent of note Bb (16/9).

Because of this phenomenon of enharmonic equivalence, there are times when the usage of a septimal tone may be missed, and the precise chord left unidentified. There is an excellent example of this in the C Minor prelude (1839) by Frederick Chopin (1810 - 1849). In bar 5 there is a septimal chord which has not so far been discussed in this chapter:

Excerpt from Chopin's *Prelude in C Minor* (1839)

CHOPIN: Prelude in C minor, Op. 28 No. 20.
@ 1955 by the Associated Board of the Royal Schools of Music. Used by permission.

The septimal chord concerned is the third chord of the first bar. The fifth of the diminished seventh chord is sharpened to create the diminished third interval seen between the notes F# and Ab. Now it could be argued that because the *Ab* progresses melodically to the *F#*, that the true chordal tone is *Ab*, in which the *F#* is simply a rising appoggiatura up to the *G*. The diminished third interval tends to give this impression, for if the *F#* was an *F*, there would be no hesitation at all in seeing in this figure an arpeggiated third belonging to a diminished seventh chord.

Such arguments aside, when this chord is viewed as a complete tetrad, it represents a chromatically altered diminished seventh chord (tetrad 2d). Yet the heard effect of the progression contradicts its implied function as an agent of tonicisation of the ensuing first inversion G minor triad. This seems highly illogical, as the primary function of the chord as spelled would be to offer tonical support for the tonic chord itself.

Here is a prime example of that analytical problem pointed out by Parks (1976) where *chromatic ornamentation complicates analysis, as does the composers occasional use of chord spellings which conflict with their function.*[1]

How is this illogicality in the chord progression to be explained? One way is through an examination of the voice leading. The linear chromatic descent in the bass line moves from the tonic note C steadily down to the dominant note G. Examination of the bass line reveals that at least one of the notes has been misspelled. The first is note B. As this is a descending passing note between *C* and *Bb*, it should be written as a *Cb*. This complements the leading tone effect of *F#* up to *G*, whilst reinforcing the declining tone effect of *Ab* down to *G*. Therefore the correct spelling for this chord is *D F# Ab Cb*.

Spelled in this way the chord is much easier to understand for it is a secondary dominant seventh chord the fifth and seventh of which have been chromatically flattened (Vb7b5 of V). So it tonicises the G minor chord that follows because it is its dominant. The chromatic alterations bring the seventh and fifth a semitone nearer to the notes of their destination, and in so doing offer a very interesting chromatic variant of the dominant seventh.

Bearing in mind the way in which the chord is originally spelled, it is noteworthy that the ear recognises the implied tonicisation of the G minor chord, even though notationally speaking, the chord is presented as a chromatically altered dominant of the C minor triad. This serves to demonstrate that even on a tempered instrument, the ear is capable of recognising and appreciating the distinction between a perfect fifth, i.e. *B* to *F#*, as found in Chopin's original chord, and a super-augmented fourth, i.e. *Cb* to *F#*, as found in the functionally correct chord. This is because of the strong functional difference between the intervals, a difference which finds its natural expression through the voice leading.

---

[1] Richard S. Parks, Voice Leading and Chromatic Harmony in the Music of Chopin, in: JMT 20/2, 1976.

Derivation of Chromatically Altered Dominant Seventh Chord

The septimal chord as spelled in the Chopin extract (*B D F# Ab*) will be recognised as an example of one of the most famous chromatic chords in musical literature, sometimes known as the 'Tristan chord' on account of its occurrence at the beginning of the Prelude to Wagner's opera *Tristan und Isolde* (1860):

Utilising the pitches *F G# B* and *D#*, this chord is enharmonically equivalent to a half-diminished seventh chord. The factors that distinguish it from the half-diminished seventh chord are purely enharmonic features, that is, features directly attributable to the influence of the prime number seven. These become apparent in the augmented sixth interval (7/4) between notes F and D#, from which it may be readily inferred that such a chord is a chromatically altered dominant: a diminished seventh chord in third inversion, the fifth of which has been chromatically sharpened.

The chromatic sharpening of the seventh of the dominant may be seen as a complete contradiction of the entire function of the dominant pillar. Yet with the diminished seventh chord it seems to work, for the tension created between the root and seventh of the chord is strong enough for it to be able to support the inclining tone effect created by the sharp fifth. Furthermore, the sharpening of the seventh brings into play the augmented sixth interval whose pull is so strong, and exerts such a powerful influence in whatever chord it may be found.

Merely to mention the 'Tristan' chord is to become embroiled in the long standing debate about its validity as a harmonic sonority. One of the most popular views of the 'Tristan chord' is exemplified by Andrews, author of the *Oxford Book of Harmony,* who disclaims it entirely, considering the note G#, which gives the chord such an interesting profile, to be *simply a long appoggiatura of the A.*[1] To Andrews therefore, it is simply a chromatically embellished French sixth chord. Cecil Hill similarly describes the note G# as but *a long rising appoggiatura.*[2] He also observes that *careful listening can give no other impression, quite apart from the theoretical non-existence of the chord of F - G# - B - D# in A minor (or indeed in any key) in diatonic harmony.*[3]

However, these arguments cannot hold any water with the same chord as it appears in numerous other pieces of music. Examples of this are the Scherzo of Bruckner's Ninth Symphony (1891 - 6) where it figures quite considerably:

The 'Tristan Chord' as it Appears in Bruckner's 'Ninth Symphony'.

An even earlier example of exactly the same chord can be found in Haydn's *The Creation:*

The 'Tristan Chord' as it Appears in Haydn's *The Creation* (1796 - 8).

Here it appears as the first chord of the second bar, and in this position and key its derivation from the diminished seventh chord is much more apparent than in Wagner's 'Tristan'. Aware of this example, having been conspicuously pointed out by Prout,[4] Andrews later contradicts his previous assertion

---

[1] Andrews, The Oxford Book of Harmony, Vol. Two, Oxford University Press, London 1950, 56.

[2] Cecil Hill, That Wagner-Tristan Chord, in: MR45, 1984, 7 - 10.

[3] Ibid.

[4] Prout, Harmony: Its Theory and Practise, 280.

observing that in this example of Haydn the chord concerned *is the Tristan chord without any doubt about the augmented seconds legitimacy'*.[1]

When viewed in isolation, the 'Tristan Chord' can appear to be extremely problematic.[2] In the light of other examples of the chord as shown above, it is much easier to understand and to place, for both the Haydn and the Bruckner examples confirm it to be a chromatically altered diminished seventh chord. Those objections that have been made against it are therefore entirely valid when viewed from the standpoint of the three-dimensional diatonic system of tonality, for as Hill quite rightly points out, the 'Tristan' chord is essentially foreign to the territory of the diatonic system. So far as the four-dimensional chromatic tonal system is concerned, it simply represents one of many possible septimal sonorities.

Consequently, it is a chord which can be constructed upon other degrees of the scale as well. Schoenberg observes this, pointing out that a chord enharmonically equivalent to the supertonic seventh chord of the minor mode can be used in an approach to the Neapolitan Sixth. Because of the chromatic nature of this approach Schoenberg quite uncharacteristically observes that the *D* would be best spelled as an *Ebb*.[3] The resulting tone - note Ebb - would represent another addition to the series of septimal tones needed to complete the key. This particular tone (*Ebb* in the key of C) would have a ratio of 8/7, since 7/4, the augmented sixth between *Ebb* and *C*, leaves an interval of 8/7 (the inversion of 7/4) between *C* and *Ebb*.

Suffice to say, the 'Tristan' chord as it appears in either position, highlights numerous septimal tones as they occur within the given key:

The "Tristan' Chord in Relation to the Chromatic Scale

Note	Ratio	Interval	Chordal Tone	
C	1/1	Prime		C
Db	16/15	Minor Second		
D	9/8	Major Second	D	
Ebb	8/7	Diminished Third		**Ebb**
Eb	6/5	Minor Third		
E	5/4	Major Third		

---

[1] Andrews, The Oxford Book of Harmony, 56.

[2] For a resumé of some of the conflicting opinions which surround this chord see The 'Tristan Chord' : Some Reflections, by Martin Wilson, in: Wagner 10/3, 1989, 83 - 95.

[3] Schoenberg, At the Frontiers of Tonality; Other Augmented and Vagrant Chords, Theory of Harmony, 256.

Fb	9/7	Diminished Fourth		
F	4/3	Perfect Fourth		F
F#	7/5	Augmented Fourth	F#	
G	3/2	Perfect Fifth		
Ab	8/5	Minor Sixth	Ab	Ab
A	5/3	Major Sixth		
Bb	16/9	Minor seventh		
B	15/8	Major Seventh	B	
Cb	40/21	Diminished Octave		

From the example of the 'Tristan' chord, one area of confusion surrounding septimal chords becomes apparent, which is their enharmonic equivalence to other chords which occur within a purely diatonic framework. In the case of the 'Tristan' chord it is the half-diminished seventh chord, whilst with the preceding Chopin example, it is again the half-diminished seventh chord which provides the nearest diatonic parallel. Yet it is clear from the examples given, that such chords are subtly different from their diatonic counterparts. Schoenberg mentions this, observing the different ways in which a half-diminished seventh chord might resolve. In his example it is possible to perceive not one, but numerous chords:

Schoenberg's Resolutions of the 'Half-diminished Seventh Chord'.[1]

Judging by its mode of resolution the first chord is an augmented sixth tetrad, which should have been spelled as *Db Fb G* and *B*: that chromatic variant of the dominant seventh shown in the Chopin example above. The second would receive the same spelling, except that, given the chord of resolution, it can be interpreted from a different pathway. It is a chromatically altered diminished seventh of the key of Ab (*Db Fb G Bb*) the third of which has been chromatically raised (*Db Fb G B*).

The third chord derives from F minor, the diminished seventh chord in third inversion (*Db E G Bb*) the fifth of which has been chromatically sharpened (*Db E G B*) In this case it progresses to chord iii of the corresponding harmonic minor mode. It is a 'Tristan' chord in other words. The fourth chord is a half-diminished seventh chord, chord ii7 of the B harmonic minor mode progressing

---

[1] Schoenberg, Ex. 190, Theory of Harmony, 258.

to chord III. The last chord is too, deriving from E minor, where it constitutes the submediant seventh of the ascending melodic minor mode, progressing to chord III of the harmonic minor mode.

Of the five chords given by Schoenberg therefore, the first three may be regarded to be septimal chords, their identity being betrayed each time by the voice leading. Therefore, despite having to operate within the strictures of equal temperament, composers have been employing chord structures whose implied range of intervallic modalities has breached both the confines of the harmonic form of the chromatic scale, and the theoretically recognised ratio limit of the prime number five.

As such, it is necessary to recognise that although theoretically the West uses a twelve-tone scale, that actual musical usage points to the emergence of a more advanced scale structure which embraces those intervals which involve the prime number seven. This process has already happened without our awareness because of the theoretical impediment brought on through the surrender of an understanding of acoustical reality for the convenience, both theoretical and practical, of the equally tempered twelve-tone scale. It is fortuitous that because of the clear harmonic context in which septimal intervals occur that the tempered intervals are accepted by the ear as fair approximations. The important point is that it is not so much the purity of septimal intervals that matters in the first instance, but being able to recognise the unique tonal functions that they create and support.

THE IDENTIFICATION OF SEPTIMAL TONES IN TONAL MUSIC

In the last chapter it was possible to come to the reasonable conclusion that composers of tonal music have been quite unknowingly employing chords which in their construction presuppose the influence of the prime number seven. Because the excerpts shown used sonorities which were the common stock of the Romantic musical vocabulary, that is chromatic chords of the augmented sixth, means that there is nothing contentious about the existence of such chords, or the fact of their usage.

The contentious point was that through the use of such chords the boundaries of the chromatic scale have been ruptured, thus leading to the necessity thus for the theoretical formulation of a new scale which both accommodates those additional septimal tones, and accounts for their precise function within a tonal framework. This is a contentious point because it challenges the belief that the basis for nineteenth century music is a twelve-tone chromatic scale. Yet this belief in the supremacy of the chromatic scale derives from no more than a limited three-dimensional perspective of the music in question. Once it is recognised that through chords of the augmented sixth the influence of a new, fourth dimension has been making itself felt, then the concept of a scale that transcends the three-dimensional chromatic scale is much easier to accept.

In making such an observation a number of immediate problems arise. The prime number seven seems to have been utilised in tonal music without the awareness of either the composers who wrote it, or the theorists who formulated the principles whereby it could be understood, contextualised, and perceived within the framework of an overall system. Considered in retrospect, the major practical reason for this was the influence of equal temperament. Providing a fair approximation of any number of acoustically pure intervals, equal temperament obviated the need for an accurate distinction between them. The task of distinction was thus relegated to the listener who perceived the implied intervals by virtue of the context in which they were presented. As Roger Bullivant has observed *any given interval, as represented by two notes on the keyboard, may perform quite different functions according to the context in which it occurs.*[1] At a notational level it thus became irrelevant whether a minor seventh was spelled as an augmented sixth, or vice versa. The listener simply heard a standardised interval which could be interpreted in a number of ways depending upon the precise context.

In this way, context became the last vanguard of an acoustical reality with both the musical scale and the method of musical notation had become increasingly at odds. Now because context itself became a sufficiently reliable vehicle of intervallic interpretation it attained a self-sufficiency where it was no longer necessary to understand the acoustical realities behind it. In simple terms, context explained all. The listener readily understood the difference between a major sixth and a diminished seventh by virtue of what preceded and followed it.

That the causes and distinctions behind these two intervals lay in the domain of acoustically pure intervals could thus be conveniently glossed over. Therefore the influence of the prime number seven in this particular direction went unnoticed, because its effects were understood and formulated in the domain of context alone. In other words, the effects were heard, but not the precise cause behind those effects. Phenomena such as the 'Tristan chord' were thus perceived as interesting, or rather curious additions to normative tonal context. Even today there are still those who regard the 'Tristan chord' as a half-diminished seventh chord placed in an unusual context.

The problems posed by this lack of awareness on the behalf of both the composer and theorist are numerous. From a composers standpoint it means that up until recently at least, the influence of the prime number seven has not been fully recognised, despite numerous observations made by theorists which could have led to a more accurate prognosis of its possibilities. This general lack of awareness means that the influence of the prime number seven has tended to manifest on an intuitive level, which means that it is an influence which has not been consciously exercised or developed in a direction which would tend to expose the unique brand of internal musical logic for which this natural agency provides a vehicle.

Indeed, those composers who have tried to use it consciously have usually been labouring under the assumption that the seventh partial forms an interval of a minor seventh. As such, for reasons already discussed, such attempts have mostly resulted in a quest for intervallic purity which has sometimes found itself at odds with the musical thinking of the times. In effect therefore, a distinct gap has opened up between the practical reality, and what should or could be, given a more enlightened awareness of the actual implications of the prime number seven. If of course, the influence of the prime number seven had been correctly

---

[1] Roger Bullivant, 'The Nature of Chromaticism', in: MR 24, 1963, 97 -129.

recognised, say for example at the turn of the present century, then of course the progress of music may have been along a different track. Tonality, rather than being seen to collapse under the weight of excessive chromaticism, may have received a vital boost, perhaps in the direction which Yasser implied in his *A Theory of Evolving Tonality*, towards a new, more advanced state of supra-tonality.

Speaking of this negative view of chromaticism as the destructive force which rended the tonal system, Kramer observes *that the transition from Classical to Romantic harmony, and ultimately to atonality, is still commonly described from the point of view that Schoenberg developed to establish the historical inevitability of his own music. Seen in this way, the force of harmonic change in the nineteenth century was a gradual heightening of chromaticism that eventually obscured tonal functions so much that tonality 'broke down'....A more fruitful approach....is to emphasise the evolutionary role of 'extended tonality' in nineteenth century music...It is possible to argue that Romantic harmony is moved by an insistent impulse to extend tonality in this sense. This is a thrust that both affirms the structural force of tonal centres and at the same time places them under considerable stress.*[1]

The more fruitful approach which Kramer describes, is of course, made eminently possible through a consideration of the prime number seven as the mathematical vehicle for the extension of tonality in this particular direction. That this extension was not recognised at the time, meant that Schoenberg's arguments concerning the historical inevitability of the breakdown of tonality could thus remain unchallenged. Therefore, from a theoretical and musicological standpoint, it means that analytical and interpretational theories have been advanced, put forward, developed and codified from a foundation that assumes the general exclusion of the prime number seven as a natural and important participant in the musical language.

Although the prime number seven may have been partially recognised in playing a purely local role within the chords of the dominant seventh, ninth, etc. that this role is entirely dependent upon the identity attributed to the seventh harmonic by Euler, Fétis, Helmholtz, Fokker, and numerous other theorists who assumed that the seventh harmonic formed an interval of a compound minor seventh with the fundamental tone.

That the interval of 7/4 may be more appropriately understood as an augmented sixth may be the cause of numerous problems so far as the tenets of established musical theory are concerned. By taking 7/4 to be an augmented sixth means that a mathematical rationale can be offered to musical phenomenon

[1] Lawrence Kramer, The Mirror of Tonality: Transitional Features of Nineteenth Century Harmony', in: 19th Century Music IV/3, 1981, 191 - 2.

which in their implication, transcend the limits of the major and minor tonal system. Yet once this is accepted it means that it must be recognised that the music of the twentieth century, emerging from that basis laid down in the previous century, has been embraced and understood from an incomplete foundation. This means that important theoretical decisions have been made which in themselves assume that the jelly has already set, when in fact it has clearly not.

A major development of the musical language has occurred along perfectly logical lines, readily explainable through reference to the prime number seven and its particular properties. It is thus vital to make some kind of re-evaluation of this body of music, and to put it into a more positive and clear perspective. The perspective that chromatic music all points inevitably towards the decay and abandonment of tonality is an extremely suspect one, for this music points quite positively towards a new, more expansive state of tonality - a chromatic state of tonality which speaks of altogether new laws, conditions and governing principles.

To be able to expose these principles and put them together into a tangible system, it will be necessary to look at a lot more music than has so far been possible within the limited space of the previous chapters. Yet before more music can be examined, it is obviously extremely important to be able to establish how to precisely identify the presence of a septimal tone or interval within a passage of tonal music. Otherwise, it will be extremely difficult to know what to actually look for. This applies on two principal levels:

1) a septimal tone as it exists as a component of an harmonic sonority;

2) a septimal tone as it is, or can be, brought into a clear relationship with a tonal centre.

Now in terms of a septimal tone as a component of an harmonic sonority, it is useful to observe that the history of harmonic theory tends to lay emphasis upon the construction of chords through the superimposition of thirds, major and minor. This view of sonorities as being composed of stacks of thirds is entirely in accordance with the principles of valency, simply because within a prime number five limit there are only two types of thirds which represent a primary valent bond between musical tones - the major third of ratio 5/4 and the minor third of ratio 6/5. Operating within their own particular dimension, the tertial chains established by these thirds cut across that dimension governed by the prime number three to create a two-dimensional (3,5) lattice of valent bonds which, on their own respective level, are responsible for weaving the entire fabric of tonal possibility. A cross-section of this fabric can be observed in the diagram below:

Bi-dimensional Fabric Encompassing Primary Valent Bonds Within Prime Number Five Limit (Excluding Prime Two)

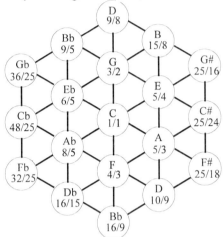

Tertial chords become important at this level because the musical tones present in such chords are bonding along the only viable pathways that are available. Looking at the above lattice, all of the tertial chords encountered in the study of harmony are to be found, clearly displayed along the various valent pathways available between musical tones. As a result of this there is a certain mathematical element involved in the generation of the exact number and type of chords actually available. Because of this implicit duality so far as thirds are concerned, means that there is an exponential increase in the possible number of different chords which follows the extension of the dyad through to the triad, the triad through to the tetrad, etc. There are thus two basic dyads, four basic triads, eight basic tetrads, and so on.

Yet running across this determinative mathematical element are the more subjective features of artistic choice and aesthetic discrimination with regard to which tones to include, and which tones to exclude from a given chord in order to obtain the requisite musical effect. Then of course, there are the parameters which derive from the fact that the chord used is a part of a tonal system in which it performs a clear and definable function. Significantly, these factors do not affect the basic principle that the chords concerned all possess that characteristic hallmark of construction relating to their derivation from the chain or pillar of thirds. Any chord, no matter how complex, can usually be reduced to a pile of thirds. The theoretical root of that chord can then be ascertained by discovering the lowest member of that chain of thirds:

Chords Derived from the Pillar of Thirds

a) Schumann: *Novelette*, Op. 21, No. 8.
b) Franz Liszt: *Nuages Gris*.
c) Domenico Scarlatti: *Harpsichord Sonata*, K. 119.

When the prime number seven is brought into the picture it significantly transforms this view of chordal possibilities owing to the fact that it represents the generating principle of a fourth dimension of tonal space. Therefore, there is an altogether new dimension at play, in which the bi-dimensional (3,5) fabric as defined above becomes transformed into a three-dimensional (3,5,7) fabric. The general key to the complex latticework of four-dimensional tonal space lies in the original 7/4 relation which converts the major triad of ratio 4:5:6 into the consonant septimal tetrad of 4:5:6:7. In order to account for this relation an augmented sixth (7/4) is placed within the original triangular unit defined by the major triad. This converts the original triangular unit into a tetrahedron of which the diagram below represents the plan view:

Tetrahedral Unit Defined by 4:5:6:7 Tetrad

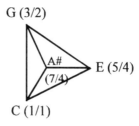

Representing the positive polarisation of four-dimensional frequency space, means that it is necessary to posit another tetrahedral unit which represents the equivalent negative polarisation. This can be simply obtained by producing the mirror image of the 4:5:6:7 tetrad:

Positive and Negative Polarisations of Four-dimensional Frequency Space

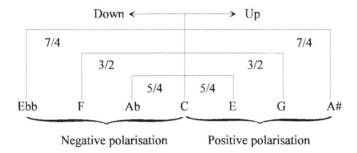

Observe that the result of this is the 'Tristan' chord as discussed in the last chapter, which thus bears the same relationship to the German Sixth as the minor triad does to the major. This unit also manifests as a tetrahedron, the difference being that it is thus pointing the other way. This can be appreciated when the original harmonic cell, or two-dimensional (3,5,) heptad, is converted into three-dimensional (3,5,7) tridecad, obtained through the conversion of each component triad to the requisite tetrahedral unit. The latticework of four-dimensional frequency space is subsequently defined by the replication of this unit upon each point of the original two-dimensional (3,5) tone lattice:

Three-dimensional Harmonic Tridecad

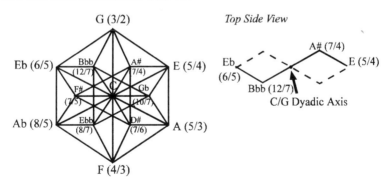

Each line within the above cell represents a primary valent bond. Septimal tetrads represent specific aggregations of these valent bonds:

Septimal Tetrads as Aggregations of Valent Bonds

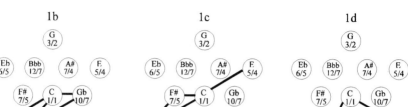

Because of the influence of this fourth dimension, the basic structure of the chords themselves are significantly changed. The interval between the seventh and eighth harmonics (*A#* to *C*) brings the interval of the diminished third to bear in the process of chord construction. This in its turn leads to the creation of a whole new category of chromatic chord types not accounted for, or explained within the terms of the three-dimensional model of Classical diatonic tonality. The interval between *C* and *A#* is one which at a diatonic level cannot be obtained unless chromatic alteration is countenanced.

Immediately therefore, the prime number seven implicates a larger and more pervasive harmonic system, in which each tertial chord that forms a part of the diatonic system of tonality can be modified to include those intervals deriving from the prime number seven. Once a chord has been altered in this way, it is significant that it becomes automatically functional as a dominant variant, or a dominant substitute.

By looking at the major and minor dominant seventh, ninth, eleventh and thirteenth sonorities it will become apparent that virtually any note can be feasibly altered to produce such septimal chromatic variants. Such variants are not being advocated upon a theoretical level as potential new sonorities, for they are all chords which are found in actual musical practice. This excludes those chords which conform to the diatonic territory of another key, i.e. sharpening the root of the dominant seventh to produce a diminished seventh chord, or sharpening the ninth of a dominant minor ninth to create a dominant major ninth chord. When any of the notes of a complex dominant sonority are altered, an infallible principle of chromatic alteration will be encountered. This principle manifests in two ways:

a) If the lower note of a minor third (6/5) is sharpened, or the upper note flattened it will produce a diminished third (8/7).

b) If the upper note of a major third (5/4) is sharpened, or the lower note flattened, it will produce an augmented third (21/16).

The application of chromatic alteration to dominant sonorities thus results in chords which deploy augmented and diminished thirds. In this way, composers never needed to be consciously aware of the prime number seven, for its presence resulted from the application of chromatic alterations to conventional chords of dominant function. Simple experimentation with the possibilities of chromatic harmony was enough to yield such possibilities. These factors remain theoretically untraceable while tone seven of the harmonic series is identified as a *Bb-*. They only become apparent when it is identified as an *A#*, because then the septimal matrix that supports these alterations become evident. That matrix, as it stands in relation to the dominant chain can be viewed as follows

Septimal Alterations of the Dominant Pillar

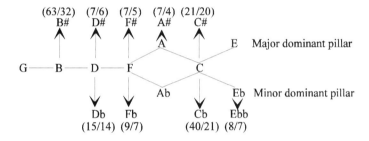

That such chromatically altered chords have played a significant part in 18th, 19th and 20th century tonal harmony is a decisive factor, the difference so far as the latter is concerned being the trend towards the use of complex chromatically altered sonorities as such as the ninth, eleventh and thirteenth:

Chromatically Altered Dominant Sonorities [1]

---

[1] Ludmila Ulehla, Contemporary Harmony: Romanticism through the Twelve-tone Row, The Free Press, New York 1966, 59-114.

Although there are many more chords to be obtained through the process of chromatic alteration, the precise categorisation of every single septimal chord does not matter at this stage. The important point is that because of the application of chromatic alteration to conventional chords of dominant function septimal chords are thus obtained. In the first chord it is the augmented sixth between *Ab* and *F#*, in the second chord the augmented sixth between *F* and *D#*, etc. Comparing a random sample of these chords with the scheme of chromatic alteration given above it will be seen that the septimal matrix provides the basis for such alterations:

Pathways of Typical Chromatically Altered Dominant Sonorities

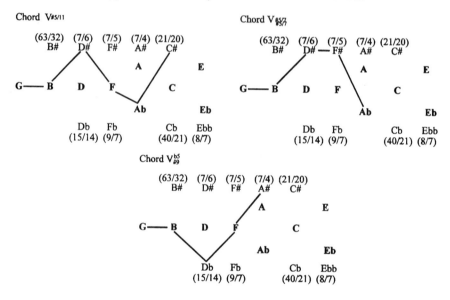

It becomes clear from this, how and why the prime number seven entered into tonal music. As soon as the chord of the dominant seventh was recognised as an independent sonority in its own right the septimal matrix was brought onto the horizons. The observed similarity in profile between the first seven harmonics and a chord of the dominant seventh is an obvious symptom of this. Yet the thrust of the progression of tonal music into the domain of the prime number seven occurred in a slightly different direction. It occurred through the chromatic alteration of the dominant chord and its various derivatives of the seventh, ninth, eleventh and thirteenth.

Now when all of these chromatically altered chords (as seen in the above list of representative examples) are transposed into the key of C, it becomes evident that the chromatic scale of that key does not serve to contain that scheme of alteration. Simply, it does not have enough notes. Examples are the fifth of the dominant chord, note D, which can also appear as note Db (15/14) or *D#* (7/6) - a scheme of alteration which presupposes three modal positions for the supertonic degree. The chromatic scale it will be noted, possesses no *D#* for that key. Similarly, the ninth of the dominant - note A - can also appear as note *A#* (7/4): there is no such tone in the chromatic scale of the key of C either.

As such, the chromatic practices of eighteenth, nineteenth and early twentieth century tonal harmony automatically presupposes the use of a more complex scale than the chromatic scale defined at a three dimensional level. Such are the basic principles which have, for so long, remained hidden behind the veil of equal temperament.

The principal distinguishing factor of a septimal chord is an implied diminished and/or augmented third. Consequently the tone which forms that relationship will nearly always fall outside of the province of the chromatic scale. In the full chromatic scale there are only two diminished thirds, and one augmented third. In the key of C these are the diminished thirds which lie between notes B and Db, F# and Ab, and the augmented third which lies between notes Db and F#. The existence of these intervals gives a special significance to the notes Db and F#, as the links between the diatonic (three-dimensional) and the chromatic (four-dimensional) spheres of tonality. As such they are two members of the chromatic scale which can on occasions be ascribed septimal ratios. These are 15/14 for the tonic declining tone Db, and 7/5 for the dominant inclining tone F#.

All other diminished and augmented thirds fall outside of the province of the chromatic scale. Therefore the use of augmented and diminished thirds in chord formations invokes those other scalar members which contribute to the formation of the basic scale of the chromatic tonal system. In the following diagram the various diminished thirds available from a given chromatic tone are charted.

In general diminished thirds are foreign to the chromatic scale. Therefore, use of any chord involving, or at least implying in its structure, a diminished or augmented third will not only evoke a septimal relationship to other chord members, but will also evoke a septimal relationship to the actual tonic note. It is this which explains why the prime number seven does not manifest itself functionally in ordinary chromatic music, that is music which makes much motivic use of the chromatic scale.

Diminished Third Relationship of Enharmonic to Chromatic Tones

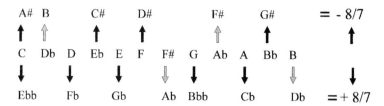

This can be demonstrated particularly well in chromatic music which precedes the nineteenth and twentieth centuries. The overtly chromatic organ piece *Ricercar Chromatico* (1635) by Girolamo Frescobaldi (1583 - 1643) provides a good case in point. The opening subject employs some six chromatic notes arranged motivically into two groups of three pitches each, the second group presenting a retrograde version of the chromatic motive introduced by the first group:

Chromatic Motives in Frescobaldi's *Ricercar Chromatico*.

Any element of tonal ambivalence suggested by this subject is immediately dispersed when the tonality of the piece is considered. Ostensibly, the order of entries suggests the Hypodorian mode, the subject entering first on the fifth of the mode, *A,* and secondly on the final, *D.* When viewed against the pitch of the final, the six chromatic notes place themselves into a clearly defined relationship to it. Looking at the first three note motive, the A represents the fifth of the Dorian species, whilst the *Bb* and *B* represent the minor and major forms of the sixth modal degree. Similarly, in terms of the second motive, the *E* represents the second modal degree, whilst the *F* and *F#* constitute the minor and major forms of the third modal degree. As such, the pitches which Frescobaldi uses, do not in any way exceed the constraints of a chromatic octave constructed upon the pitch of D.

Looking now at the polyphonic and harmonic context in which the chromatic motive is embedded, it will be seen that at all points it occurs within the firm framework of consonant triadic progressions. In this extract, two types of motivic placement can be observed:

Opening of Frescobaldi's *Ricercar Chromatico*.

In a) the motive manifests through the minor and major forms of the third of a harmonic triad, whilst in b) it manifests through a root to third displacement, the root of a triad rising a semitone to become the major third of another chord. Consequently, it can be seen that despite the highly chromatic profile of this particular subject, there is no particular evidence to be seen for the functional usage of septimal tones. On the contrary, Frescobaldi is employing a linear chromaticism the harmonic implications of which are clearly accountable within the domain of consonant triadic progressions.

That such a deliberately designed chromatic motive brings into play some distinctly unusual and novel chord progressions is one of the fascinating features of this particular piece. Yet those progressions, and the motives which the composer uses, do not necessarily implicate a fourth dimension of tonal space. Furthermore, in terms of Frescobaldi's music as a whole, it has already been noticed that because of the limitations of meantone temperament, sometimes a septimal minor seventh or tritone may be used. But it can be seen that this is not a strictly functional use of the prime number seven, simply an intonational consequence of the use of certain pitches. It is thus a curious example of a four dimensional influence being used and interpreted from the constraints of a three dimensional standpoint.

Looking now at a later chromatic piece, *Praeludium XX* in A minor, from the second volume of J. S. Bach's *The Well-Tempered Clavier* - a strongly related observation can be made. Although this music is indeed highly chromatic, those notes which do not belong to the key of A minor are notes which have been borrowed either from the parallel minor (*C#* and *F#)*, or the dominant major key (*D#*). The harmonic context in which they occur easily suggests this, for the *D#* of bar 1 is presented as a part of chord III of the dominant key, whilst the *C#* and *F#* are presented as a part of chords I and vi respectively, of the parallel major key. The exception to this perhaps, is the note Bb, which constituting the flat supertonic degree, is borrowed from the subdominant minor key. The harmonic context in which it occurs is thus explainable as belonging to chord ii of that key.

Excerpt from J. S. Bach's *Praeludium XX* (Vol. II of the *Well-Tempered Clavier*).

BACH, J.S.:Prelude No. 20, BWV 889/1, from The Well Tempered Clavier, Vol. II
@ 1994 by The Associated Board of the Royal Schools of Music. Used by permission.

Looking at those chords suggested by the arpeggiated dyads occuring with the given bass notes of bar 1, and the treble of bar 2, shows that they are all well known triadic formations: either minor, major or diminished triads fully accountable within a valent limit of five. As an exercise in the borrowing of harmonies from closely related keys it displays a great deal of skill, especially in the way in which the composer retains a strong sense of tonal coherence. This is mainly accomplished in the broad outlines of the music, in which a gradual descent from the tonic to the dominant, seen in the bass line of bar 1, is counterbalanced by a similar descent from the dominant back down towards the tonic in bar 2.

Both of these examples, chosen at random, show that the use of chromaticism is never a sure sign of the influence of the prime number seven. It is when that chromatic usage leads to an actual mutation in the structure of the chords themselves, to result in those unusual chords with augmented and diminished thirds, that the influence of the prime number seven makes itself most felt. Because of that mutation, the notes acquire a gravitational leaning up or down as the case may be; a naturally ordained force of impulsion which provides more than an analogy with the forces of dominant harmony. This magnetic force enables septimal tones, intervals and chords to acquire a function within a given tonality.

Curiously, so far as most diatonic tonal music is concerned, these septimal elements cannot be said to be of the most vital importance. Many pieces of music written before the mid-nineteenth century make no or very little reference to the prime number seven at all. And those that do, often do so in small ways. Recalling Chopin's C minor Prelude discussed in Chapter 12, the amount of exposure given to septimal tones amounts to about 7% of the playing time of the entire piece. Because of their distinctive nature, such events often stand out as being of particular expressive importance. Septimal influences are a rarity which acquire a colouristic and expressive value because of that rarity.

This highlights one of the dangers of reductive analysis, where the most sublime harmonies used in a piece of music are quickly eliminated from the analysis because the notes concerned are diatonically dependent. In this way, the fundamental basis for an entirely new system of tonality - the chromatic system - has been eliminated too.

A DEFINITION OF THE BASIC NINETEEN-TONE SCALE OF THE CHROMATIC TONAL SYSTEM

To be in possession of a reliable means for the recognition of the presence of septimal tones in music is very important, for otherwise it would be impossible to determine to what degree the prime number seven has actually managed to invade the territory of tonal art music. Yet such means are not always infallible, for they assume that the composer is aware of, or has a care for precise methods of functional pitch notation, which of course is not always the case.

Occurring in the first instance through the interval of the augmented sixth, the manifestations of the prime number seven in tonal music are often more difficult to track down than need be owing to the possibility that a composer may write an augmented sixth, or another septimal interval after the fashion of its enharmonically equivalent interval. Difficulties encountered in this respect are exacerbated in passages characterised by much chromatic movement between the parts, for there the note functions concerned are often defined by nothing else than the context in which they occur. A very good example of this can be found in the majestic opening of the slow movement to Dvořák's *Symphony for the New World*:

Here, the highly chromatic root movement underpinning the succession of essentially triadic sonorities can feasibly put one off the trail of a very simple and explicit example of a septimal sonority seen in the second half of bar three. Note that the augmented sixth interval, manifesting in the fourth crotchet of the third bar, is spelled as a minor seventh - *Gb* to *Fb*. The presence of an augmented sixth interval in this case, only becomes detectable by virtue of the characteristic mode of resolution of the chord in which it occurs. Employing the first inversion of the supertonic seventh of the Db minor tonality - *Gb Bbb Db Eb* - Dvorak raises the root note Eb, to an apparent *Fb*, thereby setting up a chromatic tendency tone which rises smoothly up to the third of the tonic triad of Db major.

Ideally this chord should be spelled *Gb Bbb Db E* in order to offer recognition to the inclining tone effect thereby invoked. Probably Dvořák did not notate it in this fashion because he was unaware that such a chord even existed. From the standpoint of conventional harmonic theory - which devolves around the three-dimensional construct that is the chromatic scale – this chord does not, and cannot exist, for there is no note E in the chromatic scale of the key of Db.

From a four-dimensional perspective this chord is just one of many sonorities, which along with the infamous 'Tristan' chord, presuppose the use of septimal intervals in their construction. Only through observation of the voice leading, and the context which this offered to the note Fb as a chromatic tendency tone up to the *F*, that this particular septimal tone was capable of being detected.

Rather than trying to eliminate chromatic notes from the tonal analysis, either because they complicate the process of analysis, or do not appear to be important to the overall structure of a particular piece of music, it is clearly important to expose such chromatic notes. The principle reason for this is that they may be viewed to be the manifestations of a new dimension of tonal possibility which, arriving from a relatively unexplored fourth dimension of frequency space, harbours within it distinct possibilities for the further progression of the musical language.

So far septimal tones have been considered in relative isolation as they manifest within specific chord progressions. This exercise useful in order to demonstrate that septimal tones have been used by composers. Having collated evidence that points to the usage of such notes, it is now time to bring that knowledge to bear for the purposes of much more far-reaching theoretical considerations.

Through the intuitive usage of septimal tones, late eighteenth and nineteenth century composers have each contributed in their own way towards the formation of a musical scale which extends beyond the harmonic form of the chromatic scale. In the Dvořák example as given above, the septimal tone is note E, otherwise spelled as an *Fb*. Now what is it that qualifies this note as being a septimal tone? A septimal tone is one which bears a ratio to the tonic note which involves the prime number seven (but no higher prime number). Involving the prime number seven, it thus represents a movement in frequency space which is unique to its level. Being unique, means that any such movement will fall outside of the province of the chromatic scale as defined by the three dimensions of frequency space signified by the prime numbers two, three and five. Accordingly, the criterion that establishes the note E as being a septimal tone is that it forms an interval of an augmented sixth with the subdominant note Gb. Consequently it brings into play a note which bears a septimal ratio to the tonic (7/6).

Through usage of this septimal tone therefore, a subtle extension of the chromatic scale is being implied in a particular direction. The nature of that direction is towards the inclusion of those septimal tones as an annex to the original chromatic scale. Arrived at by a process of combining the resources of the major and minor diatonic tonalities, the chromatic scale of the key of C may be viewed thus:

Chromatic Scale (Harmonic Form) of the Key of C

Degree	Note	Ratio	Tonal Function
1	C	1/1	Tonic
2	Db	16/15	---
3	D	9/8	Supertonic
4	Eb	6/5	Minor mediant
5	E	5/4	Major mediant
6	F	4/3	Subdominant
7	F#	45/32	---
8	G	3/2	Dominant
9	Ab	8/5	Minor submediant
10	A	5/3	Major submediant
11	Bb	16/9	Subtonic
12	B	15/8	Leading note
1	C	2/1	Tonic

Observe that no function has been offered for either of the notes Db or F#. The reason for this is that when viewed from a three-dimensional perspective, the ratio ascribed to the note F# is 45/32, a ratio obtained through the addition of a harmonic major third (5/4) to the supertonic degree or ratio 9/8. Any common triad constructed upon the supertonic degree cannot be a major triad, for this would contradict the subdominant function of the key. Whenever a major triad is used on the supertonic degree therefore, it may count as a borrowing from a closely related tonality. In this context, the term supertonic serves to define the location of the chordal root, but not its function. In functional terms the supertonic major triad is the dominant triad of the dominant key, in which case the supertonic is performing a secondary function as the dominant of the dominant.

Accordingly, the inclusion of a sharp fourth degree within a tonally functional chromatic scale is illogical for the note F# does not belong to the key of C. Admittedly, this note occurs so often in music written in the key of C that it is tempting to include it as a functionary of that key and therefore accord it due recognition as a primary member of the chromatic scale of the key of C. Yet it is a note which performs only a secondary function i.e. one which derives from another key or keys. So from a tonal standpoint, it is inappropriate to count the note F# as a primary member of the key of C.

In seeking to extend the chromatic scale in order to account for musical practice, this represents a problematical element, for as the potential representative of the resources of the monotonality of the key of C, the scale itself possesses an inherent inconsistency in its representation of tonal functions. Any extension of the chromatic scale from this standpoint therefore, can only serve to promulgate this inconsistency, and ensure its continuance on a more complex level.

In order to build upon the possibilities of the chromatic scale this inconsistency must be cleared up, for analogous to the building of a house on a faulty foundation, the entire structure built upon that foundation may become suspect. Towards this end observe that the septimal tritone of ratio 7/5 is only 7 cents lower than the dominant leading note of ratio 45/32. Representing a primary valent bond between musical tones, it might be more appropriate to substitute 7/5 for the dominant leading-note of 45/32.

Christian Huyghen's, comments upon this interval as it occurs in his 'Harmonic Cycle of 31'[1] are particularly interesting: *I would also here like to note in favour of this new temperament that everywhere in it the interval of the tritone is contained in the relationship of 7 to 5; in this numerical relationship only 1/12th of a comma is missing.... I now find that this interval 7 to 5, if one tests it carefully - and one may count it among the consonances, no matter what their lordships, the composers, who counted it more often among the false tonal relationships, may say against it.*[2]

To substitute 7/5 for 45/32 would give a consonant sharp fourth degree, one which would bring the note F# into a more direct relationship with the tonic note C. Ye to bring in the septimal tritone in favour of the dominant leading note is to effect a change which is more conceptual than real. The difference in the implied pitch of these two notes is almost negligible.

---

[1] Christian Huyghens, Oeuvres complétes, vol. XX, La Haye 1940, 160.

[2] Adriaan Fokker, New Music with 31 Notes, 16.

Nonetheless, this small difference in pitch belies the significant theoretical distinction between them. As the dominant leading note (45/32), *F#* represents a borrowing from another key. However, as occurring within the context of the various augmented sixth chords constructed upon the minor submediant degree, it is a note which can no longer be seen to be borrowed from another key. From which key is the augmented sixth between the notes Ab and F# borrowed from? There is no key in which such an interval occurs.

As the augmented sixth of the minor submediant, the note F# of ratio 7/5 has thus started to perform a *primary* function for the key itself. This represents a significant difference because the note F# no longer counts as a borrowing from the dominant key. It is now part of the tonality of C, and its inclusion in the harmonic form of the chromatic scale is justified. In this context, the note F# (7/5), embodies the secret of the septimal system and the chromatic level of tonality which it serves to generate. Through the ratio of 7/4, what was the representative of a secondary function in the key of C, has now become the representative of a primary function untraceable to any other key. In this way it is possible to see the birth of an altogether new compositional element: the primary chromatic note function.

A similar argument can be applied to the flat supertonic degree - note Db. As providing the theoretical root for the Neapolitan sixth triad it possesses a ratio of 16/15 (obtained by taking a minor sixth (8/5) above the subdominant - note F (4/3). It too is a foreigner to the key of C in that it represents a borrowing from a closely related key - in this case either the submediant major key of the minor mode in which it is chord IV, or the subdominant minor key in which it occurs as chord VI.

Like the note F# its inclusion within the harmonic form of the chromatic scale is warranted by the frequency of its usage, and the fact that fills in the gap between the tonic and supertonic degrees. But lying outside of the terms of both of the major and minor keys, it too, performs only a secondary function for the key.

Yet the flat supertonic degree occurs in other contexts in which it is difficult to assert that it represents a loan from a closely related key. When the fifth of the dominant seventh chord is chromatically flattened to create a chromatic tendency tone down to the tonic degree, the interval of a diminished third occurs between the leading note B and the flat supertonic note Db. The ratio of the note Db as it occurs in this context is 15/14. Lying 7 cents above the customary flat supertonic degree of ratio 16/15 the difference between them is quite insensible to any listener. But again, the theoretical distinction between them is considerable, for in the latter case it can no longer be construed to be a borrowing from the subdominant key. On the contrary, it represents a note which, because of its participation in a chromatically altered dominant seventh chord, performs an integral function for the key itself.

Through these slight adjustments in the ratios of the notes Db and F# a harmonic form of the chromatic scale can be constructed in which all twelve of the notes may be regarded as being fully functioning members of the tonality of C:

Chromatic Scale of the Monotonality of the Key of C

Note	Ratio	Function
C	1/1	Tonic
Db	15/14	
D	9/8	Supertonic
Eb	6/5	Minor mediant
E	5/4	Major mediant
F	4/3	Subdominant
F#	7/5	
G	3/2	Dominant
Ab	8/5	Minor submediant
A	5/3	Major submediant
Bb	16/9	Subtonic
B	15/8	Inclining tone
C	2/1	Tonic

The notes Db and F# participate in a type of chromaticism in which diatonically referable elements are borrowed from other keys in order to provide harmonic support for chromatic notes within the confines of a given key. Embracing the usage of such chords as secondary dominants, diminished seventh chords and augmented triads, this particular vein of chromatic usage devolves essentially upon the three-dimensional plane of operation of a diatonic tonality. Consequently, its chromatic elements are simply a collage of diatonic elements present in other keys.

Through recognising the septimal ratios of the notes Db and F# means that two linkage points have been set up within the confines of the tonality of C to a fourth dimension of frequency space. Of necessity, this moves in a different direction to the three-dimensional unit established at a diatonic level. Accordingly, the change effected to the notes Db and F# becomes significant of a progressive movement or thrust towards the exploitation of the resources of that fourth dimension.

As demonstrated by examples presented so far, those resources are chromatic in their orientation. By virtue of the simple ratios offered by the septimal nexus, the chromatic tones together with the chords used to accompany them are now functionaries of the key itself. In this sense the fourth dimension of frequency space offers a significant growth or upsurge of tonal possibility, beyond the strictures of the diatonic scale, and towards a more liberated usage of all twelve notes of the chromatic scale and the various septimal supplementaries which exist as an annex to that scale.

Having defined the chromatic scale it would be expedient at this stage to define these septimal supplementaries. Recall the Dvořák example given earlier. Transposing the septimal chord that he uses into the key of C, it has the apparel of a subdominant minor triad to which has been added an augmented sixth: *F Ab C D#*. However, the derivation of this chord is slightly more complicated. It derives from the first inversion of the supertonic seventh of the harmonic minor mode (a) in which the root itself has been chromatically raised in order to give an inclining tone up to the mediant degree (b).

Chromatically Altered Sonority Used in Dvořák's *Symphony for the New World*.

Here is an example of a septimal tone which uses an intervallic modality foreign to the twelve-tone chromatic system of the key of C. In the chromatic scale of the key of C there is either the declining tone - note Db (15/14), or the supertonic degree itself - note D (9/8). Consequently, there is no suggestibility within the chromatic scale for the possibility of a chromatically raised supertonic degree.

Usage of the note D# automatically suggests a new note which is not present in the chromatic scale. It cannot be construed as a secondary leading note either, because it would need to be regarded as the seventh scale step of the key of E. Given the accompanying harmony this cannot be suggested. Here can be seen the definitive use of a note which although having no place in the chromatic scale of the key of C, performs a primary function within that key. This chromatic chord thus points to a more complex scale than is currently recognised .

Recognition that the chromatic scale cannot embrace the chromatic practices which it has always been believed to represent, brings with it a feeling of uncomfortability. An easy way of dealing with this is to dismiss the note D#, and pretend that it is really an Eb. Then the chord as given above could be construed to be a minor seventh chord. Thus being dismissed, the phenomenon is easy to explain through the limited terms of the chromatic scale.

However, to do so is to create further problems. The semitone movement of *Eb* up to *E* is not problematical to explain, for it does not make any functional sense. The harmonic sensibility of this chord derives from the characteristic interval of the augmented sixth between the notes F and D#. To activate the particular directive offered by this interval, Dvořák ensures that the *F* falls to the *C*, whilst the *D#* rises up to the *E*. By so doing, a major triad whose third is doubled is avoided, a factor which Dvořák no doubt took into account.

To dismiss the note D# would be unwise, because it would ignore both the function and behaviour of the chord - an action does not do justice either to the subtlety of chromatic chord progressions, or the way in which they are being used by composers. It is obvious that the interval between the notes F and D# is not a minor seventh but an augmented sixth. Constituting an augmented sixth, means that any scale presented as a summary of the practice of chromatic harmony in tonal music, would have to include the possibility of an augmented sixth interval being used on the subdominant degree of the scale. This, of necessity, would mean the inclusion of the note D# in addition to the note Eb which, in equal temperament is its enharmonic equivalent. In plain terms, the chromatic scale would need to be supplemented to account for the usage of this note, or any other notes which might occur in similar circumstances.

In making such an expansion, the original scale is being upgraded from a three-dimensional to a four-dimensional format. The first septimal tone which would be added to the chromatic scale is the note D# (key of C). Lying an augmented sixth above (or a diminished third below) the subdominant note F, means that it has a ratio of (4/3 plus 7/4 =) 7/6.

Like the note F# (7/5), the note D# (7/6) manifests as a chromatic intermediary note between whole tones. This does not mean that it has to manifest as a chromatic passing note. It may also occur as a chromatic substitute for the original note. In the following example Grieg uses an augmented sixth constructed upon the subdominant degree as a means of chromatically enriching a plagal cadence to the tonic chord of Bb major:

Excerpt from Grieg's 'Scherzo-Impromptu', Op. 73, No. 2.

Reprint with permission of C.F. Peters, Frankfurt/M., Leipzig, London and New York.

Having taken that initial step, the scale implied by the usage of such chromatic notes starts to unfold as a matter of course. A perfect fourth above note D# (7/6) lies the septimal augmented fifth degree - the note G# of ratio 14/9. A prime example of a sonority which underlines the use of this particular note is the augmented 6-4-3 chord constructed upon the flat supertonic degree (*Db F G# B*). An example of this chord was provided in the chapter before last, where Schumann uses the sharp fifth degree (*E#* - 14/9) as an inclining tone up to the submediant degree (*F#* - 5/3):

Excerpt from Schumann's 'Novelette', Opus 21, No. 7.

Another septimal supplementary which needs to be considered as a part of the annex to the original chromatic is the 'seventh harmonic' itself - note A# of ratio 7/4. Lying between the submediant and leading note degrees, it often occurs as a tendency tone up to the leading note itself, as demonstrated in this example, which is also by Schumann:

Excerpt from Schumann's *Bunte Blätter*, Op. 99.

Reprint with permission of C.F. Peters, Frankfurt/M., Leipzig, London and New York.

Although Schumann does not use the note D# in the context of an augmented sixth chord, the context in which it occurs automatically suggests the septimal relationship of the augmented sixth (7/4) to the tonic note F. Otherwise, the chord must be interpreted as an incomplete diminished seventh chord *D# F# A C*. This would cast up note D# as the leading note of the key of E, a quite unacceptable proposition considering the context in which it is presented.

Alternatively, it could be asserted that Schumann has misspelled what in reality is a note Eb. Yet the context in which it occurs tends to refute this, the note D# entering as a quite logical tendency to raise the submediant chromatically in order to give a smooth chromatic ascent up to the leading note E. Overall therefore, it seems more appropriate to accept Schumann's notation, and see in this example a prime demonstration of the augmented sixth scale degree - ratio of 7/4.

The three septimal supplementaries considered so far share a common feature. After the initial example of the note F# (7/5), they manifest as a chromatic intermediary note between two notes a whole tone apart.

Sharp Septimal Tones as Chromatic Intermediaries

To the original chromatic scale therefore, an additional three notes need to be added in order to account for the presence within the tonality of these particular septimal tones:

The Chromatic Scale and Septimal Supplementaries

Note	Ratio	Function
C	1/1	Tonic
Db	15/14	
D	9/8	Supertonic
D#	7/6	
Eb	6/5	Minor mediant
E	5/4	Major mediant
F	4/3	Subdominant
F#	7/5	
G	3/2	Dominant

G#	14/9	
Ab	8/5	Minor submediant
A	5/3	Major submediant
A#	7/4	
Bb	16/9	Subtonic
B	15/8	Inclining tone
C	2/1	Tonic

Observe that the extra septimal tones all form an augmented interval in relation to the tonic note C, in which case they count as manifestations of the positive polarisation of four-dimensional frequency space. Here the note F# (7/5) is a positively polarised septimal tone which part of the chromatic scale. It thus constitutes the internal representative of the septimal nexus and thus the anchorage point for further septimal annexes.

Those notes pertaining to the negative polarisation of four-dimensional frequency space are those for which the internal septimal terminus of note Db (15/14) provides an anchorage point. The first to be considered is the note Gb (10/7) obtained as a perfect fourth (4/3) above the note Db (15/14). This note is perhaps unique in that it is the only septimal tone which manifests as the enharmonic equivalent of another septimal tone (F# - ratio of 7/5). Consequently, any interpretation of the manifestations of this note must be guided by caution.

Generally, the difference between the two is that whilst the former (Gb) tends to fall a semitone to the subdominant degree, the latter (F#) tends to rise a semitone to the dominant degree. Whilst the difference between them is very small in terms of pitch, they thus possess diametrically opposite chromatic functions.

A clear example of the diminished fifth scale degree can be seen in this extract from Chopin's highly chromatic *Prelude in E Minor*:

Excerpt from Chopin's *Prelude in E Minor*, Op. 28.

CHOPIN: Prelude in E minor, Op. 28 No. 4

Occurring in the second bar of the extract (note Bb in the key of E minor), the context in which it occurs suggests the dominant seventh chord of the key of F major. Considering the surrounding environment in which the chord occurs – the tonality of E minor - it could not be construed to be a borrowing from the key of F. Being approached through chord VI of the E minor tonality, it is more appropriately understood as an incomplete septimal tetrad derived by way of flattening the seventh and raising the fifth of chord VI7 (a), in order to create chromatic tendency tones both upwards and downwards to the root of the first inversion subdominant chord that follows (b). It appears to be an incomplete dominant seventh chord because the fifth is missing, but the implied missing fifth is not G but the note G# (c):

The ratio of Bb can thus be deduced by subtracting an augmented sixth (7/4) from $G\#$ (10/7). The same chord, appearing in a different position, occurs in the final bar of the extract. However, progressing as it does to V7, indicates that it is a wrongly spelled German Sixth chord, occurring in a rather rare 'third inversion'. Consequently the Bb, rather than passing down to A, rises instead to the dominant of the key.

In this extract there are two septimal chords spelled identically, the first correctly and the second incorrectly. This is an important factor to bear in mind when endeavouring to divine the septimal influences present within an excerpt of music. The manifestations of the seventh harmonic are often masked by the notation, in which case the score as written needs to be closely examined in the light of what is actually *heard*.

Often the two are not contiguous with one another. This can be demonstrated through the following excerpt in which the septimal supplementary tone Fb (9/7) becomes evident. The excerpt concerned comes from the tenth piano Prelude (1943) by the Russian composer Dmitri Kabalevsky (b. 1904). Those features which serve to indicate the participation of the prime number seven are the Bb major triad of bar 1, the G minor triad of bar 3, and the F minor triad of bar 4. The usage of such triads combined with Kabalevsky's use of the key signature of C# minor would serve to suggest that although the composer is consciously operating within a particular tonality, that the chords he uses are not restricted to the diatonic scale. On the contrary, the composer would seem to be selecting his chords from the entire resources of the monotonality of C#. However, numerous features do not concur with this idea. These generally devolve around the way in which the music is notated, and how that notation does not accurately reflect the musical logic of the chord progressions which Kabalevsky uses.

Excerpt from Kabalevsky's Tenth Prelude

An example is the apparent Bb major triad in bar 1. The placing of this suggests an intermediary chord between what is otherwise a simple bII - III - iv progression. The terms of its function derive mainly from the contrary motion between the upper and lower lines, the D occurring as a passing-note between the E and the C#, and the F occurring in the bass as a chromatic passing note between the E and the F#. Here it becomes immediately obvious that the F should be written as an E# and that some kind of mild tonicizing process is occurring in relation to the F# minor triad. From this it logically follows that the apparent Bb major chord is a septimal triad obtained by chromatically lowering the seventh of a diminished seventh chord. The precise derivation of this particular chord can be understood as follows:

Derivation of Apparent Bb Major Chord

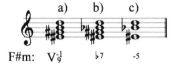

a) The diminished seventh chord of F# minor.
b) The diminished seventh with flattened fifth.
c) The diminished seventh with flat fifth, and omitted root and fifth.

When construed from the tonality of the chord thus tonicized (F# minor), the diminished fourth degree of the scale is invoked - note Bb (ratio 9/7). However, within the overlord tonality of C#, the same note manifests as the diminished seventh degree of the scale, a septimal supplementary for that key which has a ratio of 12/7.

Observe the way the sub-diminished fifth (*E# - Bb*) passes up to a perfect fifth, instead of shrinking down to a third as may be ordinarily expected. This gives the music a solid angular feel, backed up by the doubled octave texture. The chord in bar 1 is quite obviously a chromatically altered septimal chord. It is perhaps in this sense that *Bb* appears in bar 3 of the extract. Here however, it appears as the third of a G minor triad. Yet there is definitely something amiss here. In bar 4 can be seen chord iv of F# minor - a triad of B minor. The voice leading thus suggests that the *Bb* of bar 3 is functioning as an inclining-tone to the *B*.

Therefore it seems inappropriate to read this as a reappearance of the diminished fourth scale degree. Instead, the note is an *A#*, in which the triad of G minor is simply a false triad - *G A# D* - a derivative of the dominant thirteenth of the key of B minor (*F# A# C# E G B D*). Corroborating evidence for this lies in the way the left hand arpeggio lightly touches upon the root note F# and its fifth, note C#, instead of simply doubling the right-hand arpeggio It is this which gives it the feel of a straight secondary dominant harmony in which no septimal tones are actually implied.

The apparent F minor triad in bar five is also worthy of scrutiny. Observe that fifth of the *C#* minor chord to which it progresses offers a direct enharmonic continuation of the third of the F minor chord. As such, instead of reading into this microtonal intentions which are not evident, it would be more appropriate to spell the *Ab* as a *G#*. The *C* of the F minor chord is also suspect, for the way in which it passes upwards to the root of the C# minor chord. Given the voice leading, it would be more accurate to spell this note as a *B#*. The F minor triad is thus an incomplete septimal tetrad. It derives from the dominant seventh of C# minor (a), the seventh of which has been chromatically flattened (b). Being flattened, the diminished fourth scale-degree (ratio of 9/7) is invoked, which declines smoothly down to the mediant note E. Omission of the fifth gives this chord the apparel of a minor triad (c):

Derivation of Apparent F Minor Chord

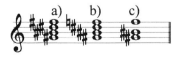

This example subsists upon two septimal tones - the diminished seventh degree - note Bb (ratio 12/7), and the diminished fourth degree - note F (ratio 9/7). Although only two are involved, their use contributes greatly to the character of the music, creating a sense of drive, harmonic impulsion, and an inevitability which can be explained through reference to the hidden manifestations of the prime number seven.

Each departure Kabalevsky makes from the scheme of diatonic tonality is explainable in terms of mutations of dominant chords brought about by the influence of septimal intervals. Therefore although composers may have expressed themselves through the medium of the equally tempered chromatic scale, another more complex scale is implied, one which allows a rational and mathematical explanation of the musical logic at work behind the chord progressions.

Although the above example may be interpreted as representing a significant break away from the diatonic tonal system of Classical tradition, through observation of the use of septimal supplementaries, it becomes apparent that there is a hidden element of continuity at work in this music. Through the unconscious utilisation of septimal influences, the system of diatonic tonality is being expanded and stretched in a new direction. In the absence of guided knowledge concerning the prime number seven, this appears to be a break in the tradition. But it is not a break. Tonality has been growing through the assimilation of the next level of valent relationships - those arising from the prime number seven. Unaware of these implications, composers wrote their music in a way that suited equal temperament, and the kind of notation that has been evolved for this.

Understanding that the septimal supplementaries offer a logical extension of the system of tonality allows the explanation of phenomenon which up until now have been regarded to be either a curiosity, or simply enigmatic phenomenon. Within the domain of septimal triads there are many examples, one of which will now be examined from Wagner's *Tristan und Isolde*.

Observe first, the demonstration of the consonant sharp fourth degree - note F# (7/5) - as seen in the two occurrences of the 'Tristan' chord in bars 1 & 8. Also observe that all chords can be accounted for within the prevailing tonality, except for the chord of A major in bars 5-6. Citing this example in his book *Harmony in Western Music*, Goldmann explains Wagner's it to be a result of continuance of the minor third motive which prevails throughout the passage. He states *The A major of measures 11 and 12 is a startling departure; it is structurally explicable in terms of the continued reference to the minor third:*

note that the melody with its wide skips, is still Eb-C-A, all minor third intervals.[1]

Extract from Wagner's *Tristan und Isolde*, Act I, Scene 2

This is an important point, for underlying the use of that A major triad is an element of melodic continuity which seems to justify its usage. Yet this is hardly a complete explanation of Wagner's use of such a curious chord in the key of C Minor. The note A is endemic to the melodic minor mode of C, and for the purposes of continuance of the motif there is no need for the introduction of foreign chromatic tones in the accompanying harmony. Consequently, it may be deduced that Wagner used such a chord for expressive purposes.

When the chord is heard in the context presented, it does not come as a shock to the ear. It comes as a shock to the analyst trying to explain it within the terms of a C minor tonality. Despite the illogicality of the use of an A major chord in the key of C minor, a hearing of the passage concerned persuades the ear that it is a progression which has a logic of its own. If so, in what does this logic lie? The logic lies in the observation that the A major chord is really a

---

[1] See the appendix to Richard Franko Goldmann's Harmony in Western Music, Barrie & Rockcliff, The Cresset Press, London 1965, where this example can be found, together with a discussion of the tonal implications of this particular chord.

septimal triad that has been misspelled. The septimal chord being referred to is a chromatic variant of chord vii of iv, whose theoretical derivation may be understood as follows:

Stage One: Chord vii ^{7} of F Minor

Stage Two: Flatten the Fifth

Stage Three

Stage Four: Omit the Third

Stage Five: Logical Voice Leading

F Minor:	V$^{b_5}_9$	i$_6$
C Minor:	V$^{b_5}_9$	iv$_6$
	iv	

This explains why the apparent A major chord progresses so well to the following F minor chord: it is a septimal chord which, being a chromatic variant of a dominant sonority, has the effect of tonicising the chord that follows. This effect is exacerbated by the three semitonal movements: the secondary leading note E to *F*; the diminished seventh degree *Bbb* (12/7) to *Ab*, and the declining tone Db to *C*. This chord is not even unusual for the time. It is Wagner's spelling of the chord that makes it look unusual. In real terms it is identical with an augmented 6-4-3 chord in which the augmented sixth is missing. In this way, an apparently foreign chord is explicable as a part of the tonality of C, but at a higher level of tonality - the chromatic level of tonality at which level the various septimal supplementaries come into operation.

In this example the augmented fourth (7/5) and diminished seventh (12/7) degrees of the scale provide the salient points of contact with the fourth dimension of frequency space. Wagner, well known for having composed at the piano, instinctively recognised the function of such a chord, yet, in the absence of any conscious logic which would explain its function, notated the nearest equivalent. A triad of A major.

A consideration of the range of septimal supplementaries can continue with the diminished third degree, signified by the note Ebb (8/7). Being enharmonically equivalent to the supertonic degree means that it is often spelled as such, which means that its usage is difficult to detect. The major reason it is spelled as the supertonic is that it forms a chromatic intermediary between the minor mediant and the flat supertonic degree: *Eb - Ebb - Db*, which itself is a chromatic tone. Its occurrence as a descending passing note thus tends to be obviated by the simpler notational solution of passing from the minor mediant - *Eb* - to the supertonic - *D* - and thence to the flattened supertonic itself - *Db*. This solution however, does not offer recognition to the importance of the augmented sixth interval implied between the diminished third and tonic degrees - *Ebb* to *C* - an interval which may be used as a splendid approach to the augmented sixth which lies a diatonic semitone below - *Db* to *B*.

There is a excellent example of this in what is curiously yet another piano prelude, Rachmaninoff's extremely well known *Prelude in C# Minor*. In a rather interesting chromatic chord progression suspended over a tonic pedal point and occurring twice in successive bars, Rachmaninoff arpeggiates a series of chords in each of the four crotchets of the bar. The implied five-part progression presented in each bar may be reduced for convenience thus:

Bar 1:

The first chords is the tonic seventh, the last the tonic triad itself. The latter is approached through a well-known type of augmented sixth chord - the German Sixth constructed upon the flat supertonic degree of the scale: *A B# D F#*. Although a consonant septimal sonority defined by the ratio of 4:5:6:7, its suspension over the tonic pedal offers it a gritty dissonant quality owing to the simultaneous clash which ensues between the *B#* and *D* and the *C#* in the bass.

Notably occurring on the flat supertonic degree, no septimal supplementaries are invoked, so any further interest in this chord immediately ceases. Instead the interest lies with the chord which precedes it. Here Rachmaninoff spells it as the dominant seventh chord of the dominant (V₇ of V) in third inversion (*C# D# Fx A#*). Looking at the behaviour of the chord as determined by its progression to the German Sixth chord that follows, Rachmaninoff's precise spelling needs to be questioned.

This can begin with the lowest part projected over the pedal. Operating in the minor key, means that *A#* is functioning as a chromatic passing note between the seventh and sixth degrees of the minor mode. That it is descending, indicates that it should be spelled as a *Bb* in order to accord recognition to its precise chromatic function. Spelled as an *A#* would be fine on ascent, especially considering the harmonic context provided for by the dominant seventh of the dominant key, for then the *A#* would acquire a perfectly logical tendency to rise up to the mediant of the implied tonic triad of G# minor.

If spelled as a Bb however, means that the other parts are now misaligned from any recognisable harmonic relationship with that note. This however, need cause no concern, as the notation of the three upper parts is also questionable owing to the way in which it depicts the chromatic orientation of the four note descending figure. A good example is the second part up from the bass, in which the note Fx occurs. Again, this note would be fine on ascent, because it would accord quite naturally with its perception as the leading note of the dominant triad. However, its descent to the note F# is illogical, for it represents a descending chromatic passing note between the dominant and subdominant degrees. Falling down towards the subdominant, it would not be appropriate to view it as a raised or sharpened subdominant degree, which is the way Rachmaninoff presents it. Accordingly, this note may be more appropriately identified as a G, one of the septimal supplementaries already considered (the flat fifth degree of ratio 10/7).

Bearing in mind these important issues of chromatic procedure, the upper part becomes questionable in the light of comments made so far. Occurring as a descending passing note between the minor mediant and flat supertonic degrees, the note D# would be more appropriately spelled as an *Eb*. This would accord with its use as a chromatic tendency tone down to the *D*:

Reviewed Chord Progression

Looking at the spelling as modified in accordance with functional pitch notation shows that the chord in the second beat of the bar is another German

Sixth chord whose generator lies a semitone above the flat supertonic degree. This makes much more sense harmonically, for it explains the tendency of the *Eb* to fall down to the *D*, and why the *C#* falls down to the *B#*. It is a parallel movement of diminished thirds (8/7). Thus can be explained one form of the appearance of the highly elusive and quite rare septimal supplementary identifiable as the diminished third degree of the scale (8/7).

Four septimal tones deriving from the negative polarisation of four-dimensional frequency space have now been named and identified: the notes Ebb (8/7), Fb (9/7), Gb (10/7) and Bbb (12/7). The septimal annex to the chromatic scale includes three supplementaries deriving from the positive polarisation of four-dimensional frequency space, and four deriving from the negative polarisation. A musical scale which fairly represented these possibilities as they apply to a four-dimensional tonality, would thus have twelve plus seven equals nineteen notes. This scale may be termed the enharmonic scale:

The Enharmonic Scale of Nineteen Notes

Degree	Note	Interval	Ratio	Cents
I	C	Prime	1/1	0
bII	Db	Minor second	16/15	112
II	D	Major second	9/8	204
bIII	Ebb	Diminished third	8/7	231
#II	D#	Augmented second	7/6	267
III	Eb	Minor third	6/5	316
#III	E	Major third	5/4	386
bIV	Fb	Diminished fourth	9/7	435
IV	F	Perfect fourth	4/3	498
#IV	F#	Augmented fourth	7/5	583
bV	Gb	Diminished fifth	10/7	617
V	G	Perfect fifth	3/2	702
#V	G#	Augmented fifth	14/9	765
bVI	Ab	Minor sixth	8/5	814
VI	A	Major sixth	5/3	884
bVII	Bbb	Diminished seventh	12/7	933
#VI	A#	Augmented sixth	7/4	969
VII	Bb	Minor seventh	9/5	1018
#VII	B	Major seventh	15/8	1088

The enharmonic scale fulfils the basic requirement necessary to successfully upgrade the chromatic scale in accordance with the dictates of the influence of a fourth dimension of frequency space. The major requirement is that it would represent a logical extension of the chromatic scale (three dimensional construct) in such a way that those extra notes used by composers, and shown in numerous examples through the course of this book, are accounted for. In this sense, the enharmonic scale should not be viewed as being a construct which represents the possibilities of septimal intervals should they ever be used by composers. On the contrary, it represents the results of the observation of musical practice.

The various stages that have led to the formulation of the enharmonic scale as given above are simple both to understand, and to trace. The first was to identify the seventh harmonic according to the reasonable and mathematically grounded criterion presented here. Having identified the seventh harmonic, the identities of all of the other septimal intervals became clear. Then it became apparent that these have all been used in the music of the eighteenth and nineteenth centuries. From there it was a short step to see that septimal intervals offered a logical extension of the chromatic scale through an expansion of the intervallic modalities of the seven scale degrees.

Through observation of musical practice it is thus possible to disprove the theoretical axiom that *the* scale of European art music is a twelve-note chromatic scale. Although this may have been true in Bach's time, it is certainly not true in relation to the nineteenth and twentieth centuries. From the arguments and observations presented here, the scale implied by European art music is a nineteen-note scale whose possibilities are only crudely accommodated within the confines of twelve-tone equal temperament.

INCLINING AND DECLINING TONES AS THE FUNCTIONAL
MANIFESTATION OF SEPTIMAL POLARITY

The methodology of study so far as part three of this book has been
concerned, has been to show that by following up the observation that the
interval whose ratio is 7/4 provides the acoustical backbone behind the various
chromatic chords of the augmented sixth, a key is thereby provided which opens
up a means to understand and systematize the rather complex and enigmatic
chromatic world of harmony associated with the Romantic movement in music
in general.

Through observation of chromatic elements as they manifest within the music
of that general period, it has been possible to show that septimal elements are
not by rights a borrowing from the territory of another tonality, but unique
elements obtained as an outgrowth of tonality into a fourth dimension of tonal
possibility. From this perspective, it has then been possible to show that the
assumed inevitability of the breakdown of tonality was itself a highly suspect
concept, for it failed to take into account the thrust of tonal forces into this new
dimension.

When that thrust is taken into account, and its precise direction plotted and
charted, the inadequacy of the chromatic scale to provide a proper foundation
for this expanded tonal language becomes self-evident. Hence the necessity for
the formulation of the enharmonic scale of nineteen notes which serves both to
embrace and summarize the agents by which tonality did expand, and at the
same time to provide a firmer and more coherent platform for further study.

The next stage, having formulated the enharmonic scale, is to begin to
become familiar with it, to study its particularities, and observe the way in
which it represents a natural organic extension of the chromatic scale. Here it is
important to look not just at the notes themselves, but the tonal functions
generated and supported by these notes. The importance of this cannot be
underestimated, for it has long since been understood that the prime number
seven offers the tangible basis for an extended system of just intonation.[1] Yet an
extended scale system can do little to assist in the understanding of the growth

---

[1] Eric Regener, The Number Seven in the Theory of Intonation, in: JMT19, 1975, 140 - 154.

of tonality through the domain of that particular prime number. It is when such a scale can be shown to result from a growth of tonal functions that it can become a truly valid scale. In this chapter the tonal functions represented by the notes of the enharmonic scale will be considered.

The fundamental distinction between the enharmonic and chromatic scales is that the former recognises the intuitive use of septimal tones within the context of tonal harmony. As each septimal tone within the scale is an expression of a clearly definable tonal function, means that any observations made about these septimal tones can only assist in the process of coming to a better understanding of the matrix of tonal functions supported by them.

Septimal tones recognised in the enharmonic scale all share a common feature. They are accessible through a chromatic alteration of either a perfect or imperfect degree of the chromatic scale. In the case of the augmented scale degrees (notes D#, F#, G# and A# in the key of C) these are obtained by raising a perfect or major degree of the scale, whilst the diminished scale degrees (notes Ebb, Fb, G, Bbb in the key of C) can only be obtained by flattening a perfect or minor scale-degree. The upshot of this is that the enharmonic scale embraces three levels of scale-degrees:

The Three Levels of Scale-Degrees Implicit to the Enharmonic Scale

Prime Number Three	Prime Number Five	Prime Number Seven
Perfect scale degrees	Major and minor	Augmented and diminished

A clear threefold pattern of tonal expansion is indicated here, in which the three levels represents the growth of tonality through the second, third and fourth dimensions of tonal space. First there are the perfect degrees of the scale which, operating within a prime number three limit, and obtained through the cycle of fifths, represent the two-dimensional foundations of tonality, reflected both in its primeval origins in the cycle of fifths, and the triangle of tonality itself which represents the threefold expression of the tonal principle: the tonic, dominant and subdominant functions. This may be termed prototonality.

The imperfect degrees of the scale, operating within a prime number five limit, represent the terms of a three-dimensional tonality: the major and minor polarisations of three-dimensional frequency space which were exploited under the mantle of the Classical tonal system in general. Called the diatonic level of tonality, which in theory precludes the prime number seven, this provided the foundation for the further expansion of tonality into the realms of the chromatic world, whose dualistic polarisation may be further formulated under the terms provided for by the augmented and diminished scale degrees. These, providing the basis for the chromatic, as opposed to the diatonic tonal system, constitute the salient features of tonal expansion, and therefore the present target of understanding.

Having its tentative origins in the Pythagorean method of scale construction, and therefore a prime number three limit, the diatonic scale offers one position for each of the seven scale degrees. The chromatic scale in which the prime number limit is five, appears as a logical continuation of this pattern for it offers up to two positions for each of the scale degrees. As a further stage in the unfoldment of an organic pattern, the enharmonic scale offers up to three positions for each of the scale degrees:

The Threefold Progression of Scale Step Positions

Scale:	Diatonic	Chromatic	Enharmonic
Steps:	7	12	19
Degree Positions:	One	Two	Three
Prime Number Limit:	Three	Five	Seven

The enharmonic scale thus represents a precise summary of the four-dimensional pitch matrix. The septimal tones present in this scale are not just a septimal frequency relation to the given tonic note, but the representative of a very specific tonal function within the expanded network that is the chromatic tonal system. Because these functions have a clear and tangible basis within the fourth dimension of tonal space, means that having become aware that they do actually exist, it is remarkably easy to offer a precise description of each one.

Each septimal tone resulting from the sharpening of a diatonic scale degree exerts a tendency to progress smoothly upwards to the next diatonic note. Conversely, each septimal tone resulting from the flattening of a diatonic scale degree exerts a tendency to pass downwards to the next diatonic scale degree. It is true to say therefore, that the context through which septimal tones entered the language of music was through the characteristic disguise of the chromatic decorative note.

From this perspective, a septimal tone is no different to any other chromatic tone brought in to chromatically enhance music written within an essentially diatonic framework. The feature that distinguishes them is the harmonic context in which they occur. Forming part of a septimal chord, in which intervals are present which originate from outside of the terms of the diatonic complex, they become functional as the entry ports for those unique and distinct chromatic relations characteristic of the world of the prime number seven.

From the territory covered so far it is clear that septimal chords derive from the same family and have similar functions. Understanding and defining those functions has presented great difficulty to theorists. Faced with such difficulties, Schoenberg concluded that they were *homeless phenomena, unbelievably adaptable and unbelievably lacking in independence; spires, who ferret out weaknesses and use them to cause confusion; turncoats, to whom abandonment of their individuality is an end in itself; agitators in every respect, but above all: most amusing fellows.*[1]

Viewed from the perspective of the chromatic scale, such chords do seem to be homeless, because the scale offers no place for them. When, however, the enharmonic scale as based on the interweave of the prime numbers three, five and seven is recognised as the legitimate successor to the chromatic scale, then such chords can be easily and logically explained as a part of rational and coherent tonal system.

Initially resulting from a basic mutation of the principle of dominant harmony, the precise function of such chords is to offer tonal support for the various degrees of the chromatic scale. Like secondary dominants, they have the effect of chromatically enhancing the chord progression, creating a sense of inevitability in terms of the semitonal movement that they support. Consequently, precise spelling is very important, because it indicates the degrees of the enharmonic scale being used. In the following example, what on a tempered instrument may be regarded to be the same chord, is used to offer support to the tonic and dominant degrees in the first resolution, and the tonic and subdominant degrees in the second:

Conflicting Resolutions of Enharmonically Equivalent Septimal Sonorities

At the level of the enharmonic scale there is a significant difference between these two chords. Both are chords of the augmented sixth, except that in the first chord a septimal note is being used whose tendency is to incline up to the dominant degree (*F#* - 7/5). This tendency is explainable through the presence of the septimal interval of the augmented third between the flat supertonic and sharp fourth degrees of the scale (*Db* - *F#:* ratio 21/16). In the second chord a

---

[1] Arnold Schoenberg, Theory of Harmony, 258.

septimal note is being used whose primary tendency is to decline down to the subdominant (*Gb* - 10/7), again a tendency imparted by the presence of that augmented third, which this time occurs between the notes Gb and B.

This is why spelling is so important. It is not a matter of altering music to fit in with the theory, but a case of correcting the spelling of a given chord in order to precisely accord with its heard function. Here it becomes evident that those tones resulting from the sharpening of a diatonic note perform the function of inclining tones to the note above, examples of which are *C#* (ratio of 21/20), *D#* (ratio 7/6), *F#* (ratio 7/5), *G#* (ratio 14/9) and *A#* (ratio of 7/4). Conversely, those septimal tones which result from the flattening of a diatonic note perform the opposite function, namely as declining tones to the note below. These are the notes *Ebb* (8/7), *Fb* (9/7), *Gb* (10/7), *Bbb* (12/7) and *Cb* (40/21).

From this basis, amply demonstrated in the musical examples shown in previous chapters, the precise function of each septimal tone within the enharmonic scale can be accurately defined. As it occurs in the chord given above, the note F# (7/5) is an inclining tone, in the sense that it tends to rise upwards to the next diatonic scale degree. The scale degree to which it rises is the dominant. In the context of the key of C, the note F# is thus the *dominant inclining tone*.

Similarly, the note Gb (10/7) as it appears in the chord given above, is a declining tone tending to fall downwards by a semitone to the nearest diatonic scale degree. The degree to which it falls is the subdominant. Note Gb, as it occurs in the key of C, is thus the *subdominant declining tone*. In this way, each and every septimal tone may be accorded a clear and readily definable function within the tonal scheme.

Looking at the diagram below, each septimal tone of the enharmonic scale offers a strong tonal support to a particular note of the original sub-chromatic scale. Observe that for the minor degrees of the scale, it is support from above through the corresponding declining tone. For the major degrees of the scale, it is support from below, through the corresponding inclining tone.

In this sense, the prime number seven presents an extremely positive view of chromaticism, a process of expansion of tonal relations that supports the primary functional centres. That such a functionally complex scale is realised in compositional practice has already been demonstrated. In most cases however, owing to temperament, and the weak and functionally unspecific notation composers intuitively operating within this system have tended to use, there are subtle ingredients at play which tend to make analysis difficult.

Septimal Note Functions Within the Context of the Chromatic Tonal System

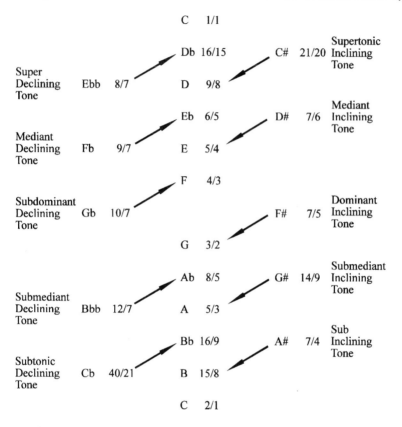

There is a very clear example of this to be seen during the opening few bars of Beethoven's *'Eroica' Symphony'*(1803):

Used with the express permission of the publishers Alfred A. Kalmus Ltd; Universal Edition (London) Ltd.

The two declamatory major chords at the beginning stridently announce the tonality of Eb major. There then follows a first subject based on an arpeggiation of the tonic triad. Against the context of this very ordinary melodic figure, Beethoven introduces an unusual turn, for the two descending diatonic semitones which follow, bring a most unusual note into the tonality of Eb major - the note C#.

When viewed from a theoretical foundation deriving from the equally tempered chromatic scale this observation is an irrelevance. Because of the extremely useful facility which equal temperament offers, it would have been possible to spell that note as a C# or a Db depending upon the required context. Now if it is taken to be the note which Beethoven writes an immediate problem is posed. The note C# has no place in the diatonic keys of either Eb major or minor. A successful way of evading the problem posed by this note is thus to assume that the composer has misspelled what in reality is a Db. Viewed thus, it may be accounted for as a 'borrowing' from the parallel minor mode - a very common practice indeed.

However, this view also poses problems. These derive from the harmonic context in which the note occurs. Viewed as Db, the accompanying G and Bb cast it up as the fifth of a chord of vii of IV, thus implying an immanent tonicisation of the triad of Ab major. However, what follows is the unexpected rise of C#, back up to the leading note D, and thence up to the tonic Eb. On these grounds, based on an observation of the behaviour of Beethoven's melodic line it must be ceded that C# is the correct spelling for this particular note.

Accepting that this note should be regarded as a C#, Roland Jackson sees in it a reminiscence of a Neapolitan progression: *Beethoven begins his 'Eroica' symphony with what can only be considered a Neapolitan progression. In this instance the opening Eb major chord...is re-interpreted as the Neapolitan chord in the key of D minor, after which it resolves to the dominant of this key, here taking the form of a diminished seventh chord on C#...Beethoven fails to carry through the Neapolitan progression to its own tonic...and abruptly turns us back once again to the key of Eb major via the V7 chord. Thus the 'dark shadow' (as Tovey expresses it) cast over these opening measures is brief in duration.* [1]

Beethoven would thus seem to up to the same sort of trickery which he used in the slow movement to the *'Waldstein'* Sonata belonging to the same period. This interpretation however, belies the sense of tonal unity which pervades the entire passage, in which the note C# somehow seems to contribute. As an integral feature of the first subject, it elevates the entire passage from an

[1] Roland Jackson, The Neapolitan Progression in the Nineteenth Century, in: MR30, 1969, 36 - 7.

otherwise perfectly straightforward chord progression in Eb major to a musical statement of great distinction.

Furthermore, if a function was ascribed to the note C#, born of unbiased observation of this particular musical passage, it could be said that it was acting as a chromatic support to the leading note D. From whence does this uniquely functional tone originate in the key of Eb major is thus the salient question that remains to be answered?

Obviously, the answer does not lie in equal temperament, but, in the sphere of, as Ellis puts it, *the indefinite number of intervals' which 'temperament renders possible.*[1] To discover an answer it is necessary to return to the simple but effective tool of the note ratio. The note C# lies a diatonic semitone (16/15) below *D*, which itself is a diatonic semitone below the tonic note Eb. The ratio of note C# to the tonic note Eb is thus 16/15 plus 16/15 which equals 256/225. The significance of this ratio has already been discussed for it has been shown that by virtue of its almost exact correspondence with the interval of 8/7, that the ear takes it for the latter.

From this it is possible to see why the note C# is hard to explain in conventional terms. It is an example of a septimal tone, the seventh harmonic of the tonic note Eb which represents that supplementary note to the chromatic scale defined above as the sub-inclining tone. Its ratio to the tonic is 7/4, and it derives not from the twelve-tone chromatic scale (in which it is unaccountable at any level) but the nineteen note enharmonic scale.

In this way, the opening of the 'Eroica' can be seen to present yet another isolated fragment of evidence in support of the fact that behind the convenience of equal temperament, a subtle metamorphosis has been taking place, a gradual expansion and proliferation of tonal relationships which goes beyond the three dimensional pitch matrix of theoretical convention, to embrace an altogether new domain - the chromatic world of the prime number seven.

This example raises an interesting issue which has so far not been discussed. The harmonic context in which the note C# occurs invokes a curious harmonic triad - *G Bb C#*. Within the domain of equal temperament it is easy to dismiss this chord as a diminished triad the upper note of which has been spelled as a *C#* to account for the voice leading. However, when looking beyond the sphere of equal temperament, the necessity for making a theoretical commitment as to whether this note should be viewed as a *Db* or *C#* has already been commented upon. The conclusion that the correct spelling of this note is C# again raises some interesting problems, for the chord concerned - G Bb C# - can, as Jackson suggests, only be regarded to be the root, fifth and seventh of a diminished

---

[1] Helmholtz, On the Sensations of Tone, 431.

seventh chord - *C# E G Bb.*   There is no other interpretation within the bounds of conventional harmony.

However, looking again at Beethoven's treatment of the chord, to identify it as an incomplete diminished seventh chord is illogical.   Viewed thus it must be cast up as the dominant minor ninth of the key of D.   Yet there is no real sense of modulation about this passage, or indeed, of the use of secondary dominant harmony.   The tonality is firmly anchored within the key of Eb, despite the intrusion of the apparent stranger - note C#.

Evidently therefore, the logical system of tonality would appear not to apply to this example. Yet there is another interpretation, which is that the missing note of this particular chord is not *E*, but the tonic note *Eb*. The logic of this lies in the distinct sense of the harmonic series which this three note chord offers.   If the note C# is given a ratio of 7/4 to the tonic note Eb, this would place the notes G and Bb as harmonic numbers five and six in the following way:

Harmonic Triad Implied by Harmonics Five, Six and Seven

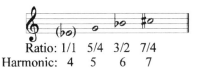

Ratio: 1/1   5/4   3/2   7/4
Harmonic: 4   5   6   7

Viewed from this standpoint the 'Eroica' symphony presents an initial musical statement which conceals a deeper significance than is at first apparent: it presents a grand symphonic exposition of one of the basic terms of an altogether new tonal system: the chromatic tonal system as it derives from the foundation of a four-dimensional pitch matrix.

Yet to put this in its proper perspective, the chord used by Beethoven in this example is not particularly rare. For a composer working within a tempered format, yet guided by their ear, it is perhaps inevitable that a chord naturally implied by the harmonic series should find a place in the musical language. Another example of exactly the same chord was presented in the last chapter - the excerpt from Schumann's *Bunte Blatter.*

Here the super inclining tone occurs as a passing note between the submediant note D and the leading note E. Schumann's treatment of the chord is very similar to Beethoven's too, except that Schumann passes straight to the dominant seventh chord, whilst Beethoven does so through the intermediary of the mediant triad.

Extract from Schumann's *Bunte Blätter*, Op. 99

On the piano keyboard the note D# as used by Schumann could easily have been spelled as an *Eb*. This is one reason why the basic outlines of the chromatic tonal system have been obscured. The principal facility of temperament during the Classical Era was to allow the playing of music in all keys without a great degree of aural discomfort. In this respect temperament worked admirably well, allowing an expansion in the number of keys which it was practicable to use.

However, since then, there has been an expansion in the pitch relations used within the province of each of those single keys. The direction of that expansion has always been assumed to be towards the full use of the chromatic scale. Yet the examples presented in this book show that twelve notes are not only insufficient to account for the relationships actually brought into play and used by composers within the province of a given key, but that they are also insufficient to provide for the maintenance of tonality within a chromatic context.

The enharmonic scale of nineteen notes is a necessary formulation because the matrix of chromatic relations used within a single key has expanded way beyond the bounds of the ordinary chromatic scale. An example is note D# as it appears in the key of F in the above example. Because the expansion of relations in a given key was along these lines, meant that the equally tempered scale started to perform a similar function for each individual key as it had performed for the body of keys overall. In other words, the notes D# and Eb as belonging say, to the key of F, were being successfully catered for through the phenomenon of enharmonic equivalence. In this way, a gradual transformation in tonality and key relations actually occurred, yet went mostly unnoticed, simply because the equally tempered scale offered a crude yet passable facility for it.

Despite temperament therefore, there is a new and important governing structure underlying nineteenth and twentieth century tonal music: not the chromatic scale of twelve notes, but the enharmonic scale of nineteen notes. In this respect it is interesting to note A. R. Mc Clure's comment that *Long experience has decided that a keyboard octave of twelve notes fits better than any other into the human pair of hands, and that, of all methods of tuning such a series, equal temperament gives by far the widest range of keys. On the other hand, history suggests that the raw ingredients of melody and harmony, although relatively stable, are in the long run subject to evolutionary changes.*[1]

The 'raw ingredients' referred to by Mc Clure are those intervals which, being represented by simple ratios, represent primary valent bonds between musical tones. The 'evolutionary changes' can only be the utilisation of those higher prime numbers which offer valent bonds which are unique to their level. Thus being unique, the musical language that utilises those bonds must change to accommodate them. Here it may be considered fortunate that temperament offered a fairly passable facility for the enharmonic scale:

Tempered Twelve-Tone Scale: a Passable Facility for the Enharmonic Scale

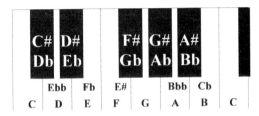

Equal temperament has thus been solving a fundamental problem in advance of any awareness of the problem itself. Through the facility of enharmonic equivalence, two given pitches are forming more than one interval. An example of this is the minor seventh and the augmented sixth. No composer or theorist could seriously deny the marvellous qualities of the augmented sixth interval, as contrasted with the interval of the minor seventh. To try to reduce these to a single interval class is a tragic loss, both for music itself, and for our appreciation of it.

An understanding of this conflict between the tempered compromise and the pure enharmonic realm has numerous ramifications in terms of the tenets of established musical theory. In his *Theory of Harmony* Schoenberg discusses the possibility of the adoption of the chromatic scale as the basis for musical composition. This assumed however, that, as Schoenberg puts it, *the raw material of all forms produced by the connecting of tones is a series of twelve tones.*[2]

From the content of the preceding pages it can be seen that this statement is illogical, for Schoenberg is confusing the cause with the consequence. The 'raw

---

[1] A. R. Mc Clure, Studies in Keyboard Temperaments, in: GSJ1, March 1948, 28 - 40.
[2] Schoenberg, Theory of Harmony, 384-389.

material' of which Schoenberg speaks derives from the properties of the tone, and its inherent harmonics by which one tone connects with another. Temperament, by its very nature, can never accurately express those relationships, because in essence it is a compromise, a reduction of the possibilities for the expression of the infinitude of musical relationships to a few more manageable ones. To imply that such a reduction is the inevitable synthesis of those relations is not only to raise temperament above the natural relations, but it is to misconstrue, both the nature of temperament, and the original relations themselves.

SEPTIMAL INFLUENCES AS SUBVERSIVELY MANIFESTING THROUGH THE GUISE OF TRIADIC SONORITIES

Because the music of the eighteenth and nineteenth centuries can be demonstrated to employ septimal elements in chord progressions means that although the pitch content of such music has been generally embraced, studied and understood from the three dimensional perspective of the diatonic level of tonality i.e. from the assumption of a prime number five limit, that it nonetheless contains within it a strong thrust towards that new fourth dimension of tonal occupation represented by the prime number seven.

The implications of that thrust are important, for they provide a parallel to the situation encountered in the Middle Ages where, in practice, the music of the times possessed a similar thrust towards the third dimension of tonal space, whilst the theory of the time only recognised the two dimensional model provided by Pythagoreanism.

Generally this thrust of the Romantic composers towards an altogether new dimension of tonal logic is explained from a negative standpoint; from a desire for rebellion and escape from the constraints of the major and minor system. The breakdown of the tonal system, and its replacement with the system of atonality may be regarded as the apotheosis of this negative standpoint. Yet from a more positive standpoint such attempts to find new frontiers for the tonal language forged the outlines of a new system of tonality, whose principles were later to become crystallised in the music of twentieth century composers such as Debussy, Bartók and Stravinsky (to name but a few).

For the present it is enough to continue the process of trying to map out the different types of septimal chord which characterize the chromatic system of tonality. Although septimal sonorities can be extremely complex, their essential elements can and often do, manifest through the guise of triadic harmony. So far in this study an emphasis has been placed on septimal tetrads, and for a very good reason. The two-dimensional pitch matrix as defined by a prime number three limit, offers only three intervals which represent a primary valent bond between musical tones - the octave (2/1), the perfect fifth (3/2) and the perfect fourth (4/3). Beyond these, the two-dimensional pitch matrix produces intervals of comparatively complex ratios such as the whole tone (ratio 9/8), the cyclic major sixth (ratio 27/16), and the cyclic major third (81/64). It is thus quite appropriate that at this level the two-dimensional reference point of the duad is proffered as the basic consonant unit of harmony.

To go a stage beyond this is to enter the terms of the more complex three-dimensional pitch matrix where, because of that extra dimension, the unit of the triad tends to arise as the basic unit of harmony. Simply, three pitches are required to represent all three-dimensional aspects - the prime (1/1), the prime number three (3/2) and the prime number five (5/4). Additionally, the fifth harmonic gives rise to those consonant forms of third and sixth which in conjunction with the perfect fifth and fourth give rise to other consonant triads.

If therefore, the prime number seven is included in the schemata of chordal design, the notion of tetradic harmony starts to come to the forefront owing to that additional dimensional factor. A complete chord at the four-dimensional level thus presupposes four notes, one representative for each of the mathematical frequency spectra which contribute to that matrix:

The Prime Number Seven as it Implicates the Harmonic Tetrad

Prime:	One	Three	Five	Seven
Chord:	Unison	Duad	Triad	Tetrad
Component:	Root	Fifth	Third	Augmented sixth

The strong implications of a tetradically based harmony existent at this level does not, and cannot exclude the domain of triadic harmony, any more than it precludes the appearance of more complex chords of five, six or seven notes. The problem with considering complex chords is that the chordal possibilities are so numerous that it is difficult to deal with them in a limited space. For this reason, in this particular chapter a short perusal will be made of septimal triads, especially those which may be readily identified as chromatic alterations of common triads. Here there is a great wealth of material to be considered, together with an abundance of examples of the use of such chords in the repertoire of tonal music.

The Italian Sixth can be regarded to be a septimal triad. This is because the augmented sixth interval of ratio 7/4 occurs between two of its three notes. The other interval which it utilises is the major third of 5/4, the remaining interval being left over to the septimal tritone (7/5). In the case of the Italian Sixth therefore, the prime number three is conspicuously absent.

The first seven members of the harmonic series apparently imply two archetypal septimal triads - *C E A#* configured by harmonics four, five and seven, and *E G A#* configured by harmonics five, six and seven. In its unaltered state, the latter chord is an incomplete seventh chord. Consequently it cannot be resolved into two superimposed thirds as can the Italian Sixth. In this context it is the other half of the triad *C G A#* configured by harmonics four, six and seven. Both of these last named chords are thus incomplete appearances of the septimal tetrad of *C E G A#.* Therefore the only true archetypal septimal triad is the Italian Sixth.

Septimal chords are fundamentally different from other chords. The concept of chordal roots is extremely problematic, owing to the fact that septimal chords may be regarded to be chromatic alterations of dominant sonorities. Therefore, in the case of the Italian Sixth, it derives from numerous points in the chain of dominant harmony, depending upon the mode of alteration applied thereto. Although implying dominant functions therefore, the same chord can possess different tendencies depending upon the context in which it occurs, and its precise position in the dominant pillar:

Various Derivations of the Italian Sixth in the Chain of Dominant Harmony

Each derivative originates from a different chromatically altered dominant chord, thereby implicating different septimal tones within the key in question. Therefore, in the case of the above chords, some five septimal tones are required - the tonic declining tone Db - ratio 15/14; the mediant declining tone Fb - ratio 9/7; the mediant inclining tone D# - ratio 7/6; the dominant inclining tone F# - ratio 7/5, and the sub-inclining tone A# - ratio 7/4.

Septimal triads may be of two kinds: apparently complete triads implied by the superimposition of two thirds (of whatever denomination), and incomplete chords of the seventh, ninth, eleventh, etc. The first group are characterised by the presence of two adjacent thirds in the chain of dominant harmony. To obtain this group of septimal chords it is necessary to refer to the primary group of usable septimal intervals, which is:

Primary Septimal Intervals

Augmented			Diminished	
Augmented Second	7/6	....	Diminished Seventh	12/7
Augmented Third	21/16	....	Diminished Sixth	32/21
Augmented Fourth	7/5	....	Diminished Fifth	10/7
Augmented Sixth	7/4	....	Diminished Third	8/7
Augmented Fifth	14/9	....	Diminished Fourth	9/7

These intervals, fundamentally chromatic in their constitution, attain a relevance either as alterations of, or substitutes for, pre-existent diatonic intervals. Any chord belonging to the three-dimensional pitch matrix can be altered to incorporate septimal intervals. On this basis, an empirical process of deduction can be applied to these chords in order to ascertain the spectrum of material available, regardless of their usage/non-usage within an historical context.

In conventional tonal terms there are four recognised triads: the major, minor, diminished and augmented. Their common feature is that they are composed of a combination of two superimposed thirds, major or minor. As there are two thirds, and two types of thirds means that there are four types of triad. The evidence of the Italian sixth chord demonstrates that the domain of septimal harmony involves an extension of this principle in the form of an expansion of the modalities of third available for the purposes of chord construction. The septimal domain offers the diminished third of ratio 8/7, and the augmented third of ratio 21/16. A triad, being composed of two thirds, means that at a septimal level there are, theoretically at least, sixteen possible triads:

Septimal Triad Table[1]

	Pitches	Composition
1	C Ebb Gbbb	Diminished plus diminished third.
2	C Ebb Gbb	Diminished plus minor third.
3	C Ebb Gb	Diminished plus major third.
4	C Ebb G	Diminished plus augmented third.
5	C Eb Gbb	Minor plus diminished third.
6	C Eb Gb	Minor plus minor third.
7	C Eb G	Minor plus major third.
8	C Eb G#	Minor plus augmented third.
9	C E Gb	Major plus diminished third.
10	C E G	Major plus minor third.
11	C E G#	Major plus major third.
12	C E Gx	Major plus augmented third.
13	C E# G	Augmented plus diminished third.
14	C E# G#	Augmented plus minor third.
15	C E# Gx	Augmented plus major third.
16	C E# G#x	Augmented plus augmented third.

Of the sixteen triads presented here four are already accounted for within the provenance of traditional harmonic theory - the major, minor, augmented and diminished triads. There are thus twelve types of septimal triad, ranging from the minimum triad composed of two superimposed diminished thirds, to the maximum triad composed of two augmented thirds. Not all of these have entered into common usage owing to the rather remote modalities of the fifth which ranges from the infra-diminished fifth of triad 1 to the ultra-augmented fifth of triad 16.

Such chords are *possible* in the enharmonic scale. The first triad on the list, the minimum triad, occurs between the notes A# C Ebb of the enharmonic

---

[1] Theorists have often commented upon the curious nature of the chords seen in this group. Schoenberg, in his Theory of Harmony, pp. 351-2 discusses nearly all of them, and shows how they can be obtained by chromatically altering ordinary triads. Similarly, Roger Sessions discusses most of these triads on page 339 of his Harmonic Practice, (Harcourt, Brace and Company, New York 1951.) They are a group of chords which, although vaguely recognised by theorists, nonetheless do not conform to conventional harmonic theories.

scale, whilst the sixteenth member of the group does not occur at all.[1] Another factor affecting the usage of such triads is their accessibility within a diatonic format. Some of the triads imply a double alteration, that is a chromatic alteration of a note which itself is already chromatically altered. This includes triads 1, 12, 15 and 16. Approached from a diatonic standpoint it is extremely doubtful that such triads would occur. It would take a conscious and deliberate exploration of the resources of the enharmonic scale to make full use of such possibilities, and as the composers whose music implied such a scale were probably unaware of its implication in their own music, this is a remote possibility.

Nonetheless, it is quite surprising how many of these triads have been used incidentally by composers. One of the problems which has tended to hamper their recognition as a related group is their relative abundance. Yet all of the twelve septimal triads as a group can be understood from the standpoint of one singular unifying principle the nature of which became apparent when septimal tetrads were being considered. The principle is this: all septimal chords can be regarded to be chromatic alterations of dominant sonorities.[2]

To understand the nature and function of a septimal chord it is thus necessary to locate its place and position in the pillar of dominant harmony. Running across this idea is the fact that a septimal chord can only be brought into play through a process of chromatic alteration. This does not just apply to the chords of dominant function however. Any chord constructed upon any scale degree can be altered to produce a septimal chord. Once altered that chord will then acquire a dominant tendency, or at least a function the nearest analogy to which is that of a dominant function.

This explains why some of the twelve septimal triads are used more often, or are more well known than others. Some pathways of chromatic alteration are more directly accessible. This becomes evident in the second chord of the group denoted by the pitches *C Ebb Gbb*. Apparently, a rather cumbersome triad, it acquires a more acceptable profile as a diminished triad the fifth and third of which have been chromatically flattened. Here it is put with the third in the bass in order to highlight the strong presence of the augmented sixth in this particular triad:

---

[1] Whilst not being implicit to a nineteen tonality, this does not preclude its functional use in a 31-tone tonality.

[2] This view will be surpassed in the next section of this book. It does however serve as a useful window through which to view septimal sonorities.

Realisation and Progression of Triad 2

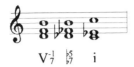

$$V_7^{-1} \quad \flat_{\flat 7}^{5} \quad i$$

In this position it invokes the declining tone Db (15/14), and the mediant declining tone Fb (9/7). In his *Twentieth Century Harmony*, Persichetti refers to this triad as a *color variant of the Italian augmented sixth with the major third.*[1] The Italian Sixth, a septimal triad already mentioned, is of course triad 3 of the Triad Table. Persischetti also mentions a chord denoted by the pitches Ab C# and F#, that is triad 4 resulting from the superimposition of a diminished and augmented third.[2]

Ratios of the Intervals of Triad 4

	7/4	
21/16		4/3
Ab	C#	F#
8/5	21/20	7/5

Because of its enharmonic similarity to a quartal triad, Persichetti suggests that it proves eminently useful in a quartal context.[3] No doubt he is referring to the tendency of the augmented sixth to expand outwards to the octave, giving a useful cadential chord. This only goes to show the great flexibility which the prime number seven levers upon chords of dominant function, as can be seen by comparing the two progressions overleaf, both of which present a vii - I progression.

One of the more interesting features about this chord is that the seventh of the dominant is sharpened to give an inclining tone to the dominant degree, whilst the fifth is flattened to give a declining tone to the tonic. It is this factor which prompts the description of note F#, having a ratio of 7/5, in the key of C, as the dominant inclining tone, as opposed to the dominant leading note. As the dominant leading note, the note F# carries the implication of another key. As the dominant inclining tone however, no other key is implied. This differential of function is expressed mathematically through the difference between the

[1] Vincent Persichetti, Twentieth Century Harmony, Faber and Faber Ltd. London 1961, 111.
[2] Ibid.
[3] Ibid., 120.

ratios of 45/32 for the dominant leading note, and 7/5, for the dominant inclining tone.

Implied Progression of Triad 4

In triad 5 the seventh of the implied dominant is flattened - *B D Fb* - an alteration which brings into play the mediant declining tone of Fb (ratio of 9/7). At the simplest level this is a septimal triad which results from the flattening of the fifth of the diminished triad. Yet the example shows this to be one of two possible interpretations of the chord (a). It can also be regarded as a chromatic alteration of chord ii of the harmonic minor mode. Here though, the chord is obtained by sharpening the bass and third. From this perspective it appears as an augmented six-four-three chord the seventh (note C) of which has been omitted (b):

Realisation and Progression of the Doubly-diminished Triad

Chords 6 and 7 of the Triad Table are conventional triads generated at a three-dimensional level: the diminished and minor triad respectively. The triad *C Eb G#* however, is extremely interesting. Its profile on the keyboard would serve to suggest the first inversion of the major triad. However in the case of this particular chord, the minor sixth is actually an augmented fifth (ratio 14/9). In terms of the chain of dominant harmony, it can thus be seen to derive either from the augmented ninth of the major dominant chain, or the augmented eleventh of the minor dominant chain:

Functional Derivation of the Minor Augmented Triad

The implication of the *A#* (7/4) is that, constituting the sub-inclining tone, it progresses upwards to the leading note. This becomes evident in this example from Beethoven where the progression of the sub-inclining tone up to the leading note can be clearly seen:

Extract from the Third Movement of Beethoven's 'Sonata Pathétique'

BEETHOVEN: Pianoforte Sonata in C minor, Op. 13, 'Pathetique'
@ 1932 by The Associated Board of the R.A.M. and the R.C.M. Used by permission.

Another type of septimal triad is the dominant chord as it occurs when the fifth is chromatically flattened - the half-diminished triad which is triad 9 in the above table. Being thus flattened, it brings into play the flat supertonic degree, that is note Db in the key of C. A prime example from one of the Mazurkas of Frederic Chopin follows.

This particular septimal triad, sometimes referred to in theoretical writings as the *defective triad*,[1] arises when the major third is omitted from the chord of the French Sixth. It resolves to the tonic chord on a par with the usual dominant, except that the voice leading implied by the diminished third, or, when inverted, the augmented sixth, leads to a double statement of the tonic note. It is also noteworthy, that the presence of the Db, as seen in this example, gives the profile of the lower tetrachord of the Phrygian mode.

---

[1] As described by Sorge in his Vorgemach der Musikalischen Komposition, Lobenstein 1745, 7.

320

Extract from Chopin's *Mazurka in C Minor*, Op. 56 No. 3.

CHOPIN: Mazurka, Op. 56 No.3
@ 1952, by The Associated Board of the Royal Schools of Music. Used by permission.

Here there are two observations of interest to be made. First, it is the use of such modal subtleties in the melodic lines of Chopin's Mazurkas that gives to the music much of its distinctive charm. Secondly, it is through the use of septimal sonorities, that modal colours can be offered harmonic support within the terms of the tonal system. Accompanying the expansion of chordal types made possible by the prime number seven, there is thus an equivalent expansion of modal resources too, a subject discussed in chapter 30.

Triads 10 and 11 are the major and augmented triads of traditional harmonic theory, and thus there is no need to discuss them. Triad 12, the doubly-augmented triad, is particularly curious because it superimposes an augmented third over a major third. As such its application is not immediately obvious, because it derives through the sharpening of the fifth of the augmented triad. That the fifth is already sharpened in the augmented triad (from a diatonic standpoint) means that it implies a double alteration.

In triad 13 is a chord which carries a similar profile to triad 4, in that, being denoted by the pitches *C E# G*, it uses the same notes on the keyboard as a quartal triad. This chord, along with the super-augmented triad, has often been noticed by theorists, but not as arising from any definitive scheme of triads. Marpurg (1718 - 1795) mentions a number of septimal triads in his theoretical writings,[1] notably *C Ebb Gb* (chord 3), which he calls the *doubly-diminished triad*; and *C E Gb* (chord 9) which he calls the *hard diminished triad*. He also mentions *C E# G* (chord 13) as arising from the combination of a perfect fifth with an augmented third, and *C E# G#* (chord 14) as arising from the augmentation of both the third and the fifth.

---

[1] Marpurg, Handbuch bei dem Generalbass, Berlin 1755-8, 48.

Although theorists have often mentioned such chords, they generally prove difficult to classify. This is because septimal triads would seem to be essentially rootless. They have a theoretical root in the sense of the root of the dominant chain of which they form a part, but their harmonic effect seems due to the character of the septimal intervals that they embody.

Therefore, triad 13 can be seen to derive from two distinct pathways. At the first level it can be understood to be the manifestation of a chromatically altered chord of the dominant major eleventh, the ninth of which has been augmented to set up the inclining tone to the leading note (a). At the second level it can be seen to derived from the chromatic alteration of the chord of dominant minor thirteenth, the eleventh of which has been augmented to set up the supertonic inclining tone:

Derivation and Application of Triad 13

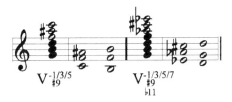

As such derivations are necessarily complex, it is probably simpler to look at septimal chords as aggregations of particular voice leading tendencies imparted by the presence of the septimal intervals present within them. Triad 14 is a good case in point. Here is an example of a triad which is enharmonically the same as the minor triad. It distinguishes itself from the minor triad by virtue of its mode of resolution, the *C#* and *E* (of the triad *Ab C# E*) tending to rise upwards by a semitone. This can demonstrated in the following example by Beethoven. Here he uses the triad with augmented third and fifth by way of the chromatic alteration of the dominant thirteenth. There is however, another pathway for this chord via the augmentation of the ninth and eleventh of the dominant major eleventh chord. The latter chord omits the root, third and fifth, to result in the pitches *F A# C#*, the *A#* and *C#* acting as inclining tones to the leading note and supertonic degrees respectively.

322

Excerpt from Beethoven's Piano Sonata in C Minor, 1st. Mvt., Opus 13

BEETHOVEN: Pianoforte Sonata in C minor, Op. 13, 'Pathetique'
@ 1932 by The Associated Board of the R.A.M. and the R.C.M. Used by permission.

Septimal triads usually result from chromatic voice leading. As such, they could be dismissed as products of chromatic voice leading being paraded as chords. Therefore, in the case of the above example, the C# and E could be viewed as paired chromatic apoggiaturas rising up to the D and F, which along with the Ab are the real harmonic tones.

Such an analysis however, does not do justice to the ingenuity of the combination as heard against the G pedal point. The progression itself has a brilliant and fiery logic which, it can be asserted, can only be properly understood through reference to the chromatic tonal system, and the various septimal intervals which it embraces.

The important point is the existence of such logic, and the best way to expose it. Because the prime number seven is primarily a chordal agent, the approach has tended to be through the sonority. This does not mean that voice-leading issues are considered redundant. It means that emphasis is placed upon the vertical element in order to expose septimal influences.

Minimum Triad (B# D Fb) as Product of Chromatic Voice Leading

A further factor which may eventually encourage a sensible theory of voice leading, is that the number of chords at this level is so large:

Triads Within the Enharmonic Scale (Key of C)

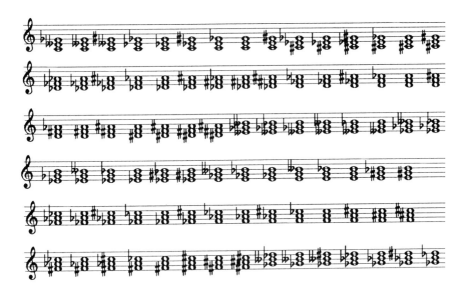

Apart from those common triads (major and minor) constructed upon the tonic, supertonic, minor and major mediant, subdominant, dominant, minor and major submediant, and subtonic - all other triads seen here may be tentatively regarded to be an extension of the dominant principle. This also includes those apparent common triads constructed upon unusual degrees, an example of which is the B major triad as given above. In the key of C, the B major triad can be regarded as an incomplete septimal tetrad denoted by the pitches *B D# F# Ab*, in which case it is simply part of a chromatically altered dominant ninth chord.

The spectrum of chords which rightly belong to the sphere of encompassment of a single tonality is thus quite vast, especially when it is considered that no attempt has been made here to include all of the septimal triads which are direct derivatives of chords of the ninth, eleventh, thirteenth, etc. There is a huge number of these, although their appearance within a musical work is often (but by no means always) masked by the musical notation. The score as written therefore, needs to be closely examined in the light of what is heard. Often the two are not contiguous with one another.

Temperament is extremely problematic in this respect. Many septimal chords are enharmonically identical with other, more conventional sonorities. Composers, being unaware of those septimal sonorities, except by reason of the ear that subtly guides them towards their usage, spell them as conventional sonorities. The only way such sonorities can be detected, is by virtue of their treatment, which will always differ from their conventional counterparts.

The writing of chords in such a fashion is extremely common in the repertoire of tonal music, a factor which can lead to a misapprehension of the underlying basis of a chord progression. A good example is the majestic opening to Vaughan Williams's *A Sea Symphony* (1903 - 9).

Extract from Vaughan Williams's *A Sea Symphony*.

In this example can be seen a curious fusion of the old and the new. The presence of a key signature of D major reveals a strongly tonally based conception of the music. Yet the first chord characterises the music as belonging to the twentieth century. The chord of Bb minor has no obvious connection with the key of D major. The connection is a rather tenuous one, obtained through a flattening of the third of the parallel minor submediant triad. The psychological connotations of this progression probably relate to the vastness and depth of the sea, expressed in the use of a minor triad related to the tonic chord by a chain of subdominant connection extending down four fourths.

Listening to this passage reveals that the ear is persuaded of a distinct logic to the progression that defies the usual concepts of key and key association. An explanation of this logic lies in the realms of the septimal triad. The *Db* of the Bb minor chord acts as a leading note to the tonic *D*. As such, in honour of its function, it could be more appropriately spelled as *C#*. Secondly, the *Bb* itself falls to the note A as the minor submediant of the key of *D* does to the dominant.

Here can be detected sure signs of dominant function - the diminished seventh interval between the notes C# and Bb which bespeaks of a chord of the dominant minor ninth of the key of D. The problem is the *F* of the Bb minor chord. Observation shows it to be an inclining tone to the mediant degree *F#*, thus revealing its identity to be an *E#*. At this stage therefore, the logic behind this progression becomes clear. Notationally a Bb minor triad is seen. Yet functionally a chromatic variant of the dominant ninth is implied.

This variant is easily explainable from the chord explained earlier, where the fifth of the dominant seventh chord is chromatically sharpened to create an inclining tone up to the mediant - *A C# E# G*. When the minor ninth is added, or substituted for the root the basis for this distinctive septimal chord can be seen – *C# E# G Bb*. Vaughan Williams uses it without the seventh: *C# E# Bb*.

A chord progression which at first sight seems at odds with the prevailing tonality, can thus be seen to fall well within the sphere of encompassment of that tonality. Indeed, in essence, such a progression is a further manifestation of a simple V - I progression. In using this chord Vaughan Williams is hearkening back to a well known Classical practice of opening a piece on the dominant prior to an announcement of the tonic triad.

The reason that septimal sonorities often remain hidden therefore, is that they are interpreted as enharmonically identical chords belonging to the diatonic tonal system. The use of a septimal sonority is thus often revealed through a differential of function when compared to another enharmonically equivalent chord – a differential usually exposed by the type of voice leading employed.

NINETEEN TONE EQUAL TEMPERAMENT AND ITS RELEVANCE TO THE CHROMATIC TONAL SYSTEM

Whether appearing under the guise of triadic, or the more usual tetradic chord formations, the gradual appearance of septimal chords in the music of the eighteenth century, coupled with the growth of chromatic invention supported by such chords during the nineteenth century, marked an event of the greatest importance. The system of tonality was beginning to outgrow the three-dimensional diatonic format originally prescribed for it by the likes of Rameau and Descartes. Entering into the terms of a new fourth dimension of tonal space, those theoretical certainties previously established for it no longer proved to be valid.

The gradual decentralisation of the major and minor system, and its subsequent recovenance under the terms of a single chromatic monotonality is an infallible example of this. It is unfortunate that the influence of this fourth dimension was not properly recognised at the time, for then it would have been clearly understood that underpinning this new and daring chromatic world of music was a matrix of septimal intervals which themselves belonged to and formed a part of an altogether new host structure: the enharmonic scale of nineteen tones to the octave.

That such a scale may be regarded to be a logical result of the intuitive use of septimal intervals can be understood through pondering the various levels of tonal influence as signified by the numbers one, two, three, five and seven:

The Multidimensional Growth of Tonality

Dimension	Prime		Unit	Scale
First	Two	2/1	Monad	---
Second	Three	3/2	Duad	Seven tone diatonic
Third	Five	5/4	Triad	Twelve tone chromatic
Fourth	Seven	7/4	Tetrad	Nineteen tone enharmonic

The number one, significant of the prototypical tone, has already been divulged as representing the very seat of the tonal principle. In theory it is dimensionless, because it represents nothing a single point in tonal space. Only when this point is brought into a perceivable relationship with another point is it possible to speak of a dimension of tonal space. The interval which belongs at this level is thus the prime of ratio 1/1, for this interval signifies the tonal principle in relation to itself, and therefore, by extension, any other tone in relation to itself. That this involves a mutual reflection of the same pitch class means that it is dimensionless.

The number two signifies the first dimension of tonal space as manifested through the interval of the octave - ratio 2/1. It is the first dimension because it represents that natural perceptual principle to which all intervallic combinations presented in subsequent dimensions are subject: the principle that is octave equivalence. Serving to configure the pitch continuum into a helix of seven or eight turns, the octave interval designated by the ratio of 2/1 is classified as a perfect interval, for it cannot be altered, changed or erased in such a way as to alter that basic format.

The number three signifies the second dimension of tonal space in which there are two possible intervals which represent a primary valent bond: the perfect fifth of ratio 3/2, and the perfect fourth of ratio 4/3. Considered in conjunction with the tonal principle (and its octave which represents the sphere over which that principle has governance), the perfect fifth and fourth represent the three primary epicentres of the musical octave which, providing the very foundations for tonality, are designated as being perfect.

The fifth of ratio 3/2 is perfect because it alone represents the generator of the second dimension of tonal space. The fourth of ratio 4/3 is also perfect because it alone represents the negative reflection of that generator which enables the prototypical tone to act as its representative. In this way, the triangle of tonality itself is completely inviolable, an immutable unit forever locked in tonal space by virtue of the mutual reinforcement offered by its representatives.

The number five represents the generator of the third dimension of tonal space. Responsible for producing valent forms of the major and minor intervals, this is the point where the forces of tonality divide into two polarised forms of expression: major and minor. Its intervals are thus designated as being imperfect, on account of the fact that they admit of this duality, of that positive and negative polarisation of frequency space so perfectly embodied in the form of the major and minor common triads.

That this is a phenomenon of the third dimension can be understood through the observation that when a major third is inverted, the result is a minor sixth, whilst when a minor third is inverted, the result is a major sixth. That reversal in the characteristic polarisation of the interval concerned represents a movement in three-dimensional frequency space. Because there are only four points in the octave where these intervals can occur, means that a full expression of tonality at this level represents the union of the triangle of perfect intervals, with the square of imperfect intervals under the overall terms of the septenary.

The complete scale thus has seven notes in order that all available terms may be thereby represented. Yet the tetrad occurs in two forms, major and minor, which means that the ultimate expression of tonality at this level is obtained as the sum of the triad, and the major and minor tetrads, which means to say that it generates a complete chromatic scale bar the central point as represented by the enigmatic interval of the tritone:

The Sub-chromatic Scale as Sum of Tonal Triad and Major and Minor Tetrad

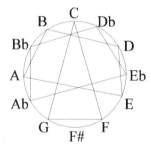

This brings the discussion to the prime number seven. To go beyond the point represented by the sum of $3 + 4 + 4 = 11$, is to proceed beyond the bounds of tonality as understood within a three-dimensional context. To do this deliberately without conscious knowledge of the fourth dimension, is to push tonality into regions where it is incapable of renewing itself. The results of such an action are well attested for by the last eighty years or so of Western musical history: the system of tonality breaks down.

In this way, the tritone representing that crucial central point of the octave, becomes the very symbol and token of that new fourth dimension of tonal possibility, for to proceed into the fourth dimension, is to bring that tritone (7/5) into the terms of a proper tonal function, and thereby complete the chromatic circle. Hence the very deep significance which may be attributed to the chord of the augmented sixth constructed upon the flat submediant degree.

With this addition (*F#* - 7/5) the chromatic circle becomes fully circumscribed, an apparently complete self-contained sphere of operation for the forces of tonality. Yet at this point a rather unique theoretical paradox presents itself, one whose solution provides the general key to the precise nature of the four-dimensional tonal possibility. Immediately the chromatic circle is closed by the septimal tritone (7/5), it is forced open again by the *sonido trece*,[1] - the thirteenth sound represented by the note Gb (10/7). The dilemma that this poses can be understood by trying to decide as to whether it is the note F# as the inclining tone to the dominant, or the note Gb as the declining tone to the subdominant that completes the chromatic circle. Which one is it?

An answer to this question is impossible for both functions are equally necessary. Endeavouring to discover an answer, the basic terms underlying the polarity of the fourth dimension of tonal space present themselves, for the note F# represents an augmented fourth in relation to the tonal principle, whilst the note Gb represents a diminished fifth. Generating valent forms of augmented and diminished intervals therefore, the forces of tonality are able to break free of the chromatic circle, and extend their dominion to the chromatic resources as summed up by that necessary differentiation between the sharp and the flat: the notes F# and Gb.   In this way, the enharmonic scale is born of the necessity to recognise this important distinction, a distinction imposed by our inability to close the chromatic circle. Because there are six valent intervals at this level (7/4, 7/5, 7/6, 8/7, 10/7, 12/7) means that any new scale which does arise in respect of this four-dimensional tonality, must have at least 17 notes: the most basic and rudimentary form of enharmonic scale.

The idea that a more advanced scale may result as a logical extension of the chromatic scale is extremely common in theoretical writings over this last century. Naturally there are different ideas and approaches to the subject, and in many cases conflicting ideas with regard to the precise nature of that extension. That such a change has been regarded in some quarters to be inevitable, becomes apparent from Schoenberg's statement upon this subject in his *Theory of Harmony*: *Moreover, it is not to our scale alone that we owe the evolution of our music. And above all; this scale is not the last word, the ultimate goal in music, but rather a provisional stopping place. The overtone series, which led the ear to it, still contains many problems that will have to be faced. And if, for the time being we still manage to escape those problems, it is due to little else than a compromise between the natural intervals and our inability to use them - that compromise which we call the tempered system, which amounts to an indefinitely extended truce. This reduction of the natural relations to manageable ones cannot permanently impede the evolution of music; and the ear will have to attack the problems, because it is so disposed. Then our scale*

---

[1] This was the term used by the Mexican composer Julián Carrillo to describe microtones.

will be transformed into a higher order, as the church modes were transformed into major and minor modes...It is certain that this movement is now afoot, certain that it will lead to something.[1]

Here Schoenberg seems well aware of the problems, and even the direction in which the most sensible solutions may be found - the so-called 'overtone' series. Significantly, Schoenberg casts up the equally tempered twelve-tone scale as being nothing more than an avenue of escape from the problems which the 'overtone' series presents, and thus a safe and secure sanctuary which enabled him to carry on composing without any more concern for the fundamental realities underlying the musical language. Consequently, his own work led to the entrenchment of an equal twelve-point octave which tended towards the elimination of those finer enharmonic distinctions between musical tones that are the essence of a four-dimensional system of tonality.

Hence he recognises the chromatic scale as the basic foundation for tonality, yet refuses to accept anything which goes beyond that: *the raw material of all forms produced by the connecting of tones is a series of twelve tones. (That there are twenty-one note names here, and that their presentation begins with C, is consistent with and derives from our imperfect notation; a more adequate notation will recognise only twelve note names and give an independent symbol for each).*[2] He then presents a series of twenty-one note symbols, which, by their nature fully sum up the possibilities of the enharmonic tone system:

Schoenberg's Note-Symbols[3]

C		D		E		F		G		A		B
Cb	C#	Db	D#	Eb	E#	Fb	F#	Gb	G#	Ab	A#	Bb
B#												

Yet his thinking leads him to reduce these to twelve. For Schoenberg the note F# is the same as the note Gb, an approach which casts up the equally tempered twelve-tone scale as the only fundamental reality. That it is simply a compromise upon those natural relations by which that fundamental reality may be found, is however, soundly evident from his earlier statement. Schoenberg's stance therefore, is a very conservative one.

In contrast to this, stands the work of Joseph Yasser, a theorist who not being content to rest with the theoretical conventions represented by the equally-tempered twelve tone scale, sought to logically expand the chromatic

---

[1] Arnold Schoenberg, Theory of Harmony, 25.

[2] Ibid., p. 387.

[3] Ibid.

scale through an extension of those natural relations implied by the harmonic series. However, rather than observing and studying that extension as it occurred in the actual body of music Yasser aimed his endeavour towards attempting to divine the tissue and organic substance of the music of the future. Towards this end he believed that the number of steps of the musical 'scale of the future' could be predicted from a pattern already established by the progression of tonal music from a seven-note to a twelve-note scale. According to this pattern, the musical scale which future generations will use with equal fluency is a scale of nineteen notes - the so-called 'supra-diatonic' scale:

Yasser's Prediction of the Number of Steps in the 'Scale of the Future'.[1]

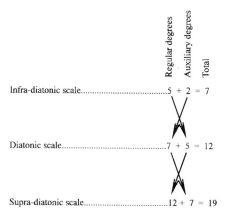

By the term 'infra-diatonic' Yasser means the heptatonic scale as viewed to consist of five principal notes plus two auxiliaries. The 'diatonic' scale he mentions is the chromatic scale of twelve notes, consisting of seven regular degrees and five chromatic alterations. The 'supra-diatonic' scale is thus viewed as a natural extension of these two scales - the next step in what Yasser sees to be a logical progression in the increasing complexity and sophistication of musical scales. Curiously Yasser does not directly implicate the prime number five, as the natural successor to the prime number three as the basis for the diatonic scale, and the prime number seven as the basis for its extension into the supra-diatonic scale. Instead, he constructs his 'supra-diatonic' scale from a section of eighteen perfect fifths, i.e. according to a retrogressive Pythagorean

---

[1] Joseph Yasser, A Theory of Evolving Tonality, 115.

intonation. Aware of the distinct disadvantages of this he then goes on to advocate a nineteen-note equal temperament.

As if this were not enough for future generations to contend with, in Chapter XI, he goes on to try to anticipate the basic consonant chord of the 'supra-diatonic' system. This amounts to a chord of six notes which is suspiciously similar in its profile to the whole tone scale, whose musically properties, as Yasser was no doubt aware, had been rather well exploited in the thirty year period prior to the publication of his book (1932). In order to make this fact less evident, he develops an extremely complex and difficult system of notation involving the addition of the letters V W X Y Z, and invokes the support of the harmonic numbers 8, 9, 10, 11, 13 and 14 in order to obtain natural ratification for this chord:

Yasser's Consonant Hexachord for the 'Music of the Future'[1]

Overtones: 8   9   10   11   13   14
C 102 D 91 E 83 F# 145 Ab 64 Bb 115 (c)

Using this chord in various transpositions he reconstructs the 'supra-diatonic' scale according to the principles of how he perceives 'just intonation'. The result, further complicated by his even more difficult and obscure system of intervallic classification, is so fraught with complexities and contradictions that its very value becomes questionable. Through developing a consonant hexachord which also involves the prime numbers eleven and thirteen, Yasser seems to be well in advance of himself, for he is invoking yet further dimensions of tonal space in support of his theory, and trying to pass off a nineteen tone scale as the summary of their possibility. This attempt is evidently not very successful, for at various times through the course of his work he advocates three separate bases from which such a scale may be built: Pythagorean intonation, just intonation and nineteen tone equal temperament.

Such perhaps are the difficulties of trying to divine the basis for the music of the future. There being nothing upon which the hypothesis can be tested, means that all possible options need to be covered. One of the redeeming features of Yasser's work is the exposure of those regular patterns which do point to a more complex scale than the chromatic scale. However, on the one hand those patterns are taken extremely literally in Yasser's work leading to a fixed presentiment of what the future of music might bring, and on the other hand, he chooses at times to ignore even the most simple pattern. As a result, Yasser did

[1] Ibid., pp. 116-123.

not implicate the prime number seven as the sole basis for extending the twelve-note into a nineteen-note scale.

Yet his grounds, stated at the outset of his work, are all quite reasonable: *Whatever one's attitude toward the radical musical tendencies of today, and whatever the absolute artistic value of modern musical compositions may be (most of them, unquestionably, mere 'creative experiments'), yet considering all the manifold historic, theoretic and acoustic data accumulated up to the present time, one can hardly doubt that those radical tendencies are signs or reflections or at least anticipations of some profound and volcanic process in musical art which will ultimately lead to the practical adoption of a new, tonally more complicated and, consequently, more subtle scale.... Our diatonic scale, and later the chromatic scale, were not established in music at one stroke either, but were preceded by less complex scales which, as a rule have now been abandoned.... We should not lose sight of the fact that a genuine musical scale (or tonality, in a more fundamental sense) is, in a way, an organic phenomenon, a materialised product of our inmost psychic functions, which, like everything else live and organic, is bound to grow and expand, to evolve continuously. It is essentially an evolving, not a static phenomenon....It would be rash therefore, to believe that our present musical scale, for instance, will be replaced in the future by a more complex one, as soon as such a scale has been theoretically found and is accessible practically.....It was probably due to the natural leisureliness of the evolutionary process indicated and to the resultant meagerness of corresponding records that the inherent laws which govern this slow, though continuous, structural development of scales, and which could thus give us a clue as to the structure of the scale of the future, have not been revealed so far.*[1]

Subsequent work, based on Yasser's initial investigations has tended to concentrate and improve upon his lapses of logic. The authors Kraehenbuehl and Schmidt advocate the evolution of more complex tonal systems, progressing through the various prime numbers of the harmonic series. The diatonic scale in its original form is based on the prime number three, the chromatic scale on the new prime of five. The next scale to emerge, described by the authors as the 'hyperchromatic', will use the prime number seven as the leading agent. After this a scale of 41 steps, which the authors describe as the 'ultrachromatic' will emerge, using the prime number 11 as the leading agent. So, according to the authors, are the next steps for the future of music.[2]

---

[1] Ibid., 3.

[2] David Kraehenbuehl and Christopher Schmidt, On the Development of Musical Systems, in: JMT6, 1962, 32 - 65.

In this study, no such claim is being made for the enharmonic scale. On the contrary, endeavouring to divine the 'scale of the future' can only be viewed to be a pointless and disheartening exercise. Here perhaps, it is apt to hearken back to Sir Hubert Parry's famous and oft quoted observation that *scales are made in the process of endeavouring to make music and continue to be altered and modified generation after generation, even till the art has arrived at a high stage of maturity.*[1] To endeavour to divine the scale before the music has actually been created, is surely the wrong way around.

The aim of this study has been to try to show that the nineteen tone enharmonic scale, together with the septimal intervals it implicates, had already been established well before the time theorists such as Schoenberg or Yasser were even writing. In this respect, both theorists were anticipating developments which had in fact already occurred in the actual music. It is just that it was not noticed at the time. All that was noticed is that some kind of change was going on.

Looking at these changes from the perspective afforded by the prime number seven, those changes were not primarily towards the breakdown of tonality, but towards the building up of a new system of tonality: the chromatic tonal system which utilises a scale of nineteen notes. The process of scalar expansion which ensued occurred by way of an expansion in the realms of tonal function. Yet this is perhaps the only feasible way for an expansion to occur. It would be quite pointless to expand systems of intonation unless the tonal functions were there in the first place.

Here it has been shown that such tonal functions are indeed there from a comparatively early stage. Yasser points out above that *a genuine musical scale (or tonality, in a more fundamental sense) is, in a way, an organic phenomenon, a materialised product of our inmost psychic functions, which, like everything else live and organic, is bound to grow and expand, to evolve continuously.*[2] The process of expansion he refers to has already happened - at the level of function. Unfortunately, twelve-tone equal temperament provides for that matrix of functions in a very imperfect way. Looking at the enharmonic scale, the salient septimal intervals are some one-third of a semitone larger or smaller than their tempered equivalents:

---

[1] Sir Hubert Parry, The Art of Music, London

[2] Yasser, Op. Cit.

Differentials Between Septimal Intervals and Their Equally Tempered
Counterparts

Degree	Note	Interval	Ratio	Cents	Diff.
I	C	Prime	1/1	0	
bII	Db	Minor second	16/15	112	
II	D	Major second	9/8	204	
bIII	Ebb	Diminished third	8/7	231	+31
#II	D#	Augmented second	7/6	267	−33
III	Eb	Minor third	6/5	316	
#III	E	Major third	5/4	386	
bIV	Fb	Diminished fourth	9/7	435	+35
IV	F	Perfect fourth	4/3	498	
#IV	F#	Augmented fourth	7/5	583	−17
bV	Gb	Diminished fifth	10/7	617	+17
V	G	Perfect fifth	3/2	702	
#V	G#	Augmented fifth	14/9	765	−35
bVI	Ab	Minor sixth	8/5	814	
VI	A	Major sixth	5/3	884	
bVII	Bbb	Diminished seventh	12/7	933	+33
#VI	A#	Augmented sixth	7/4	969	−31
VII	Bb	Minor seventh	9/5	1018	
#VII	B	Major seventh	15/8	1088	
I	C	Octave	2/1	1200	

This shows how powerfully persuasive context can be, for to appreciate the
often complex chromatic harmony of the music of the nineteenth century,
context is all that the ear has to rely upon. Some keyboards have designs which
are better suited for portrayal of the reality of a nineteen-note tonal system.
Involving intervals smaller than the semitone, these necessitate the use of
microtones.

Some of these were arrived at long ahead of the task, although for quite
different reasons. A good example is the Clavicymbalum Universale, seen by
Praetorius and described in his *Syntagmatis Musici Tomus Secundus de
Organographia* of 1619.[1] Tuned according to the meantone system, it gives
very good approximations of the septimal intervals present in the enharmonic

---

[1] The reprinted 1884 edition which utilises seven white and twelve black keys, 74-

scale.[1] It was however, designed for use of the diatonic scale and its transposition in different keys:

Nineteen Note Scale of the *Clavicymbalum Universale*.

Note	Cents	Nearest Ratio	Cents	Difference
C	000	1/1	000	
C#	76	21/20	85	+11
Db	117	16/15	112	+5
D	193	9/8	204	+11
D#	269	7/6	267	−2
Eb	310	6/5	316	+6
E	386	5/4	386	0
E#	462	21/16	471	+11
F	503	4/3	498	−5
F#	579	7/5	582	+3
Gb	621	10/7	617	−4
G	697	3/2	702	+5
G#	773	14/9	765	−8
Ab	814	8/5	814	0
A	890	5/3	884	−6
A#	966	7/4	969	+3
Bb	1007	16/9	996	−11
B	1083	15/8	1088	+5
B#	1156	49/25	1165	+9
C	1200	2/1	1200	0

The largest difference to an equivalent septimal interval is 11 cents which is the acceptable difference between the whole tone of 9/8 and the mean tone itself. What does this mean? Does it mean that such a scale should be practically adopted? Not necessarily.

Keyboards have been designed which are more suitable for the accurate presentation of septimal intervals. The keyboard as given above however, would be useful for one or two keys of the enharmonic scale. To be able to use the enharmonic scale in all of the keys a much more complex scale would be required, or some kind of tempered scale which gave better approximations of septimal intervals.

---

[1] Ellis describes the nineteen notes thus C c# db D d# Eb E e# F f# Gb G g# ab A a# bb B b# C, small letters being the white keys. Helmholtz, Op. Cit., 320.

Equal nineteen-tone is a prime example, a temperament which has been around for a very long time. Its use was first advocated by the blind Spanish organist and theorist Francisco Salinas (1513 - 1590).[1] Since then, its qualities have been admired by many theorists and composers. Even Yasser, aware of the problems created by his complex 'supra-tonal' scale in just intonation eventually opted for an equally tempered nineteen-tone division of the octave. The hypothetical keyboard he designed for this purpose provides an interesting example of the intended use of split keys:

Yasser's Nineteen-Tone Equally Tempered Keyboard[2]

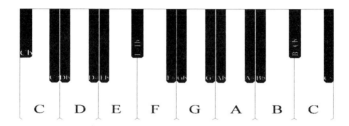

In his *Studies of Keyboard Temperaments* (1948), A. R. Mc Clure makes a thorough examination of the possibilities of nineteen-tone equal temperament, as advocated by Woolstone, Yasser and others. He observes that it gives *a surprisingly smooth German Sixth (representing the frequency ratio 4:5:6:7), and on the other hand a surprisingly rough chord of the dominant seventh with no trace of the sentimental about it.*[3] This distinction between the German Sixth being represented by the 4:5:6:7 configuration, and the rougher dominant seventh chord, is the very type of distinction required for the successful realisation a four-dimensional system of tonality. Examining nineteen-tone equal temperament against the enharmonic scale, it does offer fair approximations of some septimal intervals:

---

[1] James Murray Barbour, Equal temperament, its history from Ramis (1482) to Rameau (1737), 95.

[2] A. R. Mc Clure, Studies in Keyboard Temperaments, in: GSJ1, March 1948, 28.

[3] Joseph Yasser, Op. Cit., 281.

Comparison of Nineteen-Tone Equal Temperament with the Enharmonic Scale

	Equal Nineteen			Enharmonic Scale			
Note		Cents	Note	Cents	Ratio		Diff.
1	C	00.00	C	000.00	1/1		
2	C#	063.1	C#	084.47	21/20		−21.31
3	Db	126.3	Db	111.73	16/15		+14.59
4	D	189.4	D	203.91	9/8		−14.44
--	--	---	Ebb	231.17	8/7		---
5	D#	252.6	D#	266.87	7/6		−14.24
6	Eb	315.7	Eb	315.64	6/5		+00.06
7	E	378.9	E	386.31	5/4		− 7.41
8	Fb	442.1	Fb	435.08	9/7		+ 7.02
9	F	505.2	F	498.04	4/3		+ 7.16
10	F#	568.4	F#	582.51	7/5		−14.11
11	Gb	631.5	Gb	617.49	10/7		+14.01
12	G	694.7	G	701.96	3/2		− 7.26
13	G#	757.8	G#	764.92	14/9		− 7.12
14	Ab	821.0	Ab	813.69	8/5		+ 7.31
15	A	884.2	A	884.36	5/3		−00.16
16	Bbb	947.3	Bbb	933.13	12/7		+14.17
---	---	---	A#	968.83	7/4		---
17	Bb	1010.5	Bb	996.09	16/9		+14.41
18	B	1073.6	B	1088.27	15/8		−14.67
19	Cb	1136.8	Cb	1115.53	40/21		+ 21.5

The average discrepancy is about 14 cents, a gap whose significance depends upon the interval concerned. For the leading note it is a rather large discrepancy, especially in light of the modern tendency to try to raise the pitch of the leading note nearer to the target tone. The perfect fifth is not very well provided for either, for having an extremely simple ratio, it can tolerate far less deviation than an interval of more complex ratio. Most of the septimal tones are some 14 cents off, either way, a discrepancy which is not without its problems, although at least equal-nineteen offers some type of representation of the difference between a septimal interval and its enharmonic equivalent within a twelve-tone format.

Aside from these discrepancies, one problem is that it does not offer a functional sub-inclining tone (7/4), or indeed, the inversion of the sub-inclining tone - the super-declining tone (8/7). Instead it offers a supertonic inclining tone (C# - 21/20), and subtonic declining tone (Cb - 40/21). Because the seventh harmonic of the tonic is not very well represented, the German Sixth referred to by McClure was no doubt the chord constructed upon the minor submediant degree (*Ab C Eb F#*) which is almost perfectly realised in 19 tone equal temperament.

Despite these points of objection, when nineteen-tone equal temperament is compared with the enharmonic scale a rather interesting series of conclusions result. From the musical examples which have been presented in this book so far, it becomes apparent that the chromaticism of the music of the nineteenth century represents a transitionary element between two essentially stable tonal systems: the diatonic system of tonality as rooted in a prime number five limit and founded upon the twelve note chromatic scale, and a chromatic tonal system rooted in a seven limit and founded upon the nineteen note enharmonic scale.

Twelve tone equal temperament provided the basic solution to a problem which was encountered initially at the diatonic level of tonality: the problem of how to modulate freely between keys without overly affecting the purity of the requisite intervals. For this purpose it did a good job. Since Bach's time however, the situation has changed. The major tonality gradually combined its resources with the minor tonality, the pair being gradually drawn together in the slipstream of a unified monotonality which gave composers the option of either major or minor polarisations as and when required.

Additionally, the resources of chromatic harmony were significantly expanded to produce a large number of new chord forms; septimal sonorities whose very intervallic constitution caused the rupturing of the closed circle of the chromatic scale and thereby opening the gateway to the mysterious and enigmatic effects of enharmony whose principal characteristic was a keen distinction between the sharp and the flat, or the rising and falling chromatic note.

The way the situation changed is that the territory of each individual key expanded beyond all recognition to gradually embrace a complex and sophisticated nineteen-tone system. If the problem that faced Bach was reassessed on these grounds, it would have to be upgraded in accordance with these changes. The problem would be how to accommodate this expansion in the resources of a single key whilst at the same time preserving the freedom to modulate from any key to any other key. Twelve-tone equal temperament fails miserably in this respect, because it offers no audible recognition for the distinction between sharp and flat within the confines of a single key that the chromatic tonal system calls for. A simple example is the difference between note D# (7/6) and Eb (6/5) in the key of C, pitches which perform contrasting functions in the tonal network, the former performing the function of the mediant inclining tone, the latter the minor mediant scale degree.

A glance at the above comparison shows that equal nineteen performs admirably in its ability to offer that recognition. Because of its equal interval system, it enables the composer to modulate freely between keys. It thus offers a solution to the same problem as equal-twelve, the difference being the level of application, the former belonging at the chromatic level, the latter at the diatonic level. In this respect, equal-nineteen is far from perfect, although it does represent a step in the right direction.

One of the fundamental problems which arises with nineteenth century chromatic music is that it functionally implies one scale system whilst being crudely expressed through another more rudimentary scale. This helps to explain some of the problems which arose with regard to the notation of this music, for the composer was always faced with a contradiction. Because equal-twelve was the medium of expression it didn't matter how a composer spelled a given chromatic note, yet because the voice leading tended to implicate a sharp or flat as the preferential option in a given situation, somehow it did matter. The composer therefore was caught in the middle, hesitating between these two conflicting concerns.

This helps to explain why context became such an important feature of modern musical theory, for in the absence of any audible distinction between the sharp and the flat, the only arbiter that could offer a decision either way was the contextual setting of the given note or chord form. It is unfortunate that whilst the music of the nineteenth century literally cried out for a more fitting medium of expression such as nineteen-tone equal temperament could offer, it never actually materialised. Instead, twelve-tone equal temperament tightened its stranglehold, eventually to attain the dogmatic status as the scale of Western art music.

Therefore, the chromatic subtleties of nineteenth century music were offered only a declentive address through a scale system which was ill suited to their expression. For a musical theory which took twelve-tone equal temperament as the standard therefore, the augmented sixth was eventually considered to be the same as a minor seventh, and the Tristan chord the same as a half-diminished seventh chord. Whilst equal-nineteen therefore affirms a distinction between these chord or interval categories, equal-twelve continually defies that distinction, leading in the end to a convergence of opposing chromatic functions upon a neutral tone that favoured neither one nor the other.

That merger however, was not a constructive merger, guided by a sound unifying principle, it was a collapse of functions because the twelve-tone medium could no longer support the direction in which the tonal language was expanding. So one or the other had to surrender. In the end, tonality surrendered, collapsing in on itself in favour of an infinite freedom obtained at the expense of the nullification of those original tonal functions.

THE RELEVANCE OF THE PRIME NUMBER SEVEN TO THE BREAKDOWN OF TONALITY

So far in this study it has been shown that music of the eighteenth and nineteenth centuries contains within it the portent of a larger encompassing system: the chromatic system of tonality. From a reading of that music it has been shown that the chromatic tonal system presents significant features not inherent to the diatonic tonal system: an extremely wide range of chromatically altered sonorities that considerably increases the colouristic range and harmonic palette of the composer, and a matrix of septimal note functions, supported by those chords, which allows a diversification in the network of tonal relations usable within the confines of a particular key. Consequently, it also possesses a more refined and sophisticated musical scale which serves both to summarise and embrace those increased possibilities.

Yet these features, which have been obscured by the assumption of equal temperament into a position of theoretical autocracy, are not the chromatic tonal system itself, but signs of the impending arrival of that system. To view the chromatic tonal system in its full splendour it is necessary to move on to the topic of late nineteenth and early twentieth century music, where its principles start to become clarified. The music considered so far, mostly written within the period 1800 - 1885, rather than representing the last vestiges of the appearance of tonality before its final abandonment in the face of the 'historical inevitability' of atonality, may be regarded as representing a transitional phase between the diatonic system of tonality of the Classical era and the chromatic system of tonality of the twentieth century. Because there are strong elements of continuity between all three of these phases of musical history, means that it is impossible to draw a clear demarcation line as to where the diatonic system ends and the chromatic system begins. Consequently, it is equally impossible to draw a demarcation line in the music itself.

That stage of musical history when the system of tonality was starting to be stretched to breaking point i.e. the late nineteenth century, represents an important staging post towards the manifestation of the chromatic system of tonality. Here the uncharted role which septimal chords played in the perceived breakdown of tonality needs to be pondered. The highly chromatic language of Wagner's 'Tristan' is often cited as one of the major influential factors which encouraged the breakdown of tonality.[1] The highly chromatic elements of this language depended very much on the tonal itinerance and ambiguity of those septimal chords such as the 'French sixth', or even the 'Tristan' chord itself.

Consequently the seventh harmonic may have provided one of the contributory factors towards the breakdown of tonality. Yet the prime number seven is a constructive principle. Therefore if it was influential towards the breakdown of tonality, it can by the same token, be influential in the building up of a new tonality. In this sense, the prime number seven starts to bear an increasing relevance to both of the apparently opposing trends of the music of the twentieth century. Simply, for a new tonality to be built up, the old must first be broken down.

Discussing the breakdown of tonality in general Antokeletz observes that: *with the dissolution of traditional tonal functions in the early part of this century composers of divergent stylistic backgrounds and influences were evolving a new concept of the relations contained in the chromatic continuum. The trend towards equalization of the twelve tones led to a tonally acentric system that underwent developments primarily in the work of the Viennese composers Schoenberg, Berg and Webern, and also to a body of musical compositions that were deeply rooted in a sense of tonal centricity. These compositions, which have some connections with certain works of the Viennese composers, are significantly represented by the works of Bartok, and other non-Germanic composers.*[2]

Here, Antokeletz makes a general distinction between those composers who opted for atonality and serialism, and those who, like Bartók or Debussy, opted for the retention of some kind of tonal centricity. Although this is a rather broad categorisation it does contain an important point - that connecting both, what would appear to be diametrically opposite approaches is the chromatic continuum as represented by the twelve notes of the tempered scale. This is the important area that both tonal and atonal approaches to twentieth century music share in common. They both advocate the breakdown of the old diatonic scale system, and its replacement with the chromatic scale system.

---

[1] Donald Jay Grout & Claude V. Palisca, A History of Western Music (3rd Edition), J. M. Dent & Sons, London and Melbourne 1980, 634.
[2] Elliot Antokeletz, The Music of Bela Bartók: A Study of Tonality and Progression in Twentieth Century Music, University of California Press, London 1984, 2.

It is here that the strongest sign of the ascension of the chromatic tonal system over the old diatonic tonal system presents itself. Already it has already been postulated that despite the general use and theoretical acceptance of the equally tempered twelve tone scale, the practice of composers pointed towards a more refined network of tonal functions which only crudely accommodated by that scale.

The dangers of this are now beginning to achieve some kind of recognition. As Ben Johnston says: *A more harmful, it more subtle effect of temperament is the inadequate conceptual model it presents to the composer. So long as musical usages are based on a rational scale, the out - of - tuneness of temperament is a largely negligible consideration. But when many of these usages become outmoded and a search for new principles of musical organisation begins, as happened in the twentieth century, the one-sided model provided by temperament becomes a serious but largely unrecognised limitation.*[1]

Here the dangers that temperament presents have become all too apparent, for behind that scale, hidden at first, exists a lattice of septimal intervals that have served to transform the musical language from the simple triadic functions of the major and minor modes, to the more complex and enigmatic sphere of the chromatic tonal system. There thus exists the intimation that composers of the twentieth century, building and enlarging upon the foundations laid down in the previous century, have unknowingly entered the domain of this larger encompassing system.

This may explain why much of twentieth century tonal music has tended to defy systematic analysis - the chromatic tonal system from which such music takes its departure point has not been properly defined. All that has been successfully charted is the way in which composers have reacted against the constraints of the original diatonic tonal system. So no wonder tonality appeared to have broken down. The snake has shed its skin and now lies elsewhere. Left with nothing but the skin, a rather negative view of the entire process has resulted.

From the examples shown so far it is clear that nineteenth century composers are utilising a functional scale which has more than twelve notes; and that where strange or unusual chords are used which seem to point to a free or even anarchic use of any of the twelve notes of the chromatic scale, examination has shown that these are simply chords belonging to the diatonic tonal system whose function has been mutated, extended and upgraded in accordance with

---

[1] Ben Johnston, Scalar Order as a Compositional Resource, in: PNM2/2, 1964, 60.

the dictates of the prime number seven. Consequently, the bones of the original system are still there, and what has been taken to be a radical departure from it is nothing of the sort - it is a transformation of the original system caused by the unconscious utilisation of a new harmonic resource.

The emphasis of this study has thus been based largely on the harmonic sonority, for it is through sonority in the first instance, that septimal strains of influence have surreptitiously crept their way into music. Beginning comparatively early with the arrival of the Italian Sixth chord, the prime number seven has been exerting an increasingly powerful influence upon music and its further development.

The most potent effects can be seen in the sphere of dominant sonorities, where the prime number seven has supported the creation of a veritable host of dominant empowered chromatically altered sonorities. Through the hidden power of the prime number seven, the dominant tetrad and its derivatives has mutated, hybridised, variegated, and in so doing opened up harmonic support within the province of the sphere of tonality for a new expanded matrix of tonal functions.

Although the sonorities which involve the use of septimal tones offer a certain degree of support for Wagner's technique of 'creeping about' melodically by semitones, this is only a limited resource. The chromatic system of tonality was never meant to be an unbridled universe of homogeneous chromatic effects. Unfortunately, in the absence of any clear knowledge concerning the prime number seven this is eventually what it became. Substitutes were then developed, artifices which, pretending to be the next vital step in the evolution of the musical language, were paraded before an unwitting and increasingly hostile musical public.

Yet there is something fundamentally suspect in the argument that atonality represents the inevitable historical successor to the principle of tonality. The major flaw lies in the fact that atonality is not, in itself, a positive principle underlying the composition of music. It is the effect or consequence of a principle. To affirm that tonality is a principle is to immediately posit the existence of the opposite principle that is atonality. However, that counter principle can no longer serve to replace the original principle, than a monarchically controlled state can be replaced by a system of 'anti-monarchy'. Once monarchy has passed away, what is there to justify it? There is nothing. The counter principle thus disappears along with the principle. Atonality is thus not, and never can be a true compositional principle.

But of course this is simply arguing over the validity of the term itself. Schoenberg chose to dissociate himself from this particular term, preferring instead the term *pantonality*, which projects a much more positive image of what he was trying to achieve. Yet entering into this recipe for total confusion, the term pan-tonality - the prefix 'pan' signifying 'all' - implies not the absence of tonality but the simultaneous presence of all tonalities. As different as black is from white, it seems paradoxical that both terms could be used to describe the same music.

Problematically, even the concept of pantonality presents a fundamental flaw. Tonality itself is not identifiable with the key in which it operates. Key is the domain of expression of the principle of tonality. To say that there are twelve keys is not to say that there are therefore twelve tonalities. Each key is a replication of the others, the difference between them being a relative one of pitch. There is thus one tonality which is replicated in the many keys or domains of its expression.

The concept of pantonality mistakenly assumes the expression to be the same as the principle, where it is clear that the two are distinct. Consequently, it is impossible to simultaneously project all tonalities, because there is only one tonality. Key is the domain of its operation, and modulation is the principle of its maintenance. The very concept is thus flawed, in that it devolves upon the misidentification of the singular principle of tonality, with the plural domain of its manifestation.

That such cherished terms of twentieth century music do not stand up to the most superficial logical inspection suggests that somewhere, and somehow, something has seriously gone wrong. The chromatic tonal system which promised the continuance of tonality upon a higher and more elevated level of operation has collapsed, and the principles brought in to replace it are themselves deeply flawed.

A clue to what has gone wrong, may lie in the observation that unbeknown to Schoenberg and his followers, the prime number seven was entering the musical discourse in subtle ways that defied detection. It led to a transformation of musical keys and tonal functions; the generation of a whole body of chromatically altered chords; and perhaps most importantly, a new scale.

That none of these were recognised at the time means that the very concept of atonality was founded upon an assumption, a basic misapprehension of the music of the past that cast up the equally tempered twelve-tone scale as the quintessence of music. For this reason, any compositional system based on atonality as a first principle will always remain an incomplete expression of musical reality. [1] At this point therefore, it might be apt to ask the question that

---

[1] Martin Vogel, The Denial of Tone Relation in Atonal Music, On the Relations of Tone, 277-279.

if indeed, the concepts that led to the development of twelve-tone writing are founded upon an historical assumption, does that assumption extend to the music itself? Does the concept of atonality accurately account for the musical phenomenon which it pretends to embrace?

At a general level, this question has already been approached by writers such as Sylvia Milstein, who, through an in depth study of some of Schoenberg's twelve-tone pieces, has shown evidence for the existence of hierarchical pitch relations reminiscent of tonal structures.[1] Here, however, the question is being asked at a deeper level. Is the prime number seven relevant to such music? If the prime number seven was involved, this would indicate that atonal music itself was dependent upon a more complex scale than the theory itself actually recognised. In other words, the fundamental premise of atonality language would be called into question, simply because there would be *more than twelve tones involved.*

One way to begin to answer these questions is to look at a short piece of atonal music to see whether or not the presence or influence of the prime number seven can be detected. The piece chosen is the last of Schoenberg's *Six Little Piano Pieces* written in 1911, chosen both because it stems from a period when Schoenberg was starting to clearly define the parameters of the atonal language, and for its brevity and overt harmonic sensibility. Many of Schoenberg's atonal compositions tend to be contrapuntally based, making a clear harmonic analysis difficult. This piece is extremely useful as a demonstration of Schoenberg's approach to the vertical sonority within an atonal context.

---

[1] Silvia Milsten: Arnold Schoenberg: Notes, Sets, Forms, Cambridge University Press, Cambridge 1992.

The Sixth of Schoenberg's *Six Little Piano Pieces* (1911)

Sehr langsam

A quick perusal of this piece will show that it is based mostly on the juxtaposition of three note chords, with the occasional introduction of short melodic fragments. The first chord, utilising the pitch classes of *A, F#* and *B* is a very prominent feature of the piece, in that it sounds for some six of the total number of nine bars which make up the piece as a whole. It is interesting to observe that this chord has distinct tonal implications. These becomes apparent from a consideration of the intervallic constitution of this particular chord. Composed of a major sixth to which has been added a perfect fourth, it possesses no chromatic intervals which may have an effect of offsetting the obvious diatonic implications present within it.

On the surface it looks very much like a third inversion dominant seventh chord of the key of E, the third of which has been omitted. Although this impression may come as a surprise in what is ostensibly an atonal composition, it is vindicated by the arrival of the missing third of that dominant seventh chord in the third bar (note D#). Here the third is doubled an octave higher in the left-hand part, dispelling any impression that this may not have been a deliberately move on the composers part.[1]

So in what does the anti-tonal sense of the music lie? This lies in the deliberate introduction of the quartal triad $G \, C \, F$ in the left-hand part of the first bar. Heard against the right hand chord, it is obviously intended to dispel, or at least allay the tonal implications of the dominant seventh chord implied by the right hand part. Here, the F pitch class of the quartal triad clashes with the $F\#$ of the dominant chord, whilst the G pitch class of the quartal triad, lying a semitone above the pitch class of $F\#$, brings in an equally pungent dissonance.

Through the juxtaposition of two chords Schoenberg seems to be to trying to convey something, for the dominant seventh chord, the known object of that tradition so highly prized by Schoenberg, has been brought into a direct conflict with the quartal triad - the very symbol and token of the new modernist trend. Even the first bar is thus fraught with emotion, depicting elements of conflict, nostalgia and a certain element of self-sacrifice; of a tradition that has been passed over and superseded by more compelling historical necessities. It is interesting in this respect, that Schoenberg composed this piece in memory of Gustav Mahler, who had died a month earlier.

The suggestion in the first bar of the juxtaposition of two familiar objects, the one traditional, the other modern, is only one level of appreciation of the musical content. Beyond this, exist deeper levels of appreciation which tend to belie the surface deployment of known objects as seen and manifested through the musical score. When the two chords are played together on the piano, although the result is indeed dissonant, the ear is persuaded of a cogent sense of logic caused by the fusion of the respective sounds belonging to the two chords. Whether Schoenberg was consciously aware of this logic or not it is difficult to say.

In what does this logic lie? Sounded together the two chords project a dissonant hexachord which possesses definable qualities. From what do these qualities derive? Here a strong clue may lie in the D# which enters in the third

---

[1] This chord is obviously an example of what Richard S. Parks describes as a 'tonal analogue' : 'a tonal analogue is a pitch combination in an atonal context that is familiar from its frequent and conspicuous occurrence in tonal contexts'. Richard S. Parks, Tonal Analogues as Atonal Resources and their Relation to Form in Debussy's Chromatic Etude, in: JMT29/1, 1985, 35.

bar. In the left hand, the note E enters as an auxiliary to the *D#*. This means that Schoenberg has used all seven notes of an E harmonic minor scale with the addition of the declining tone F. The first chord of the right hand is the dominant seventh of that key. Therefore the *G* and *C* of the quartal triad are accountable as the ninth and thirteenth of that dominant. The *F* thus counts as a chromatically lowered fifth. In this way, all of the pitches present in the first bar can be accounted for as the projection of an unresolved chromatically altered dominant sonority: *B D# F# (F) A C - G*. The tension present in the combination arises from the doubly-inflected fifth.

In bar five Schoenberg reverses the pattern set up in bar one: the quartal triad arrives first, in the right hand, whilst the dominant chord arrives second in the left hand. The other major difference is that the source of tension has changed. The chord resulting from the combination of the dominant and quartal triads is the same basic chord that occurs in the first few bars. This time however, it has been transposed a perfect fifth down: *E G# Bb D F# (F) - C*.

The felt source of tension is thus the doubly-inflected ninth, which occurs in its major form in the dominant triad, and in its minor form in the quartal triad. Inevitably, the implication here is of an *A* tonal centre. Schoenberg obviously has to avoid any overt reference to this because to do so would run against the grain of expressive intent present within the music. Yet it seems that Schoenberg was definitely influenced by this because the melodic fragment that follows conforms almost entirely to the A major tonality:

Implications of A Major Tonality in Bar 7

Degree: IV   III - - - IV   VI   ♭V

At this point in the piece tonal implications are becoming increasingly evident in spite of Schoenberg's attempts to restrain them. As if sensing this, in the bar that follows occur the most cryptic harmonies of the entire piece (bar 8). The key to the explanation of these seems to lie in the trace of the music so far: both chords are dominants, to which tension has been added through the use of double–inflection. The first chord is a dominant of *A*, the double-inflection arising on the thirteenth; the second is a dominant of *D*, the double-inflection arising on the third:

Chord 1 (of Bar 8):   E G# B D F# - C# (C)   Chord 2 : - C# (C) Eb G B D

In this way the two chords belonging to this bar contain in microcosm the content of the previous seven bars, for they consist of a dominant which drops a perfect fifth:

Tonal Scheme of Bars 1 - 8

Bars 1 - 7   *Bar 8*

Dominant of E   Dominant of A

Dominant of A   Dominant of D

The way in which Schoenberg achieves a state of atonality in this piece thus manifests upon two basic levels: the first in terms of known harmonic objects - dominant and quartal chords brought into a close and often uncomfortable juxtaposition with one another. Yet the second level is just as important too: the use of unresolved dominant tension. In projecting states of dominant tension, the use of double-inflection is extremely effective, allowing the creation of harmonies characterised by a high degree of biting dissonance. In using double-inflection however, Schoenberg has unknowingly brought into play a series of septimal sonorities: dominant chords chromatically altered and mutated in accordance with the prime number seven.

The implication in this example therefore, is that the prime number seven may actually have a bearing upon the state of atonality, as well as the state of tonality. In so far as a state of atonality can be achieved though the use of unresolved dominant tension, the prime number seven, through providing the basis for the alteration of these sonorities, yields the very elements which enables that language to achieve a degree of sophistication: an infinite variety of dominant permutations which, forever being unresolved, suspend the sense of tonality.

Inevitably, problems arise when the music is looked at in this way. The analysis as given above, hinges upon the validity of interpreting separate and successive chords as belonging to a unified harmonic field of reference that is the unresolved dominant variegate. And that the example shown is only one piece by one composer, means that it would certainly be premature to draw any significant conclusions from it. It is approached from the standpoint of intrigue as to whether septimal influences may be filtering through from a subconscious level. If there are, then of course the argument begins anew, for the chromatic scale itself is not an adequate summary of these.

In defence of this reference to only one small piece of atonal music, the point being made is a general one, which is that through the use of unresolved dominant tension within chords mutated by the influence of the prime number seven, the piece shows signs of the influence of a larger encompassing system of which Schoenberg himself was unaware. That such dominant elements as can be extricated from this music derive from the chromatic tonal system itself, may also point to the rather interesting possibility that the tonal/atonal conflict which has besieged the music of the twentieth century may yet find an adequate reconciliation within the terms of that governing system. But of course, to discover whether this is possible or not, it is first necessary to define that system in clear and simple terms.

At a general level there are many clear signs which act as further pointers towards the possibilities of a larger governing system.   Even Schoenberg himself admitted that: *What today is remote can tomorrow be close at hand; it is all a matter of whether one can get closer. And the evolution of music has followed this course: it has drawn into the stock of artistic resources more and more of the harmonic possibilities inherent in the tone.*[1]

According to Schoenberg the increased complexity of modern harmony is due to the exploitation of new pitch relations present within the tone, and implied by its respective harmonics. In view of this, it is surprising that Schoenberg denied such resources in favour of the equally tempered twelve-tone scale. Yet it in defence of Schoenberg's position, he viewed the twelve-tone scale as an adequate summary of these resources.

This becomes apparent from his article *Problems of Harmony* (1934), in which he saw in the array of partials up to the thirteenth the natural genesis of the twelve-toned chromatic scale.[2] Here, he regards the partial spectrum of the tonic, dominant and subdominant degrees as being sufficient to generate this scale, the 'white notes' being generated by the major triad constructed upon those degrees, and the 'black notes' deriving from higher harmonics: notes Bb, F# and Ab deriving from the 7th, 11th and 13th partials of the tonic C; notes Eb, and Db deriving from the 7th and 13th partials of note F; and notes Eb and Db appearing again as the 13th and 11th partials of the dominant G respectively. The twelve-tone chromatic scale according to this view would appear as follows:

---

[1] Arnold Schoenberg, Consonance & Dissonance, Theory of Harmony, 21.

[2] Arnold Schoenberg, Problem's of Harmony, in: Modern Music 11, 1934, 167 - 187.

Implied Ratios of the Chromatic Scale According to Schoenberg

Degree	Note	Ratio	Interval
1	C	1/1	Prime
2a	Db	33/32	Minor second
2b	Db	13/12	Minor second
3	D	9/8	Major second
4a	Eb	7/6	Minor third
4b	Eb	39/32	Minor third
5	E	5/4	Major third
6	F	4/3	Perfect fourth
7	F#	11/8	Augmented fourth
8	G	3/2	Perfect fifth
9	Ab	13/8	Minor sixth
10	A	5/3	Major sixth
11	Bb	7/4	Minor seventh
12	B	15/8	Major seventh
13	C	2/1	Octave

This may be viewed as a very naive manipulation of the raw materials of the harmonic series. Musically, it could not work, as it does not respect the full scalar implications of the triadic functions which Schoenberg assumes as the foundation for the seven 'white notes'. The tonic, dominant and subdominant triads which provide the foundation for Schoenberg's intended system would need to be able to appear in their minor forms, as defined by the harmonics 10, 12 and 15, and implicated by the notes E, G and B of Schoenberg's twelve toned scale. This would give grossly conflicting ratios for the notes Eb, Ab and Bb of 6/5, 8/5 and 9/5 respectively.

Possibly aware of that branch of theoretical thinking which pointed to the prime numbers seven, eleven and thirteen as agents of immanent musical expansion, Schoenberg probably sought to explain the chromatic scale this way in order to validate the historical and evolutionary inevitability of his twelve-note system. Yet to bring in harmonic numbers seven, eleven and thirteen as Schoenberg has done, is to implicate not a chromatic scale, but a vast expansion of the three-dimensional chromatic scale to a much more complex six-dimensional scale which would need at least 50 notes. Schoenberg's scheme thus does little to help solve any of the problems associated with these spheres.

This view of the further progression of the musical language being linked to the use of those prime numbered members of the harmonic series beyond the fifth has been put forward by other twentieth century theorists. Henry Cowell observed that: *Since we have seen the development of the use of chords from the simple ones in ancient times, through somewhat more complex ones later, and still more complex ones in present day music, all following the overtone series on upwards, it seems inevitable that the system of building up chords must eventually include the next overtones after those related in thirds, namely, from the seventh overtone upwards. There seems to be need of such a system to further the understanding of contemporary material.*[1]

According to this, the seventh, and other prime numbered harmonics may prove relevant to the change of established norms in musical harmony. Generally, those harmonics up to the seventh are seen to form a seventh chord, up to the ninth a chord of the ninth, up to the eleventh a chord of the eleventh and so on. An idea propounded by turn of the century theorists such as Georg Capellen[2] it has since become an important axiom of popular music theory.

Chordal Implications of the Harmonic Series

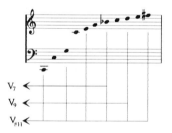

Therefore, at a general level the proposition that the seventh harmonic has played a part in the evolution of modern harmonic materials undoubtedly has some validity. However, from the arguments put forth in this book so far, there would seem to be more to this than at first appears Not only did the prime number seven enter much earlier than was suspected, but theorists have underestimated the fact that the implications of the harmonic series do not depend upon vague resemblances between tempered and natural intervals, but

---

[1] Henry Cowell, New Musical Resources, Alfred A. Knopf Inc, New York 1934, 113-4.

[2] David W. Bernstein, Georg Cappelen's Theory of Reduction: Radical Harmonic Theory at the Turn of the Century, in: JMT37/1, 1993, 85 - 116.

absolutely precise mathematical criteria whose nature is backed up and ratified through both the property of valency, and the workings of the inner ear.

As such, the idea that harmonists, seeking new and exciting chord progressions, have gradually 'ascended' the ladder of the harmonic series, may hold true at a general level, but such an ascent depends upon very much more than vague referential elements introduced in acknowledgement of these higher harmonics. And for a harmonic system in which the seventh harmonic plays an integral part the triad can no longer be accepted as the basic unit of harmony. A system of harmony extending to the seventh harmonic requires at least the tetrad as the basic unit.

That this step has already been taken in practice is confirmed by the relinquishment of the need for both the preparation and resolution of the comparative dissonance which the tetrad automatically implies.[1] Such chords can be attacked freely in an atmosphere which is thoroughly infused with harmonic tension. Here Leigh Gerdine observes that *the history of musical theory may be regarded as an exploration of harmonic possibilities of combinations of ever-closer intervals occurring higher in the natural harmonic series. To the simple octave, in which men's and women's or men's and boy's voices must naturally have sung, have been progressively added the fifth and the fourth, the major third and the minor third, the major and minor sixths: the mathematical relation of vibration ratios acceptable to the ear has become increasingly complex. The great upheaval in music which began about 1900 may be considered ...as an inevitable step in the admission of the seconds and sevenths, both major and minor, as 'consonant' intervals. The implications of this statement are enormous. For one thing, it adopts a point of view in which the music of Stravinsky, Bartók, Schoenberg and, indeed, every other experimental composer of the twentieth century finds a place. Further, it reduces the controversy which divided atonalists from the defenders of tonality, to somewhat the same status as the Brahms - Wagner controversy of the nineteenth century.*[2]

This view of a gradual ascent up the Jacob's ladder of the harmonic series finds an indirect corroboration in the trace of this study so far. Yet it is not enough to make vague observations, because the system of tonality as it arises from, and is a faithful reflection of the laws of valency, has an exactitude and

---

[1] See Roy Travis's Toward a New Concept of Tonality? (in: JMT3, 1959, 257 - 84,) where he tries to show 'prolongation' (in a Schenkerian sense) of non-triadic sonorities in the music of Stravinsky and others. Also see Robert P. Morgan's Dissonant prolongation: Theoretical and Compositional Precedents, (in: JMT20/ 1, Spring, 1976, 49-92) where he discusses the possible foundations 'for a theory of twentieth century tonal structure based on 'dissonant tonics'.

[2] Leigh Gerdine, A General Theory of Music, in: JMT2/1, April 1958, 105.

level of certainty which makes it possible to distinguish between what is tangible and real so far as tonality is concerned, and what amounts to a vague aspiration. The chromatic tonal system is quite tangible, but it is not a result of the exploitation of the upper regions of the harmonic series. It is a result of the gradual exploitation of the next level of valent possibility after the prime number five. Its sensibility, indications, and systematic elements are therefore exact, and leave no room for vague theories which implicate higher harmonics.

KEY POLARITY IN THE CHROMATIC TONAL SYSTEM

Having put forth the concept that the music of the nineteenth-century represents a phase of transition between the diatonic and the chromatic tonal systems, it is now time to begin the consideration of the chromatic tonal system as it gradually reached its maturity, within the approximate period 1890 - 1930. Embracing the tonal music of composers such as Stravinsky, Strauss, Bartók, and Debussy, the chromatic tonal system represents a complete rational system which when understood in its proper context, offers the possibility of the unification of many diverse aspects of the twentieth century musical language into a single and coherent whole. The key for this process of unification will already be understood be the 7/4 relation.

Both the diatonic and the chromatic tonal systems devolve around the presence of a functioning tonic pole which is both the point of attraction for the entire mass of tone, and the point of origination of the web of relationships which binds that mass into a unity. Whether speaking of the diatonic or chromatic level of tonality therefore, both systems utilise a set of keys or keynotes deriving from the different pitches of the tonal network that can serve as prospective tonics.

Yet a key for the chromatic tonal system is a more complex entity than the relatively simple model provided for by the diatonic system of tonality. A key at the chromatic level has at least nineteen notes each of which performs a precise tonal function under the cover of that tonality. Consequently, the internal structure of a chromatic key, when compared to its diatonic precursors, is not only much more complex and sophisticated, but it generates an equal complexity in terms of the unity of its system of keys and the modulatory pathways by which one key may connect with another.

To a large extent, the terms of that unity are defined by the internal properties of a single chromatic key. The precise definition of those terms is thus itself dependent upon an appreciation of those properties, and the way in which they enable one key to forge an audible link with another. Yet the consideration of the resources of a single key is itself dependent upon an appreciation of the network of keys within which it finds itself. The result is a closed cycle of mutual dependence which in theoretical terms, is extremely problematic to penetrate.

For this reason, any appreciation the reader may have of the resources of a single key of the chromatic tonal system can only depend upon the extremely limited view provided for by this study so far. That these resources (as the next chapter will serve to show) are infinitely more complex, both in terms of their application and possibilities, means that it will only be possible to consider the unity of the system of keys belonging to the chromatic tonal system in a limited way. But in so doing, that closed loop of tonal interdependence will at least be broken, so paving the way for a more advanced and fuller appreciation of the chromatic tonal system.

The consideration of this system of keys can start with a very simple question which is just this: what is a keynote? In answer to this it may be observed that a keynote is simply a musical tone, and therefore no different in its essentials to any other musical tone. Yet as the prefix 'key' suggests, it is a tone which carries a priority over all other tones. This is because it signifies the pitch of the chosen tonic, that note which, lying at the very centre of the web of tonal relations, imparts to all other musical tones their precise meaning and significance.

That the terms of this web are entirely defined by the laws of valency, means that any tonal system that utilises such a keynote will belong to a certain level, whose nature is fundamentally determined by the number of dimensions of tonal occupation which it chooses to exploit. That, in the chromatic tonal system, there are four such dimensions, signified by the prime numbers 2, 3, 5 and 7, means therefore that the chromatic tonal system offers a four-dimensional or essentially tetradic organ of expression for that tonal principle or keynote.

Because therefore, the chromatic system of tonality offers an additional dimensional perspective to the diatonic system of tonality, means that the terms of reference surrounding the use of these keynotes is slightly different in the chromatic tonal system. This difference is not just dependent upon those objective factors determined by the laws of valency, but also upon the more subjective factors of the historical and practical usage of those keynotes within the system of tonality to date. Therefore, to say that a piece of music is written in A major, is not only to identify the relative pitch of the tonic - note A - but it is also to inform of the precise modality of the key. Being informed of a modality in this fashion, immediately shows that the music being spoken of takes its departure point not from the chromatic system of tonality, but from the diatonic system of tonality that represents its natural precursor.

The principle reason for this is that at the chromatic level a key embraces the entire resources of the chromatic scale, together with the septimal supplementaries. There are thus no diatonic constraints as would call for the definition of a key as being either major or minor. Therefore, all that can be said about the tonality of a piece of music, given that its primary keynote is *A*, is that it is *in* or, as Halsey Stevens has put it in reference to Bartók's unique methods of handling tonality,[1] *on* the keynote of A.

Now although such a keynote is in theory, a single tone, as a representative of the tonic function, it embodies within itself those links by which it may connect to, and transfer by proxy, the function of tonic to another related tone. When this process of transfer occurs a modulation is said to have taken place. In any modulation therefore, there are always four essential aspects to consider. There is the keynote of the original key, the keynote of the key of destination, the route by which the modulation is effected, and finally the relationship between the two keynotes.

This general point as it applies to the diatonic system of tonality can be well demonstrated in the excerpt given overleaf where Mozart modulates from the tonic key of F (the keynote of the original key) to the dominant key of C (the keynote of the key of destination), using chords vi and V as the initial pivots (in which they are reinterpreted as ii and I of the new key). The vii to I progression in the dominant key that follows offers the first wind of an impending modulation, in which the basic route undertaken to the new key is through a protracted ii - V - I cadence in the dominant key of C major (bars 9 - 22 of the excerpt).

As a keynote is a single note, so the relationship between two keynotes may be cast up as an interval between two tones. Given therefore, that the modulation proceeds from the tonic key up to the dominant, the interval between the two keynotes is a perfect fifth - ratio of 3/2. Therefore the link between keynotes activated in this example is prompted by the third partial, in that the ratio between the two keynotes is 3/2. In terms of a modulation to the mediant key, this represents a shift of the tonic axis in a different dimension to the dominant key, in that the link between the keynotes of F and A is a major third of ratio 5/4. Consequently, it occurs along a channel provided for by the fifth partial of the original tonic note. The importance of this observation for the chromatic tonal system, is that it shows that the possibilities for the transfer of the tonic function from one tonic axis to an other is tantamount to a movement in frequency space.

---

[1] Halsey Stevens, The Life and Music of Béla Bartók, 2nd ed., Oxford University Press, London & New York 1964, 172.

Excerpt from the Third Movement of Mozart's *Pianoforte Sonata in F Major*, K 280 (1775).

MOZART: Pianoforte Sonata in F major, K280 (third movement)
@ 1978 by The Associated Board of the Royal Schools of Music. Used by permission.

That in the chromatic tonal system there are three dimensions of possible movement (those motivated by the prime numbers three, five and seven) means that the tonic axis may shift in one of three possible dimensions. The general mechanism that activates a link between keynotes, and enables a new keynote to become established will thus differ depending upon whether the matter is viewed from the diatonic or the chromatic levels of tonality. For the diatonic tonal system the principle mechanism is the V7 - I cadence (and its variants) as it occurs in the new key.

Whether arrived at through the use of pivot chords or introduced in abrupt fashion, the dominant seventh chord offers the composer a reliable agent for the control and direction of tonality, solely by virtue of its unique capacity to satisfactorily define the tonic triad. Therefore, although the intention of the composer may be to move say, from the tonic to the mediant key, the actual target of the chord progression will undoubtedly be the dominant seventh chord of the new key.

At the chromatic level of tonality, no simple cadential formulae can be relied upon. This is because such formulae have connotations which suggest the diatonic level of tonality. The chord of V7 in the key of C utilises some four notes which are *G B D F*. Given that the tonic triad is major, the remaining notes would be spelled as *C E (G)*, whilst if minor *C Eb (G)*. In this way, although the V7 - I cadence provides a reliable means for the processes of tonicization, it tends to implicate the two basic modal forms suggestive of the diatonic level of tonality - the major and the minor.

To escape such suggestions, and acquire the possibility of being ejected into the new sphere of a chromatic tonality, these formulae must be avoided, and replaced by new equally powerful mechanisms for the purposes of tonicization, suitable for operation within the terms of that more demanding context. As the chromatic tonal system is essentially four-dimensional, means that it can be reasonably expected that those mechanisms which composers did develop would themselves arrive from the fourth dimension of tonal space.

And so they did, although this was a rather slow process which gradually accelerated through the course of the nineteenth century. One very important factor which paved the way for the eventual supercession of the dominant seventh chord as the sole agent of tonicization, was the deliberate stabilization of the tonic principle through reference to the keynotes which lay a semitone either side of it. A very fine example of this is the introductory Largo to the grand fugue of Beethoven's *Hammerklavier* Sonata. The three sections of this prelude are each characterised by a change of key signature, the first key established being the main key, mainly Bb major. After that there is a section in B major (enharmonic Cb major), the key which lies a semitone above, which is then immediately followed by a section in A major, the key which lies a semitone below.

As a result of this chromatic procedure, the tonic principle itself is being defined as a central keynote, either side of which are displaced the keynotes a semitone above and below. This feature of supporting the tonic through reference to a supersemitone and subsemitone, also occurred within the more local terms of harmonic progressions, the most obvious participant of which was the Neapolitan triad as used in contradistinction to the conventional dominant.

In Chopin's Mazurka, Op. 7, no. 2 the Neapolitan triad is approached by way of its own dominant seventh chord, introduced through the addition of a seventh to the submediant triad. After a pause there follows the regular dominant in which the leading note is brought into sharp focus. The result is that the tonic note A is firmly established as the note which lies between the super- and subsemitonal notes of Bb and G# respectively:

Excerpt from Chopin's *Mazurka*, Op. 7, No. 2.

CHOPIN: Mazurka, Op. 7 No. 2.
@ by The Associated Board of the Royal Schools of Music. Used by permission.

The significance of this can be gauged by looking at the super- and subsemitone functions within the context of the chromatic complex. Looking at the chromatic scale as it applies to the key of C, both the tonic and dominant degrees are automatically implicated as being the most important degrees of the scale. This occurs by what Gillies describes as the process of *chromatic encirclement*:[1]

Chromatic Encirclement of Tonic and Dominant Degrees of the Chromatic Scale

Only the pitches of *C* and *G* are encircled by notes which in themselves are independent scale degrees. However, this factor could be dismissed as an element which arises from the way in which the chromatic scale is notated. The notation of chromatic relationships is never entirely consistent. In his study of chromaticism, Mitchel observes that: *Our system of notation is essentially a diatonic system, fitted for the 'correct' notation of only diatonic and, by extension few chromatic relationships. Thus although it can be said with assurance that there is only one proper way to notate the major and minor scales, no such assurance is forthcoming with regard to the notating of the chromatic scale.*[2]

Here however, it is again necessary to distinguish between the convenience of tempered pitch notation and functional pitch notation. Tempered pitch notation takes equal temperament as the standard, so it does not really matter if a

---

[1] Malcolm Gillies, Notation and Structure in Bartók's Later Works, Garland Publishing, Inc. New York & London 1989, 27.

[2] William J. Mitchell, A Study of Chromaticism, JMT 6/1, 1962, pp. 2 - 31, p. 2.

composer spells a *Db* as a *C#*, or visa versa. Now if Db, as seen and displayed in the above diagram is spelled as a *C#*, then the supertonic degree would be thus encircled. Therefore at this level, the concept of chromatic encirclement is not such an important signpost.

In this study the methods of functional notation have been strictly adhered to. Here a pitch is notated according to its precise function in a tonal context. Because many composers have not been bothered with this, it has often been necessary in the musical examples being presented, to point out the correct functional notation for a particular chord or chromatic inflection. This becomes especially necessary since the looseness of tempered pitch notation has become one of the theoretical blind spots of modern musical theory. Preventing a clear overview of the orderly expansion of tonal functions from the chromatic to the enharmonic scale, it has developed an acute incapacity to explain chromatic musical resources, and the precise system from which they originate.

The notation of the chromatic scale as given above is the correct functional notation. Therefore, the semitone above note C is spelled as a *Db* (and not as a *C#*) because it performs the general function of a declining tone down to the tonic C. Similarly, the semitone below note C is spelled as *B*, because it performs the general function of an inclining tone up to the tonic. In this way, being a precise expression of function, the notation becomes a clear and orderly expression of functional interrelationships.

Consequently, the process of chromatic encirclement is something which is integral to the character and constitution of the chromatic scale. For a note to be chromatically encircled, means that it stands as the point of resolution of a given augmented sixth interval. That there are two such intervals in the chromatic scale, whose respective resolutions are to the tonic and dominant degrees, means therefore that the augmented sixth interval itself displays a rather unique capacity to highlight and define the tone to which it resolves. This occurs through a semitonal shift in contrary motion, in which one note manifests as the inclining tone, the other as the declining tone to the implied and respective note of resolution.

In this fashion the interval of the augmented sixth (7/4) offers unique possibilities for the control and direction of tonality in a purely chromatic environment. That no diatonic scale simultaneously contains both an inclining and declining tone, shows that the simultaneous use of these two notes as they converge upon the tonic, is an effect which belongs at the chromatic level of tonality. Bela Bartók's final cadence of the first movement of his *Music for Strings, Percussion and Celesta* is an exemplary example of this, in which the diminished third is used as a direct substitute for the old diatonic dominant seventh chord:

Cadence to the First Movement of Béla Bartók's *Music for Strings, Percussion and Celesta.*

Therefore whilst at the diatonic level of tonality the interval of the augmented sixth was not a particularly important interval, at the chromatic level it starts to take on a much deeper significance. Forming the binding relationship between the super- and subsemitone, it starts to play an increasingly important role in the processes of tonicisation. Here there are many examples to be found which demonstrate that this 7/4 relation has provided composers with an important alternative to conventional dominants.

In this example, Sibelius avoids use of the conventional dominant seventh by chromatically flattening the fifth, thus bringing the super- and subsemitonal functions to work within the one sonority. Note also his use of the German Sixth chord as an important vehicle for achieving tonal stability:

Excerpt from Sibelius's *Finlandia*, Op. 26, No. 7.

But of course, it is not always felt necessary to deploy the super- and subsemitones within the province of a single sonority. In the following excerpt from Stravinsky's *Rite of Spring* the music scillates etween two minor triads constructed respectively upon the super- and subsemitonal poles in order to offer tonal stability to the tonic D minor triad which is sustained by the horns:

Excerpt from Stravinsky's *Rite of Spring*

In this example, from Benjamin Britten's *Ad majorem Dei gloriam* (1939), a more sparse polyphonically oriented texture is evident in which the super- and subsemitones approach the tonic from the context of their own respective parts. Although spelled as a Db, the function of this note, as it rises up to the tonic, betrays the usage of the subsemitone (note C#):

Excerpt from Benjamin Britten's *A.M.D.G., Seven Settings for SATB, Prayer II.*

@ 1989 Faber Music Ltd. Reproduced by kind permission of the publishers.

That the ratio of the augmented sixth interval which connects the super- and subsemitones may be regarded to be 7/4 means that the fourth dimension of tonal space is providing those agents which enable the precise tonal control of the other three dimensions within a chromatic context. This means that it provides not only for the maintenance of tonality within a chromatic context, but the means whereby modulation may be achieved. Within the terms of the enharmonic scale, every single note of the original sub-chromatic scale has been chromatically encircled:

Processes of Chromatic Encirclement in the Enharmonic Scale

A#	B	C	Db	Ebb

C#	D	Eb	Fb

D#	E	F	Gb

F#	G	Ab	Bbb

G#	A	Bb	Cb

Serving to extend a pattern of chromatic encirclement which is already implicit to the chromatic scale, the enharmonic scale represents a growth or logical progression of tonality in a particular direction. Through this extension, the septimal matrix is extending a significance not just to the tonic and dominant degrees, but to each and every independent chromatic function. This therefore speaks of an immanent expansion of tonal principles just as significant as the expansion witnessed in the progression of tonality from the seven-tone diatonic to the twelve-note chromatic scales.

One of the most important features underlying this process of expansion, is the way in which the septimal matrix serves to modify the system of key relations belonging to the Classical system of tonality, and in so doing, offer an upgrading of that original system in accordance with the dictates of the fourth dimension of tonal space. The primary clue as to the precise nature of that upgrading lies in the observation that wherever in the enharmonic scale this chromatic circle is found, a doorway to another related key is being presented in which the notes of the augmented sixth (or diminished third as the case may be) are capable of being reinterpreted as the super- and subsemitones of the new key.

That, in the enharmonic scale, there are nine such intervals, means that at a chromatic level, excluding the tonic oriented B - Db chromatic circle (which serves to define the keynote of C), there are six immediate doorways to a closely related key. From the standpoint of the key of C, these are the keys of Db, Eb, E, F, G, Ab & A, and B:

Closely Related Chromatic Keys to the Key of C

Controlling Interval	Keynote
Ebb - C	Db
Fb - D	Eb
F - D#	E
Gb - E	F
Ab - F#	G
Bbb - G	Ab
Bb - G#	A
C - A#	B

Observe that this group of eight keys automatically divides up into four pairs of keys, in which the central tonic note C functions as the shared common axis of symmetry: the super- and subsemitonal keys of B and Db are a minor second above and below the original tonic; *Eb* and *A* are a minor third above and below the original tonic; the keys of E and Ab are a major third above and below, whilst *F* and *G* are a perfect fourth above and below:

Eight of the Most Closely Related Keys in the Chromatic Tonal System

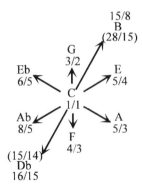

Of the four pairs, those connections between keys motivated by the prime number three are the easiest to trace, simply because they occur along those conventional channels as defined by the cycle of fifths/fourths. As the scale in general use by twentieth century composers is the equally tempered chromatic scale, means that at the first level, there are twelve recognisable keynotes capable of operating within that closed circuit as defined by the cycle of fifths/fourths. Any more than this, is to exploit the possibilities which the tempered scale offers for enharmonic equivalence between those keynotes separated by a cycle of twelve fifths i.e. *C* to *B♯*.

Theoretical convention defines the key of C as being the starting point of the cycle of fifths. Mainly, this is because of the primacy of the major mode in the diatonic tonal system, and the fact that the C major tonality possesses no sharps or flats in the key signature. The key of C major thus represents the perfect point of balance between those keys with flats in the key signature, and those with sharps. Within the chromatic tonal system it becomes apparent that the days of the primacy of the major mode are long since past. Where, however, is the cycle of fifths considered to begin in the chromatic tonal system? Here, a single key has at least nineteen notes, so accidentals cannot possibly be avoided. Looking at the enharmonic scale as it is constructed in all twelve keys, each key has either twelve or thirteen accidentals:

The starting point of the circle of fifths can be deduced as the point of balance between those twelve keynotes, a position readily ascertained by observing the range of accidentals present in each key. Lying between the key of Ab (which has five double-flats, seven flats and one sharp) and the key of G♯ (which has two flats, seven sharps and four double-sharps) the perfect point of balance is the key of D, for amongst its range of twelve accidentals some six are sharps and six are flats. So in the chromatic tonal system, the pitch centre of *D* counts as the rightful beginning of the cycle of fifths:

The Cycle of Fifths as Defined by the Chromatic Tonal System and Expressed Within the Province of Twelve-tone Equal Temperament

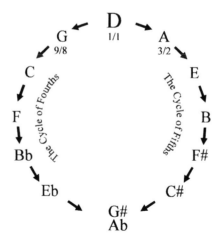

Observe from the table of keys given above that the dominant (*A*) and subdominant keys (*G*) differ from the key of D by only one accidental. In the dominant key of A the note Ab drops out to be replaced by the note Fx. Similarly, in the subdominant key of G the note G# drops out to be replaced by the note Db. In this sense, on a par with the diatonic level of tonality, the dominant and subdominant keys are those which, sharing the most notes in common with the central key, are undoubtedly the most closely related keys to it. Although this diatonically oriented scheme of key connection is therefore retained within the chromatic tonal system, it will be readily understood that there is no place in such a system for that conventional 'tick-tock' between the tonic triad and dominant seventh chord, which characterised the diatonic system of tonality.

As this practice represents nothing more than a reversion to a past model of tonal procedure means that the spectrum of keys belonging to the cycle of fifths is reformulated under new terms provided for by the weft and warp of the fourth dimension of tonal space. Now the augmented sixth interval (7/4) occurs at two points in the chromatic scale - on the declining tone and upon the flat submediant degree. The upper augmented sixth is at the same time the lower augmented sixth of the dominant key, whilst the lower augmented sixth is at the same time the upper augmented sixth of the subdominant key. Through the inherent tonal ambiguity offered by that shared augmented sixth, the prime number seven serves to support an extremely powerful bond between keys which occurs between successive members of the cycle of fifths:

The Prime Number Seven as it Ratifies the Circle of Fifths

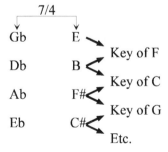

Within the chromatic tonal system the dominant and subdominant keys may be considered to be just as important as they were before. The major difference is that each key, embracing within itself a more complex and demanding resource, offers more subtle, chromatically oriented pathways to those keys.

A good example of this is *Mars - the God of War* movement of Gustav Holst's *The Planets Suite* (1916) where, after some 39 bars of a *G* tonic rhythmic pedal, the music shifts to a *C* tonic rhythmic pedal. His pathway to the new key occurs by way of an immanent alternation between the triads of Db and B major. The roots of these triads correspond respectively to the super- and subsemitones of the new key note, thus offering the *G* rhythmic pedal a new interpretation as dominant rather than tonic pedal point. As in the Stravinsky example offered above, the augmented sixth interval used to define the new keynote is thus occurring between the roots of the triads themselves.

In contrast to those connections between keys occurring along a predefined channel determined by the prime number three, there are also those connections between keys motivated by links arising from the prime number five. These proceed along those valent channels offered by the major and minor thirds. Accounting for some four of the six closely related keys offered above, these links serve to generate some of the most interesting and fascinating features of the key system belonging to the chromatic system of tonality. These can be appreciated through a consideration of some of the basic limitations of the diatonic system of tonality.

Now in the minor tonality there is a strong link to the submediant major key, a link both supported and enhanced by the fact that the submediant major key is at the same time the relative major of the subdominant key. In Chopin's *Prelude in C minor* he deliberately exploits this link in bar 2 in order to prepare the listener for the point in bar's 8 and 12 where chord IV of the submediant key, is reinterpreted as the Neapolitan triad of C minor:

Bars 1-2 and 7-8 of Chopin's *Prelude in C Minor,* Op. 28, No. 20.

CHOPIN: Prelude in C minor, Op. 28 No. 20
@ 1955 by The Associated Board of the Royal Schools of Music. Used by permission.

This link occurs along a channel which moves in a different direction to the cycle of fifths. Whilst the cycle of fifths offers a link between keys which occurs in the second dimension of tonal space, the link to the submediant major key occurs through the third dimension of tonal space in that the submediant of the minor key is a major third (5/4) down from the original tonic. The same strength of link does not exist to a key which lies a major third above.

Given that the original tonic note was C, the key of E major is implied - a key with which C minor shares nothing in common. Therefore, to approach the tonality of E major from C minor, a clear pathway is not immediately evident, except perhaps, by way of a third key which shares notes in common with both keys i.e. the parallel major mode. This would work because in the major tonality, there is a strong link to a tonality which lies a major third above (the key of E minor from the standpoint of C major). This link is also reinforced by the fact that E minor is the relative minor of the dominant major key of G - one of the most closely related keys to C major.

Tertial Links Between Keys Occurring in Opposite Directions

$$\text{Ab Major} \longleftarrow \text{C Minor}$$
$$\text{C Major} \longrightarrow \text{E Minor}$$

Whilst the major tonality implies a link in one direction, the minor thus implies a link in quite the opposite direction. So what does this say about the possibility for such links in the chromatic tonal system, where the major and minor tonalities are subsumed under the terms of a singular monotonality? It says that all such links which were previously exclusive to either the major or the minor key, are now shared under the terms of the new co-operative that is that tonal singularity.

Therefore at the chromatic level of tonality, there is no major or minor key. There is simply a domain which represents the collective pool of possibilities surrounding the use of a particular note as a central tonic or reference point. Consequently, at this level the link to a key a major third above the original tonic, is matched by an equal and opposite link to a key which lies a major third below the tonic.

Therefore, let the key which lies a major third above the tonic be called the super-major key in which the term major is used to designate not the nature of the tonality, but the nature of the link itself. Then let the key which lies a major third below the tonic be called the sub-major key. This unit of three related keys i.e. the keys of C, E and Ab as for example, can then be termed a trine.

Trine Based on Three Connected Keys a Major Third Apart

Key:	Sub-major	Tonic	Super-major
Pitch:	Ab	C	E

The existence of such a unit, prompted by the nature of a chromatic tonality, considerably modifies the possibilities of key connection as represented by the original scheme of keys defined by the cycle of fifths. This is because the trine is capable of duplication within the tonalities defined by the original trine, so that both the super- and sub-major keys are themselves pinioned at the centre of two keys which are the respective super- and sub-major keys for them.

In terms of the super-major key of E, this invokes the keys of C (sub-major) and G# (super-major), whilst in terms of the key of Ab (8/5), this invokes the keys of Fb (sub-major) and C (super-major). Now when it is recalled that the keynote of Fb is enharmonically equivalent to the keynote of E, whilst the keynote of G# is enharmonically equivalent to the keynote of Ab, it will be seen that within a tempered format, the presentiment is offered of a closed cycle of three interlinked keys separated by a uniform major third.

Closed Cycle Involving the Keys of C, E and Ab

Keys:	C	E	Ab
	Tonic	Super-major	Sub-major
	Sub-major	Tonic	Super-major
	Super-major	Sub-major	Tonic

Accounting for the notes C, E and Ab, such a cycle can be invoked anywhere along the cycle of fifths. Consequently, through the enharmonic equivalence of certain notes, the twelve keys provided for by the cycle of fifths can now be reconfigured as four connected groups of three related keys:

Scheme of Four Trines in Twelve-Tone Scale

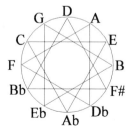

The relationship between the declining and inclining tones of a given key is an augmented sixth with an implied ratio of 7/4. In the super-major key of E, the declining and inclining tones are the notes F and D#, whilst in the sub-major key of Ab they are the notes Bbb and G. The notes F and D#, the tonally controlling factors of the key of E, are at the same time the subdominant and mediant inclining tone of the key of C. Similarly, the notes Bbb and G, the tonally controlling factors for the key of Ab are the submediant declining tone and dominant of the key of C. Accordingly, the link between chromatic keys a major third apart is activated by the interval 7/4, as it appears in its representative form of the augmented sixth interval common to both keys, but performing a different function within each:

Augmented Sixth Intervals Belonging to the Key of C as they Interlink the Super-major and Sub-major Keys

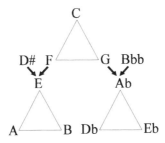

This does not mean that the augmented sixth defined by the super- and subsemitones provides the only pathway to a new key. It provides the main channel, which may or may not be used by the composer concerned. In the example overleaf, Debussy moves from the sub-major key back to the original tonic key, through use of a septimal chord which is enharmonically equivalent to the chord of the dominant seventh of the sub-major key. Yet its function betrays this false identity which the unwary may ascribe to it. Devolving around the properties of the septimal interval of the diminished fourth (*E - Ab*) Debussy uses the *Ab* as a declining tone to the dominant note G, whilst preserving the use of the regular inclining tone (note B) which satisfactorily defines the pitch of the tonic note.

An entirely similar set of links evolves from the other strong key connection which occurs at this level - the link between tonalities a minor third apart. Like the major third link between keys, this link is entirely modally dependent when viewed from the standpoint of the diatonic system of tonality. The key of A minor bears a strong connection to the key of C major, in that the former is the relative minor of the latter, and the latter is the relative major of the former. A

374

similar strength of connection however, cannot be said to exist between the key of C major and the key which lies a minor third above - the key of Eb major. Yet there is a strong link between between the tonalities of C minor and Eb major based on that relative major/minor relationship.

Excerpt from Debussy's *Children's Corner Suite, I, Doctor Gradus ad Parnassum.*

Reprint with permission of C.F. Peters, Frankfurt/M., Leipzig, London and New York.

Within the singular terms of a chromatic tonal system the key of C bears an equally strong connection to both the keys of Eb and A. Accordingly, at the level of the chromatic tonal system, yet another symmetrical link between keys is set up, a minor third above and a minor third below the original tonic. Let the key which lies a minor third above, be called the super-minor key, and the key which lies a minor third below be called the sub-minor key. The group of three notes thus formed gives rise to a trine of different orientation to the first trine considered, and may be termed the minor as opposed to the major trine.

An explicit example of the use of the minor trine is the Bartók work referred to above - his *Music for Strings, Percussion and Celesta.* As Donald Grout has already observed in reference to this work: *the main tonality of the first and last movements is A with an important secondary centre at the augmented fourth D# (substituting for the conventional dominant E); the second movement is in C, with a similar tritonic subcentre on F#; the Adagio is indeterminate, fluctuating in the region C - F# (the two keys equidistant on either side from the principle tonality of the work).*[1]

What are the unique set of links that activates the minor trine? These arise from a similar set of circumstances to those of the major trine. Taking the trine represented by the keys of A, C and Eb, it will be seen that the declining and inclining tones of Eb, are the notes Fb (9/7) and D (9/8) - the mediant declining tone and supertonic of the key of C. Similarly, the declining and inclining tones of A are the notes Bb (16/9) and G# (14/9) - the subtonic and submediant

---

[1] Donald Jay Grout & Claude Palisca, A History of Western Music 1980, 689.

inclining tones of the key of C. The link between these keys is thus activated by the augmented sixth (7/4) that adjacent keys of the trine share in common.

When the trines of each of the super- and sub-minor keys (the keys of Eb and A) are brought into consideration, a strong chain of connection between keys a minor third apart is set up which extends through the keynotes of Gb, Eb, C, A, and F#. Like the chain of major thirds set up by the major trine, this also leads to the presentiment of a closed cycle of tonalities, the difference being that this time it is a cycle of four keys respectively separated by the interval of a minor third. Let such a cycle be called a square:

Square of Tonalities a Minor Apart as it Appears in Twelve-Tone Equal Temperament

Keys:	C	Eb	F# (Gb)	A
	Tonic	Super-minor	---	Sub-minor
	Sub-minor	Tonic	Super-minor	---
	---	Sub-minor	Tonic	Super-minor
	Super-minor	---	Sub-minor	Tonic

This cycle, being replicated upon the dominant and subdominant degrees, yields a third scheme of twelve keys, one which is divisible into three groups of four. The trine therefore, as it represents a pair of keys symmetrically disposed around a common axis, may be regarded to occur in three basic forms: the major, minor and perfect trine:

Major, Minor and Perfect Trines of the Chromatic Key of C

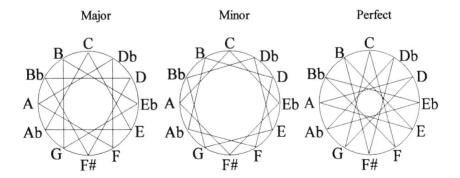

Such relationships, worked out and calculated in respect of the natural implications of those septimal intervals present in the enharmonic scale, yields a system of key polarity in which the central keynote functions as the axis of symmetry in three respective dimensions. The diatonic level of tonality tends to block the manifestations of key symmetry through its own inherent modal polarity. Therefore at the chromatic level of tonality, the phenomenon of axial polarity takes over priority of place to the modal polarity which was so important at the diatonic level. The place of the prime number seven in this process is to offer the tonally controlling factors that activate that polarity.

THE RESOURCES OF A SINGLE KEY OF THE CHROMATIC TONAL SYSTEM

The chromatic tonal system constitutes a unity of twelve basic keys interlinked through the existence of various modulatory pathways provided for, validated and supported by the new found tonicising properties of septimal sonorities. A fuller understanding of this system depends on an appreciation of the resources of a single key as it belongs to the chromatic tonal system.

Here it becomes evident that what counts as a key in the diatonic tonal system, is not necessarily valid for the chromatic tonal system. Although both systems offer deference to a central tonic note, the increased complexity and sophistication of the chromatic tonal system leads to a more diffused and generalised sense of tonality. Primarily, this is because of an increase in the resources which are available under the cover of a single key.

Each individual key now contains not just the major mode or the minor mode, but the entire chromatic scale implied by the fusion of their separate resources, together with numerous additional tones deriving from the participation of the prime number seven. A single key of the chromatic tonal system is thus a rather complex entity which at first sight is rather difficult to both envision and understand.

One way of understanding the nature and constitution of a key at this level is as a series of enclosures. Starting at the very centre, each enclosure represents a self-contained scale system, yet is itself subsumed within the terms of a larger system. Proceeding from the pentatonic to the heptatonic to the chromatic and finally to the complete enharmonic scale, a single key is thus a multi-leveled pitch structure which, embracing those resources which begin with the simplest and most elementary offers a graduated progression through some four complete levels of possibility.

Examining this scheme more closely reveals that it embodies within it important observations on the way in which tonality has tended to expand. If the direction of growth is defined by an increase in the number of mathematical dimensions operable within a given tonal system it becomes apparent that any progression which a given dimension may represent as the current factor of tonal advancement can only occur through a process of functional reciprocation. All previous dimensions provide the foundation upon which the new dimension may build, whilst the new dimension in its turn, offers a fresh perspective from which the possibilities of those previous dimensions may be reinterpreted.

Four Levels of Key in the Chromatic Tonal System

Level One: Pentatonic (5 toned)
Level Two: Heptatonic (7 toned)
Level Three: Chromatic (12 toned)
Level Four: Enharmonic (19 toned)

A simple example of this is the difference between the two-dimensional dyad that is the perfect fifth, and the three-dimensional unit that is the triad. The triad took the foundation provided for by the dyad, and added a new element. That new element in its turn, offered to the dyad a fresh significance within the overall tonal scheme. Progress was not achieved by rejecting the original dyad, and starting completely afresh, but assimilating the dyad into an altogether new and original constitution which offered it an altogether fresh perspective.

The simple conclusion is that the way forward for the musical language is not to reject everything from the past, but to assimilate it into a fresh perspective provided for by the current factor of tonal advancement. It only this which could eventually guarantee the integrity of a new common language: the fact that it embraced the entire musical cosmos from an altogether new perspective.

An appreciation of the mutual relationship between the various dimensions of tonal space considerably helps towards understanding the significance of the various enclosures of tonal possibility embraced by the enharmonic scale. First there is the pentatonic level which embraces those five notes of the enharmonic scale which have ratios involving no prime number higher than three.

Core Pentatonic Structure Embraced by the Enharmonic Scale

Ratio:	1/1	9/8	4/3	3/2	16/9
Interval:	Prime	Major 2nd.	Perfect 4th.	Perfect 5th.	Minor 7th.

Serving to bind the tonally functional degrees of the tonic (1/1), dominant (3/2), subdominant (4/3), supertonic (9/8) and subtonic (16/9) into the terms of a complete self-contained scalar entity, it represents the two-dimensional foundation for the enharmonic scale structure as a whole. Here it may seem curious to observe that lying at the very core of the enharmonic scale exists what is probably the oldest scale system on Earth, surviving completely intact in its purest form as tuned according to a segment of four fifths.

As this is important, it is worthwhile pondering for a moment, what this actually means. For at least the last millennium, the pentatonic scale has taken second place to the more complex diatonic scale. Surviving as a relic or vestige of a much more primitive tone system, the artistic and intellectual interest of European art music has always been with more advanced scale structures. Considering this type of interest, it is perhaps rather illogical that, when viewed from the perspective of twentieth century art music, there has been a significant resurrection of interest in the pentatonic scale, especially as it derives from the province of ethnic, exotic and folk music in general.

Here one of the most definitive pointers towards the possibilities of an entirely new status being accorded to the pentatonic scale, is the pentatonic opening to Gustav Mahler's *Das Lied von der Erde* (1911). Being used as the basic foundation stone of a grand symphonic plan, the pentatonic scale is obviously being placed in a context far removed from its early and exotic beginnings, in which it becomes capable of both initiating and supporting musical processes which in their complexity far surpass the more limited possibilities presented by the diatonic tonal system.

Therefore, although in this way, the chromatic tonal system may be seen to subsume the pentatonic possibility as found in ancient reference, exotic sources, folk music, and in the art music of composers such as Debussy, Bartók and Stravinsky, modern usage carries with it the full range and weight of techniques available within the four dimensional pitch matrix, which means to say that the pentatonic scale is thus a known or familiar object operating in a new chromatic context.[1] Observe that the array of semitones present within the enharmonic scale tend to radiate out from the five primary pitch centres as represented by its five notes. In this sense the pentatonic scale represents that core exclusion zone into which all chromatic possibilities are denied access. Analogous to a hard stone at the centre of a fruit, it is signifies those scale degrees which represent the immutable matrix of primary tonal functions upon which the chromatic tonal system subsists.

---

[1] Concerning this Lendvai makes the salient observation that 'at first it may seem astonishing that in Bartók's music pentatony is so closely allied to chromaticism...' Ernö Lendvai, Béla Bartók: an Analysis of his Music, Kahn & Averill, London 1990., 50.

Pentatonic Scale as Representing the Five Primary Pitch Centres of the Enharmonic Scale

A#	B	(C)	Db	Ebb
	C#	(D)	Eb	Fb
D#	E	(F)	Gb	
	F#	(G)	Ab	Bbb
G#	A	(Bb)	Cb	

The ascendancy of the pentatonic scale in twentieth century music is not a sign of regression, but a signal of an overall expansion of tonal possibility. This is because in the chromatic tonal system, both pentatonic and heptatonic elements are themselves subsumed by a basic overlord structure which represents not only their host, but the environment in which they are both capable of being offered a fresh significance.

In terms of the heptatonic level of possibility embraced by a single key of the chromatic tonal system there are numerous problematic features. The attested history of the usage of the heptatonic scale within Western culture embraces not only the major and minor modes, but also the various Church modes, which themselves are rather dubiously linked to earlier ancient Greek models. It also embraces various heptatonic scales derived from folk sources, or used by twentieth century composers specifically for the purposes of a particular musical work.

A single key of the chromatic tonal system embraces all of these resources because they derive from a rather free use of the chromatic scale, which is itself, only a part of that larger governing structure which is the enharmonic scale. Consequently, the major and minor scales of Classical tonality gradually move off the screen to be replaced by a more balanced view of diatonic and heptatonic resources as they derive from the overlord perspective of the chromatic scale of a given key.

Primarily, this is because, dealing at the level of the chromatic, as opposed to the diatonic tonal system, the seat of organising musical consciousness is no longer anchored at the diatonic level, but operates from that general overlord provided by the chromatic scale. Accordingly, any heptatonic scale that is used or envisaged for the processes of musical expression is itself but a limited selection or set of pitch classes derived from that scale as a whole. This means that diatonic scales themselves, although a part of the chromatic tonal system, are no longer the principal means for the organisation of musical material.[1] There are thus more possibilities available at this level owing to the removal of that basic constraint.

Each mode is but an isolated fragment of a larger chromatic possibility which subsumes both pentatonic and heptatonic scales in its wake. When a seven-note mode has been used, this still means that those other notes of the enharmonic scale are available for usage at any time according to the specific context. A fine example of this can be found in the piano piece *The Little Shepherd* from Debussy's *Children's Corner Suite*. Here the composer makes prominent use of a mode whose third is major and whose sixth is minor. This mode he constructs upon the keynote of *A*.

His choice of mode however, does not preclude reference to other tones present in the enharmonic scale as a whole. In this excerpt excellent use is made of the tonally controlling powers of the septimal supplementary of the subtonic declining tone (note Ab - 40/21) in the key of A. Although such a note can crudely be confused as a misspelling of the leading note (*G#*), looking at the context in which it occurs, and the way in which it passes smoothly down to the subtonic, Debussy's own spelling of the note concerned amply demonstrates that here a functional septimal tone is being used:

Excerpt from Debussy's *The Little Shepherd*.

Reprint with permission of C.F.Peters, Frankfurt/M., Leipzig, London and New York.

Within the chromatic tonal system therefore, seven note scales do not represent the prime objects of expression. They are a facet of that object, the true nature of which is the chromatic consciousness brought into full flowering and fruition through the external assistance of the septimal supplementaries. One of the difficulties which any understanding of that orientation tends to present is the place of the septimal tones in a single key of the chromatic tonal

---

[1] Igor Stravinsky mentions this in his Poetics of Music, Trans. by Knodel and Dahl, Harvard University Press, Cambridge 1947, 35.

system. Being somewhat overshadowed by their enharmonic equivalents in the chromatic scale they are often extremely difficult to either perceive or evaluate.

A fruitful way of understanding the place of such notes is through the realisation that the level of tonal development in which the chromatic scale is to be viewed as a diatonic scale to which has been added five supplementary chromatic notes has long since passed. The diatonic scale itself has now become simply one of those referential elements within a larger governing system. From the standpoint of the chromatic tonal system, and the more elevated position which its four-dimensional status allows, all of the notes of the chromatic scale may thus count as potential equals. As this point is liable to cause confusion it will be discussed further, for it immediately tends to shadow issues relevant to the concept of free dodecaphony.

Although dodecaphonic music endeavoured to offer functional equality to the twelve notes of the chromatic scale, that it does nonetheless possess a fundamental failing which readily identifies it as a delusive successor to the system of tonality: it does not recognise the fundamental principle which establishes the twelve notes of the chromatic scale as being functional equals. That principle is the prime number seven as represented and embodied in the various septimal tones which make up the complete enharmonic scale.

Constituting the fundamental directive of a new force of tonality, the prime number seven and its representatives serves to galvanise the matrix of tonal functions upon which this new force may find a secure anchorage point. In this sense the notes of the chromatic scale become equal partners as the core representatives of tonality, whilst the septimal tones serve as the representative agents of that directive which, issuing forth from a new dimension of tonal space, arrives from the outside.

Consequently, a rather neat twofold division of the complete enharmonic scale becomes apparent, in that its notes divide up into two orders - the basic chromatic scale, and the septimal tones which now serve as the supplementaries to that scale. In order to demonstrate this point a musical example will be used which perfectly demonstrates this peculiar relationship of the septimal tones to the twelve notes of the chromatic scale. The extract concerned is from one of the string quartets of Bela Bartók (1881 - 1945).

In his study of Bartok's precise methods of pitch notation Malcolm Gillies observed that *Bartók strove to represent the tonal structures of his music in his pitch notations.*[1] In this extract which, like the rest of the unique movement is played pizzicato throughout, the notation certainly has an unerring exactitude which greatly assists the process of both analysing his use of septimal tones and

---

[1] Malcolm Gillies, Notation and Tonal Structure in Bartók's Later Works, Garland Publishing Inc. New York & London 1989, 21.

demonstrating their supplementary role to the notes of the chromatic scale. Unfortunately, given the space available, only a small extract can be considered. Yet even this extract is enough to show that Bartók himself was operating fully and uninhibitedly within the terms of the chromatic tonal system.

Excerpt from the Fourth Movement of Bartók's *Fourth String Quartet* (1928)

Bartók - String Quartet No 4, Sz 91. @ Copyright 1929 Boosey & Hawkes, Inc. Used by permission.

Here Bartók temporarily establishes a point of tonal stability around D, as can be seen by the repetitive tonic ninth chord which occurs throughout in the cello part. The viola part is also highly repetitive, introducing a chord on the off-beat which features a double inflection of the second and third degrees of the scale. In the viola there is thus an *Eb* as against the *E* in the cello, and the *F* as against the *F#* in the cello. This gives the impression of two alternating secundal major triads a semitone apart, the triad in the cello part being built upon note D, the triad in the viola part note Eb. So far as these two accompanimental parts are concerned, Bartók is thus employing a chromatic hexachord composed of the first six notes of the harmonic form of the chromatic scale as built up from the principal note D:

384

Chromatic Hexachord Implicated in the Above Excerpt

The most notable feature here is Bartók's clear spelling of the first half of a chromatic scale constructed upon note D. This offers a significance to the melodic content of the violin parts. These are mostly based around the interval of a diminished third, presented either in simple or compound fashion, and resolving unto a unison. The diminished third is a valent septimal interval. Being the inversion of the augmented sixth defined by harmonics four and seven, it has a ratio of 8/7 - i.e. it is the interval between the seventh and eighth harmonics. With this important septimal interval, the upper note tends to fall a semitone, whilst the lower note tends to rise a semitone, both notes thus converging upon the unison. Bartók's treatment of the diminished third is exemplary in this respect:

Bartók's Treatment of the Diminished Third

This example refers to the first diminished third which Bartók uses, which occurs in the second violin part of the first bar of the extract. It will be recalled that the note Cb has no place in a chromatic scale constructed upon note D, as it implies a third modality for the seventh degree. Note Cb, lying a diminished third above note A, has a ratio of 3/2 plus 8/7 equals 12/7. In the enharmonic scale this note performs the septimal function of the submediant declining tone. It thus counts as one of the septimal supplementaries.

The next diminished third which Bartók uses is in bar two of the extract which is constructed upon note B. Invoking the septimal tone Db, its ratio is 5/3 plus 8/7 equals 40/21, which is the ratio of the subtonic declining tone - another septimal supplementary tone. For the next few bars Bartók repeats these diminished thirds in their respective parts. It is not until bar seven of the extract that any new diminished thirds arise. At this point there is a veritable flourish of them. The first is in the second violin part and is constructed upon note E#. Note E# also has no place in the chromatic scale of D. Its ratio, lying a diminished third below note G, is 4/3 minus 8/7 which equals 7/6 - the ratio of the mediant inclining tone. After that, there is a further diminished third constructed upon note C#. This is one of the only two diminished thirds present in the chromatic scale - the diminished third between the inclining and declining tones - notes C# and Eb in the key of D. There is thus no need to discuss this interval any further. The last diminished third of the extract is constructed upon note A# - a note which has no place in the chromatic scale. It has a ratio of 16/9 minus 8/7 which equals 14/9 - the ratio of the submediant inclining tone.

In this extract can be seen a clear distinction between the primary tones as represented by the notes of the chromatic scale constructed upon note D, and the various supplementary septimal tones. These Bartók introduces as diminished thirds constructed upon five separate pitches: the pitches of A, B, E#, C# and A#. In doing so, Bartók has transcended the limitations of the chromatic scale - a scale which he himself is clearly aware of, as can be seen through its crystal clear definition in the accompanimental parts.

The exact manner in which he is transcending the chromatic scale is through the use of numerous supplementary septimal tones. This particular passage demonstrates the existence of these supplementaries extremely well, Bartók using some sixteen notes of the complete enharmonic scale of the key of D. The salient supplementary notes, those originating from the septimal sphere of influence, are the submediant declining tone Cb (ratio 12/7); the subtonic declining tone Db (ratio 40/21); the mediant inclining tone E# (ratio 7/6) and the submediant inclining tone A# (ratio 14/9). That, in all cases, Bartok's treatment of the septimal notes conforms entirely to their prescribed function, soundly demonstrates that Bartók is here operating within the terms of the chromatic tonal system.

The division of the resources of the enharmonic scale into a basic chromatic core upon which is attendant numerous septimal supplementary notes also serves to highlight an important functional distinction between two spheres. An understanding of the fundamental nature of that distinction may be approached initially through the observation that the prime number seven is an exact but finite resource. In terms of the unconscious Western exploitation of that resource this has occurred mainly in the unparalleled expansion of the possibilities of the dominant function. This in itself is an exact application, and in turn leads to an equally exact result.

The exact result being referred to is the release of the dominant tetrad from the role of sole agent of tonicization In the place of the dominant tetrad the prime number seven offers any number of unique and specific chromatically altered sonorities which carry the franchise of the original dominant tetrad. Thus the constraints of the V7 - I progression no longer exert such an imposing grip upon chord progressions, the power and authority for tonicization becoming relegated to the septimal tones that are the supplementary principles to the chromatic scale.

Through this the sphere of tonality represented by the chromatic scale becomes sealed off and purified through a process of tonal catharsis. Through the prime number seven and its influence it has become purged of any necessity for chord progressions to be unerringly guided towards the inevitability of the V7 - I cadence upon which the maintenance of tonality had previously depended. It is in this vital sense that the notes of the chromatic scale now become equals. They are equal because they are now linked by a common purpose - collectively they represent the static or passive elements of the key, a three-dimensional sphere of relative tonal stasis that is both self-contained and complete in itself. The septimal supplementaries, now responsible for tonal control and direction thus represent the four-dimensional sphere of tonal dynamism.

The web of tonal functions embraced by the enharmonic scale thus possesses two distinct orders of function. First there are the static tonal functions represented by the notes of the chromatic scale. They are termed static because they do not exert any leverage upon the tonal centre. On the contrary, they are the vital functions which support and protect that tonal centre against the presence of hostile chromatic elements which may serve to disrupt the tonality. Second, there are the dynamic tonal functions represented by the septimal supplementaries.

Dynamic is the term used to denote chromatically dependent notes whose function is to enrich and diversify melodic and harmonic possibility whilst offering support for the static tonal functions. Their dynamism lies in the way they tend to progress up or down to a tonally functional note of the chromatic scale.

Tonally Static and Dynamic Intervals

Tonally Static	Tonally Dynamic
Perfect Intervals	
Major Intervals	Augmented Intervals
Minor Intervals	Diminished Intervals

Intervals such as the tritone, the augmented sixth and diminished seventh are characterised by a sense of tonal instability and restlessness. Being unstable, they progress to tonally stable elements in a most convincing fashion. This is a very advantageous quality. Each of the augmented and diminished intervals can be viewed to be positively charged with tonal force, and like the opposite poles of a magnet which are forever attracted to one another, tonally dynamic intervals require the counterpart of their equivalent tonally static interval in order to discharge their tonal energy.

This is the interval or intervals to which, in a conventional sense, they find a satisfactory mode of discharge. This amounts to the projection of their tonal energy upon the interval that succeeds it. Thus being discharged the succeeding interval acquires a degree of tonal centricity which will remain unaffected by the presence of other tonally static intervals. It is not until another tonally dynamic interval occurs that this enhanced state of tonal centricity will either be reinforced or cancelled.

Either way, the tonally static interval has for the moment acquired a new prominence in the tonal scheme which distinguishes it from other tonally static intervals - it has temporarily acquired a quality of tonal centricity. In this sense, the operation of the force of tonality requires three terminal points - tonally static, tonally dynamic and tonally centric, the latter being the result of the interplay between the first two.

Historically speaking the efficacy of the V7 - I cadence caused a reduction in the number of viable modes to only two: the major and the minor. The prime number seven, through providing the substantive basis for the sphere of tonal dynamism, removes that constraint entirely. This means that the wealth of modal scales known to and used by the ancients is again on tap.

This wealth emerges from a new standpoint. Septimal sonorities are extremely virulent and powerful. Operating in a sphere which is their own, they bear no allegiance to the more limited diatonic system to which they are attached, and in relation to which they acquire a function. They are a virulent influence, and analogous to the invasion of an organism by a virus, lead to significant mutations of basic diatonic structures. These mutations, wherever and whenever they appear, belong to their own particular sphere - a sphere of tonal dynamism which carries with it as much a destructive as a constructive power.

Thus is caused a division between two spheres, a basic antagonism, polarity or dialectical interplay. This interplay between two contrasting spheres of influence provides one of the fundamental bases of the chromatic system of tonality. In simple terms the chromatic tonal system is the field defined by the interplay between these two spheres - the three dimensional sphere of tonal stasis as represented by the notes of the chromatic scale, and the four dimensional sphere of tonal dynamism as represented by the supplementary principles.

So far as the sphere of tonal stasis is concerned there is an obvious characteristic which arises and that is the absolute purity of its component structures. Purged of the necessity for manipulating, controlling or directing tonality, it means that a resurgence of basic modal structures is possible. These however, are able to appear from a much more elevated standpoint than has hitherto been possible.

They are no longer the masters of the music, but its servants, for each modal form is simply one of the crystalline forms or facets of the sphere of tonal stasis defined by the twelve notes of the chromatic scale. In this sense the modes themselves have an illusory quality, for they are simply partial projections of the total nature that is the fundamental unity of the chromatic scale. Like the frequencies of the colours of the rainbow contained within the totality that is white light, so the modes themselves derive from and are an integral part of that unity. All of these modes thus possess a common property - they are functionaries of that pure three-dimensional tonal sphere. To maintain that pure state it is of course necessary to avoid direct reference to the V7 - I cadence and the matrix of traditional harmonic functions in which it is embroiled. Otherwise, the very foundations of the chromatic tonal system are liable to collapse, leading either to a retrogressive tonality, or a negation of the principle of tonality itself.

Automatically precluding the dominant seventh and its derivatives, this sphere of related passive elements performs a very important function in the chromatic tonal system. Forever surrounded and encircled by the tonally active elements, it represents the state of a tonality at rest, with no sense of conflict, demand or pressure for change. Consequently, the intrusion upon that sphere of a tonally dynamic element can only imply the opposite state - the de-stabilisation of tonality in accordance with a fresh directive.

Some tonally dynamic elements are implicit to pitch structures right from the very beginning. This is the phenomenon of inherent dynamism, an example of which is the dynamic element between notes 'si' and 'fa' of the major scale. Constituting the only dynamic element of that system means that it alone provides the major factor responsible for the control and direction of tonality. Embedded in the diminished triad, the dominant seventh chord, the half-diminished and diminished seventh chords, it represents the fundamental tonicising element of the key concerned. Through a change of the chordal context in which this interval occurs it can equally serve as the tonicising element of the relative minor mode.

One of the negative attributions of the diminished fifth in the diatonic scale is that its fixed placing gives to certain of the seven diatonic modes a sense of tonal instability. The Lydian and Locrian modes are obvious examples here, for in both cases the implied modal tonic is itself part of that dynamic element - the augmented fourth in the case of the Lydian mode, and the diminished fifth in the case of the Locrian mode.

To use these modes successfully it is a matter of neutralising that dynamic element through recourse to more persuasive dynamic elements that sway tonality in the favour of the intended tonic. In any case, the focus of activity shifts to a chromatic level where such problems are less acute. For this reason, these two modes are not, and can never be, a part of the sphere of tonal stasis.

The sphere of tonal stasis precludes all dynamic elements, which includes the diminished and augmented triads of conventional tonality. The diminished triad possesses that diminished fifth, whilst the augmented triad possesses an augmented fifth. From the standpoint of the chromatic tonal system therefore, they belong to the sphere of tonal dynamism in which case they count as chromatically altered chords. Of the four triads recognised in conventional tonality two triads are recognisable as being tonally static - the major and the minor triads, whilst two triads are tonally dynamic - the diminished and augmented triads.

Now so far as basic triadic harmony is concerned, these tonally static triadic elements are not just a random array of triads from which a composer haphazardly selects what he requires. They are a purposive group of triads which perform a very specific function for the key concerned.

Common Triads in the Chromatic Scale of the Key of C

Numeral	Triad			Function
I	C	E	G	Tonic major triad
i	C	Eb	G	Tonic minor triad
ii	D	F	A	Supertonic triad
III	Eb	G	Bb	Minor mediant
#iii	E	G	B	Major mediant
IV	F	A	C	Subdominant major triad
iv	F	Ab	C	Subdominant minor triad
V	G	B	D	Dominant major triad
v	G	Bb	D	Dominant minor triad
bVI	Ab	C	Eb	Minor submediant
vi	A	C	E	Major submediant
VII	Bb	D	F	Subtonic triad

There are twelve triads presented here, those triads which become available through the combined resources of the major and minor scales. Other common triads represent some form of an extension to that pre-existing body of triads originally provided for by the diatonic system of tonality. In terms of the diatonic system, an extension is feasibly possible through the incorporation of applied dominants. However, at the chromatic level, where conventional dominant sonorities are no longer pre-eminent, such an extension is quite pointless.

This explains why the resurrection of the old modes in the chromatic system of tonality is in part illusory: it is a coincidence brought about through the controlled manipulation of the tonally static elements of the key - the array of common triads as presented above. Ensuring that the root progression conforms to tonally static constraints ensures the emergence of a basic diatonic modal formula. A good example of this is provided for in Ralph Vaughan-Williams *Mass in G Minor*:

Excerpt from Vaughan Williams *Mass in G Minor*:

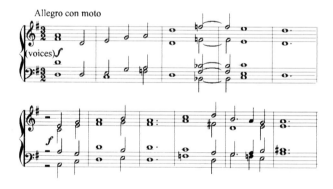

Modeling itself on the plaintive homophony of pieces such as Palestrina's *Stabat Mater*, the music operates within a purely diatonic curve. Here the upper line traces the Dorian mode belonging to the key of D. To offer appropriate harmonic support to that line there are points in the middle parts where notes which depart from the pure diatonic Dorian mode are used - the notes Bb, F# and C#. As a result of this it will be seen that this passage uses the entire chromatic mode as defined by the table of triads above, except for degree bII.

It thus provides a perfect example of the rejuvenation of the old modes within a basically chromatic format. At no point in this progression of root position common triads does Vaughan-Williams make recourse to tonally dynamic phenomenon. The music thus operates within a pure sphere of tonal stasis where there is no sense of tension. This can be seen especially in the scheme of root movement which the composer employs. Movements from one root to another are all restricted to major, minor or perfect intervals. There is a complete lack of tonally dynamic root movement.

The extract as given above serves to demonstrate some of the important features and qualities of the sphere of tonal stasis. One feature which deserves consideration is the intriguing phenomenon of chromatic alteration. Constituting the demarcation line that divides the sphere of tonal stasis from the sphere of tonal dynamism, there is a radical shift with regards to what is and is not considered to be a chromatic alteration

Viewed from the perspective of a diatonic tonality the passage above is directly referable to the Dorian mode. Those points at which Vaughan-Williams departs from the strict seven note Dorian formula - evident in his usage of the triads of D major, Bb major and A major - would generally be viewed to involve chromatic alterations of diatonic modal degrees. Thus the D major triad requires a sharpened third, the Bb major triad a flattened sixth, and the A major triad a sharpened seventh.

At the chromatic level of tonality however, all tonally static elements may be considered to be basic unaltered structures. Simply, all occurrences of major, minor and perfect intervals cannot by their very nature involve chromatic alteration. Chromatic alteration may be only considered to occur when a dynamic element is brought into participation. In others words, it only occurs when either an augmented or diminished interval manifests harmonically, melodically or through the harmonic root progression.

The passage above, involving only tonally static elements, does not implicate any chromatic alteration, apart from the odd incidence of cross-relation in which the intrusion of a dynamic element is unavoidable. This may seem curious seeing that it uses nearly the entire chromatic scale of the key of D. Yet a tonally static interval is by its very nature an unaltered element. This includes all major, minor and perfect intervals in the chromatic scale. These, in aggregate, comprise the sphere of tonal stasis. All augmented and diminished intervals thus belong to the sphere of tonal dynamism.

In looking at the tonally controlling powers of the prime number seven it is thus necessary to distinguish between the internal and external vehicles of tonal control. The external vehicles of tonal control are the septimal supplementaries. They are external simply because their usage depends upon references to notes which mostly fall outside of the sphere of the chromatic scale. A prime example is the note Fb - 9/7 - described as the mediant declining tone - which has no place in the chromatic scale of the key of C. Additionally, there are the internal manifestations of septimal influences in the chromatic scale. These become evident in those places in the chromatic continuum where dynamic elements occur.

An example is the 'si'-'fa' diminished fifth as present in the major mode, and its inversion the augmented fourth. Another example is the augmented sixth as generated between the declining and inclining tones of the chromatic octave. Yet another is the diminished fourth interval between the major mediant and the minor submediant. These represent the inherent dynamic elements of the chromatic scale system i.e. those dynamic elements which do not directly involve the septimal supplementaries.

All of these can be construed to have ratios which can be defined through the prime numbers two, three and five. Therefore there is the 'si-fa' diminished fifth which has a defining ratio of 64/45, the bII - #VII augmented sixth which has a ratio of 225/128, and the diminished fourth between #III and bVI which has a ratio of 32/25. However, being dynamic intervals, means that, theoretically at least, they should all have ratios which somehow involve the prime number seven.

And so they do, it is just a matter of understanding the principles which determine the ratios of these intervals. Within the sphere of the chromatic scale there are a number of important septimal termini which function as the vehicles for the internal control of tonal forces. The principal septimal terminus is that point in the chromatic octave where the interval of the augmented sixth tends to manifest itself - note Db, known in the diatonic system of tonality as the flattened supertonic, and in the chromatic system of tonality as the supersemitone.

Here the augmented sixth interval (7/4) occurs in relation to the leading (inclining tone) note B. Within the terms of a diatonic tonality, the note Db initially constitutes the altered note, which means that it carries a septimal ratio of 15/14 (obtained as a result of subtracting 7/4 from the ratio of the leading note 15/8), as defined by that particular harmonic context.

A second, and equally important terminus is the sharp fourth degree of the scale - note F# - which has a ratio of 7/5. This terminus is obtained when an augmented sixth interval is used on the minor submediant degree, and its ratio is obtained as a result of the addition of 7/4 to the ratio of the minor submediant which is 8/5. As to which terminus is participating in the generation of a given dynamic interval is determined by the way in which that dynamic interval is obtained.

A dynamic interval automatically implies a state of chromatic alteration. The augmented sixth between notes Db and B can be obtained from two directions of alteration. Either the *Bb* can be sharpened to give the requisite note B, or the *D* can be flattened to give the requisite note Db. When the *B* is sharpened, it is brought into a dynamic relationship with the bass note Db. It is thus the *B* which carries the septimal ratio, in this case 28/15 obtained as the sum of 16/15 - the normal ratio of the declining tone Db - and 7/4. In this case the relevant terminus involved is thus note F# - 7/5. However, if the augmented sixth is obtained when the *D* is flattened, then it is the bass note itself which is responsible for the dynamic relationship generated in relation to the upper note B. In this case it is thus the *Db* which carries the septimal ratio of 15/14.

Although this explains how the termini are generated in the first instance, it does not explain how they generate the entire array of dynamic intervals present in the chromatic scale. This they do through a domino effect along the harmonic chains that form the chromatic scale. Note Db, having a ratio of 15/14 is then brought into a direct valent relationship with other notes of the chromatic scale. To the major submediant note A (5/3) it forms an interval of a diminished fourth - ratio 9/7 - whilst to the major mediant note E (5/4) it forms an interval of an augmented second - ratio 7/6. The result is a harmonic triad in which, like the major or minor triads, all of the notes bear a direct valent relationship to one another:

Septimal 'Major' Triad Obtained as the Sum of 9/7 and 7/6

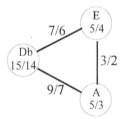

From this basis it can be seen that other triads can be similarly constructed. The augmented second between notes Db to E is an interval whose ratio is 7/6, whilst the perfect fifth between notes Db to Ab is an interval whose ratio is 3/2. The diminished fourth between notes E and Ab therefore, gives a ratio of 9/7. In this way a septimal triad of the same intervallic components, but different profile is generated in which all of the notes bear a valent relationship:

Septimal 'Minor' Triad Obtained as the Sum of 7/6 and 9/7

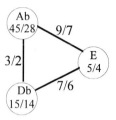

Placing all of these interrelationships into the form of a diagram it will be seen that the septimal terminus ratios of 15/14 and 7/5 bring all of the dynamic intervals into a direct valent relationship with one another:

Valent Relationships Generated by the Septimal Termini 15/14 & 7/5

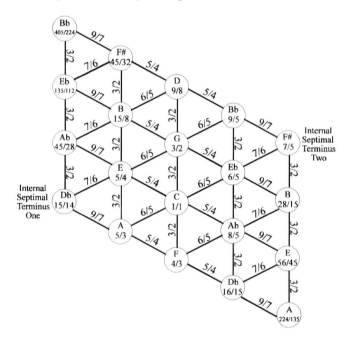

In the centre are the three columns of fifths which generate the three dimensional chromatic scale. Either side, to the left and right, are the septimal shadow tones generated by harmonic chain progression, by the two septimal termini. The first terminus, note Db, generates a series of three fifths, whilst the second terminus, note F#, generates a series of three fourths. In this way, all of the dynamic intervals present in the chromatic scale are present and accounted for, together with the reasons for, and the manner of, their septimal derivation.

The triads formed by this lattice of septimal intervals are aptly termed 'false triads', for the simple reason that they provide enharmonic equivalents to more conventional common triads. Being dynamic in their nature however, they perform an important function in terms of the internal control of tonality. A very fine example of this is the use of the septimal major triad as a substitute for the conventional dominant by Vaughan Williams at the end of his sixth symphony:

Cadence Used in Vaughan-Williams *Sixth Symphony* (1948)

Ostensibly, an enharmonic Eb major triad operating in an E minor tonality the use of a false triad is betrayed by the voice leading, the notes D# and A# acting as inclining tones up to the tonic and dominant degrees respectively.

In this example, a septimal false minor triad is used, the notation again being that used by the composer:

Excerpt from Leos Janácek's *Láska Opravdivá* (for male voices)

Those dynamic elements which do occur within the chromatic scale are the three-dimensional presage of what is in effect a four-dimensional phenomenon. This is why the theory of the natural seventh (7/4) is so at odds with the fundamental grounds of a four-dimensional tonality, in that it casts up 7/4 as a static element - the minor seventh between 'so' and 'fa'. The acoustical basis for the dynamic elements of the key is completely missed, and the ruling and controlling powers of the prime number seven upon the sphere of tonality bypassed. The seventh harmonic, as a new prime number after the fifth, represents a dynamic frequency shift whose sphere lies beyond the staticity of the elements controlled by the prime numbers five, three and two.

THE TRITONE BIPOLE AS A MANIFESTATION OF SEPTIMAL POLARITY

The principles underlying the scheme of keys belonging to the chromatic tonal system are based on the observation of the logical implications of the fourth dimension of tonal space as embodied both by the enharmonic scale, and intuitive use of that scale by various composers. It is inevitable that contact with that dimension has brought into play new tonal bonds and new tonal circuitry which are as integral to the chromatic tonal system as the tonic and dominant functions were to the diatonic tonal system.

Although the particularities of the mathematical dimension from which this circuitry originates may not be generally recognised, the presence of such circuitry, visibly evident in very much of the tonal music of the twentieth century, has thankfully received much comment. In endeavouring to explicate this circuitry it is convenient that ground has already been covered by musicologists endeavouring to solve the problems posed by the individual musical languages of specific twentieth century tonal composers. Salient, although by no means strictly compatible examples are Berger,[1] Van den Toorn[2] and Straus's[3] work on the music of Stravinsky, and Ernö Lendvai's studies of the music of Kodaly[4] and Bartók.[5]

Highlighting some of the unique problems presented by the musical languages of the composers whose work they are addressing, the writings of such individuals have proved invaluable in an attempt to define the basic outlines of the chromatic tonal system. In this respect, both Berger and Van den Toorn's work on the importance of the octatonic pitch collection in Stravinsky's music is interesting, exposing as it does, salient issues which any attempt to define the chromatic tonal system must satisfactorily address. Straus's work is

---

[1] Arthur Berger, Perspectives on Schoenberg and Stravinsky, 19th Century Music X3, 1987.

[2] Pieter van den Toorn, Some Characteristics of Stravinsky's Diatonic Music, in: PNM 14/1, 1975, 104 - 138 and 15/2, 1977, 58 - 96.

[3] Joseph Straus, Stravinsky's Tonal Axis, in: JMT2, 1982, 261 - 290.

[4] Ernö Lendvai, Modality; Atonality; Function, in: Soundings 6, 1977, 24 - 27.

[5] Ernö Lendvai, Béla Bartók: An Analysis of his Music, Kahn & Averill, London 1990.

also illuminating for the way in which he points to those polarities inherent within particular chordal sonorities. This has had a strong influence on the way in which septimal chords have been both viewed and analysed, especially the bipolarised dominant hexachord which will be discussed in this chapter.

Relevant to this, are those comments Stravinsky made on the subject in his Poetics of Music: *Having reached this point beyond Classical tonality, it is no less indispensable to obey, not new idols, but the eternal necessity of affirming the axis of our music, and to recognise the existence of certain poles of attraction. Diatonic tonality is only one means of orienting music towards these poles. The function of tonality is completely subordinated to the force of attraction of the pole of sonority. All music is nothing more than a succession of impulses that converge toward a definite point of repose.*[1]

In referring to a point beyond 'Classical tonality', Stravinsky is offering intimations of a new system of tonality in which the diatonic level no longer constitutes the principle means of 'orienting music towards these poles'. Unfortunately Stravinsky never defined what these poles were, so leaving room for theoretical debate on the subject.

Rather than entering into this debate, the intention in this chapter is to make further enquiries concerning those poles which become naturally evident through a consideration of the septimal matrix and its manifestation in the music of the nineteenth and twentieth centuries. Therefore it is not necessary to take sides; to implicate either the octatonic collection or sonority as the most significant feature in the generation of tonal polarities, for in all probability both viewpoints are correct within the terms of the overlord view provided by the chromatic tonal system as a whole.

Here must be acknowledged that lucid, convincing and logical exposition of the scheme of key polarities arising from the chromatic continuum as originally put forward by Ernö Lendvai in his highly perceptive and cogent *An Analysis of Béla Bartók's Music*. Intended to explicate the basic principles by which Bartok organised the tonalities of his music, Lendvai's axis system[2] exposes objective tonal polarities arising from the chromatic tonal system. As such his system offers not only a penetrating insight into the music of one of the twentieth centuries greatest composers, but it is a system which in its bare bones fully accords with the logical implications offered by the mathematically based criterion of the prime number seven itself.

In this respect, Lendvai's 'axis system' would appear to have a strong basis in the natural powers of tonal valency, and therefore possesses an application not

---

[1] Igor Stravinsky, The Poetics of Music, trans, by Knodel and Dahl, Harvard University Press, Cambridge 1947, 35.
[2] Ernö Lendvai, Béla Bartók: An Analysis of his Music, The Axis System, 1-16.

just to the music of Bartók, and his contemporary Kodaly, but to the music of virtually every twentieth century tonal composer. Consequently, any further discussion of key polarities, especially those pertaining to the prime number seven, cannot take place without reference to the numerous groundbreaking concepts which Lendvai has introduced.

Yet here the concern is not just with the music of Bartók, it is with the chromatic tonal system in general. To go any further therefore, it is necessary to make a broad sweep through a fairly wide territory before some of the more specific concepts introduced by Lendvai, and their relevance to the chromatic tonal system can be successfully broached. This surveillance can begin with the consideration of the following chord progression from the *March au Supplice* movement from Berlioz's *Symphonie Fantastique* (1830):

Extract from Berlioz's *Symphonie Fantastique*

Ostensibly in the key of G minor, this passage is distinctive for the way in which it rocks back and forth between the tonic triad and a triad of Db major. Viewed in conventional tonal terms the chord of Db major performs no obvious and identifiable function within the tonality of G minor. It is thus a chromatic chord, although bearing in mind the type of chord that Berlioz uses here, even this type of classification is problematic. This is because chromatic common triads are ordinarily borrowed dominants which serve to temporarily tonicise the implied chord of destination. Here there is no such preparation, and apparently no such resolution. It thus begs the question: In what is the logic of this binary chord progression based?

One answer is to assert that it has no logic, in which case it may be possible to find agreement with Schumann, who saw in this progression nothing more than a sign of the immaturity of its composer.[1] To dismiss it in this fashion is evasive, for a listening of the passage in question reveals that it possesses a majestic aural logic which defies our inability to explain this chord within the conventional terms of the diatonic tonal system.

Yet it is in this observation that the answer lies. Viewed from the standpoint of the diatonic tonal system Berlioz's progression seems illogical. Yet viewed

---

[1] Heinrich Schenker, Harmony, 113.

from the perspective of the chromatic tonal system it appears as nothing out of the ordinary. The extraordinary quality of this progression lies in the fact that it represents a trend setting example of nineteenth century composers tendency towards the exploitation of unusual root progressions in which the tritone, or 'diabolus in musica' offered a prime subject for experimentation.

In this respect Berlioz has anticipated some of the salient features which characterise the use of a tritonal link between chordal roots found in later music. Examples of this are abundant. In his studies of the more unusual harmonic procedures found in the music of Berlioz, Friedheim observes that a similar progression (lasting for some 42 measures) can be seen in the *Coronation Scene* of Mussorgsky's *Boris Gudonov*.[1] Here, the composer alternates between two 'seventh' chords constructed respectively upon the roots of *Ab* and *D*. Freidheim points out a similar progression in the third movement of Bruckner's ninth symphony, where the composer juxtaposes the triads of B and F minor. And of course, the same pair of chords figure prominently in Strauss's *Elektra*.

Something which has been read into the use of chords whose roots lie a tritone apart is that it implicates a chromatically flattened dominant degree.[2] This is an interesting explanation, for if this is how to explain it, it demonstrates the use of a tonal relationship which speaks of an altogether new level of harmonic operation, far removed from the major and minor scales of the Classical Era. Yet this is not the only avenue of explanation of this phenomenon.

Another explicit example of the use of the tritone in twentieth century music is Stravinsky's *Petrushka*, where the composer cleverly juxtaposes the chords of C major and F# major. Viewing these chords referentially as familiar objects of expression it might be tempting to read bitonal implications into the way in which the composer brings these two chordal identities into such close juxtaposition. Eric Walter White views the issue this way, and to add to the 'familiar objects' interpretation he points out that the F# major triad originates from the 'black notes' of the piano keyboard, the C major chord from the 'white notes: *in view of Stravinsky's well known habit of composing at the piano and the fact that in this score the piano was originally intended to play a concertante role, the combination of a black note chord and a white note chord clearly results from the composers preoccupation with bitonality.*[3]

[1] Philip Freidheim, Radical Harmonic Procedures in Berlioz, in: MR21, 1960, 282 - 296.

[2] Bryan Simms, Choron, Fétis and the Theory of Tonality, in: JMT19, No. 1. 1975, 112 - 139. For a study of the flat dominant degree as used by Russian composers of the time also see Richard Taruskin's Chernomor to Kaschei: Harmonic Sorcery; or Stravinsky's 'Angle', in: JAMS38, Spring 1985, 72 - 142.

[3] Eric Walter White: Stravinsky: the Composer and his Works, Faber and Faber, London and Boston 1979, 198 - 200. See also Richard Taruskin, Chernomor to Kaschei: Harmonic

The problem with this view is that tonality depends upon more than the perceived presence of a tonic triad. The triad itself is backed up by its dominant, which in its turn is counterbalanced by the subdominant, etc. To implicate C major as the tonic chord of one key, and F# major as the tonic chord of another is not sufficient justification for the establishment of bitonality. In the sense of two keys being used at once, bitonality implies the use of two diatonic scales belonging to separate keys. Looking at 'Petrushka' it would seem that rather than constituting the terms of two equal and opposite tonalities, that the chords concerned are actually complimentary to one another in the sense of polarity.

Here the most telling factor is the hexatonic pitch collection that Stravinsky evolves through the combination of the two chords:

Generative Materials Used in Stravinsky's 'Petrushka'

Resulting from the fusion of the F# and C major chords, the indications of this pitch collection are that the chords concerned have merged to create a specified harmonic state which could be considered to be analogous to a modality. This is certainly the view upheld by Berger too, who sees the two chords as being *subsumed under a single collection with a single referential order*.[1]

Melodically speaking, the tritone has provided the basis for many interesting musical discourses. A prime example is Sibelius's fourth symphony, in which the tritonal motive (suggestive of the Lydian mode) introduced at the very beginning of the first movement, recurs again and again through all four movements, thus giving the impression of a work that provides a precise and close-knit musical study of the various attributes and properties of this extremely curious interval. And of course, a further strident example, is *Mars, the God of War* movement of Holst's *The Planets Suite* where the rising fifth motive *G - D* presented at the beginning of the movement is sinisterly echoed a diminished fifth higher: *Db -Ab*.

Sorcery; or Stravinsky's 'Angle', in: JAMS38, Spring 1985, 72 - 142 for a further assessment of this statement.

[1] Arthur Berger, Perspectives on Schoenberg and Stravinsky, in: 19th. Century Music X/3, 137. Also see Richard Taruskin's Chéz Petrouchka: Harmony and Tonality chéz Stravinsky in the same volume, 268.

Claude Debussy's *Prélude à 'L'après-midi d'un faune* is characterised by a melodic use of the tritone, particularly the opening subject in which a melodic figure, repeated twice, descends chromatically from the tonic note C# down to the note G and thence back up again to the point from which it started.

Concerning this characteristic opening subject Paul Griffifths observes that *Debussy's 'Prélude' undoubtedly heralds the modern era. Gently it shakes loose from roots in diatonic (major-minor) tonality, which is not to say that it is atonal or keyless, but merely that the old harmonic relationships are no longer of binding significance. At times Debussy leaves the key in doubt, as he does in the first two bars of the flute melody - where he fills in the space between C# and G: all the notes are included, and not just the selection which would point to a particular major or minor key. Moreover, the outline interval, a tritone, is that most inimical to the diatonic tonal system, the 'diabolus in musica' as it was called by Medieval theorists.*[1]

From this standpoint, Berlioz's rather innocent employment of the tritone is the beginning of what amounts to a perennial fascination amongst composers with regard to the peculiar properties of this interval. As an interval in its own right it is extremely interesting. Enharmonically speaking, it is the only interval which when inverted replicates itself a tritone higher. This is because within the tempered scale it represents the exact midpoint of the musical octave. Looking at this central point with respect to the octave as a closed circle it can be seen that the tritone relation represents the furthest possible point away from the starting point. In this sense, the two notes which form the interval of the tritone appear as diametrically opposite points on the chromatic continuum:

Tritone Interval as Representing Diametrically Opposite Points of the Octave

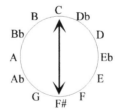

Another fascinating feature of the tritone is that within a tempered context the same tritone offers a resolution to chords whose roots are themselves a tritone apart. Therefore assuming enharmonic equivalence for the moment (for

---

[1] Paul Griffifths, Modern Music - A Concise History from Debussy to Boulez, Thames and Hudson, London 1986, 7-8.

this is how composers operating within the equally tempered scale would view the matter) the notes B and F conceived as being part of the dominant seventh chord of C (*G B F*), are also a part of the dominant seventh chord of the key of Gb (*Db F Cb*). The tritone itself therefore serves two keys which are themselves a tritone removed from one another. Now when these keys are placed on the circle of fifths they occupy diametrically opposite points of the tonal circle:

Keys of C and Gb as Diametrically Opposite Points in the Circle of Fifths

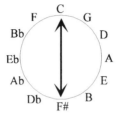

So from whichever standpoint the tritone is viewed, it is an interval possessed of a great mystique, suggesting two equal points on the chromatic continuum poised in a relationship of perpetual opposition. Thus speaking of the balance or equilibrium of equal and opposite forces, the two notes are as opposite to one another as the Summer and Winter Solstices of the circle of the year. It is not surprising that composers have sought to explore the possibilities of this fascinating interval, a fascination made all the more vivid for its provocative and diabolical nickname.

As one of the more enigmatic features of modern musical theory, the tritone is an interval which incites theoretical interest. Leading to the creation of tonal links which fall outside of the sphere of governance of the major and minor modes, suggests that it is an interval which has an extremely strong relevance to the chromatic tonal system. Confirmatory to this suggestion is the observation that it figures quite prominently as a feature of those septimal chords which have already been considered. It is expedient at this stage to reconsider these chords, and review their properties in relation to the tritone interval inherent within them. When this has been accomplished a curious feature relevant to the tritonal relationship will become apparent.

When the fifth of a dominant minor ninth chord is flattened the result is a chromatically altered chord of dominant functions. Through flattening the fifth the common triad on the dominant degree becomes a half-diminished triad *C E Gb*. At the same time the alteration has led to the creation of a major triad on the flat supertonic degree: *Gb Bb Db*.

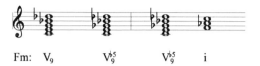

Fm: V_9 V_9^{b5} V_9^{b5} i

The alteration causes a distinct shift in the overall balances of the sonority. Whilst the function of the chord remains essentially the same, the difference being one of chromatic colouring and inflection, observe that the alteration sets up a distinct conflict between two essentially stable harmonic areas: the original dominant triad, and the newly created flat supertonic triad:

Should a composer require a dominant minor ninth chord with an extremely high level of harmonic tension, all that remains to be done is to reintroduce the D and thereby create an extremely powerful doubly-inflected dominant sonority. Here it is extremely interesting to see that there are many examples of the use of such complex septimal chords in twentieth century tonal music. Strauss's opera *Elektra* makes significant use of such a chord, whilst a further example can be found in the Prologue to scene ii of Mussorgsky's *Boris Gudonov* (measure 36). This particular example is from Paul Hindemith's second piano sonata (1936):

The resolution to the E minor triad is particularly effective in terms of voice leading. The diminished fifth of the chord, appearing as the declining tone F, progresses smoothly down to the implied tonic *E*, whilst at the same time the perfect fifth - *F#* - rises smoothly upwards to the minor third of the implied tonic chord. It is undoubtedly the simultaneous presence of both the notes F and *F#* that imparts to this chord that tensile factor which is so effectively discharged through the contrary motion of the implied tendency tones. In this respect it is a chord which could easily be dismissed as an incidental result of the voice leading. Yet it appears so many times in other contexts that it would be problematic to try to dismiss it in this way.

The intrusion of septimal influences upon the nature and constitution of the dominant principle has gradually led to a three-tiered evolution of the original dominant ninth chord. The first stage is the introduction of chromatic alteration, mitigated and supported by the septimal matrix. Because of such alterations, specific chromatic functions are being offered to notes which in conventional diatonic terms, do not belong to the tonality in question. Examples are the dominant inclining tone (note F# - 7/5) or the subdominant declining tone (note Gb - 10/7). The enharmonic scale offers a necessary summary of those particular functions.

The second stage is the introduction of double-inflection, thereby introducing septimal intervals of the diminished or augmented octave. This is an important stage, for although through double-inflection conflicting definitions of particular scale degrees are being offered, through the participation of the septimal matrix, each of those tones are possessed of a different function.

An example may be given to illustrate this point. In the first chord the fifth of the dominant ninth of the key of F is being presented in both its unaltered (note G) and chromatically flattened form (note Gb). Rather than serving to contradict the note G, the alteration compliments it through the portrayal of a different harmonic function. The G represents the supertonic degree, and thus the note which offers stability to the dominant, whilst the Gb represents the declining tone, whose chromatic function is to fall to the tonic. The dissonant interval of the augmented octave implied by their combination, imparts to the supertonic its tendency to rise up to the mediant, and thus give rise to an extremely lucid and effective resolution:

Resolution of Doubly-inflected Dominant Ninth Chord

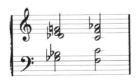

The use of double-inflection in chordal sonorities thus results from an instinctive recognition of the different chromatic functions performed by different versions of the same scale degree. This possibility arises solely through of the action of the septimal matrix which offers its support to these chromatic functions.

Therefore, the third and perhaps most fascinating stage in the gradual evolution and metamorphosis of the dominant function is the way in which the septimal matrix serves as the generator of an internal conflict between chordal strengths, roots and identities within the same sonority. This process may be considered analogous to the process of cell division in that, as a result of processes of chromatic alteration being applied to the original dominant sonority, the chord has actually split up between two conflicting poles of influence. The dominant function has *bipolarised* along a tritonal axis:

Bipolarisation of the Dominant Along a Tritonal Axis

Tritonal Axis

In this way the very important function of the declining tone is born, a note which serving the tonic from the opposite direction to the inclining tone, nonetheless also performs a dominant function. That this process is directly due to the hidden influence of the prime number seven can easily be seen when the bipolarised dominant sonority is represented diagrammatically for there the septimal links become well apparent:

Septimal Links Within Bipolarised Dominant Sonority

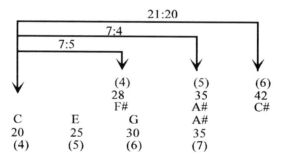

The relationship between the chordal roots is determined by the septimal tritone of ratio 7/5, a ratio which is duplicated in the relationship between the thirds and fifths of the two respective triads. The upper triad is the lower triad which has been replicated a septimal tritone higher. Also, the seventh harmonic of the lowermost triad is at the same time the fifth harmonic of the uppermost triad. Finally, the relationship between the C and C# is the septimal semitone of ratio 21/20.

The pathways of valent connection between the two respective triadic units ensures that the bond between them is a strong one. The use of the prime number seven, first in the chromatic alteration of dominant sonorities, second in the use of double inflection, and third, in the bipolarisation of the dominant sonority, has thus led to the forging of a bond between two areas of the tonal network which in the diatonic tonal system quite literally possessed a diametrically opposite relationship to one another. In this light it is interesting to see that the bipolarised dominant hexachord presupposes a fusion of two distinct triadic separations: the original dominant triad, and the 'Neapolitan' triad.

The latter, in works such as Beethoven's F minor piano sonata, Op. 55 (the *Appassionata*), is a chord which attains a significant structural importance that tends to belie its appreciation as a local chromatically inflected sonority. Concerning this triad Jackson observes that *what appealed perhaps most strongly to nineteenth century composers was the peculiar movement of a tritone between the lowered supertonic chord and the dominant chord...that invariably followed.*[1]

As to whether the Neapolitan triad should be deemed to be a flattened supertonic triad is highly questionable. Its occurrence in the bipolarised dominant hexachord suggests that whilst it fulfils a dominant related function for the key concerned, it also stands as a natural counterpole of the original dominant triad. The tendency of composers to switch or alternate between these two triads may thus be viewed as a pendular motion between two complimentary yet conflicting terms of the bipolarised dominant function.

In this way, the bipolarised dominant proves analogous to a magnet with its North and South polarity. Outwardly there is a dual principle at work seen in the repulsion of like poles and the attraction of unlike poles. Yet underlying this duality is a singular principle represented by the magnetic field in which both poles perform their respective functions.

The chord of C major thus calls for the complementation of F# major, whilst the chord of F# major calls for the complementation of the chord of C major, the two ever revolving around one another in a display of mutual need and attraction.

It is this notion which so admirably supports Ernö Lendvai's observation that the flat supertonic degree may be considered the *dominant counterpole* of the conventional dominant.[2] In the key of C, *G* is thus the 'dominant pole' whilst *Db* is the 'dominant counterpole'. The ratio which cements this particular relationship being 7/5, indicates that the emergence of these principles as seen and manifested in tonal works of twentieth century composers is itself another

---

[1] Roland Jackson, The Neapolitan Progression in the Nineteenth Century, in: MR30, 1969, 35.

[2] Ernö Lendvai, Béla Bartók: An Analysis of his Music, 4.

symptom of the intuitive exploitation of the resources of the prime number seven.

In corroboration of this both triadic separations can and do perform dominant functions upon their own respective levels. Here Lendvai refers to what he describes as the Kodaly cadence: *Chords based on D flat (the minor second degree of the tonic) have...acquired a dominant character in Bartók and Kodály because 'leading note' steps predominate in them, just as in the G seventh chord.*[1] He then observes that *The Phrygian minor second step downwards - by its frequent occurrence - could also be called the 'Kodaly' dominant....In the Kodaly dominant, just as in the classical V7 - I cadence, the 'leading' role is played by the notes sensibles: 'ti' and 'fa'.*[2]

Expressed within terms already laid out so far, the Kodaly dominant is the triad defined by the ratios of 4:5:7. To generate it the dominant pole (*G*) is simply swapped for the dominant counterpole (*Db*). This says much about the chords of C and F# major used in Stravinsky's 'Petrushka', for viewed in these terms they represent a finalised stage of development of the dominant chord in its relationship to the septimal matrix. The state of bitonality would seem to be apparent, because the triads concerned are a single dominant sonority whose forces have become bipolarised along that septimal axis (7/5). Simply, the music which Stravinsky uses to characterise the figure of Petrushka thrives on a state of unresolved dominant tension.

The logic of the music does not lie in one tonal field as heard against another (the bitonal interpretation) but in the projection of two polarised forces implicit to the dominant function itself. The 'Petrushka' scale is simply a scalar projection of the internal conflict set up in the dominant principle caused by the perturbing influence of the seventh harmonic.

The role played by the prime number seven as a catalyst for such developments can be well understood within the terms of the dominant principle. What however, does this mean for the tonic principle? This question can be partly answered when it is realised that the dominant counterpole is at the same time the dominant triad of a keynote which lies a diminished fifth above the original tonic. Therefore, in the key of C, the triad *Db F Ab* is at the same time interpretable as the dominant of the key of Gb. To perform this function a reversal of polarity is required in which the dominant counterpole is then treated as the dominant pole. Now when the dominant counterpole is calculated in relation to this new key it produces a triad which is enharmonically equivalent to the original dominant pole. By way of enharmonic substitution the

---

[1] Ernö Lendvai, Modality: Atonality: Function, in: Soundings 6, 1977, 1 - 41.
[2] Ibid., 24-7.

same bipolarised dominant hexachord thus serves two keys a tritone apart through the principle of the reversal of polarity:

Bipolarised Dominant Hexachord as Medium of Connection Between Keys a Tritone Apart

$$G \quad B \quad D \quad Db \quad F \quad Ab$$
$$(Abb \quad Cb \quad Ebb)$$

dominant	dominant counterpole	➤ Key of C
dominant counterpole	dominant	➤ Key of Gb

In this way the bipolarised dominant hexachord serves to relate the key of Gb to the key of C in a similar sense, an observation which offers outright confirmation of Lendvai's supposition that the note Gb may be regarded to be the 'tonic counterpole' of the note C.   In support of this he provides us with some fine examples from the music of Bartók in which he shows that *the inner form of Bluebeard's Castle was conceived in pole-counterpole tensions.   It starts at the dark F♯ pole, rises to the bright C major chord (the realm of Bluebeard) and descends again to the gloomy F♯.*[1] He also observes that the *B major tonic of the violin concerto is replaced in the development by its counterpole F. Similarly the F major tonic of the Divertimento is replaced by B in the development.*[2] Such observations tend to quash the idea that the tonic counterpole is, or ever was a 'flattened dominant' triad.

In support of this, the triads involved in such processes of connection are not always major. In the Berlioz example, one was major whilst the other was minor, whilst in the *Elektra* example, both triads were minor. The tritone that provides the link between the roots of the two chords is still 7/5, but the derivation is different. The salient sonority is the ninth chord built upon the inclining tone - *B D F Ab C* where the fifth has been chromatically sharpened to give the chord *B D F♯ Ab C*. When the original fifth is reintroduced as a double inflection the result is another form of bipolarised dominant hexachord: *B D F♯ F Ab C*, in which the two triads are minor.

---

[1] Erno Lendvai, Béla Bartók: An Analysis of his Music, 4.

[2] Ibid., 4.

Pathways of Valent Connection Between Two Minor Triads Whose Roots are a Tritone Apart

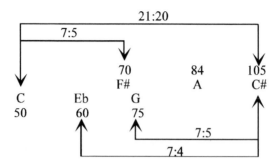

The pair of minor triads linked according to the tritone bipole, thus provide a direct mirror image of the pair of major triads, showing one to derive from the positive polarisation of four-dimensional frequency space, the other to derive from its reflection in the negative polarisation of four-dimensional frequency space:

Tritonally Linked Paired Major and Minor Triads as Mirror Images

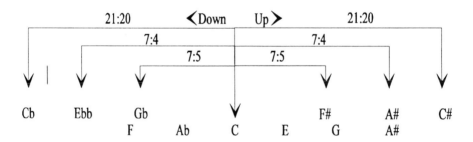

In this way, the importance offered to the tritone within the domain of 20th century tonal music, may be read yet another symptom of the emergence of the musical language into the fourth dimension of tonal space.

TRIADIC HARMONY IN THE CHROMATIC TONAL SYSTEM

The spectrum of twelve common triads considered in chapter 24 belonged to the sphere of tonal stasis. Including all of the common triads available through the combined resources of the major and minor modes, they are limited in their representation of the complete possibilities available within the chromatic circle as a whole. An examination of virtually any piece of twentieth century tonal music suggests that it should be possible to use any degree of the chromatic scale as the root of either a major or a minor triad.

An excellent model of a free, and even experimental approach to the use of triadic harmony in a chromatic context is the music to Richard Strauss's opera *Elektra* (1906-8). The musical language which Strauss (1864 - 1949) used for this opera - with its characteristic terseness and apparent tonal acentricity, is well suited to the portrayal of the themes of revenge, anger and hatred which figure so strongly in this particular opera. In terms of the chromatic materials which Strauss developed for this purpose, *Elektra* provides a veritable gold mine of analytical opportunity. Here is an example of the type of free triadic technique which Strauss uses here:

Extract from Strauss's *Elektra*

Here the composer employs a scheme of root movement difficult to explain within the terms of the diatonic scale. Although the progression retains a sense of tonality, bearing in its broad outlines a progression from chord I to chord V, the scheme of root movement sets it apart from a diatonically controlled harmonic environment. The 'strangers in the village' which tend to undermine a purely diatonic analysis are the D minor, G minor and E minor triads. Looking at this scheme, there is a strong suggestibility of equal root movement by thirds,

412

seen in the progression from *D#* up to *G*, and thence from *G* down to *E* down to *C#*. This kind of progression not only has a motivic coherence, but it cuts cleanly through the sphere of diatonicism, to reveal a root logic which is seemingly more at home within the more expansive terms of the chromatic scale:

Implications of Chromatic Sphere in Schemes of Root Movement By Thirds[1]

Major Triads   Minor Triads

Consequently, the composer seems to be selecting his chords not from the diatonic scale, but the entire resources of the chromatic scale. The chords of D minor, G minor and E minor have no place in the key of F# major. Yet they do have a place in the chromatic key of F#, based on the chromatic scale and its septimal supplementaries. The chromatic scale offers the composer a much greater and wide-ranging selection of chords to choose from than the diatonic scale. In terms of common triads alone, there would be twelve major and twelve minor triads to choose from. As such it would seem to have the merit of being a superior system.

However, a question must be asked: Is this a valid tonal system? In the diatonic scale (major or minor), each chord has a definable function within the tonality as a whole. Within the chromatic scale system, where each note is viewed as the prospective root of a harmonic sonority, there is no clear scheme of definable functions to guide the composer. What is the function of the G minor triad that Strauss uses in the key of F#?

One answer might be that it is a minor chord constructed upon the flat second degree of the scale. Yet this answer does not define its function, it merely defines its apparent derivation. So far as the chromatic scale system is concerned there is a distinct problem with regard to root logic and for this reason: in the absence of an objective scheme of chordal functions the composer has nothing to rely upon to guide the progression, to give it a goal, an impetus or a compelling direction. It is perhaps this state of potential chaos which the chromatic scale system presents which caused Strauss to take a step

---

[1] See Hans Tischler's Chromatic Mediants - A Facet of Musical Romanticism, in: JMT 2/1, 94 - 96. Also see Richard Taruskin's Chernomor to Kaschei: Harmonic Sorcery; or Stravinsky's 'Angle', (JAMS 38, Spring 1985, 72 - 142) for a study of root movement by thirds as used by Russian composers such as Rimsky-Korsakov, and Glinka.

back from the tonal ambiguity of *Elektra* into what Griffifths describes as the *comfortable pastiche of 'Der Rosenkavalier'.*[1]

When arriving at such chord progressions the composer has their own ear to rely upon as a guide. This particular progression, even when played through on the piano, has a majestic logic of its own. Yet in what is that logic based? As Alden Ashforth has observed in his studies of the music of Beethoven *it is the very rightness in sound of these events, however puzzling analytically, which suggests the existence of some systematic element, however deeply hidden, which gives rise to their employment.*[2]

This statement could just as easily be applied to this example. However, to assert that the logic of the music lies in a chromatic as opposed to a diatonic sense of tonality says nothing. It simply displaces the question into a more complex and less well understood area. The possibility that the chromatic scale may offer a logical extension of the range of common triads is certainly suggested by this music. However, one of the central problems which confronts any attempt to extend this group of triads, is the accorded place of those triads in the diatonic system of tonality.

A good example is the major chord constructed upon the supertonic degree. This chord is very difficult to use as an independent triad because in the Classical tonal system it represents the dominant of the dominant. Its use not only suggests this association, but it is difficult to justify its inclusion in the key concerned, because it is borrowed from the closely related diatonic key of G.

Some kind of mitigation is possible through the observation that the dominant chain of influence (of which applied dominants are the direct agents), may be superseded by the tonally controlling powers of septimal sonorities whose authority lies elsewhere. Accordingly, the dominant chain as represented by chord V of V (for example) is no longer of such importance. The problem here is being able to transcend the influence of that chain in such a way as to claim those triads into the terms of the unified field that is the chromatic key.

One solution to this problem stems from the fact that the dominant chain of fifths belongs to the three-dimensional system of tonality. Through the application of principles which stem from the ruling powers of the fourth dimension, the dominant chain may be reconfigured in such a way as to make available that more extensive range of triads actually required. The agent by which this is accomplished is the septimal tritone of ratio 7/5, that pitch relationship which provides the underlying basis for the 'pole-counterpole' axis. The importance of this relationship, both in terms of being able to transcend the

---

[1] Paul Griffifths, Modern Music: A Concise History from Debussy to Boulez, 26.
[2] Alden Ashforth, The Relationship of the Sixth in Beethoven's Piano Sonata, Opus 110, in: MR 32, 1971, 93.

414

limits of the diatonic scale, and in being able to expand the domain of a given key to include common triads originating from the entire territory of the chromatic circle, cannot possibly be overestimated.

In conventional diatonic terms, the roots of two triads constructed upon the notes C and F# are the furthest points away from each other on the chromatic circle. Representing diametrically opposite points means that at a three-dimensional level they are distantly related to one another. At a four-dimensional level however, a valent link can be set up between these two apparently opposite points in such a way as to forge a strong bond between them. That link is the 7/4 relation.

This excerpt from Kodaly's *Psalmus Hungaricus* provides an explicit example of this link, for observe that the fifth harmonic of the tonic note E (note G#), is at the same time represented as the seventh harmonic (augmented sixth) of the tonic counterpole *Bb* (again note G#):

Excerpt from Kodaly's 'Psalmus Hungaricus' (1924)

As a direct consequence of that link the triads concerned are no longer distantly related through the cycle of fifths, for they have now become inextricably linked through the medium of the fourth dimension of tonal space. Thus being linked, the two triads become locked into a binary axis in which the one serves to ratify and support the other. This occurs by the reciprocation of the same relationship back to the original pole (or its enharmonic equivalent).

In terms of the respective spheres of tonal stasis and dynamism, the tonic pole itself belongs to the sphere of tonal stasis. The tonic counterpole, by virtue of its augmented fourth root relationship to the C major triad, represents itself as a functionary of the sphere of tonal dynamism. Therefore, although the triad of F# major is the negative reflection of the tonic principle on the opposite side of the chromatic circle, because it represents the dynamic state of tonality it has a positive effect i.e. it ratifies the C major chord in its accorded position as the primary tonal centre.

As the C major chord is ratified in this fashion, then so must every other chord belonging to the sphere of tonal stasis. Therefore every chord belonging to the sphere of tonal stasis possesses its own negative reflection on the opposite side of the chromatic circle. Because there are twelve triads belonging to the sphere of stasis, means that there twelve representatives of these triads, in the form of their counterpoles, belonging to the sphere of dynamism.

To generate the complete possibilities available to the chromatic system it is thus necessary to construct the counterpoles of each of the triads presented in the triad table given in the last chapter. When this is accomplished a very interesting feature emerges:

Common Triads and Their Counterpoles Within the Chromatic Tonal System

Sphere of Stasis (Pole)			Sphere of Dynamism (Counterpole)		
C	Eb	G	F#	A	C#
C	E	G	F#	A#	C#
D	F	A	Ab	Cb	Eb
Eb	G	Bb	A	C#	E
E	G	B	Bb	Db	F
F	Ab	C	B	D	F#
F	A	C	B	D#	F#
G	Bb	D	Db	Fb	Ab
G	B	D	Db	F	Ab
Ab	C	Eb	D	F#	A
A	C	E	Eb	Gb	Bb
Bb	D	F	E	G#	B

The sum of all of the common triads available within the major and minor modes, together with their counterpoles produces a set of 24 triads, 12 major and 12 minor, each of which takes a different degree of the chromatic scale as its implied root:

System of Twenty-four Common Triads in the Chromatic Tonal System

	Major					Minor			
I	C	E	G		i	C	Eb	G	
bII	Db	F	Ab		bii	Db	Fb	Ab	
II	D	F#	A		ii	D	F	A	
III	Eb	G	Bb		iii	Eb	Gb	Bb	
#III	E	G#	B		#iii	E	G	B	
IV	F	A	C		iv	F	Ab	C	
#IV	F#	A#	C#		#iv	F#	A	C#	
V	G	B	D		v	G	Bb	D	
bVI	Ab	C	Eb		bvi	Ab	Cb	Eb	
VI	A	C#	E		vi	A	C	E	
VII	Bb	D	F		vii	Bb	Db	F	
#VII	B	D#	F#		#vii	B	D	F#	

Thus can be defined the basic set of common triads belonging to the chromatic tonal system. Superficially, this set of triads appears to result from a rather free and loose use of common triads within the terms of the more expansive chromatic continuum. Yet from a deeper perspective, it is a logical extension of the resources of Classical tonality through the application of septimal principles of chord connection.

Belonging to a unified system of tonality means that each of the above triads performs a definite function, and occupies a certain place in that system. The nature of that system can be understood when it is realised that each triad can be allied with its counterpole, and that each resultant bipole itself, occurs within the overall context of a square of chordal roots which represents the balanced sum of two such bipoles:

Square as the Sum of Two Bipoles

III	F#	A#	C#
IV	A	C#	E
I	C	E	G
II	Eb	G	Bb

In the case of the above square the root note A represents the axis of symmetry between the points C and F#. In this way it represents not only a midway point between the pole and counterpole, but a point which is common to both poles, for A is the sub-minor pole of C, and also the super-minor pole of

F#. The above case shows the tonic square, in that it represents the tonic triad, its counterpole, the relative tonic triad and its counterpole. That there are three such squares in the chromatic tonal system means that the unity of the system of common triads is reducible to a trine of squares:

Unity of the System of Twenty-four Common Triads

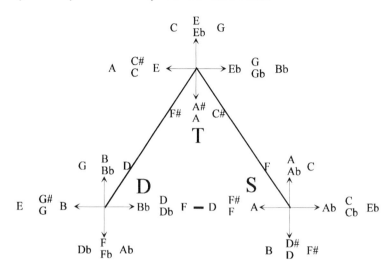

That such a system is needed to explain twentieth century tonal practice is self-evident. The provision of examples is problematic because there are so many. For those who are unsure how to spot examples, one which may be examined at the readers convenience is the chromatic use of common triads seen in sections II to 8 bars after III of the fifth movement (*Saturn, the Bringer of Old Age*) of Holst's *The Planet's Suite*. In a passage which is in the chromatic key of C, the composer utilises some fifteen of the twenty-four possible triads. Here the prominent use of the tritone as a feature underlying the root movement between these triads is the factor which identifies this passage as a clear manifestation of the principles being discussed:

Common Triads Used in the Fifth Movement of Holst's *The Planets Suite*.

This example, in which the chords have been extracted from the orchestral context in which they are presented, provides an excellent illustration of some of the principles already discussed, as well as a timely warning of the various traps which can be encountered when taking the composers notation at face value.

The 22 bars of music represented here are divisible into four sections of 4, 8, 4 and 6 bars (as determined by the reappearance of the tonic minor triad of C as it begins a new phrase). At no point is the conventional dominant seventh chord employed as an agent of tonicization. Instead Holst relies upon septimal sonorities which in the chromatic tonal system replace the dominant seventh chord as the sole agent of tonicization.

A good example is the second chord of section A in which the subsemitonal triad (B minor) is projected over the dominant root. Another example is the fourth chord of section A (*Bb F# A D*). This chord does not belong to the chromatic key of C, for it is a chromatically altered dominant of the super-minor pole of *Eb*, in which the fifth and seventh have been chromatically sharpened in order to bring the mediant and dominant inclining tones into play (ratios of 7/6 and 7/5 respectively):

Derivation of Chromatically Altered Dominant in Bar Two of the Extract

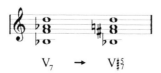

With the next appearance of this particular chord (bar 5 or the first bar of section B) it is resolved deceptively to a triad of Cb major. Observe the contradiction between the *B* in the treble and the Cb in the bass, and the fact that Holst has spelled this chord as a false triad: *B Eb F#*. That it is not a false triad can be readily determined by the chords behaviour.

Progressing to the subdominant major triad, it is the subdominant counterpole, an axial progression reaffirmed in the next bar. In bar 5 of section B the subdominant counterpole passes on to a chord which Holst again spells as a false triad: *Db E A*. The behaviour of the chord informs us that this is not a false triad. The triad as written by Holst possesses very particular tendencies imparted by the intervals of the augmented second and fifth present within it. Either the *Db* would tend to fall to the *C*, or more likely, both the *E* and *A* would pass up by a semitone to *F* and *Bb* respectively.

In the triad used by Holst no tendencies become apparent. Holst spells the following chord as a false triad too: *C Eb G#* over an *F#* in the bass. The *G#* has some logic as it passes up to the *A* of the subsequent false triad: *Db E A* over a *G* in the bass. In bar seven of section B Holst does try to spell the chord properly, in that it is presented as an A major triad, which suspended over the bass note F#, gives it the apparel of an F# minor seventh chord.

Having reached this point Holst has landed himself in trouble, for although the subsequent E major triad is a logical consequent of the F# minor chord, its cadential resolution to the tonic C minor chord at the beginning of section C is problematic to explain. In this particular section therefore, although the chord progression is sound, the notation does not do justice to what is actually happening in the music. This is probably because Holst was unaware of the particularities of the system through which the intrinsic logic of this chord progression can be easily explained.

The problem starts with the false spelling of the Cb major chord in bar 2 of section B. Being spelled falsely in bar four as well, it lands Holst into difficult territory. Understood as a Cb major chord, the chord in bar 5 (section B) is the sub-minor counterpole (*Db Fb Bbb*), a chord which harnesses two declining tones - the mediant declining tone of Fb (9/7) and the submediant declining tone of Bbb (12/7). From this, it becomes clear that the chord to which it progresses is an Ab major triad suspended over its own minor seventh (*Gb*) in the bass. The *Gb*, being interpreted enharmonically as the augmented sixth of the root note Ab passes smoothly up to the *G* which is the augmented sixth of the previous triad: *Db Fb Bbb*. This explains its smooth resolution to the Ab major triad that follows, for it has now become a German Sixth chord (*Bbb Db Fb G*) whose chord of resolution is quite naturally Ab major.

Summary of Bars 4,5 and 6 of Section B

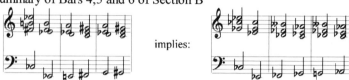

implies:

Having reached the minor submediant chord (Ab major) by bar seven, the confusing appearance of E major is now easy to understand. The chord concerned is Fb major, the subtonic counterpole, and the *D* which would otherwise convert the E major triad into a E dominant seventh chord, is really the augmented sixth (7/4) of the Fb major triad. The fifth of this triad, note Cb is interpreted enharmonically as the inclining tone of C, which means that the cadential chord by which the tonic minor triad is approached is not an E dominant seventh chord. It is a chromatic alteration of the diminished seventh chord of the key of C, where the fifth has been flattened (*B D F Ab* becomes *B D Fb Ab*) in order to invoke the mediant declining tone - note Fb (9/7). Thus can be explained the dominant function performed by this particular chord.

Now Roger Bullivant has observed that *no aspect of theory is more subject to the jibe of academicism than notation. To argue as to whether a key is 'really F# or Gb' is regarded as betraying either a highly technical or, even worse, a merely pedantic attitude to music.*[1] In reinterpreting the notation of this particular passage along these lines, this accusation could probably be made here. Nonetheless, he also admits that *the naming of a note, chord, or key can be a definite aid to a faithful description of what the ear hears.*[2] Bearing this in mind, together with the comments which have been made concerning this passage, it would perhaps be more appropriate to view this passage in the following way:

Summary of Bars 4-9 of Section B

---

[1] Roger Bullivant, The Nature of Chromaticism, in: MR xxiv, 1963, 97-129/279 -304.
[2] Ibid.

Although the repeat of section A deserves no further comment, section C uses numerous counterpole triads. In bar 3 of that section the subdominant counterpole is heard in relation to its axial partner the subdominant triad. In bar 4 the axis shifts to the tonic major triad (*C E G*) and its minor counterpole (*F# A C#*). This axis is repeated in bar 5, whilst in bar 6 can be seen an appearance of the super-minor pole, as represented by the minor mediant triad *Eb G Bb*, and its minor counterpole, the triad of A minor. In bars 4, 5 and 6 therefore, can be seen a complete appearance of the tonic square. The passage ends, it will be noted, on the super-minor pole itself.

Whilst it may be accepted that at a chromatic level, the array of common triads is far more extensive than those provided at a diatonic level, what does this say about the other two types of triad recognised in the original Classical system of tonality - the diminished and augmented triads.

These are similarly reconfigured in accordance with the requirements of their place in a new system. The diminished triad has a very strong association with the dominant seventh chord, so strong in fact that it has often been described as a dominant seventh chord with omitted root. Clearly in a system in which the dominant seventh chord is no longer pre-eminent, means that the diminished triad looses some of the status it has already required as the partner of the dominant seventh.

Occurring on the degree of the scale immediately below the tonic it has now been replaced by a subsemitonal sonority which may have many different profiles depending upon the exact requirements being made of it. Here the triad is more likely to be minor, major, chromatically altered, anything in fact except for the conventional diminished triad with its Classical dominant to tonic associations. And where a diminished triad does become evident it is more likely to be embedded in a more complex sonority where it is less recognisable.

To a large extent, the same argument can be applied to the augmented triad. Not being present in the diatonic scale, means that it was already a chromatically altered chord for the diatonic system of tonality. In the chromatic tonal system it retains the same significance - it is a chromatically altered chord, and as such only subject to consideration as a member of an extremely large group of chromatically altered chords in which it appears as only one option. For this reason, like the diminished triad, it is not particularly necessary to focus upon it, for it is simply one of many chromatically altered chords which form a part of the sphere of tonal dynamism.

Therefore, as some chords drop out of consideration, other chords, quite new to the list of available sonorities necessitate a more thorough and exacting theoretical recognition. For example, the system of triads depicted above is incomplete without due reference being offered to the mutable triad. The nature

422

of this chord can be understood through the concept that the chromatic tonal system represents an upsurge of tonal forces into the domain of a fourth dimension of tonal space. One of the symptoms of that upsurge is the drawing together of the major and minor tonalities by what at first seemed to be an invisible force, but in reality was the influence of that fourth dimension beginning to make itself felt:

Upsurge of Tonal Forces into the Fourth Dimension of Tonal Space Resulting in a Drawing Together of the Major and Minor Tonalities

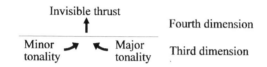

As the point of unification of the major and minor tonalities under the controlling terms of a fourth dimension, the chromatic tonal system demands its own representation within the sphere of triadic sonorities in general, by which the terms of that unique and specific merger may be identified. That triad is the mutable triad, obtained as a result of the merger of the major and minor triads.

The usage of this triad, especially favoured by Stravinsky, and used by virtually every twentieth century tonal composer since, firmly points towards that chromatic orientation which signaled the general arrival and establishment of the chromatic tonal system as a whole.[1] The augmented octave between the two forms of third gives it a dissonant quality which gives the common triad an altogether new status which quite befits its place in the new system. It now becomes the equal of those septimal chords which employing the facility of double-inflection, present comparable levels of harmonic tension.

---

[1] A fine example of the use of a mutable triad was presented earlier in this chapter in the form of the excerpt from Kodaly's Psalmus Hungaricus.

TERTIAL, QUARTAL AND SECUNDAL HARMONY AS INTEGRAL RESOURCES OF THE CHROMATIC TONAL SYSTEM

The instinctively felt necessity to avoid specific reference to the V7 - I cadence, and the sphere of conventional functional triadic harmony in which it plays such an important part is undoubtedly one of the motivating forces that has inspired twentieth century composers towards a veritable plethora of harmonic invention and versatility. The fact that the tyranny of the dominant seventh could be overcome, and the powers of tonicisation relegated to new harmonies was itself a signal of the arrival of an altogether new system of tonality, one unfettered by the restrictions of conventional triadic harmony, and the constraints of the major and minor key system.

One of the ways composers found a certain degree of freedom from the constraints of the diatonic level of tonality was through the use of triads whose roots could seemingly derive from any of the twelve notes of the chromatic scale. Another was the use of increasingly complex sonorities obtained by the addition of the seventh, ninth, eleventh and thirteenth to basic triadic formations. Yet another was through the creation and usage of a whole roster of altogether new chords types which by their very nature tended to dissociate from conventional functional harmony.

These included the use of equivocation (mutable triads), quartal and quintal chords, secundal chords and tone clusters, and the use of added note sonorities where familiar chords were spiced up through the addition of dissonant and apparently non-harmonic tones.

Although from a composers standpoint the development of such alternatives led to an expansion of the range of harmonic resources, such an expansion did not, and could not, occur outside of the bonds of valent connection which naturally exist between musical tones. From a theoretical standpoint therefore, such resources both stemmed from, and contributed to the emergence of a logical and coherent system. The subject to be considered in this chapter is exactly how these resources were relevant to that new emergent system - the chromatic system of tonality.

In the chromatic tonal system, the triad can no longer be considered the basic unit of harmony. Because the chromatic tonal system is four-dimensional means that the tetrad must be counted as the basic unit of harmonic control. That this stage has already arrived is extremely obvious. When Bartók ended the second movement of his *Concerto for Orchestra* (1943) on a D dominant seventh chord which was not resolved to the appropriate G major triad he was clearly making a statement concerning the nature of harmony and the state of evolution of the tonal system. By virtue of the fact that he does not resolve this chord may be viewed on a superficial level to be a statement concerning the invalidity of the basic syntax of Classical tonality in the twentieth century.

But there is surely more to this gesture. First, it can be viewed as an affirmation of the tetrad as the controlling unit of harmonic organisation. Hence it is not resolved, because at that level, it is complete in itself. It does not need a triad to release its tension, simply because there is no tension in the tetrad to resolve anymore. Tension is a relative term, and can only derive from the norm which a composer sets up and establishes at the outset of a work. In an atmosphere characterised by continual harmonic tension, the tetrad must rank as a relatively mild contributor.

The type of chord Bartók used is significant as well. It is not a dominant seventh chord. The functional characteristic that defines the dominant seventh chord is its ability to tonicise the triad that follows. Projected as an autonomous sonority outside of the context of its dynamic relation to the tonic triad, it can no longer count as a dominant seventh. The terms have to change to do justice to its newfound function. That it does not resolve is Bartók's way of indicating that this is not the chord of the dominant seventh. From this it may be inferred that the chord being alluded to is that defined by the configuration of harmonics 4, 5, 6 and 7 - the consonant tetrad.

The ramifications of this fact are considerable, for they directly affect the way in which basic harmonic materials may be viewed. In terms of the diatonic system of tonality, the tetrad, or chord of the seventh, may be viewed as a triad to which has been added that dissonant factor which is the seventh above the chordal root. Being dissonant, it was once considered customary to resolve that dissonance to an appropriate point of concordance. Within the diatonic tonal system therefore, the distinction between concord and discord was of great importance. Discord represented those points of harmonic tension and instability which, through their resolution, gave way to a state of harmonic repose.

In this sense, discords were the carriers of latent potential musical energy, whilst their resolution represented the expenditure of that energy in the appropriate melodic movement which determined their resolution. This musical energy, manifesting through the alternation of the musical impulses of tension and relaxation respectively, constituted the basic dynamo of the harmonic motor, the factor that gave chord progressions their drive, zeal and impetus.

In a system where the tetrad is taken as the basic unit of harmony, the seventh can no longer be regarded to be a factor which is additional to the harmonic unit of the triad. Instead, the seventh becomes an intrinsic and stable part of the unit itself. This represents a significant step, for if the seventh is considered a stable part of the harmonic unit, so therefore is the ninth. The seventh represents the step below the octave of the root, whilst the ninth represents the step above.

This point was referred to by Leigh Gerdine in his *General Theory of Music* of 1958: *the history of musical theory may be regarded as an exploration of harmonic possibilities of combinations of ever closer intervals occurring higher in the natural harmonic series.... To the simple octave, in which men's and women's or men's and boy's voices must naturally have sung, have been progressively added the fifth and the fourth, the major third and the minor third, the major and minor sixths: the mathematical relation of vibration ratios acceptable to the ear has become increasingly complex. The great upheaval in music which began about 1900 may be considered ...as an inevitable step in the admission of the seconds and sevenths, both major and minor, as 'consonant' intervals. The implications of this statement are enormous. For one thing, it adopts a point of view in which the music of Stravinsky, Bartók, Schoenberg and, indeed, every other experimental composer of the twentieth century finds a place. Further, it reduces the controversy which divided atonalists from the defenders of tonality, to somewhat the same status as the Brahms - Wagner controversy of the nineteenth century.*[1]

To take the tetrad as the basic unit of harmony however, is to create a problem. It is to remove the dynamo from the harmonic motor. Dissonance need no longer resolve to consonance, and consonance need no longer require the contrast of dissonance. In the place of a well oiled and serviceable harmonic motor, the composer is now left with nothing but a series of dissonant chord piles whose high and relatively constant level of harmonic tension makes the prior functional distinction between consonance and dissonance irrelevant. The vital dynamic factor that was once the seventh chord, has now become relegated to being a passive harmonic agent. Similarly, the passive harmonic agent that was once the triad, begins to disappear off the screen to become an incomplete tetrad.

This says very much about the newfound sensibility of the dominant seventh tetrad. Previously, the resolution of its tensions to the tonic triad had been a principal factor in the process of tonicization. Being viewed as a stable

---

[1] Leigh Gerdine, A General Theory of Music, in: JMT 2/1, April 1958, 105.

harmonic unit means that it has lost both its power and its sting. It is now a chord whose level of tension, when compared with other seventh chords, is comparatively mild. This therefore, creates yet another problem. How to provide for the processes of tonicization.

Both of the major problems associated with the adoption of the tetrad as the basic unit of harmony find an adequate solution in the fundamental tetrad of the chromatic tonal system - the 4:5:6:7 tetrad, whose four respective tones represent the four dimensions of tonal space accountable in the chromatic system of tonality. The figures 4:5:6 represent the major common triad that was the basic unit of the diatonic tonal system. The figure 7 represents the thrust of that unit into a new dimension of tonal occupation. Through 7, the basic unit has evolved, been increased by a vital term which serves to differentiate it from the plain 4:5:6 triadic unit.

The difference which the prime number seven makes to that basic unit is that the tonally static unit has acquired a directive, a tonal momentum which allows the force of tonality to be harnessed and controlled. Rather than providing the basis for the chord of the dominant seventh, as was once thought, the prime number seven provides the very opposite - the basis by which the dominant seventh may be superseded.

In the final cadence from Ravel's song *le Réveil de la Mariée* (1909) the redundancy of the dominant seventh tetrad is made clear, the composer using instead a clear and simple 4:5:6:7 tetrad (*Ab C Eb F#*):

Excerpt from Ravel's *Cinq Mélodies populaires Grecques: Le Réveil de la Mariée*.

Constituting the generator of the world of dynamic intervals the prime number seven serves as new fuel for the harmonic motor. The passive and dissonant chord piles of the chromatic tonal system have acquired the possibility of a new dynamism and impulsion through the participation of the prime number seven. In this context, 7 is thus both the destroyer of the old system of tonality, and the creator of the new.

But this does not mean that the dominant seventh chord no longer has a place in the system. Because its resolution to an appropriate tonic triad is no longer felt to be essential, means that it simply loses its prior status so far as the chromatic tonal system is concerned. If the impression is not to be created of a lapse back to the diatonic level of tonality, such chords must be handled very carefully (if not avoided) or else transformed through chromatic alteration.

Both Ravel and Debussy were masters of the creation of new contexts in which such chords could be used. It was probably due to their combined influence that such chords actually retained a place in the new system, not as tonally functional entities participating in a conventional dominant to tonic context, but as chords enjoyed more for their own particular sonorous qualities.

Here it is important to observe that if a dominant seventh chord is persistently refused resolution to its respective tonic, it ceases to be perceived as a dominant seventh. The problem which arises then, is how to distinguish it from the 4:5:6:7 tetrad. This can be accomplished by looking at the context and treatment of the respective chords.

Here, the music of the English composer Brian Dennis provides us with some fine insights, for Dennis is a composer who consciously strived to use the 7/4 relation in his music. In this first extract from Brian Dennis's *The Boatman's Song* (1989) a chain of three connected dominant seventh chords are used whose roots are on *D, G* and *A* respectively. His use of dissonant appogiaturas and chromatic decorations, coupled with his refusal to let the chords resolve in a conventional sense is enough to inform us that the chords being used are indeed dominant seventh chords:

Excerpt from Brian Dennis's *A Little Water Music, Six Short Piano Pieces: 1. The Boatman's Song* (1989).

Reproduced by kind permission of the publisher Forward Music Ltd.

In a passage which occurs some seven bars later he does use the 4:5:6:7 tetrad, and in so doing brings into play two of the septimal supplementaries.

The chord is detectable by virtue of its mode of treatment, in that melodically, Dennis brings out the chromatic tetrachord implied by harmonics 12, 14 and 15 in both cases. The septimal supplementaries that he uses are note E# (7/6) - the mediant inclining tone of the key of D, and note G# - (7/5) - the dominant inclining tone of the same key:

Brian Dennis, *The Boatman's Song*, (bb. 20 - 24).

Reproduced by kind permission of the publisher Forward Music Ltd.

Another of the important consequences of the adoption of the tetrad as the basic unit of harmony, is that in accordance with modern harmonic practice, sevenths and seconds may be considered relatively stable harmonic units. It is thus no longer necessary to build vertical aggregates from thirds alone. All seven notes of the diatonic scale may be used in a chord which possesses a certain degree of tonal stability. Therefore, vertical aggregates built up from any combination of intervals become feasible. As there are six types of interval (excluding the octave), and three of these are the inversion of the others means that there are thus three levels of chord construction devisable according to this particular criterion:

Three Levels of Chord Construction

Seconds	Sevenths	Secundal harmony
Thirds	Sixths	Tertial harmony
Fourths	Fifths	Quartal harmony

A tertial chord, composed of superimposed thirds, is essentially a three-dimensional construct. In the case of the major triad it offers a reference point to each of the tonal dimensions signified by the prime numbers one, three and five. Therefore the root has a ratio of 1/1, the third a ratio of 5/4 and the fifth a ratio of 3/2. As against the consonant dyadic unit of the perfect fifth or fourth, the triad thus represents a progressive movement into a new dimension of tonal space. Now by piling more thirds onto the triad the result is an increase in the complexity of the sonorities so obtained. A seventh chord is a more complex harmonic entity than a triad, whilst a ninth is even more complex still.

Accompanying this increase in complexity is an increase in dissonance levels, a process which represents a growth or expansion of harmonic possibilities in a particular direction. However, no matter how many thirds are piled onto the basic root, this does not represent a movement into a new dimension of tonal space. From a tertial standpoint therefore, the trend of twentieth century music towards the use of more complex sonorities such as the ninth, eleventh and thirteenth, usually taken unprepared and unresolved, does not constitute an evolution of harmonic possibility. All that it represents is a more pervasive and complete occupation of the three-dimensional space that is already available.

This observation has a direct relevance to other types of harmony, such as quartal and secundal harmony. A quartal chord uses the fourth as the basic unit of chordal generation, whilst a secundal chord uses the interval of the second. Because both types of chord pile arise against the general backdrop of the tertial chains that underpin the system of triads, the newness of these sonorities is only apparent. They are, and always were implicit to the three-dimensional model of tonality in that their generation does not lead to a specific projection into a new dimension of tonal space.

This is an extremely important point because the development of such chords in the early twentieth century are often viewed to represent an evolution of harmonic possibility. But they are not strictly an evolution, because they do not exert any thrust into a new dimension of tonal occupation. This observation calls into question the perceived separateness of secundal, tertial and quartal harmonic resources. Although the chords belonging to each category are built up from different interval classes, there is a strong inter-relationship between them which tends to defy their perception as separate compartments of harmonic organisation.

Tertial chords are built up from aggregates of thirds and sixths, quartal chords from fourths and fifths. If the intermediate thirds of a tertial chord are omitted a substratum of fifths is exposed: *C E G B D F A*. Similarly, the intermediate fifths of a quintal chord may be omitted to reveal a substratum of ninths (or seconds): *C G D A E B F*. The cycle of interdependence becomes complete when it is seen that intermediate seconds may be omitted from a secundal chord to reveal a substratum of thirds: *C D E F G A B*.

In this way, all three chord types are connected to one another within the terms of one grand cycle to reveal a fundamental unity of harmonic resources which exists at the chromatic level of tonality. That state of unity is itself dependent upon a fundamental but hidden principle. It is hidden because it lies in a different dimension. The chord types aforementioned obtain their standing

430

and stature from the three-dimensional construct that is the chromatic scale. The manipulation, control and direction of the tonal forces to which such chords can provide a vehicle for however, comes from a different dimension - the fourth dimension governed by the prime number seven, i.e.:

Septimal Sonority used as Tonally Controlling Factor in a Quartal Context[1]

(Winds) *f*

Consequently all three chords types are passive agents which have the capacity to carry and harness tonal force. Their ability in this respect is determined by the dynamic intervals set up because of their mutation by the influence of the prime number seven. The demonstration of this lies in the consideration of the many different types of augmented sixth chords which are possible:

Different Types of Augmented Sixth Chords

Looking at the above range of septimal chords, the important factor is the augmented sixth interval itself, not the original chord to which it has become attached. The augmented sixth, or indeed, any other dynamic (septimal) interval or intervals, can be added to any combination of tonally static intervals to produce a characteristically tonally dynamic (septimal) chordal sonority.

In this way, whether through chords of the augmented sixth, or other types of chromatic chord which employ dynamic intervals, the fourth dimension of tonal space becomes a great leveler of three-dimensional harmonic possibility, for whether secundal, quartal or tertial, all such sonorities are simply passive agents manipulated and controlled by septimal forces. Accordingly, the fourth dimension constitutes that singular controlling principle which unites the three chord types under the banner of a single purpose: the maintenance of tonality within the province of an advanced four-dimensional state.

---

[1] Example by Persischetti who is pointing out the uses of augmented sixth chords in a quartal context. Vincent Persischetti, Twentieth Century Harmony, 135.

SEPTIMAL POLARITY AS THE BASIS FOR DOMINANT PROLONGATION (ATONALITY)

Rather than trying to offer an encyclopedic definition of the various chords discussed in the last chapter, it would be more useful at this stage to continue with the discussion of general principles, for the ramifications and extensions of these will soon become readily apparent to the reader. A prime example is the division of the tonal world into the spheres of tonally static and tonally dynamic, an idea which is still capable of being explored. In the process of doing so, more will be discovered about both the chromatic tonal system in general, and its manifestations in the music of the twentieth century.

Tonally dynamic pitch structures are those which possess septimal intervals. There are many pitch structures in use in the twentieth century that are themselves dynamic, and perform dynamic functions. Consequently, these too must be regarded as being necessary parts or features of the chromatic tonal system. One such structure which springs to mind is the whole tone scale, a scale which, subsequent to systematic usage by the nineteenth century Russian composers Glinka (1804 - 1857) and Dargomizhsky (1813 - 1869), has since gained a pre-eminence that justifies its consideration here as an independent pitch structure.

In theoretical terms the whole tone scale is a *tour de force* of chromatic geometry, the equally tempered twelve-tone scale dividing neatly into two cyclical transpositions which between them account for all of its twelve notes. The first transposition uses the odd numbers of the twelve-tone scale, whilst the second utilises the even numbers. In sum, the whole-tone scale thus offers a hemispheric reflection of the mathematical perfection of the twelve-tone system.

From the standpoint of the equally tempered twelve-tone scale, the whole-tone scale is a closed system, a spiral of mathematically equal whole tones which, winding its way up or down the pitch continuum, offers no real sense of any beginning or ending. This lack of gravitational leanings towards other tones, is of course, due to the complete lack of semitones, and therefore the absence of any connotations of a leading note. Superficially therefore, the whole-tone scale would seem to be an artificial product of the tempered system, the result of deliberate attempts to exploit the tonal vagueness and ambiguity of equal intervals.

The Two Cyclical Transpositions of the Whole-Tone Scale

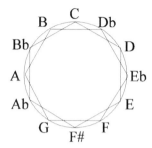

An examination of the whole-tone scale reveals that behind the gloss of mathematical perfection exist distinct irregularities which serve as pointers to the tonal and acoustic realities underlying the characteristic sound world of the whole-tone scale. When a series of pure whole-tone steps are taken from a given starting note, it is possible to ascend some five steps before the note A# is reached. A whole tone above note A# is not *C*, but *B#*. Because, in temperament, *B#* is enharmonically equivalent to *C*, the sixth step *A#/C* is lazily assumed to be coequal with a whole tone. But it is not a whole tone - it is a diminished third. Immediately therefore, the name whole-tone scale is in part illogical, as the scale is not made up of whole tones. It consists of five whole tones and a diminished third.

From this, it may be objected that the scale composers have in mind is one in which the octave is divided between six equal intervals. The naming of those intervals, and their imperfect expression in musical notation does not matter. Yet this objection misses the point. Because of the diminished third, there is a missing scale step implied. *A group of pitches may be very complexly related to each other* writes Ben Johnston, *but often all of them can be simply related to another pitch which need not even be present.*[1]

Lying between *A#* and *C* this missing scale step would be note B, in the case of the transposition *C D E F# G# A# C*. Viewed in these terms, the whole-tone scale is not even a complete scale - it is a species of hexatonic mode characterised by the presence of five adjacent whole tone steps and a diminished third.

---

[1] Ben Johnston, Scalar Order as a Compositional Resource, in: PNM 2/2, 1964, 61.

This serves to explain very much. Through omission of the seventh note B, the only point in the scale where a semitone would otherwise occur, the inherent tendencies of the scale to lead up or down to it are denied. That this tendency is implicit to the scale can be easily ascertained through the clue provided by for the diminished third. When opened out, the primary generating interval of the septimal matrix - the augmented sixth - is invoked, the interval which defines the gap between the declining and inclining tones so important for the definition of tonality at a chromatic level.

Accordingly, behind and beyond the whole-tone scale exist the shadows of firm tonal functions, the measure of which can be calculated from the missing tonic note which is B in the case of this particular transposition:

Functions of Notes in the Whole-Tone Scale

C	D	E	F#	G#	A#
Declining Tone	Minor Mediant	Subdom.	Dominant	Major Submed.	Inclining Tone

Spanning the interval of an augmented sixth between the supersemitone and subsemitone of the key concerned, it can be surmised that, like the 'Petrushka' scale mentioned earlier, the whole-tone scale represents the projection of a state of dominant tension brought about by its component dynamic intervals. Being composed of some three tritones a whole tone apart, the entire structure veritably bristles with dynamism. Looking at some of the types of chord which tend to occur within a whole-tone context, this factor is easily demonstrated:

Septimal Sonorities Present Within the Whole-Tone Scale

There, forming the backbone of each of those chords is the 7/4 relation - *C* to *A#* - which establishes the whole-tone scale both as a dynamically oriented pitch structure, and therefore a particular of the chromatic tonal system.

As a dynamic aggregate of musical tones, whose interrelationships speak of the union of some four dimensions of tonal space, it is evident that the whole-tone scale itself, possesses particular dominant leanings. Consequently, each of the chords presented above may be viewed as chromatic alterations of the chord of the dominant seventh or ninth of the key of B. Unless this book has failed in its purpose so far, the manner and method of their derivation from the dominant

434

chain, will already be evident to the reader. Suffice to say, viewing the whole-tone scale as a complete sonority, a chromatically altered dominant eleventh chord of the key of B is obtained:.

The Whole-Tone Scale as Arising from a Chromatically Altered Dominant Thirteenth

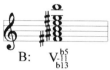

The dominant tensions present within the whole-tone scale succinctly implicate the missing tonic note of B. Accordingly, each species of whole-tone scale, depending upon the placement of the diminished third, can be attributed an implied note of resolution. This is the note which, lying between each appearance of the diminished third significant of the declining and inclining tones of the key concerned, is characteristically absent from the scale.

Because, in equal temperament, the diminished third is enharmonically identical to a whole tone, means that any one of the six whole tones can, through being thus spelled, imply an outlet to a particular note of resolution. Each of the two transpositions of the whole-tone scale thus offer potential outlets to six notes each. When the exact whole-tone scales relevant to these twelve notes of resolution are spelled correctly i.e. with recognition of the diminished third, the precise place of the whole-tone scale in the chromatic tonal system can be surmised:

The Twelve Transpositions of the Whole-Tone Scale

Implied Tone of Resolution	Transposition of Whole-Tone Scale					
Note C	Db	Eb	F	G	A	B
Note Db	Ebb	Fb	Gb	Ab	Bb	C
Note D	Eb	F	G	A	B	C#
Note Eb	Fb	Gb	Ab	Bb	C	D
Note E	F	.G	A	B	C#	D#
Note F	Gb	Ab	Bb	C	D	E
Note F#	G	A	B	C#	D#	E#
Note G	Ab	Bb	C	D	E	F#
Note Ab	Bbb	Cb	Db	Eb	F	G
Note A	Bb	C	D	E	F#	G#

Note Bb	Cb	Db	Eb	F	G	A
Note B	C	D	E	F#	G#	A#

Each transposition constitutes a species of chromatically altered dominant hexachord. There are twelve of these hexachords, one for each key of the chromatic tonal system. The function of the diminished third in each case is to act as the leader or prime representative of that dominant function.

When resolution of these dominant tendencies are persistently denied, that restless wandering quality which has been so well exploited in works such as Debussy's second piano prelude of 1910 entitled *Voiles*, begins to emerge. This wandering quality is tantamount to a state of atonality, a state achieved through a long-term prolongation of a septimal dominant

When chords based on it are resolved, it provides excellent opportunities, both for modulation, and integration with more diatonically oriented passages. This is done through treating the whole-tone scale consciously as an altered dominant, and offering it resolution to a particular tonic area. The possibilities which the whole-tone scale offers for integration with other scale systems, show that it bears a strong relationship to those systems.

The ascending form of the melodic minor mode already has four adjacent whole tones (a). Through the flattening of the second degree, the number of whole tones is increased to the full compliment of five (b). This alteration has the effect of focusing the dominant qualities of the mode along the tritonal axis aforementioned, in that it brings into play the pole of declination Observe that the scale manifests as two successive whole tones spanning a major third, constructed respectively upon the dominant pole and counterpole (c). Consequently, the whole-tone scale is an aggregation of symmetrical tonal elements built up around the dominant 'pole-counterpole' axis. This observation enables the definition of septimal ratios for the various notes of the whole-tone scale (d).

A brief examination of the whole-tone scale thus leads to the simple conclusion that it is a dynamic pitch structure, the use of which implies specific techniques of dominant prolongation. As such, it too can be claimed as part of the territory of the chromatic tonal system. What does this say of other pitch structures derived from the equally tempered twelve-tone scale? Do these too, have any basis in the network of natural relations implied by the harmonic series, or are they simply inventions of the human mind? As prime examples of structures which bear more of a kinship to the equally tempered chromatic scale, than any 'natural scale' evolved strictly from acoustically pure relationships, Messiaen's seven *Modes of Limited Transposition* come to mind.

436

The Dominant Pole and Counterpole as they Manifest in the Whole-Tone Scale

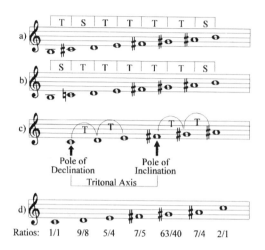

The whole-tone scale was claimed by Messiaen to be his *First Mode of Limited Transposition*.[1] Having assumed it into his modal system, Messiaen himself tended to moderate its use in his own works, observing that *Claude Debussy, in 'Pelléas et Mélisande', and after him Paul Dukas, in 'Ariane et Barbe-Bleue', have made such remarkable use of it that there is nothing more to add. Then we shall carefully avoid making use of it, unless it is concealed in a superposition of modes which renders it unrecognisable.*[2]

Despite being content to work within the confines of the equally tempered twelve-tone scale, Messiaen drew upon the natural relations implicit to the harmonic series in support of certain features of his unique modal and harmonic system. Discussing the particularities of his own musical language he offers a particular significance to the interval of the tritone, observing that *a very fine ear clearly perceives an F# in the natural resonance of a low C.*[3] Referring to the eleventh partial, he then goes on to observe that: *This F# is endowed with an attraction toward the C which becomes its normal resolution.*[4]

---

[1] For a resumeé of this system see Messiaen's Musical Language: an Introduction, by Anthony Pople, The Messiaen Companion, Edited by Peter Hill, Faber and Faber, London 1995, 17 - 30.

[2] Olivier Messiaen, Technique de mon Langage Musical, Vol. 1, Alphonse Leduc, Paris 1966, 59.

[3] Ibid., 31.

[4] Ibid., 31.

Consequently, he observes: *We are in the presence of the first interval to choose: the descending augmented fourth.*[1]

Although Messiaen presents us here with an acoustical criterion for his selection of this pitch relationship, there are shortcomings in his argument which indicate that the tritone relationship so often used in his music, and present in all seven of the *Modes of Limited Transposition* may not have any bearing on his initial observation. Exactly how the note F# is endowed with an attraction to the fundamental tone C, he omits to explain. Examples he gives do not help to explain this either. In *Example 70*, he ascribes to the eleventh harmonic the pitch class of F#, and the seventh harmonic the pitch class of Bb. The chord defined by this attribution of definitive pitch classes to the odd numbered harmonics up to the eleventh is a chromatically altered dominant eleventh chord. How it confers a sense of compelling attraction of the *F#* towards the *C* is difficult to imagine. It is more likely that the *F#* displays a tendency towards resolution to the major ninth of the implied *F* tonic chord:

Tendencies Towards Resolution of the Chromatically Altered Dominant Eleventh Chord Implied by Messiaen's 'Example 70'

Messiaen's subsequent example (*Example 71*) does even less to explain. Here, *F#* occurs in the context of an added note chord, as a major sixth above the note A. It thus manifests as a functionary of an apoggiatura chord. When resolved, the *F#* displays more of an attraction towards the note E, than note C, a tendency exacerbated by its major seventh relationship to the bass note G:

Apoggiatura Chord Presented in Messiaen's *Example 71*.

---

[1] Ibid., 31.

From the perspective of the theory of valency it is difficult to find corroboration for Messiaen's argument. The supporting six-four major triad invokes two mathematical dimensions of tone connection: the first signified by the third partial, seen in the perfect fourth (4/3), and the second signified by the fifth partial seen in the major third (5/4), and the major sixth (5/3) which results from their sum. The *A* and the *F#* manifest to the ear as that major sixth transposed up a whole tone. There is no overriding evidence in the examples which Messiaen presents, for the existence or portrayal of a new mathematical dimension of tonal space that would justify identifying *F#* with the eleventh partial.

If there ever was any sense of attraction of *F#*, viewed as the eleventh harmonic, towards the fundamental tone C, then it could only be in a conceptual sense, based on the notion that the ear resolves the mathematically regular partials of a given note into the experience of a single pitch whose frequency conforms to the fundamental tone. In this sense Messiaen seems to have created a tonal function after the example of an acoustic principle, rather than a true acoustical process.

From a consideration of the constitution of the whole-tone scale it becomes apparent that the seventh, rather than the eleventh harmonic, may have more of a bearing on Messiaen's system of modes. His 'Second Mode of Limited Transposition' is a good case in point. Known as the octatonic scale, it is readily characterised by an alternating pattern of semitones and tones:

The Octatonic Scale

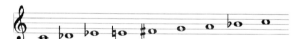

This particular scale, like the whole-tone scale that precedes it in Messiaen's system, has been used extensively by composers. Rimsky-Korsakov (1844 - 1908) used it in his opera *Sadko* of 1867, and it was used by Eastern composers such as Scriabin, Stravinsky, Kodaly and Bartók. Messiaen admits this observing that *one already finds traces of it in Sadko by Rimsky-Korsakov; Scriabine uses it in a more conscious fashion; Ravel and Stravinsky have used it transiently.*[1]

One of the interesting features of this scale, is that the unit of semitone-tone repeated every minor third brings into focus a sharp foursquare division of the

---

[1] Messiaen, Op. Cit., 59. But see Arthur Berger's Problems of Pitch Organisation in Stravinsky, in: PNM II, 1963, 11 - 42, where the author demonstrates that Stravinsky's use of the octatonic pitch collection is anything but transient.

musical octave circumscribed by the notes *C Eb F# A*. The other four notes of the scale, being a semitone higher, also invoke a diminished seventh chord: *Db E G Bb*. As there are only three diminished seventh chords in the tempered scale, and the octatonic scale uses two of them, means that, like the whole-tone scale, the octatonic scale represents a rational geometric partitioning of the chromatic continuum.[1]

The Octatonic Scale Within the Chromatic Circle

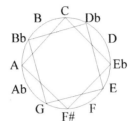

Its musical effects succinctly depend upon the presence of those dynamic septimal intervals present within it. The salient septimal interval is the tritone between the notes C and F# (ratio of 7/5). Providing the basis for the pole-counterpole relationship, the octatonic scale is an explicit product of the use of that relationship within the terms of a dynamic cycle of dominant prolongation.

In Mussorgsky's *Boris Gudonov* there is a passage already referred to in which the harmony oscillates between pole and counterpole, represented by two dominant seventh chords whose roots are a tritone apart, for some 46 measures. Representing a fascinating example of dominant prolongation, these already account for some six notes of the octatonic collection. All that remains is to bring in the other dyadic axis as implied by that complete square of tonality, to result in the full octatonic scale.

The Octatonic Pitch Collection as a Manifestation of the Square of Tonality

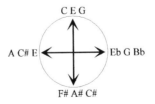

[1] Richard Taruskin; Chernomor to Kaschei: Harmonic Sorcery: or Stravinsky's 'Angle', in: JAMS 38, Spring 1985, 77 - 142.

440

Here the octatonic scale is completely defined by the sum of four major triads, whose roots define the square concerned. In this passage from *Quatour pour la fin du temps* (1941) Messiaen admirably exploits these triadic possibilities:

Excerpt from the Seventh Movement of Messiaen's *Quatour pour la fin du temps*.

Because composers employing this scale system are operating within a tempered format, means that it is possible to extend each triad into a chord of the dominant seventh, and each dominant seventh into a dominant ninth. Additionally, triads may be enriched using added note harmony, a technique which Messiaen himself was extremely fond.[1] In this respect, Paul Griffifths observes that *the second mode lends itself to the dominant seventh, diminished seventh and added sixth chords that are the main pillars of Messiaen's harmony in the Banquet Cèleste and much later music.*[2]

The important issue with the octatonic scale therefore, is not so much the type of chords used within it, for whether major, minor, dominant seventh, chromatically altered or added note, the salient feature is that perfectly balanced scheme of septimal root polarity which it presents, in which the principal dyadic axis (C - $F\#$) is counterbalanced by the secondary dyadic axis (Eb - A) to result in a dynamic fourfold cycle of dominant prolongation.

This feature of being able to suspend tonality through techniques of dominant prolongation is a property shared by the other 'Modes of Limited

---

[1] Messiaen, Volume 2, Langage, Ex. 317.

[2] Paul Griffifths, Oliver Messiaen and the Music of Time, Faber and Faber, London 1985, 30.

Transposition'. Mode three is a good example. Here the generating pattern of the mode is a tone, followed by two semitones:

In similarity to the other modes of transposition, it reveals a number of rational mathematical features which allow it to operate so well in a twelve-tone context. Unlike the octatonic scale which relates to the square and thereby an equal fourfold division of the octave, this mode may be viewed as an evolution of mode one, in that it puts emphasis upon the augmented triad, and therefore an equal threefold division of the octave.

The whole-tone scale results from the two of the four possible transpositions of the augmented triad. This mode utilises three of the four possible transpositions. In this way the development of modes one through to three can be traced through the multiplication of equal structures leading up to the complete dodecaphonic scale.

Relationship Between Modes One, Two and Three

	Threefold Division	Fourfold Division
One transposition:	Augmented triad	Diminished seventh
Two transpositions:	Mode one	Mode two
Three transpositions:	Mode three	Dodecaphonic scale
Four transpositions:	Dodecaphonic scale	- - - - - - - - - - - - - -

These features constitute only one facet of its nature. Behind the dodecaphonic element exists the tonally controlling powers of the dynamic intervals present within it. These become apparent when it is realised that each transposition of mode three is an enharmonic unification of three separate transpositions, which differ essentially in their spelling.

Unification of the Three Transpositions of Mode Three a Major Third/Diminished Fourth Apart

Transposition	As Generated from Note C
C D Eb E F# G Ab Bb B	C D Eb E F# G Ab Bb B
E F# G Ab Bb B C D Eb	C D Eb Fb Gb G Ab Bb Cb
Ab Bb B C D Eb E F# G	C D D# E F# G G# A# B

The entire idea of 'limited transposition' is thus a relative concept based on the assumption of enharmonic equivalence. This forms part of that 'charm of impossibilities' that attracted Messiaen to these modes, for if that assumption is not upheld, each mode has twelve transpositions. At the enharmonic level, one of the most important features of this mode are the tritones, of which there are three: *C/F#*; *D/Ab* and *E/Bb*. These, it will be seen, collectively define the first mode of limited transposition - the whole-tone scale.

The third mode of transposition, consists of this (the whole-tone scale) plus the three additional notes *Eb*, *G* and *B*. Now the tritone may be regarded as the simplest possible expression of the bipolarisation of dominant forces in that, of the two notes belonging to the tritone, one may be viewed as the dominant pole, the other as the dominant counterpole.

Therefore, in terms of the first tritone, notes C and F#, there is a mutual leaning towards the note B. In terms of the second tritone, *Ab* to *D*, there is a leaning towards note G; whilst the third tritone exerts a leaning towards note Eb. In this way, the tonal leanings of the three tritones implicit to the whole-tone scale, implicate the three additional notes of Eb, G and B. This can be easily confirmed through a consideration of the various types of septimal chord implied by this mode.

Septimal Chords Implied by Mode Three

This mode therefore implicates more than one tonality at the same time, thus corroborating Messiaen's theoretical observation that *they are at once in the atmosphere of several tonalities, without polytonality, the composer being free to give predominance to one of the tonalities, or to leave the tonal impression unsettled.*[1] The tonalities concerned are those belonging to the major trine, in which *G* may be regarded to be the principal tonic, *Eb* the sub-major pole, and *B* the super-major pole. Mode 3, by virtue of its extremely powerful dynamic components, is thus identifiable as being a part of the territory of the chromatic tonal system.

These observations shed much light on the other modes of transposition. Of the four remaining, mode six will be considered first, as modes four, five and seven can be considered as a group. In mode six the order of intervals is two tones, followed by two semitones, an order which is repeated twice in the octave. That the note at which this order is repeated is a tritone above the

---

[1] Messiaen, Langage, 58.

starting note, makes for a mode which at first sight looks like a hybrid of the scales of C and F# major:

The Sixth Mode of Limited Transposition

Perhaps it is in this sense that Gustav Holst used a scale coincidentally the same as the sixth 'Mode of Limited Transposition' as one of the important devices for the generation of material for *Mercury, the Winged Messenger*, movement of his *The Planet's Suite*. Possessing a hybrid character, it succinctly expresses the dual nature of the hermaphroditic divinity of Mercury.

An examination of the Sixth Mode of Limited Transposition shows that it offers a prime model of the implications of the reversal of polarity between the dominant poles and counterpoles as they relate to the septimal tritonal axis C/F# (7/5). The implications of chromatically altered dominant harmony of a whole-tone scale constructed upon note C have already been commented upon. Here can be seen a scale that not only embraces those implications, but offers the prime tone of their resolution, which of course is note B. What then, of the note F? The placement of this note can be understood as the manifestation of the tonic counterpole, brought into being through the reversal of polarity aforementioned. Through the enharmonic switch of F# for *Gb*, note C then becomes the dominant pole, and note Gb the dominant counterpole, in which the tone of resolution is *F*. This can be understood from the following diagram:

Basic Tonal Dynamics of Mode Six

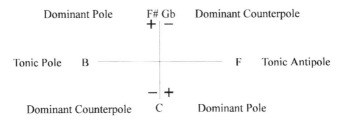

Mode six thus presupposes an enharmonic fusion of two transpositions of this mode - the transpositions on *C* and *Gb* respectively. It is this process of fusion which enables chords arising from this mode to function either as septimal dominants of *F* or *B*, or, if the necessity arises, to function ambiguously between the tonic pole and counterpole. This succinct

444

ambiguously between the tonic pole and counterpole. This succinct interbalancing of tonal forces present within these tonal models becomes especially apparent in the fourth, fifth and seventh modes, which can be considered together as a group. Here, curious though it may seem, the first mode of the group is mode five.

The Fifth Mode of Limited Transposition

Here every note can be accounted for in what to all extents and purposes represents a perfect interlocking of septimal functions. The best way to explain this is diagrammatically, it being understood that the significance of the terms used has been discussed already:

The Tonal Dynamics of Mode Five

C	Db	F	F#	G	B
TP	DCP			DP	
DP		TCP	DCP		

Note:-

TP	=	Tonic Pole
TCP	=	Tonic Counterpole
DP	=	Dominant Pole
DCP	=	Dominant Counterpole

It is the augmented sixth chords constructed either on note G or Db which enable the notes C or F# to be implicated as prospective tonic notes. Their tritone relationship casts them up as belonging to a pole-counterpole relationship. From an examination of the diagram, it can be seen just why mode five should actually precede mode four. This is because mode four involves the addition of a new polar term to the equation - the tritone between notes D and Ab.

The Fourth Mode of Limited Transposition

This means that the network of functions manifested by mode five, has been further extended and complexified in the following way:

The Tonal Dynamics of Mode Four

C	Db	D	F	F#	G	Ab	B
TP	DCP				DP		
DP				TCP	DCP		
TP	DCP					DP	
DP					TCP	DCP	

The mode, as seen in this way, embraces two transpositions of mode five a semitone apart. Its possibilities thus devolve around the pair of dyadic axes *C - F#* and *Db - G*, constituting as it does, a sum of musical impulses in which every note is mutually dependent upon every other note. The result is a perfect mathematical configuration of tonal forces which brings to mind that intricate balance of force present and participating within the world of the atom. It thus becomes apparent that the mode can be extended through the addition of further axes, and it is in this context that the final mode of transposition - mode seven can be understood:

The Seventh Mode of Limited Transposition

Here, there is yet another axis added to the previous mode, which exists between the notes Eb and A. The result, therefore, is a further complexification of the network of note functions as follows:

The Tonal Dynamics of Mode Seven

C	Db	D	Eb	F	F#	G	Ab	A	B
TP	DCP					DP			
DP					TCP	DCP			

TP   DCP   DP
DP   TCP   DCP
TP   DCP   DP
DP   TCP   DCP

This final 'Mode of Limited Transposition' leads inevitably to that unmentioned eighth mode which has only one possible transposition - the complete chromatic scale which apparently represents the host system to the seven modes considered so far. All that remains to obtain this mode is the addition of a final tritonal term to the ten notes present in mode seven. When this is done, something very interesting emerges, for the result is a picture of the tonal dynamics of the twelve-tone scale as revealed from a septimal viewpoint:

The Tonal Dynamics of the Twelve Tone Scale

C	Db	D	Eb	E	F	F#	G	Ab	A	Bb	B
DCP											DP
TP											
DP					TCP	DCP					
	TP	DCP					DP				
	DP					TCP	DCP				
		TP	DCP					DP			
		DP					TCP	DCP			
			TP	DCP					DP		
			DP					TCP	DCP		
				TP	DCP					DP	
				DP					TCP	DCP	
					TP	DCP					DP
					DP					TCP	DCP
						TP					

From this it can be seen that every note of the tempered scale may serve as the dominant pole, the dominant counterpole and the implied tonic and tonic counterpole. Here the most important observation to be made is that all twelve notes of the scale have established themselves as functional equals. In terms of the aggregate of note functions there is thus no sense of hierarchical subordination to any other note. From this perspective, the total network of septimal relations implied by the scale is thus indicative of a maternal or host state which could only be best described by the term atonality.

To be able to achieve that state many more notes are required, a complete enharmonic scale (at least) which embraces the sharp or flat required depending upon the particular instance. In this sense, the state of atonality being referred to is dependent upon that matrix of septimal functions already discussed in this book so far.

The 'Modes of Limited Transposition', are simply selections from the total network of impulses implied by the chromatic scale as a whole. The success of such a selection depends upon a successful integration of the note functions present within each mode. Here, the salient factor was discovered to be the tritonal axes which ensured that the lattice of functions remained essentially balanced. Having made that selection it becomes apparent that the composer could utilise its inherent dynamics in various ways. Here, there are a number of what could best be termed fundamental choices which devolve around the respective functions of tonic and dominant.

The tendencies of dominant forces to resolve to a particular tonal point can be exploited to give a sense of tonal centricity. Alternatively, those tendencies can be suppressed to create a sense of atonality. In doing so, the dominant principle is being subjected to prolongation techniques the most essential factor of which again, is the tritone, for it is the tritone which permitting alternation between poles without any recognisable change of function, prevents a sense of stasis. In this sense, all of the 'Modes of Limited Transposition' are simply an extension of that very principle of dominant prolongation.

All of these possibilities entirely depend upon the growth of dominant functions through the mathematical domain of the prime number seven. The extent of this growth is to create and mark out entirely new dominant possibilities and structures which by their nature allow the precise control and/or suppression of tonality. Viewed from this perspective, the tritone is representative of a bipolar oscillation which when set up, suspends either the need or desire for resolution to a tonic principle.

In that such a state can feasibly deny the tonic principle altogether, means that through the prime number seven it is possible to achieve a dynamic (as opposed to stagnant) state of atonality. From this perspective, the chromatic tonal system represents the point of flux between those two apparently opposite states: a state of tonality, which may be defined as the eternal attraction of the tonic towards the dominant, and the dominant towards the tonic, and a state of atonality which may be defined as the tonic principle which forever repels the dominant, and the dominant which forever repels the tonic. The chromatic tonal system thus constitutes the quintessential territory defined by their mutual interaction:

The Chromatic Tonal System as the Point of Flux Between the Tonal and Atonal States

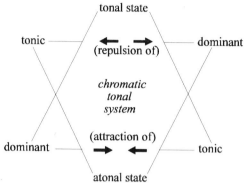

In this context tonality may be defined as being the prolongation of the tonic principle, atonality the prolongation of the dominant principle. The basic principle underlying chromatic music is that it thus represents nothing more than an extended I - V - I progression, the V in this case, being the dominant function vastly upgraded in accordance with the dictates of the septimal matrix. If Schenker's theories were eventually to be updated in order to account for chromatic and even some types of atonal music,[1] it is undoubtedly the role of septimal intervals as the generators of a dynamic universe of dominant forces, that would need to be looked at as a first principle.

From a theoretical standpoint, there are some difficulties, especially in terms of the apparent conflict between the equally tempered chromatic system, and the more dimly perceived shadow of the enharmonic system. For a composer to notate every shade and inflection of the implied voice leading in order to accurately account for the precise behaviour of every single tone would be tedious and impractical. But this is no reason to deny the reality concealed behind the notational appearance. The tempered system leads to a very simple method of musical notation which is often very convenient. Because the notational system does not have the symbols to express the exact implications of the chords used at every point, does not invalidate the nature of the chords themselves. It simply means that the complexities of septimal influences are being expressed through the medium of an imperfect scalar and notational system.

---

[1] 'theorists such as Gregory Proctor and Patrick McCreless, claim that Schenker's methods must be expanded by new theories of chromatic tonality in order to cope with this repertory'. William J. Mitchel, A Study of Chromaticism, in: JMT 6/1, 1962, 2.

THE UNIFICATION OF MODAL RESOURCES UNDER THE COVER OF THE ENHARMONIC SCALE

The trend of the last few chapters of this book has been towards the understanding and definition of the various states and conditions characteristic of the chromatic system of tonality as defined by the interweave of the second, third, fifth and seventh prime numbers. To accomplish this it became necessary to look behind the facade of equal temperament, and the loose though convenient methods of pitch notation associated with it, in order to expose the role that septimal intervals were playing within the music concerned.

The focus has never been on what might or could be, simply the interpretation of what has transpired musically during the period under consideration. Emphasis has been placed on the vertical element of harmony, not because of a desire to undermine the importance of voice leading, but because it is in this area that the influence of the prime number seven has had the most fertile effect. Here, it became important to accord recognition to the fact that the seventh harmonic is participating in many musical phenomenon, and that the sum of those phenomenon in their entirety, comprise the chromatic system of tonality.

From a consideration of the vertical element of musical harmony, a further issue arose as a by-product of those considerations, and that was the crystallisation of precise scalar functions which not only transcended the chromatic scale, but served as the basis for the establishment of a new more refined nineteen-tone scale in which septimal elements could be demonstrated to play a part. Although initially arising as a by-product this is an extremely important area for it contains within it the idea that the chromatic tonal system, like the diatonic system with its major and minor scales, possesses its own set of scales which stand as the natural successors to the major and minor modes. In this chapter the precise nature of these scales and their modal derivatives will be considered, together with how they stand and relate to their host system, the enharmonic scale.

The necessity for a precise definition of the chromatic tonal system and its body of scales is long overdue. The modal poverty of the major/minor system when compared to the modal system that preceded it is well charted. Through the nineteenth and early twentieth centuries continual attempts were made by composers to expand upon those limited resources, either through the use of chromaticism, or reference to other scalar models. One of the most celebrated and oft discussed examples is of course Beethoven's *String Quartet in A minor*, Opus 132, with its 'Lydian' first movement. Brahm's *Chorale*, Opus 62, no. 7 is similarly modeled on one of the old modes, although here the scalar model is the Dorian mode. Liszt (1811 - 1886), in his *Hungarian Rhapsodies* stretched the major/minor system through reference to Gypsy scales, characterised by their minor lower tetrachord and sharp fourth degree.

Since then, through the diverse influences of folk music, exotic sources, and Eastern influences, a veritable plethora of new scales has entered into the Western musical vocabulary, not least of which are the pentatonic scales of both Western folk and Oriental music, the 'Blues scale' of Jazz, scales based on Hindu 'raga' prototypes, or the melodic formulae of Hebrew cantillation. Then there are the loosely termed 'artificial scales', so called because, not seeming to have an outside point of reference, perform a purely local referential role in relation to a particular musical composition or group of compositions. Ferrucio Busoni (1866 - 1924) in his *Sketch of a New Esthetic Music* succinctly commented upon this trend as it appeared in his own time, observing that *some few have already felt how the intervals of seven might be differently arranged (graduated) is manifested in isolated passages by Liszt, and recently by Debussy and his followers....Yet it does not appear to me that a conscious and orderly conception of this intensified means of expression had been formed by these composers.*[1]

Busoni's attempts towards this end were accomplished empirically through raising and lowering the intervals of the seven toned scale, to result in *establishing one hundred and thirteen different scales.*[2] Since then Barbour has pointed out that according to the system devised by Busoni, there is actually more than 113 scales implied,[3] whilst Robert Mason has invoked the aid of matrix algebra in order to calculate the precise number of modes generated according to Busoni's system of evaluation.[4] The central problem with this approach is that it abstracts the issue from the innumerable musical problems in which the ideas and processes of scalar generation are embodied. Rather than

---

[1] Ferruccio Busoni, Nature, and the Reformer, Sketch of a New Esthetic of Music, 29.

[2] Ibid.

[3] J. Murray Barbour, Musical Scales and their Classification, in: JASA 21/6, Nov. 1949, 586 - 589. See also Synthetic Musical Scales, in: AMM 36, March 1929, 155 - 160.

[4] Robert Mason, Enumeration of Synthetic Musical Scales by Matrix Algebra and a Catalogue of Busoni Scales, in: JMT 14/1,1970.

solving any problems therefore, it simply evades them by placing the focus on enumeration and calculation. This in its turn prevents an overview of the single unified system from which all of these scales actually originate - the chromatic tonal system.

As a necessary upgrading of the chromatic scale, both in accordance with harmonic practice, and the new mathematical dimension of musical logic implicated by that practice (prime number seven), the enharmonic scale provides the key by which to understand, elucidate and systematise that new body of musical modes implicated by late nineteenth and twentieth century musical practice. The precise nature of that body of modes can be approached in the first instance through looking at the precise structure of the major and minor modes themselves. The major mode is comprised of two disjunct diatonic tetrachords which for ease reference can be described as the lower and the upper tetrachords:

The Major Mode and its Two Disjunct Diatonic Tetrachords

Note:	C	D	E	F	G	A	B	C
Ratio:	1/1	9/8	5/4	4/3	3/2	5/3	15/8	2/1
Tetrachord:	I	II	III	IV	I	II	III	IV
	Diatonic Lower Tetrachord				Diatonic Upper Tetrachord			

The minor modes distinguish themselves from the major by virtue of their different tetrachordal structure:

Tetrachordal Structure of the Harmonic and Melodic Minor Modes

Note:	C	D	Eb	F	G	Ab	B	C
Ratio:	1/1	9/8	6/5	4/3	3/2	8/5	15/8	2/1

Note:	C	D	Eb	F	G	A	B	C
Ratio:	---	---	---	---	---	5/3	---	---

Note:	C	D	Eb	F	G	Ab	Bb	C
Ratio:	---	---	---	---	---	8/5	16/9	---

Tetrachords:	I	II	III	IV	I	II	III	IV
		Lower Tetrachord				Upper Tetrachord		

Observe that combining all upper tetrachords leads to a full chromatic definition of the fourth between dominant and tonic. However the combination of lower tetrachords leads only to a partial chromatic definition of the fourth between tonic and subdominant, the missing note being *Db*. Through the creation of a satisfactory harmonic function for the note Db (the dominant counterpole), it becomes possible to complete the lower tetrachord and obtain a more or less full compliment of notes.

Looking at the eleven-note pitch array which results from the inclusion of the note Db, it will be seen that an equal number of tetrachords is implicated in both upper and lower halves of the octave. Excluding repetitions of the same interval category i.e. a major and a minor third being placed together in the same tetrachord, some four different types of tetrachord are possible:

Tetrachords Implied by Eleven Note Sub-chromatic Scale

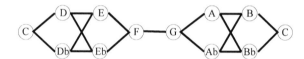

Of the four tetrachords, three are recognisable as being diatonic tetrachords, composed of two tones and a semitone, whilst one may be classified as a chromatic tetrachord, composed as it is of two semitones and an augmented second:

The Four Types of Tetrachords

C	Db	Eb	F	
	16/15	9/8	10/9	Soft Diatonic

C	D	Eb	F	
	9/8	16/15	10/9	Neutral Diatonic

C	D	E	F	
	9/8	10/9	16/15	Acute Diatonic

C	Db	E	F	
	16/15	75/64	16/15	Chromatic

Because there are four tetrachords in the lower half and four tetrachords in the upper half, means that the eleven-note chromatic pitch array automatically implicates a formative spectrum of sixteen modes. However, this offers a rather limited view of modal possibility, as it arises in relation to the foundation scale provided by a purely chromatic division of the octave. Therefore, it represents only a partial view of the complete modal scheme which arises at the chromatic level of tonality. When the available pitch resources are opened out from the chromatic to the fully formed enharmonic scale, a number of significant expansions upon the original chromatic modal possibility become apparent.

A diatonic tetrachord is made up of two whole tones and a semitone. In a chromatic tetrachord, one of the whole tones is widened to give a tetrachord which is usually described as consisting of a minor third and two semitones. However, this is illogical, as an expanded whole tone does not give a minor third. The concept of a 'tone' of whatever size, derives from the relationship between two adjacent modal degrees, whilst a minor third is an interval between three modal degrees.

A minor third may be understood as a compressed ditone, but an expanded tone is just that - a whole tone interval between adjacent modal degrees which has become enlarged or augmented. Its expansion gives an interval of an augmented second. In the harmonic minor mode this can be seen in the relationship between the sixth and seventh modal degrees - the augmented second between notes Ab and B.

The harmonic minor mode thus belongs to a different order of modes than the major, and melodic minor modes, which are composed solely of diatonic tetrachords of various derivations. The factor that establishes that it belongs to a different category is the presence of the augmented second between the sixth and seventh degrees. The augmented second is not a diatonic interval - it is a chromatic interval.

Here it proves interesting to look at the precise ratio of this interval when calculated from the ratios of the harmonic minor mode in just intonation. Its ratio is 15/8 - 1088 cents - (the ratio of the leading note) minus 8/5 - 814 cents - (the ratio of the minor submediant degree) which equals 75/64 - 274 cents. This becomes a salient observation when it is recalled that the interval between the seventh and sixth harmonics (267 cents) is only some 7 cents removed from the augmented second of ratio 75/64. The augmented second present in the harmonic minor mode, thus offers a distinct presentiment of this particular septimal interval

This presentiment is reinforced by the relationship between subdominant and submediant degrees - F and Ab - for the interval between them is a minor third of ratio 6/5. Consequently, notes F, Ab and B, considered as a unit, offer a presentiment of the fifth, sixth and seventh harmonics. When the flattened supertonic, note Db is brought into the picture, the result is the German Sixth chord defined by the fourth, fifth, sixth and seventh harmonics. Here it is noteworthy to observe that the principle feature which the septimal tones belonging to the enharmonic scale contribute to the modal scheme is chromatic tetrachords of various types.

The logic of this can be understood from a consideration of the harmonic series. When tone seven of a harmonic series constructed upon note C, is identified as note A#, this means that the interval between the sixth and the seventh harmonics is the augmented second between notes G and A#. Harmonics 6, 7, and 8 considered as a unit give rise to a three note figure defined by the notes G, A# and C. Between *A#* and *C*, the interval of a diminished third, another pitch value is implied. The identity of this pitch value can be discovered from the observation that the augmented second implies continuation upwards by a semitone, rather than progressing straight to the eighth partial. Note A# therefore invokes the use of the fifteenth partial in the following tetrachordal progression:

Chromatic Tetrachord Implied by the Seventh Harmonic

Note:	G		A#		B		C
Ratio:	3/2		7/4		15/8		2/1
Interval:		7/6		15/14		16/15	

The extra note implied is thus *B*, the fifteenth harmonic of note C. The chromatic unit represented by the notes A#, B and C thus represents harmonics 14, 15, and 16, from which it can be deduced that the seventh harmonic implies a chromatic, as opposed to diatonic tetrachord. Within the diatonic tonal system, the nearest equivalent is the chromatic tetrachord found in the harmonic form of the minor mode.

The enharmonic scale offers six possible lower tetrachords, three of which are diatonic, and three of which are chromatic:

Lower Tetrachords in the Enharmonic Scale

C	Db	Eb	F		C	Db	Ebb	F	
16/15	9/8	10/9		Soft Diatonic	16/15	15/14	7/6		Soft Chromatic

C	D	Eb	F		C	Db	E	F	
9/8	16/15	10/9		Neutral Diatonic	16/15	75/64	16/15		Neutral Chromatic

C	D	E	F		C	D#	E	F	
9/8	10/9	16/15		Acute Diatonic	7/6	15/14	16/15		Acute Chromatic

In the case of the upper tetrachord there are also six which are:

Upper Tetrachords in the Enharmonic Scale

G	Ab	Bb	C	
	16/15	10/9	9/8	Soft Diatonic

G	Ab	Bbb	C	
	16/15	15/14	7/6	Soft Chromatic

G	A	Bb	C	
	10/9	16/15	9/8	Neutral Diatonic

G	Ab	B	C	
	16/15	75/64	16/15	Neutral Chromatic

G	A	B	C	
	10/9	9/8	16/15	Acute Diatonic

G	A#	B	C	
	7/6	15/14	16/15	Acute Chromatic

There being six tetrachords in the lower half, six in the upper half of the octave, means that the enharmonic scale thus implies thirty-six basic modes.

Mode 1:1	C	Db	Eb	F	G	Ab	Bb	C
Mode 1:2	C	Db	Eb	F	G	A	Bb	C
Mode 1:3	C	Db	Eb	F	G	A	B	C
Mode 1:4	C	Db	Eb	F	G	Ab	Bbb	C
Mode 1:5	C	Db	Eb	F	G	Ab	B	C
Mode 1:6	C	Db	Eb	F	G	A#	B	C
Mode 2:1	C	D	Eb	F	G	Ab	Bb	C
Mode 2:2	C	D	Eb	F	G	A	Bb	C
Mode 2:3	C	D	Eb	F	G	A	B	C
Mode 2:4	C	D	Eb	F	G	Ab	Bbb	C
Mode 2:5	C	D	Eb	F	G	Ab	B	C
Mode 2:6	C	D	Eb	F	G	A#	B	C
Mode 3:1	C	D	E	F	G	Ab	Bb	C
Mode 3:2	C	D	E	F	G	A	Bb	C
Mode 3:3	C	D	E	F	G	A	B	C
Mode 3:4	C	D	E	F	G	Ab	Bbb	C
Mode 3:5	C	D	E	F	G	Ab	B	C
Mode 3:6	C	D	E	F	G	A#	B	C
Mode 4:1	C	Db	Ebb	F	G	Ab	Bb	C
Mode 4:2	C	Db	Ebb	F	G	A	Bb	C
Mode 4:3	C	Db	Ebb	F	G	A	B	C
Mode 4:4	C	Db	Ebb	F	G	Ab	Bbb	C
Mode 4:5	C	Db	Ebb	F	G	Ab	B	C
Mode 4:6	C	Db	Ebb	F	G	A#	B	C
Mode 5:1	C	Db	E	F	G	Ab	Bb	C
Mode 5:2	C	Db	E	F	G	A	Bb	C
Mode 5:3	C	Db	E	F	G	A	B	C
Mode 5:4	C	Db	E	F	G	Ab	Bbb	C
Mode 5:5	C	Db	E	F	G	Ab	B	C

Mode 5:6	C	Db	E	F	G	A#	B	C
Mode 6:1	C	D#	E	F	G	Ab	Bb	C
Mode 6:2	C	D#	E	F	G	A	Bb	C
Mode 6:3	C	D#	E	F	G	A	B	C
Mode 6:4	C	D#	E	F	G	Ab	Bbb	C
Mode 6:5	C	D#	E	F	G	Ab	B	C
Mode 6:6	C	D#	E	F	G	A#	B	C

Here is the main group of modes which have interested twentieth century composers, which include the five basic diatonic modes of Renaissance polyphony: the Phrygian, Aeolian, Dorian, Mixolydian and Ionian modes, the major and minor modes, various chromatic modes including the double-harmonic mode (5:5), or the harmonic major mode (3:5) so suggestive of oriental and Asian music, the leading whole tone scale (1:3) and other such heptatonic modal formulae which depend upon an advantageous placing of the dominant counterpole.[1] In explanation of the modal number system used, the thirty-six modes divide into six groups of six as determined by the nature of the lower tetrachord. Assigning those numbers to each type of tetrachord as seen in the original scheme above, means that any of these modes may be represented as a combination of numbers.

In six of these modes both numbers are the same. This means that they have the same tetrachord in both upper and lower halves of the octave. Accordingly, these modes may be described as *fixed* modes, as opposed to the *mutable* modes which have different tetrachords in each modal segment. Each group of six modes is characterised by one fixed mode, whose name defines the nature of the lower tetrachord of each group, and five mutable modes. The fixed modes, and the group of six modes to which they belong, may be assigned names because of their distinctive tetrachordal content:

Fixed Modes (with Matching Lower and Upper Tetrachords)

Mode				Note set					Name
1:1	C	Db	Eb	F	G	Ab	Bb	C	Soft Diatonic
2:2	C	D	Eb	F	G	A	Bb	C	Neutral Diatonic
3:3	C	D	E	F	G	A	B	C	Acute Diatonic
4:4	C	Db	Ebb	F	G	Ab	Bbb	C	Soft Chromatic
5:5	C	Db	E	F	G	Ab	B	C	Neutral Chromatic
6:6	C	D#	E	F	G	A#	B	C	Acute Chromatic

---

[1] The names for modes 5:5, 3:5 and 1:3 were suggested by Persichetti in his Twentieth Century Harmony, Faber and Faber Ltd., London 1961, 44.

There are six modes (one fixed and five mutable) belonging to the soft diatonic group, six to the soft chromatic group, etc. Every mode has a mirror image. The mirror image of mode 1:1 is mode 3:3, and visa versa. Some modes, when mirrored give rise to the same mode i.e. they are symmetrical. Two of the above modes, namely 2:2 and 5:5, display this property. These two belong to another group of six symmetrical modes:

Symmetrical Heptatonic Modes

1:3	C	Db	Eb	F	G	A	B	C
2:2	C	D	Eb	F	G	A	Bb	C
3:1	C	D	E	F	G	Ab	Bb	C
4:6	C	Db	Ebb	F	G	A#	B	C
5:5	C	Db	E	F	G	Ab	B	C
6:4	C	D#	E	F	G	Ab	Bbb	C

There are only two modes possessing the same tetrachordal structure in both halves, and displaying the properties of mirror symmetry. These are the primary modes of the group: mode 2:2, which represents the primary diatonic mode, and mode 5:5, which represents the primary chromatic mode. That the neutral chromatic mode results from chromatic alteration of the neutral diatonic mode, means that the basic mode of the entire chromatic tonal system is the neutral diatonic (or Dorian mode).

The spectrum of modes obtained so far is still incomplete. This is because it assumes the immutability of the three perfect degrees of the scale as they provide the basis for the tetrachordal frame. In practice, composers often use modes with a sharp fourth, an extremely obvious example of which is the Lydian mode:

The Lydian Mode with its Sharp Fourth

I	II	III	IV	V	VI	VII	I
C	D	E	F#	G	A	B	C

To sharpen the fourth is to negate the strength of the subdominant. Within the terms of the diatonic system of tonality this is problematic. Within the terms of the chromatic system such problems are lessened by those representatives of the dominant and subdominant functions as they appear in the representative forms of their corresponding counterpoles: the supersemitone in the case of the dominant, and the subsemitone in the case of the subdominant.

The facility for the use of such functions within a chromatic context solves many of the problems associated with this type of mode, especially the newfound role of the subsemitonal triad in defining the pitch of the tonic. Given that such problems can be solved, what is this note F# that tends to infringe upon the immutability of the three perfect degrees of the scale? From where does it stem, and what function does it perform? Is it a manifestation of the tonic counterpole, or is it something else altogether? Such are the types of question which arise in relation to the sharp fourth of the diatonic Lydian mode.

Having a ratio within the chromatic tonal system of 7/5, it represents the dominant inclining tone, and thus offers septimal support for that tonic-dominant axis which provides the backbone of the most popular modal forms. But there is more to it than that. As a nodal point approximately midway between the octave, it offers a counter-statement of the original axis in which the tonic then appears as the diminished fifth:

Primary and Counter Axes in the Sharp Fourth Tetrachordal Scheme

C	F#	C
1/1	7/5	2/1

F#	C	F#
1/1	10/7	2/1

The diminished fifth axis is an integral feature of certain modes, of which the much-neglected Locrian mode provides a fine example.

The Locrian Mode with its Flat Fifth

I	II	III	IV	V	VI	VII	VIII
B	C	D	E	F	G	A	B
Tonic							

The Lydian and Locrian modes thus represent two sides of the same problem. The Lydian mode compromises the triangle of tonality through the sharpening of the subdominant, whilst the Locrian mode compromises it through the flattening of the dominant. The Lydian and Locrian modes are thus strongly related, for one becomes the other through an exchange of tonic along that tritonal axis:

Connection Between Lydian and Locrian Modes Through Exchange of Tonic Along Tritonal Axis

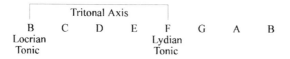

The feature both types of mode have in common is that they are both stretched across the framework of that powerful tritone bipole (7/5). Modes with a sharp fourth or flat fifth thus possess both a tonic pole and counterpole. The significance of this needs to be gauged in the light of the loss of the integrity of either the dominant or subdominant principle depending upon which type is being considered. In replacement of that lost element, the dyadic tonic axis of pole and counterpole offers an expressive impetus. A good example is provided in the opening subject of the movement *Saturn, the Bringer of Old Age* from *Holst's The Planets Suite*. Here, the melodic line gradually rises from the depths, touching as it does so, on the bare outlines of that tritonal dyadic axis:

Excerpt from the Opening Subject of Holst's *Saturn, the Bringer of Old Age.*

This offers the music a particular expressive appeal which is unique to this type of mode. Yet the generation of those modes which do possess either a sharp fourth or flat fifth would seem to occur, in all other respects, along exactly the same lines as the original set of thirty-six modes. The only feature that is different is the tetrachordal frame, which in the case of the Lydian mode, instead of being *C F G C* is now *C F# G C*. Therefore, let all such modes which possess this frame be called *acute* modes owing to the presence of that sharp fourth. There are thirty-six of these:

The Acute Modes

Mode 1:1	C	Db	Eb	F#	G	Ab	Bb	C
Mode 1:2	C	Db	Eb	F#	G	A	Bb	C
Mode 1:3	C	Db	Eb	F#	G	A	B	C
Mode 1:4	C	Db	Eb	F#	G	Ab	Bbb	C
Mode 1:5	C	Db	Eb	F#	G	Ab	B	C

Mode 1:6	C	Db	Eb	F#	G	A#	B	C
Mode 2:1	C	D	Eb	F#	G	Ab	Bb	C
Mode 2:2	C	D	Eb	F#	G	A	Bb	C
Mode 2:3	C	D	Eb	F#	G	A	B	C
Mode 2:4	C	D	Eb	F#	G	Ab	Bbb	C
Mode 2:5	C	D	Eb	F#	G	Ab	B	C
Mode 2:6	C	D	Eb	F#	G	A#	B	C
Mode 3:1	C	D	E	F#	G	Ab	Bb	C
Mode 3:2	C	D	E	F#	G	A	Bb	C
Mode 3:3	C	D	E	F#	G	A	B	C
Mode 3:4	C	D	E	F#	G	Ab	Bbb	C
Mode 3:5	C	D	E	F#	G	Ab	B	C
Mode 3:6	C	D	E	F#	G	A#	B	C
Mode 4:1	C	Db	Ebb	F#	G	Ab	Bb	C
Mode 4:2	C	Db	Ebb	F#	G	A	Bb	C
Mode 4:3	C	Db	Ebb	F#	G	A	B	C
Mode 4:4	C	Db	Ebb	F#	G	Ab	Bbb	C
Mode 4:5	C	Db	Ebb	F#	G	Ab	B	C
Mode 4:6	C	Db	Ebb	F#	G	A#	B	C
Mode 5:1	C	Db	E	F#	G	Ab	Bb	C
Mode 5:2	C	Db	E	F#	G	A	Bb	C
Mode 5:3	C	Db	E	F#	G	A	B	C
Mode 5:4	C	Db	E	F#	G	Ab	Bbb	C
Mode 5:5	C	Db	E	F#	G	Ab	B	C
Mode 5:6	C	Db	E	F#	G	A#	B	C
Mode 6:1	C	D#	E	F	G	Ab	Bb	C
Mode 6:2	C	D#	E	F#	G	A	Bb	C
Mode 6:3	C	D#	E	F#	G	A	B	C
Mode 6:4	C	D#	E	F#	G	Ab	Bbb	C
Mode 6:5	C	D#	E	F#	G	Ab	B	C
Mode 6:6	C	D#	E	F#	G	A#	B	C

Thus are obtained modes such as the 'Lydian' (Mode 3:3), the 'Slavonic Lydian' (Mode 3:2), otherwise known as Bartók's 'acoustic scale', the 'Hungarian minor' (Mode 2:5), and the 'Hungarian major' (6:5). Others of this group can be superficially related to Hindustani modal forms, examples of which are 'Purvi' (mode 5:5), 'Marva' (Mode 5:4), and 'Todi' (Mode 1:6).[1] It is completely coincidental that taking the two groups of thirty-six modes together, they exactly correspond to the 72 melas or modal scales recognised in the

[1] Charles Capwell, Southeast Asia III., Raga, The Harvard Dictionary of Music, 781.

Carnatic branch of South Asian or Indian music.[1] This is because, excepting for the modal tonic, the basic Carnatic scale also employs three intervallic modalities for each of the seven modal degrees, bar the fourth degree, which occurs only in two forms, and the fifth degree which is immutable.

The chromatic tonal system embraces the modal possibility of such a rich monophonic tradition. That such connections sometimes occur provided the basis for Frank Howe's study *Modal Harmony: Western and Indian* (1947). Here he observes that *it is when seeking the new scales that composers have sometimes used one of the Indian modes - often unconsciously.*[2] As an example he cites Ernest Bloch's *Quintet* which uses the raga 'Hindole' in the finale. The reason for such a connection, he feels, is that the scales themselves have particular musical properties which the composers discover independently of any system that they might stem from. He thus observes *that several composers, including Sibelius, have discovered oriental scales accidentally, shows that these particular scales had undiscovered characteristics.*[3] These characteristics no doubt derive from the conformity of these scales to the natural laws of valency, and the expression of those laws within the context of the chromatic tonal system.

The scheme of modes embraced by that system, is still not complete, for there are those modes with a flat fifth to consider, the basic archetype for which is the Locrian mode, stretching from *B* to *B* on the white notes of the piano. Let all modes with a flat fifth be called soft modes, in contradistinction to either the neutral or acute modes. The soft forms of the thirty-six modes are obtained by flattening the fifth of the original modes:

Heptatonic Modes with Perfect Fourth and Flat Fifth

Mode 1:1	C	Db	Eb	F	Gb	Ab	Bb	C
Mode 1:2	C	Db	Eb	F	Gb	A	Bb	C
Mode 1:3	C	Db	Eb	F	Gb	A	B	C
Mode 1:4	C	Db	Eb	F	Gb	Ab	Bbb	C
Mode 1:5	C	Db	Eb	F	Gb	Ab	B	C
Mode 1:6	C	Db	Eb	F	Gb	A#	B	C
Mode 2:1	C	D	Eb	F	Gb	Ab	Bb	C
Mode 2:2	C	D	Eb	F	Gb	A	Bb	C
Mode 2:3	C	D	Eb	F	Gb	A	B	C
Mode 2:4	C	D	Eb	F	Gb	Ab	Bbb	C

---

[1] Ibid.

[2] Frank Howes, Modal Harmony: Western and Indian, in: PRMA 74, 1947, 28.

[3] Ibid.

Mode 2:5	C	D	Eb	F	Gb	Ab	B	C
Mode 2:6	C	D	Eb	F	Gb	A#	B	C
Mode 3:1	C	D	E	F	Gb	Ab	Bb	C
Mode 3:2	C	D	E	F	Gb	A	Bb	C
Mode 3:3	C	D	E	F	Gb	A	B	C
Mode 3:4	C	D	E	F	Gb	Ab	Bbb	C
Mode 3:5	C	D	E	F	Gb	Ab	B	C
Mode 3:6	C	D	E	F	Gb	A#	B	C
Mode 4:1	C	Db	Ebb	F	Gb	Ab	Bb	C
Mode 4:2	C	Db	Ebb	F	Gb	A	Bb	C
Mode 4:3	C	Db	Ebb	F	Gb	A	B	C
Mode 4:4	C	Db	Ebb	F	Gb	Ab	Bbb	C
Mode 4:5	C	Db	Ebb	F	Gb	Ab	B	C
Mode 4:6	C	Db	Ebb	F	Gb	A#	B	C
Mode 5:1	C	Db	E	F	Gb	Ab	Bb	C
Mode 5:2	C	Db	E	F	Gb	A	Bb	C
Mode 5:3	C	Db	E	F	Gb	A	B	C
Mode 5:4	C	Db	E	F	Gb	Ab	Bbb	C
Mode 5:5	C	Db	E	F	Gb	Ab	B	C
Mode 5:6	C	Db	E	F	Gb	A#	B	C
Mode 6:1	C	D#	E	F	Gb	Ab	Bb	C
Mode 6:2	C	D#	E	F	Gb	A	Bb	C
Mode 6:3	C	D#	E	F	Gb	A	B	C
Mode 6:4	C	D#	E	F	Gb	Ab	Bbb	C
Mode 6:5	C	D#	E	F	Gb	Ab	B	C
Mode 6:6	C	D#	E	F	Gb	A#	B	C

This group contains a number of important modes such as the 'Locrian' (Mode 1:1), the 'Major Locrian' (Mode 3:1), and the mode which Persichetti describes simply as the 'Oriental' (Mode 5:2). An explicit use of mode 2:1 is found in Debussy's piano piece 'Nuages'. Mark de Voto's comments upon this reveal an interesting, although generally upheld view concerning such modes: *Debussy's modal harmony arises in part from the frequent but constantly changing use of different modal and pentatonic scales....Debussy's Nuages (Nocturnes no.1 makes extensive use of an artificial scale (B C# D E F G A) that defines an idiosyncratic harmonic environment for much of the piece.*[1]

From the standpoint of the major and minor modes, or the diatonic modes of Church music, such a scale may indeed appear to be 'artificial'. However, that the threefold scheme of heptatonic modes presented above derives from the

---

[1] Mark de Voto, Tonality, The Harvard Dictionary of Music, 368.

organic foundations of the enharmonic scale, which itself represents a natural and organic interweave of the prime numbers 2, 3, 5 and 7, infallibly demonstrates that these scales have just as strong and justifiable basis in the realm of natural tonal relations as the major or minor modes. Therefore there is no justification to describe them as artificial scales, except perhaps as a caretaker term used for the reason that the integral system from which these modes derive - the chromatic tonal system - has not been properly defined.

In total the enharmonic scale embraces 108 primary heptatonic modal forms (exclusive of those others obtained by rotation of the tonic). Further modal forms may be derived through utilising the unique properties of septimally defined fourths and fifths. Prime participants here are the diminished fourth (*Fb* - ratio 9/7), and the augmented fifth (*G#* - 14/9). When these are brought into consideration there are a total of eight possible tetrachordal frames:

Defining Tetrachordal Bases in the Enharmonic Scale

1.	C	F	G	C
2.	C	F#	G	C
3.	C	F	Gb	C
4.	C	Fb	G	C
5.	C	F#	G#	C
6.	C	Fb	Gb	C
7.	C	F#	G#	C
8.	C	Fb	G#	C

To accurately identify any mode, each number can be preceded by the number of the tetrachordal frame. In this way, can be classified modes such as the 'Super Locrian' as used in the Holst example above (C Db Eb Fb Gb Ab Bb C) - mode 6:1:1, or Verdi's 'Enigmatic scale' (C Db E F# G# A# B) - mode 5:5:6, etc. Of the eight groups, not all have thirty-six modes. The presence of the *Fb* in tetrachordal frames 4, 6 and 8, precludes the participation of note E in the lower tetrachord unless enharmonic tetrachords are being advocated as a viable musical resource. The same applies to the use of the note Ab in those tetrachordal frames which employ a *G#* - bases 5, 7 and 8. That these are impossible to realise in twelve-tone temperament is one of the inhibitory factors that has prevented music developing any further along these lines.

When the fourth or fifth is omitted from a group of modes, there arise a number of definitive species of hexatonic mode, a simple example of which is the mode *C Db E F Ab Bbb C*, described by Persichetti as the six-tone symmetrical mode.[1] When the fourth is sharp, and the fifth omitted, or the fifth flat, and the fourth omitted, hexatonic modes characterised by a tritonal division of the octave arise.

Scriabin's 'Mystic Chord' is one example out of what are potentially a great number of possibilities. The same argument can be applied to pentatonic modes: obtained by omitting two notes from a heptatonic mode, they possess a capability which is readily subsumed within the territory of the heptatonic modes already considered. Then there are various species of octatonic modes consisting of a pentachord and a tetrachord, whilst nine note modes would therefore consist of two pentachords.

The necessity here for the recording of every one of these modes is questionable. The important point is that as the foundation scale for a chromatic system of tonality, the enharmonic scale embraces a vast modal possibility which extends to just about every modal form used in the music of the West (and so it would seem, in the East too, bar the unusual tuning of certain modes such as the Indonesian forms of pentatonic mode).

Busoni had empirically calculated many of these modes and had suspicions that they derived from a larger encompassing system. Indeed, he posits the question: *But how would a lawgiver classify the tone series C Db Eb Fb G Ab B C/ C Db Eb F Gb A B C / C D Eb Fb Gb A B C / C Db E F Gb A Bb C? or these forsooth: C D Eb Fb G A# B C / C D Eb Fb G# A B C / C Db Eb F# G# A Bb C ? One cannot estimate at a glance what a wealth of melodic and harmonic expression would thus be opened up to the hearing....with this presentation the unity of all keys may be considered as finally pronounced and justified*.[2] This chapter demonstrates that the unity Busoni is alluding to is the vast expanse of the chromatic tonal system.

---

[1] Persichetti, Op. Cit., 111.

[2] Busoni, Op. Cit., 29.

CONCLUSIONS

This study began with the consideration of a musical tone, and ended with a discussion of the extremely complex tonal system defined here as the chromatic system. Through the property of valency, all possibilities discussed between these two extremes were already there, latent within the tone itself. That further possibilities still exist in relation to higher prime numbers such as 11, 13, 17 and 19 there can be no doubt. To discuss these in any detail would be premature without some evidence of their impending use by composers. In this conclusion therefore, it only remains to retrace some of the steps taken so far, and endeavour to place them in a clear perspective for the reader. The musical tone itself is an ideal place to begin.

The harmonics of a musical tone are its constituent components, in which case to speak of a tone 'and its harmonics' is to forge an untenable distinction between the whole and its parts. As the sum of those parts, the whole cannot be isolated from them. That the ear blends these parts into an overall discernible 'Gestalt' does not belie the fact that a musical tone is a complex configuration of vibrations. Within that configuration exists an intricate mathematical pattern, the most important feature of which is the fundamental that corresponds to the pitch heard. The vibrations of all subsequent harmonics are simply multiples of that fundamental frequency, which means that the relationship between any two harmonics can be described in terms of a ratio, say 3:2. That ratio, as well as being a depiction of the precise relationship between the frequencies of the two vibrations, is also a quantitative measure of the space or distance between them.

That space is at the same time the plane against which music is heard and perceived. This plane of projection is clearly multidimensional in its constitution. The first dimension is the pitch continuum as it is conceived as an unbroken array of frequencies (Helmholtz, Stumpf, etc.). As the primal raw matter from which the notes of music derive it thus sets up a basic duality perceived as the rising and falling of pitch. This constitutes movement in one dimension only.

Other significant dimensions of musical activity arise from the perceptual delineation of tonal space according to the principles of tonal geometry. An example of this is the universal experience of octave equivalence (Seashore, Revesz), the basic 2:1 relationship found between the first and second harmonics, and duplicated in the relationship between two fundamental tones an octave apart. This factor not only neatly sectionalises musical space, but configures its helical constitution. Thus in a canon at the octave, the second entry is heard to be the same melody occurring on the next turn of the spiral upwards.

Because harmonics are the multiples of a given fundamental frequency, means that at certain points one of these multiples belonging to one fundamental will coincide with a multiple belonging to another. Because of this mathematical connection the two sounds will be heard to be related in some way. Thus is the basis for the property of valency.

The simplest manifestation of valency is through the interval - the combination of two musical tones. If the ratio of that interval is known the exact basis for the bond between the two notes can be easily calculated. That such bonds are important to music is suggested by the universal selection of those intervals with simple ratios in which tonal bonds can be easily discerned. Valency is therefore a natural force of music, which means that any attempt to combine musical tones should do so in co-operation with it.

This is where it is possible to criticise twelve-tone serialism as introduced by Schoenberg. By defying this force, and combining tones in a fashion dictated only by the artificial order of the series, a music is created which, like the cells of the body replicating themselves in chaotic fashion, speaks of a musical art in a state of demise. To regenerate the musical language from such a pathetic condition it is necessary to develop ways of combining tones together in respect of this natural force.

Yet with this view comes certain basic problems. Because of the adoption of equal temperament in the West, intervals no longer correspond with their ideal simple ratios. Tempered intervals have irrational ratios, yet these are acceptable to most ears. That tempered intervals are acceptable to the ear might suggest that the basis for musical relations may not lie in tonal bonds. Yet here another problem arises. If this is true, and equal temperament is taken as the theoretical standard it becomes impossible to understand just why the same tempered interval should be heard to be one interval in one context, and quite a different interval in another.

It becomes apparent that in addition to the objective factor that is the heard tempered interval, there are psycho-acoustic and psychological processes in operation which also play a part in what is heard. These seem to indicate that the ear resolves the tempered intervals into those with the nearest simple ratio to which they can be fitted. Therefore the ear has the capacity to interpret a tempered perfect fifth as a '3/2' which possesses certain qualitative distortions. This observation allows a path to be made between the two conflicting viewpoints, for both sets of intervals are playing a part in the musical process. The pure intervals are providing the basic perceptual frameworks through which tempered intervals are heard.

To understand the intervals used in music therefore, it is necessary to look at both sides of the issue: pure intervals, together with their exact ratios, and their compromises arising through temperament. The conflict between ideologies that favour either the tempered or the pure intervals need not affect this conclusion, since both types of interval play a part in what is heard by the listener.

The conformity of pure musical intervals to those relationships found in the harmonic series has impressed so many theorists that it would be difficult to list them all. Certainly, so far as the history of musical theory is concerned, it is a correspondence which has led theorists into numerous traps, the main one being that music may thus be explained through a dependence upon purely acoustic phenomenon.

For Rameau the conformity of musical intervals to the harmonic series was a revelation, but it led him to an obsessive preoccupation with acoustics. For Tartini the objective concept of the 'chord of nature' was a remarkable phenomenon, but it too led him to put too much down to pure acoustics. His continual reference to the 'terza sona' or ' third sound' in his theoretical work the Trattado di Musica is a prime example of this.

That theorists could not find the minor triad in the lower regions of the harmonic series was a source of the utmost frustration. If music obtained its natural validation from the 'chord of nature', then why does it not reflect the equal standing of the major and minor triads? From the concept of the harmonic series the equal and opposite conception of the sub-harmonic series thus came into being - natures way of validating the minor triad. The problem here is that such a series is simply the projection of a hypothetical mirror image of the harmonic series. Therefore the principle being used to validate the minor chord is itself without validation.

Through the concept of valency it became possible to sidetrack numerous traps associated with those attempts to explain music through purely acoustical phenomenon. The harmonic series is a web of relationships which, being inherent to the very nature of tone, assists the ear in making connections between tones. Therefore after the octave, the next most elementary connection between musical tones is according to the 3/2 relation. The helical configuration of tonal space results from cyclical repetition of the 2/1 relation. The process of cyclical repetition applied to the 3/2 relation results in the generation of a unique second dimension of tonal space - the cyclical 3/2 relation.

Because the prime numbers 2 and 3 are incommensurate means that, starting from the same point, the cyclical 3/2 relation never meets up with the cyclical 2/1 relation. In this way, movement along this line (the cycle of fifths or fourths) constitutes a new dimensional movement. The result of this movement is the specific formatting of the musical octave, through which the pentatonic, heptatonic, twelve tone chromatic, enharmonic, and other basic scalar prototypes are derived.

Being formatted in this way, the octave retains that imprint with great tenacity. Here, the basic seven toned division is a prime example, having played a conspicuous part in music for many thousands of years. As well as serving to format the octave, the second dimension also serves as the primary field of the manifestation of an important musical principle. A perfect fifth up can be matched by a perfect fifth down. Thus is the basic manifestation of the duality of the first dimension.

But a perfect fifth up matched against an octave down yields an interval which bears an important relationship to the first: it is its inversion. Whilst therefore, the basic duality of the first dimension manifests through the rising and falling of pitch (a principle to which all subsequent dimensions are subject), the basic duality of the second dimension manifests through the phenomenon of intervallic inversion. Here therefore, there are two perceptual principles: the principle of octave equivalence, and the principle of inversional complimentarity.

These in their turn lead to the understanding of the basic duality of the second dimension, for the same cyclical movement (a perfect fifth up and a perfect fifth down) yields two different but related intervals through application of the principle of inversion: the perfect fifth and the perfect fourth. The duality set up by the second dimension is thus the principle of intervallic polarity, two intervals which are the same in essence but different in expression.

This therefore leads on to the consideration of the third dimension of tonal space generated by the 5/4 relation. A consideration of the passing into Western music of the 5/4 relation leads to the overriding conclusion that the exact point at which it entered, into either musical theory and/or musical practice, is extremely difficult to pin-point with any certainty. In terms of practice it is entirely feasible that it is a relation which was always there, but never recognised in theory. In the sense that for the past few hundred years at least it has been a recognised relation, it does not really matter how and when it entered into music. The brief here are the theoretical conclusions which can be drawn from musical activity extruding into this particular dimension of tonal space.

Here the most important point is that those points in the octave generated by the '5/4' relation tend to be perceived categorically within the framework of the octave format already set up by the 3/2 relation. Here there was found to be an extremely interesting process at work, which might be termed 'progressive intonation'. At certain places along the line of cyclic repetition of the 3/2 relation, there are points where it very nearly comes into contact with line of cyclic repetition of the 5/4 relation. In this way, although the prime numbers of the harmonic series are incommensurate, the various dimensions of musical space which they open up, are full of corridors where one dimension leads to, or flows into another.

Therefore according to the principle of progressive intonation, the harmonic major third with the extremely simple ratio of 5/4, came in to replace the cyclic major third with its complex ratio of 81/64. The fabric of tonal relations thus becomes modified accordingly. One of the important consequences of extrusion into this third dimension of tonal space was seen to be the creation of major/minor triadic polarity. Here it was found that the triads concerned possessed a dimensional logic and justification of their own, in that they constituted the perceptual correlates of ensuing activity in that particular dimension. This is why it is perhaps foolish to try to seek justification for the minor triad in the harmonic series. It needs no justification, as it represents the natural polar counterpart to the major triad.

Subsequent to the 5/4 relation, there is the more problematic 7/4 relation: the spearhead of a fourth dimension of tonal space. This particular relation, although recognised as far back as ancient Greece, has often evoked a negative response amongst theorists. Through an examination of their arguments it becomes apparent that there is no overriding reason for not recognising the 7/4 relation as a valid musical resource. Each theorist that avers it has done so for their own reasons, which upon examination are often spurious, frivolous or downright unreasonable, ranging from total evasion (Zarlino), avoidance on the grounds of personal taste (Rameau), that the ear cannot perceive such a relation (Descartes, Schenker), that it will unleash demons beyond our control (Daniélou), that it is too problematic (Hindemith), etc.

For those theorists who have recognised the 7/4 relation there is at least some common consent discernible between them. Marin Mersenne, in the seventeenth century could see no reason why it should be excluded from music. Kirnberger went even further, regarding the 7/4 relation as a 'natural consonance', and invented his own notational symbols so that he could incorporate it into musical compositions.

For most of the theorists who did recognise the value of the 7/4 relation, it was, above all, regarded to be a rather flat minor seventh interval. Trumpeters often used it when a minor seventh was required, using the technique of lipping to raise the pitch to an acceptable standard. Certainly in the tempered system the nearest interval to 7/4 would seem to be the minor seventh. For Leonard Euler, the 7/4 relation provided the ideal tuning for the minor seventh in the chord of the dominant seventh. At around the same time, Sorge was thinking along the same lines, except for Sorge the 7/4 relation was a fundamental dissonance which empowered the chord of the dominant seventh with its marvelous tonicizing qualities. He also saw septimal implications in the half-diminished and supertonic seventh chords.

Tartini as well, was all for the introduction of the seventh harmonic into actual practice, and like Kirnberger, devised his own notation for that relation. Helmholtz, like the historian Fétis, continued to promulgate the idea of the 'natural seventh', although Helmholtz referred to it as the 'sub-minor seventh'. Ellis thoroughly upheld Helmholtz views and defined other septimal intervals according to that fundamental identity.

Despite the many problems resulting from this view, it became so widespread that, as Mathew Shirlaw observes, it almost became an 'article of faith amongst musicians'. One of the factors that did seem to favour the minor seventh interpretation of the 7/4 relation was vocal and string intonation since the nineteenth century. Even here though, it became apparent that 'functional' intonation, in which the leading note was slightly raised and the seventh of the dominant slightly flattened, tended to be applicable in melodic contexts, and that, in vertical terms, musicians often strove to attain the ideals of just intonation. In any case, it very quickly became evident that in terms of 'functional' intonation, it is the justly intoned intervals that constitute the basic percepts that are compromised for expressive purposes.

Consequently, the best way to view the 7/4 relation is through the principles of just intonation. Here it can be seen just why the minor seventh identity ascribed to the 7/4 relation is so unsatisfactory. It is because in just intonation the nearest interval to the 7/4 relation is the interval of the augmented sixth (225/128). The difference between them is so small that it is virtually impossible to detect. A long line of theorists have observed this (i.e. Vicentino, Wallis, Serre, Kirnberger, Tartini, Helmholtz, Ellis, Shirlaw, Fokker, Regener, Vogel, etc.) although few of them deemed it necessary to make much comment upon the obvious significance of this fact i.e. that the 7/4 relation was manifesting in tonal music under the guise of chords of the augmented sixth.

One factor which no doubt inhibited an enthusiastic reaction in this direction was the influence of equal temperament, which had firmly relegated any distinction between the intervals of the augmented sixth and minor seventh to the domain of notational spelling. And even then, in the realms of notation it didn't matter that much because the listener became aware of the distinction through the precise contextual setting of the tempered intervals.

Yet even if temperament does compromise the 7/4 relation, it became apparent that it should not be allowed to contaminate theoretical reasoning with its practical compromises. To compromise reason, for whatever purpose, is to deal in untruth. Providing the underlying percept upon which chords of the augmented sixth are based, it was shown that the 7/4 relation provided the basis for a significant body of chromatically altered chords. From this it became clear that the 7/4 relation was actually purposive in a tonal context, in that it led to the upgrading and transformation of the dominant function in accordance with the matrix of septimal intervals.

This transformation was discovered to be purposive in that it led to the creation of new scalar functions, which not only transcended the limitations of the major and minor modes, but actually extended and upgraded the chromatic scale into a more advanced nineteen note scale. The scale itself implicated an altogether new level of tonality, which in this study was described as the chromatic system of tonality. Being generally implicated in the harmonic trends of nineteenth century music, it became apparent that twentieth century tonal music is based intuitively on this inherited chromatic system of tonality, and that such a system allows many of the apparently unconnected threads of musical development present in the twentieth century to be brought together in such a way as to implicate a new common practice. Some of the major features underlying this common practice are:

1) The adoption of the tetrad as the basic unit of harmony.

2) New ways for controlling and directing tonality.

3) The adoption of the chromatic, as opposed to the diatonic scale, as the base for musical composition.

4) An extension of chord types to include the 7th harmonic.

5) The development and exploitation of septimal polarities. (i.e. dominant 'pole' - 'counterpole', etc.).

6) The development of techniques of dominant prolongation (atonality) as an expressive antithesis to the defining tonal state.

7) The development of new scales defined by septimal polarities (whole tone, octatonic, Messiaen's various 'Modes of Limited Transposition').

8) The unification of global modal resources under the cover of one universally defined key.

As a tonal system still being discovered, it is largely a result of the progressive assimilation of those relationships present higher up in the harmonic series. That this process has tended to occur throughout the history of music shows that each level of tonality, rather than being a closed self-sufficient system, is forever vulnerable to invasion from the often invisible and hidden influence of these higher harmonics.

The entry of these fertilising influences into music is hardly ever a conscious process, and often goes unrecognised until much later. All that is known at the time, is that the established system is being put under threat by the weight of new phenomena which threaten to overturn the system as it stands. At the beginning of this century this became well apparent, although the consequences of the overthrow of the diatonic level of tonality were mistakenly assumed to point to the systematic exploitation of the possibilities of atonality. Yet atonality of course, was only one side of the picture - the negative reflection of the highly potent possibility that was the chromatic tonal system.

In this sense, the subsequent split of factions that occurred between the supporters of tonality on the one hand, and atonality on the other are both rooted in the same essential principle. The diatonic level of tonality was basically three dimensional, in that its phenomenon were a direct resultant of the interweave of the prime numbers two, three and five. Yet because of the existence of those mysterious corridors or 'worm-holes' between different dimensions of tonal space, new influences were able to enter which at first sight seemed to harbour the threat of the breakdown of the original system. Further examination revealed that these influences were in fact the new phoenix arising from the ashes of the old system. Tonality dies, only to be reborn at yet a higher and more sophisticated level.

APPENDIX 1

The Three-Tone Systems

1. The Seven-Tone System - Two Dimensional - 3 Pitch Matrix - Diatonic

Note	Ratio	Interval
C	1/1	Prime
D	9/8	Major second
E	81/64	Ditone
F	4/3	Perfect fourth
G	3/2	Perfect fifth
A	27/16	Cyclic major sixth
B	243/128	Cyclic major seventh
C	2/1	Octave

2. The Twelve-Tone System - Three Dimensional - 3/5 Pitch Matrix – Chromatic

Note	Ratio	Interval
C	1/1	Prime
Db	16/15	Minor second
D	9/8	Major second
Eb	6/5	Minor third
E	5/4	Major third
F	4/3	Perfect fourth
F#	45/32	Augmented fourth
G	3/2	Perfect fifth
Ab	8/5	Minor sixth
A	5/3	Major sixth
Bb	16/9	Minor seventh
B	15/8	Major seventh
C	2/1	Octave

3. The Nineteen-Tone System - Four Dimensional - 3/5/7 Pitch Matrix - Enharmonic

Note	Ratio	Interval
C	1/1	Prime
Db	16/15 (15/14)	Minor second
D	9/8	Major second
Ebb	8/7	Diminished third
D#	7/6	Augmented second
Eb	6/5	Minor third
E	5/4	Major third
Fb	9/7	Diminished fourth
F	4/3	Perfect fourth
F#	7/5	Augmented fourth
Gb	10/7	Diminished fifth
G	3/2	Perfect fifth
G#	14/9	Augmented fifth
Ab	8/5	Minor sixth
A	5/3	Major sixth
Bbb	12/7	Diminished seventh
A#	7/4	Augmented sixth
Bb	16/9	Minor seventh
B	15/8	Major seventh
C	2/1	Octave

APPENDIX 2

Some Useful Arithmetic for Note Ratios

1) Calculating the sum of two ratios.

Application: to find the ratio of the interval which results from the sum of those two intervals.

Process: the denominator of the first ratio is multiplied by the denominator of the second ratio to give the denominator of the resultant ratio. The numerator of the first ratio is multiplied by the numerator of the second ratio to give the numerator of the resultant ratio. The result is then reduced to the smallest possible number by the elimination of common prime factors.

Example: What is the ratio of the interval which results from the sum of those intervals whose ratios are 17/16 and 16/15?

Calculation:

$$\frac{17 \times 16}{16 \times 15} = \frac{272}{240} = \frac{17}{15}$$

2) Calculating the differential ratio of two other ratios

Application: finding the ratio of the interval which results from the difference between a larger and a smaller interval.

Process: Here, the numerator of the first ratio is multiplied by the denominator of the second ratio to give the denominator of the resultant ratio; and the denominator of the first ratio is multiplied by the numerator of the second ratio to give the numerator of the resultant ratio.

Example: What is the ratio of the interval which results from the difference of the two intervals whose ratios are 17/16 and 16/15?

Calculation:

$$\frac{17}{16} \diagdown \frac{16}{15} = \frac{256}{255}$$

3) Calculating the number of cyclic cents in a given interval.

Application: to find the size of an interval expressed in Ellis's system of cyclic cents.

Process: The logarithm of 2 (representing the octave of 2/1) is divided by 1200 to give the value for a single cent. The logarithm of the interval for which a cents measurement is sought can then be divided by that number to give the precise value of that interval in cents.

Example: How many cents are there in the Pythagorean major sixth of ratio 27/16?

Calculation:

$$\text{Log. } 2 = 0.301029995664$$
$$\div 1200 = 0.00025085832972 \text{ (1 cent)}$$
$$27/16 = 1.6875. \text{ Log} = 0.2272437815$$
$$\div \text{ 1 cent} = 905.865$$

There are thus 905.9 cents (to the nearest decimal place) in a Pythagorean major sixth.

BIBLIOGRAPHY

ADAMS, BYRON, Stages of Revision of Vaughan Williams Sixth Symphony, in: *MQ* 73/3, 1989.

ALDWELL, E. & SCHACHTER, C. Harmony and Voice Leading, Harcourt Brace Jovanovich Ltd., London 1989.

ANDREWS, H.K., The Oxford Harmony (Volume Two), Oxford University Press, London 1950.

ANTOKELETZ, E., The Music of Bela Bartók: A Study of Tonality and Progression in Twentieth Century Music, University of California Press, London 1984.

APEL, W., The Notation of Polyphonic Music, 5th. ed., Cambridge 1961.

ARISTOXENUS, The Harmonics, Trans, by Henry S. Macran, the Clarendon Press, Oxford 1902.

ARPS, B. (Ed.), Performance in Java and Bali, School of Oriental and African Studies 1993.

ASHFORTH, A., The Relationship of the Sixth in Beethoven's Piano Sonata, Opus 110, in: *MR* 32, 1971, 93 - 102.

ATCHERSON, W., Key and Mode in Seventeenth-Century Music Theory Books, in: *JMT* 17/2, 1973, 204 -33.

BABBIT, W. (trans.); PALISCA, C.V. (Ed.), Hucbald, Guido and John on Music, Yale University Press, New Haven and London 1978.

BAKER, J., The New in Music, in: *Tempo* 30, 1953.

BARBERA, A., The Consonant Eleventh and the Expansion of the Musical Tetractys: A Study of Ancient Pythagoreanism, in; *JMT* 28/2, 1984, 191-224.

BARBIERI P., Violin Intonation: A Historical Survey, in: *EM* XIX/1, 1991, 69 -90.

BARBOUR, J. M., Equal Temperament, its History from Ramis (1482) to Rameau (1737), Ph. D. Dissertation, Cornell University 1932.

BARBOUR, J. M., Musical Scales and their Classification, in: *JASA* 21/6, Nov. 1949, 586-589.

BARBOUR, J. M., Synthetic Musical Scales, in: *The American Mathematical Monthly* 36, 155-160.

BARBOUR, J. M., Tuning and Temperament: A Historical Survey, East Lansing: Mich St Coll Pr 1953.

BARBOUR, J. M., Violin Intonation in the 18th. Century, in: *JAMS* V/3, 1952, 224-235,

BARKER, A. (Ed.), Greek Musical Writings, Vol. II: Harmonic and Acoustic Theory, Cambridge University Press, Cambridge 1989.

BENT, M., Musica Recta and Musica Ficta, in: *MD* 26, 1972, 73-100.

BERGER, A., Perspectives on Schoenberg and Stravinsky, in: *19th. Century Music*, X/3, 1987.

BERGER, A., Problems of Pitch Organisation in Stravinsky, in: *PNM* II, 1963, 11-42.

BERGER, K., Theories of Chromatic and Enharmonic Music in Late 16th Century Italy, UMI Research Press 1980.

BERNSTEIN, D. W., Georg Capellen's Theory of Reduction: Radical Harmonic Theory at the Turn of the Century, in: *JMT* 37/1, 1993, 85-116.

BLACKWOOD, E., The Structure of Recognisable Diatonic Tunings, Princeton University Press, Princeton 1985.

BROWN, M., The Diatonic and the Chromatic in Schenker's Theory of Harmonic Relations, in: *JMT* 30/1, Spring 1986.

BULLIVANT, R., The Nature of Chromaticism, in: *MR* 24, 1963, 97-129.

BUSONI, F., Sketch of a New Esthetic of Music, Trans. by Dr. Th. Baker, Schirmer Inc., New York 1911

CAZDEN, N., Pythagoras and Aristoxenus Reconciled, in: *JAMS* XI, 1958, 97 - 105.

CHESUIT, J., Mozart's Teaching of Intonation, in: *JAMS* 30, 1977.

CLOUGH, J., The Leading Tone in Direct Chromaticism: from Renaissance to Baroque, in: *JMT* 1/1, 1957.

CATEL, C.S. Traite de l'Harmonie, Paris 1801.

COWELL, H., New Musical Resources, New York, Something Else Press 1969.

CROSS, I.; HOWELL, P. and WEST, R. (Eds.), Musical Structure and Cognition, Academic Press, London 1985.

DANIÉLOU, A., Introduction to the Study of Musical Scales, The India Society, London 1943.

DANIÉLOU, A., The Ragas of Northern Indian Music, Barrie and Rockliff, The Cresset Press, London 1968.

DESCARTES, R., Compendium of Music 1618; English trans. by Walter Robert, American Institute of Musicology 1961.

EUCLID, Introduction to the Section of the Canon, trans, Charles Davy, Bury St Edmunds: J. Rackam 1787.

EULER, L., Conjecture sur la rasion de quelques dissonances généralement reçues dans la musique (1764), in: *Opera Omnie*, Serie III, Band 1, Leipzig and Berlin 1926.

EULER, L., Tentamen Novae Theoriae Musicae, St Petersburg 1739.

FÉTIS, F., Esquisse de L'histoire de l'Harmonie, Paris 1840. (Trans. by Mary Irene Arlin, Ph.D. diss. Indiana University 1971)

FÉTIS, F., Trait complet de la theorie et de la pratique de l'harmonie, Paris and Brussels 1844.

FOGLIANO L., Musica Theorica, Venice 1529.

FOKKER, A., Neue Musik mit 31 Tonën, Im Verlag der Gesellschaft zur Förderung der systematischen Musikwissenschaft e.v., Düsseldorf 1966.

FOKKER, A., On the Expansion of the Musician's Realm of Harmony, in: *Ac M* XXXVIII, 1966, 197-201.

FONVILLE, J., Ben Johnston's Extended Just Intonation: A Guide for Interpreters , in: *PNM* 29/2, 1991,106-137.

FORTE, A. Tonal Harmony in Concept and Practice, Holt, Rhinehart and Winston, New York 1962.

FORTE, A., The Structure of Atonal Music, New Haven, Yale Univeristy Press 1973.

FORTE, A. & GILBERT, S., Introduction to Schenkerian Analysis, New York, Norton 1982.

FREIDHEIM, P., Radical Harmonic Procedures in Berlioz, in: *MR* 21, 1960, 282-296.

FULLER, R., A Study of Microtonal Equal Temperaments, in: *JMT* 35, Spring 1991.

GERDINE, L., A General Theory of Music, in: *JMT* II/1, April 1958.

GERDINE, L. (trans.): Adriaan Fokker, New Music with 31 Notes, Im Verlag der Gesellschaft zur Fördering der systematischen Musikwissenschaft e.V., Düsseldorf 1966.

GILLIES, M., Notation and Tonal Structure in Bartók's Later Works, Garland Publishing, Inc. New York & London 1989.

GILMORE, B., Changing the Metaphor: Ratio Models of Musical Pitch in the Work of Harry Partch, Ben Johnston, and James Tenney, in: *PNM* 33/1, 1995.

GOLDMAN, R. F., Harmony in Western Music, Barrie & Rockcliff, The Cresset Press, London 1965.

GODWIN, J., Speculative Music, Companion to Contemporary Musical Thought, Volume 1; Ed. by John Paynter, Tim Howell, Richard Orton and Peter Seymour; Routledge Publishers, London and New York 1992.

GOOF, I., On the Break-up of the Traditional Tonal System: A Confession and a Small Contribution, in: *MR* 48, 1988, 218-220.

GRIDLEY, M. C., Jazz Styles, Prentice Hall Inc., Englewood Cliffs 1978.

GRIFFIFTHS, P., Modern Music - A Concise History from Debussy to Boulez, Thames and Hudson, London 1986.

GRIFFIFTHS, P., Oliver Messiaen and the Music of Time, Faber and Faber, London 1985.

GROUT, D.,J. & PALISCA, C., A History of Western Music, 3rd Edition, J. M. Dent & Sons, London and Melbourne 1980.

HAAR, J., False Relations and Chromaticism in 17th Century Music, in: *JAMS* 30, 1977, 391-417.

HÁBA, A., Neue Harmonielehre des diatonischen, chromatischen, Viertel-, Drittel, Sechstel und Zwölftel-Tonsystems, Leipzig, Kistener & Siegel 1927.

HAINES, B., Beyond Temperament: Non-Keyboard Intonation in the 17th. and 18th. Centuries, in: *EM* XIX/3, August 1991, 357-381.

HALL, D., The Objective Measurement of Goodness - of - Fit for Tunings and Temperaments, in: *JMT* 17/2, 1973, 274-291.

HALLE-ROWEN, R., Music Through Sources and Documents, Prentice Hall Inc., New Jersey 1979.

HANDSCHIN, J., The Timaeus Scale, in: *MD* IV,1950.

HARRIS, S., Chord Forms Based on the Whole - Tone Scale in Early Twentieth Century Music, in: *MR* 41, 1980, 36-50.

HAUPTMANN, M., Die Natur der Harmonik und Metrik, Leipzig 1853. (Trans. by William E. Heathcote, London 1988).

HAWKINS, Sir J., A General History of the Science and Practice of Music, 2 Vols., Novello, Ewer and Co, London 1875.

HELMHOLTZ, H., On the Sensations of Tone, Dover Publications Inc., New York 1954.

HERLINGER, J.W., Marchetto's Division of the Whole Tone, in: *JAMS* 34, 1981, 203-4.

HILL, C., Mozart's French Sixth Chord in the Symphony in G Minor, in: *MR* 46, 1985, 162.

HILL, C., That Wagner-Tristan Chord, in: *MR* 45, 1984, 7-10.

HILL, P., The Chinese Song Cycles of Brian Dennis, in: *Tempo* 137, June 1981.

HILL, C., (Ed.), The Messiaen Companion, Faber and Faber, London 1995.

HINDEMITH, P., The Craft of Musical Composition, Vol. 1 (Theory), Schott & Co. Ltd, London 1945.

HOWES, F., Modal Harmony: Western and Indian, in: *PRMA* 74, 1947.

JACKSON, R., The 'Neapolitan Progression' in the Nineteenth Century, in: *MR* 30, 1969, 35-46.

JEPPESEN, K., Counterpoint, the Polyphonic Vocal Style of the Sixteenth Century, Trans. by Glen Haydon; Prentice Hall Inc. Englewood Cliffs, N.J. 1939.

JOHNSTON, B., Scalar Order as a Compositional Resource, in: *PNM* 2/2, 1964, 56-76.

JORGENSEN, O. H., Tuning, Michigan State University Press, East Lansing 1991.

KEISLER, D., Six Composers on Nonstandard Tunings, in: *PNM* 29/1, 1991.

KIRNBERGER, J. P., The Art of Strict Musical Composition, Trans. by D. Beach & Jurgen Thym; Yale University Press, New Haven and London 1982.

KIRNBERGER, J. P., The True Principles for the Practice of Harmony, Trans. by D. Beach & Jurgen Thyme, in: JMT 23/2, 1979, 164-226.

de KLERK, D., Equal Temperament, in: *AM* LI, 1979, 140-150.

KRAEHENBUEHL, D. & SCHMIDT, C., On the Developement of Musical Systems, in: *JMT* 6, 1962, 32-65.

KRAMER, L., The Mirror of Tonality: Transitional Features of Nineteenth Century Harmony, in: *19th Century Music*, IV/3, 1981, 191-209.

LEICHTENTRITT, H., MUSIC, History and Ideas, Harvard University Press, Cambridge 1966.

LENDVAI, E., Béla Bartók: an Analysis of his Music, Kahn & Averill, London 1990.

LENDVAI, E., Modality: Atonality: Function, in: *Soundings* 6, 1977.

LESTER, J., The Recognition of Major and Minor Keys in German Theory: 1680 – 1730, in: *JMT* 22/1, 1978, 65-104.

LINDLEY, M., Mersenne on Keyboard Tuning, in: *JMT* 24/2, 1980.

LINDLEY, M. & SMITH, R. T., Mathematical Models of Musical Scales: A New Approach, Verlag für systematische Musikwissenschaft GmbH, Bonn 1993.

LOEB, D., Mathematical Aspects of Music, in: *MF* II, 1970, 110-129.

MANDELBAUM, J., Toward the Expansion of our Concepts of Intonation, in: *PNM* 13/1, 1974.

MASON, R. M., Enumeration of Synthetic Musical Scales by Matrix Algebra and a Catalogue of Busoni Scales, in: *JMT* 14/1,1970.

MATHEWS, M.V. & PIERCE, J. R. (Editors), Current Directions in Computer Music Research, The Mit Press, London 1989.

MC CLURE, A. R., Studies in Keyboard Temperaments, in: *GSJ* 1, March 1948, 28-40.

MERSENNE M., Harmonie Universelle, Paris 1636-37.

MESSIAEN, O., Technique de mon Langage Musical (Volumes 1 and 2), Alphonse Leduc, Paris 1966.

MICKELSON, W., Hugo Riemann's Theory of Harmony: A Study, University of Nebraska Press, Lincoln 1977.

MILSTEIN, S., Arnold Schoenberg: Notes, Sets, Forms, Cambridge University Press, Cambridge 1992.

MITCHELL, W. J., The Study of Chromaticism, in: *JMT* 6/1,1962, 2-31.

MORTON, I. A., Numerical Orders in Triadic Harmony, in: JMT 4/2, 1960, 153-168.

NAKASEKU, K., Symbolism in Ancient Chinese Musical Theory, in: *JMT* 1/2, Nov. 1957.

OLDHAM, G., Harmonics, The New Grove Dictionary of Music and Musicians, Vol. 8, Macmillan Publishers 1995, 165-166.

de PAREJA, B. R., Musica Practica 1482.

PARKS, R. S., Tonal Analogues as Atonal Resources and their Relation to Form in Debussy's Chromatic Etude, in: *JMT* 29/1, 1985, 33-60.

PARKS, R. S., Voice Leading and Chromatic Harmony in the Music of Chopin, in: *JMT* 20/2, 1976.

PARRY, Sir H., The Art of Music, London 1893.

PARTCH, H., Genesis of a Music, Da Capo Press, New York 1974.

PARTCH, H., Harry Partch: Bitter Music: Collected Journals, Essays, Introductions and Librettos, Ed. by Thomas Mc George, University of Illinois Press, Urbana and Chicago 1991.

PERRET, W., Some Questions of Musical Theory, W. Heffer and Sons Ltd. Cambridge 1926.

PERSICHETTI, V., Twentieth Century Harmony, Faber and Faber Ltd. London 1961.

PIERCE, J., R., The Science of Musical Sound, W.H.Freeman and Co., New York 1992.

PIKLER, A. G., History of Experiments on the Musical Interval Sense, in: *JMT* 10/1, 1966, 54-95.

PISTON, W., Harmony, 4th. Ed. Rev. by Mark de Voto, New York: Norton 1978.

PISTON, W., Orchestration, Victor Gollancz Ltd, London 1978.

PLOMP R. AND LEVELT, W. J. M., Tonal Consonance and Critical Bandwidth, in: *JASA*, 38:548, 1965.

POL, B. van der, Music and Elementary Theory of Numbers, in: *MR* 7, 1946, 1-25.

PRATT, G., The Dynamics of Harmony: Principles and Practice, Open University Press, Milton Keynes 1984.

PROUT, E., Harmony: Its Theory and Practice, Augener Ltd., London 1903.

RAESSLER, D. M., The 113 Scales of Ferruccio Busoni, in: *MR* 43, 1982, 51-56.

RAMEAU, J. P., Treatise on Harmony, Trans. by Philip Gosset, Dover Publications, Inc. New York 1971.

RANDEL, D. M. (ED.), The New Harvard Dictionary of Music, Harvard University Press, London 1986.

RAPOPORT, P., Towards the Infinite Expansion of Tonal Resources, in: *Tempo* 144, March 1983, 7-11.

READ, G., 20th Century Microtonal Notation, Greenwood Press, New York 1990.

REGENER, E., The Number Seven in the Theory of Intonation, in: *JMT* 19,1975, 140-154.

REGENER, E., Pitch Notation and Equal Temperament: A Formal Study, University of California Press, Berkeley, Los Angeles, London 1973.

RIEMANN, H., Die objektive Existenz der Untertöne in der Schallwelle, Berlin 1877.

RIEMANN, H., History of Musical Theory: Books 1 and 2, Translated by Raymond H. Haggh, Da Capo Press, New York 1974.

RIEMANN, H., Ideas for a Study on the Imagination of Tone, Translated by Robert Watson and Elizabeth West Marvin, in: *JMT* 36/1, 1992, 69-116.

RIVE, T., The Dorian Origin of the Minor Mode, in: *SM* 2,1968, 21-32.

RIVERA, B. V., The Isagogue (1581) of Johannes Avianus: An Early Formulation of Triadic Theory, in: *JMT* 22/1, 1978, 43-64.

ROEDERER, J. G., Introduction to the Physics and Psychophysics of Music (Second edition), Heidelberg Science Library; Vol 16, Springer-Verlag, New York/Heidelberg/Berlin 1975.

ROSENSTIEL, L. (trans.), Musica Enchiriadis, Colorado Springs: Colo Coll Mus 1976.

SCHENKER, H., Harmony, Trans. by Elisabeth Mann Borgese, The Mit Press, London,1973.

484

SCHLESINGER, K., The Greek Aulos, Methuen and Co. Ltd., London 1939

SCHOENBERG, A., Problems of Harmony, in: *Modern Music* 11: May - June, 1934,167-187

SCHOENBERG, A., Theory of Harmony, transl. by R. E. Carter, Faber and Faber 1978.

SCHOLES, P., The Oxford Companion to Music, ed. by J. O. Ward, London 1970.

SESSIONS, R., Harmonic Practice, Harcourt, Brace and Company, New York 1951.

SEASHORE, C. E., The Psychology of Music, McGraw-Hill Book Company Inc., New York and London 1960.

SERRE, J. A., Essais sur les Principes de L'Harmonie, Paris 1753.

SHACKFORD, C., Some Aspects of Perception, in: *JMT* 6,1962.

SHINN, R., Ben Johnston's Fourth String Quartet, in: *PNM* 15/2, 1975. 145 - 173.

SHIRLAW, M., The Theory of Harmony, Novello & Company Ltd., London 1917.

SIMMS, B., Choron, Fétis and the Theory of Tonality, in: *JMT* 19/1,1975, 112-139.

SMITH, C. J., The Functional Extravagance of Chromatic Chords, in: *MTS* 8, 1986, 94-139.

STEVENS, H., The Life and Music of Béla Bartók, 2nd ed., Oxford University Press, London and New York 1964..

STOCKHAUSEN, K., Aus den Sieben Tagen, Universal Edition, Vienna 1968.

STRAUS, J., Stravinsky's Tonal Axis, in: *JMT* 26/2, 1982, 261-290.

STRAVINSKY, I., Poetics of Music, trans. by Knodel and Dahl, Harvard University Press, Cambridge 1947.

STRICKLAND, E., Minimalism: Origins, Indiana University Press, Bloomington and Indianapolis 1993

STRUNK, O., Source Readings in Musical History, Faber and Faber, London 1952.

STÜBER, J., Die Intonation des Geigers, Verlag für systematische Musikwissenchaft, GmbH, Bonn 1989.

STUMPF, C., Konzonanz und Konkordanz, Beitrage zur Akustik und Musikwissenschaft, 6, 1911, 116-150.

TARTINI, G., Trattado di Musica, Padua 1754.

TARUSKIN, R., Chernomor to Kaschei: Harmonic Sorcery; or Stravinsky's 'Angle', in: *JAMS* 38, Spring 1985, 72-142.

TARUSKIN, R., Chéz Petrouchka: Harmony and Tonality chéz Stravinsky, 19th. Century Music X/3, 1987.

TERHARDT, E., Pitch, Consonance and Harmony, in: *JASA*, 55:1061, 1974.

TISCHLER, H., Chromatic Mediants - A Facet of Musical Romanticism, in: *JMT* 2/1,1958, 94-96.

van den TOORN, P., Some Characteristics of Stravinsky's Diatonic Music, in: *PNM*14/1,1975, 104-138; 15/2,1977, 58-96.

TRAVIS, R., Toward a New Concept of Tonality?, in: *JMT* 3, 1959, 257-84.

ULEHLA, L., Contemporary Harmony: Romanticism through the Twelve-Tone Row, The Free Press, New York 1966.

VICENTINO, N., L'Antica musica ridotta all moderna prattica, Rome 1555.

VÏSHNEGRADSKY, I., La musique à quarts de ton et sa réalisation pratique, in: *ReM*, 171, 1937, 26-33.

VOGEL, M., Denkschrift zum Bau von Tasteninstrumenten in Reiner Stimmung, Verlag für systematische Musikwissenschaft GmbH, Bonn 1986.

VOGEL, M., Die enharmonische Gitarre, ibid., Bonn 1982.

VOGEL, M., Die Naturseptime, ibid., Bonn 1991.

VOGEL, M., On the Relations of Tone, trans. by V. J. Kisselbach, ed. by Carl A. Poldy, ibid., Bonn 1993.

WHITE, E. W., Stravinsky: the Composer and his Works, Faber and Faber, London and Boston 1979.

WIENPAHL, R. W., Zarlino, the Senario and Tonality, in: *JAMS* XII, 1959, 27-41

WILLIAMS, R., F., Trans. of 4th Treatise of Mersenne's Harmonie Universelle, Ph.D. Dissertation, Univ. of Rochester 1972.

WILSON, M., The 'Tristan Chord': Some Reflections, in: *Wagner* 10/3, 1989, 83-95.

WINNINGTON INGRAM, R.P., The Pentatonic Tuning of the Greek Lyre: a Theory Examined, in: *Classical Quarterly*, New Series VI, 1956.

WOOD, A., The Physics of Music (6th. Ed.), University Paperbacks, Methuen, London 1962.

YASSER, J., A Theory of Evolving Tonality, American Library of Musicology, New York 1932.

YOUNG, G., The Pitch Organization of Harmonium for James Tenney, in: *PNM*, 26/2, 1988.

ZARLINO, G., Le istitutioni harmoniche, Venice 1558.

ZARLINO, G., The Art of Counterpoint, Translated by Guy A. Marco and Claude V. Palisca, The Norton Library, W. W. Norton and Company. Inc., New York 1968.

WORKS CITED

Anon.	Sumer is Icumin In
Bach, J. S.	Cantata 31
	Prelude XX, Vol II, The Well Tempered Clavier
Bartók, Béla,	Bluebeards Castle
	Divertimento for Strings
	Fourth String Quartet
	Music for Strings, Percussion and Celesta
Berlioz, Hector,	Symphonie Fantastique
Beethoven, Ludwig van,	Diabelli Variations, Op. 120
	Piano Sonata in C Minor, Op. 13, no. 1
	Piano Sonata in C Major, Op. 53
	Symphony in Eb Major, Op. 55
	Piano Sonata in Fminor, Op. 57
	Symphony in D Major
Britten, Benjamin,	Ad majorem Dei gloriam (Seven Settings for SATB)
	Serenade for Tenor, Horn and Strings, op. 31
Anton Bruckner,	Ninth Symphony
Chopin, Frederick,	Nocturne in Bb Minor, Op. 9, no. 1
	Mazurka in C Minor, Op. 56, no. 3
	Prelude in E Minor, Op. 28
	Prelude in F Major, Op. 28
	Prelude in C Minor, Op. 28
Debussy, Claude,	Childrens Corner Suite
	Pelleas et Melisande
	Prélude à 'L'après-midi d'un faune'
	Preludes for Piano (Book2)
Dennis, Brian,	Six Chinese Song Cycles
	A Little Water Music - Six Short Piano Pieces
Dukas, Paul,	Ariane et Barbe-Bleue
Dvórak, Anton,	Symphony for the New World

Frescobaldi, Girolamo,	Ricercar Chromatico
Granados, Enrique,	12 Spanish Dances for the Piano
Grieg, Edvard,	Scherzo-Impromptu, Op. 73, no. 2
Haydn, Joseph,	The Creation
Hindemith, Paul,	Second Piano Sonata
Holst, Gustav,	The Planets Suite
Janácek, Leos,	Láska Opradivá (for male voices)
Johnston, Ben,	Fourth String Quartet
	Innocence
	Mass
	One Man
	Rose
Kabalevsky, Dmitri,	24 Preludes for Piano, Op. 38
Kodály, Zoltán,	Psalmus Hungaricus
Korsakov, Rimsky,	Capriccio Espagnol
	Sadko
Liszt, Franz,	Die Ideale
	Faust Symphony
	Nuages Gris
Mahler, Gustav,	Das Lied von der Erde
Messiaen, Olivier,	Banquet Céleste
	Quartet for the End of Time
Mozart, Wolfgang,	Piano Sonata in F Major, K.280
	Symphony in G minor
Mussorgsky, Modest,	Boris Gudonov
Penderecki, Krystof,	Polymorphia
Rachmaninoff, Serge,	Prelude in C# Minor
Rutter, John,	Gloria
Scarlatti, Domenico,	Harpsichord Sonata, K.119
Schoenberg, Arnold,	Six Little Piano Pieces
Schumann, Robert,	Humoreske, Op. 20
	Novelette, Op. 21/7
	Novelette, Op. 21/8
	Bunte Blatter, Op. 99
Shostakovich, Dmitri,	Lady Macbeth von Mzensk
Sibelius, Jan,	Fourth Symphony
	Finlandia
Stockhausen, Karlheinz,	Aus den Sieben Tagen
Stravinsky, Igor,	The Rite of Spring
	Symphonies of Wind Instruments

SUBJECT INDEX

INDEX OF AUTHORITIES

Die Bände der ORpheus-Schriftenreihe zu Grundfragen der Musik

Die Bände der ORpheus-Schriftenreihe zu Grundfragen der Musik

Die Bände der ORpheus-Schriftenreihe zu Grundfragen der Musik

Die Bände der ORpheus-Schriftenreihe zu Grundfragen der Musik

Die Bände der ORpheus-Schriftenreihe zu Grundfragen der Musik